Portrait and biographical record of Winona County, Minnesota; containing biographical sketches of prominent and representative citizens of the county

Anonymous

PORTRAIT AND BIOGRAPHICAL RECORD

OF

WINONA COUNTY,

MINNESOTA.

Containing Biographical Sketches of Prominent and Representative Citizens of the County,

Together with Biographies and Portraits of all the Presidents of the United States.

LAKE CITY PUBLISHING CO.

CHICAGO:
[illegible]

PREFACE.

THE greatest of English historians, MACAULAY, and one of the most brilliant writers of the present century, has said: "The history of a country is best told in a record of the lives of its people." In conformity with this idea the PORTRAIT AND BIOGRAPHICAL RECORD of this county has been prepared. Instead of going to musty records, and taking therefrom dry statistical matter that can be appreciated by but few, our corps of writers have gone to the people, the men and women who have, by their enterprise and industry, brought the county to rank second to none among those comprising this great and noble State, and from their lips have the story of their life struggles. No more interesting or instructive matter could be presented to an intelligent public. In this volume will be found a record of many whose lives are worthy the imitation of coming generations. It tells how some, commencing life in poverty, by industry and economy have accumulated wealth. It tells how others, with limited advantages for securing an education, have become learned men and women, with an influence extending throughout the length and breadth of the land. It tells of men who have risen from the lower walks of life to eminence as statesmen, and whose names have become famous. It tells of those in every walk in life who have striven to succeed, and records how that success has usually crowned their efforts. It tells also of many, very many, who, not seeking the applause of the world, have pursued "the even tenor of their way," content to have it said of them as Christ said of the woman performing a deed of mercy—"they have done what they could." It tells how that many in the pride and strength of young manhood left the plow and the anvil, the lawyer's office and the counting-room, left every trade and profession, and at their country's call went forth valiantly "to do or die," and how through their efforts the Union was restored and peace once more reigned in the land. In the life of every man and of every woman is a lesson that should not be lost upon those who follow after.

Coming generations will appreciate this volume and preserve it as a sacred treasure, from the fact that it contains so much that would never find its way into public records, and which would otherwise be inaccessible. Great care has been taken in the compilation of the work and every opportunity possible given to those represented to insure correctness in what has been written, and the publishers flatter themselves that they give to their readers a work with few errors of consequence. In addition to the biographical sketches, portraits of a number of representative citizens are given.

The faces of some, and biographical sketches of many, will be missed in this volume. For this the publishers are not to blame. Not having a proper conception of the work, some refused to give the information necessary to compile a sketch, while others were indifferent. Occasionally some member of the family would oppose the enterprise, and on account of such opposition the support of the interested one would be withheld. In a few instances men could never be found, though repeated calls were made at their residence [illegible] place [illegible] business.

February, 18[illegible]

[illegible] Co.

PORTRAITS AND BIOGRAPHIES

OF THE

PRESIDENTS

OF THE

UNITED STATES

PRESIDENTS.

G. Washington

GEORGE WASHINGTON.

THE Father of our Country was born in Westmoreland County, Va., February 22, 1732. His parents were Augustine and Mary (Ball) Washington. The family to which he belonged has not been satisfactorily traced in England. His great-grandfather, John Washington, emigrated to Virginia about 1657, and became a prosperous planter. He had two sons, Lawrence and John. The former married Mildred Warner, and had three children, John, Augustine and Mildred. Augustine, the father of George, first married Jane Butler, who bore him four children, two of whom, Lawrence and Augustine, reached maturity. Of six children by his second marriage, George was the eldest, the others being Betty, Samuel, John Augustine, Charles and Mildred.

Augustine Washington, the father of George, died in 1743, leaving a large landed property. To his eldest son, Lawrence, he bequeathed an estate on the Potomac, afterwards known as Mt. Vernon, and to George he left the parental residence. George received only such education as the neighborhood schools afforded, save for a short time after he left school, when he received private instruction in mathematics. His spelling was rather defective. Remarkable stories are told of his great physical strength and development at an early age. He was an acknowledged leader among his companions, and was early noted for that nobleness of character, fairness and veracity which characterized his whole life.

When George was fourteen years old he had a desire to go to sea, and a midshipman's warrant was secured for h[illegible] of his mother th[illegible] years later he was appointed surveyor to the immense estate of Lord Fairfax. In this business he spent three years in a rough frontier life, gaining experience which afterwards proved very essential to him. In 1751, though only nineteen years of age, he was appointed Adjutant, with the rank of Major, in the Virginia militia, then being trained for active service against the French and Indians. Soon after this he sailed to the West Indies with his brother Lawrence, who went there to restore his health. They soon returned, and in the summer of 1752 Lawrence died, leaving a large fortune to an infant daughter, who did not long survive him. On her demise the estate of Mt. Vernon was given to George.

Upon the arrival of Robert Dinwiddie as Lieutenant-Governor of Virginia, in 1752, the militia was reorganized, and the province divided into four military districts, of which the northern was assigned to Washington as Adjutant-General. Shortly after this a very perilous mission, which others had refused, was assigned him and accepted. This was to proceed to the French post near Lake Erie, in northwestern Pennsylvania. The distance to be traversed was about six hundred miles. Winter was at hand, and the journey was to be made without military escort, through a territory occupied by Indians. The trip was a perilous one, and several times he nearly lost his life, but he returned in safety and furnished a full and useful report of his expedition. A regiment of three hundred men was raised in Virginia and put in command of Col. Joshua Fry, and Maj. Washington was commissioned Lieutenant-Colonel. [illegible] war was then begun against the [illegible] ton took a most important part In the memorable event of July 9, 1755, known as "Braddock's defeat," Washington was almost the only officer of distinction who escaped from the calamities of the day with life and honor

Having been for five years in the military service, and having vainly sought promotion in the royal army, he took advantage of the fall of Ft Duquesne and the expulsion of the French from the valley of the Ohio to resign his commission Soon after he entered the Legislature, where, although not a leader, he took an active and important part January 17, 1759, he married Mrs Martha (Dandridge) Custis the wealthy widow of John Parke Custis

When the British Parliament had closed the port of Boston, the cry went up throughout the provinces, "The cause of Boston is the cause of us all!" It was then, at the suggestion of Virginia, that a congress of all the colonies was called to meet at Philadelphia September 5, 1774, to secure their common liberties, peaceably if possible To this congress Col Washington was sent as a delegate On May 10, 1775, the congress re-assembled, when the hostile intentions of England were plainly apparent The battles of Concord and Lexington had been fought, and among the first acts of this congress was the election of a commander-in-chief of the Colonial forces This high and responsible office was conferred upon Washington, who was still a member of the congress He accepted it on June 19, but upon the express condition that he receive no salary He would keep an exact account of expenses, and expect congress to pay them and nothing more It is not the object of this sketch to trace the military acts of Washington, to whom the fortunes and liberties of the people of this country were so long confided The war was conducted by him under every possible disadvantage, and while his forces often met with reverses, yet he overcame every obstacle, and after seven years of heroic devotion and matchless skill he gained liberty for the greatest nation of earth On Decem
address of
mission as

Continental Congress sitting at Annapolis He retired immediately to Mt Vernon and resumed his occupation as a farmer and planter, shunning all connection with public life

In February, 1789, Washington was unanimously elected President, and at the expiration of his first term he was unanimously re-elected At the end of this term many were anxious that he be re-elected, but he absolutely refused a third nomination On March 4, 1797, at the expiration of his second term as President, he returned to his home, hoping to pass there his few remaining years free from the annoyances of public life Later in the year, however, his repose seemed likely to be interrupted by war with France At the prospect of such a war he was again urged to take command of the army, but he chose his subordinate officers and left them the charge of matters in the field, which he superintended from his home In accepting the command, he made the reservation that he was not to be in the field until it was necessary In the midst of these preparations his life was suddenly cut off December 12 he took a severe cold from a ride in the rain which, settling in his throat, produced inflammation, and terminated fatally on the night of the 14th On the 18th his body was borne with military honors to its final resting-place, and interred in the family vault at Mt Vernon

Of the character of Washington it is impossible to speak but in terms of the highest respect and admiration. The more we see of the operations of our government, and the more deeply we feel the difficulty of uniting all opinions in a common interest, the more highly we must estimate the force of his talent and character, which have been able to challenge the reverence of all parties, and principles, and nations, and to win a fame as extended as the limits of the globe, and which we cannot but believe will be as lasting as the existence of man

In person, Washington was unusually tall, erect and well proportioned, and his muscular strength was great His features were of a beautiful sym-
without any ap-
as ever serious

John Adams

JOHN ADAMS.

JOHN ADAMS, the second President and the first Vice-President of the United States, was born in Braintree (now Quincy) Mass, and about ten miles from Boston, October 19, 1735 His great-grandfather, Henry Adams, emigrated from England about 1640, with a family of eight sons, and settled at Braintree The parents of John were John and Susannah (Boylston) Adams His father, who was a farmer of limited means, also engaged in the business of shoemaking He gave his eldest son, John, a classical education at Harvard College John graduated in 1755, and at once took charge of the school at Worcester, Mass This he found but a "school of affliction," from which he endeavored to gain relief by devoting himself, in addition, to the study of law For this purpose he placed himself under the tuition of the only lawyer in the town He had thought seriously of the clerical profession, but seems to have been turned from this by what he termed "the frightful engines of ecclesiastical councils, of diabolical malice, and Calvinistic good nature," of the operations of which he had been a witness in his native town He was well fitted for the legal profession, possessing a clear, sonorous voice, being ready and fluent of speech, and having quick perceptive powers He gradually gained a practice, and in 1764 married Abigail Smith, a daughter of a minister, and a lady of superior intelligence Shortly after his marriage, in 1765, the attempt at parliamentary taxation turned him from law to politics. He took initial steps toward holding a town meeting, and the resolutions he offered on the subject became very popular throughout the province, and were adopted word for word by over forty different towns He moved to Boston in 1768, and became one of the most courageous and prominent advocates of the popular cause, and was chosen a member of the General Court (the Legislature) in 1770

Mr Adams wa[s]

gates from Massachusetts to the first Continental Congress, which met in 1774 Here he distinguished himself by his capacity for business and for debate, and advocated the movement for independence against the majority of the members In May, 1776, he moved and carried a resolution in Congress that the Colonies should assume the duties of self-government He was a prominent member of the committee of five appointed June 11 to prepare a declaration of independence This article was drawn by Jefferson, but on Adams devolved the task of battling it through Congress in a three-days debate

On the day after the Declaration of Independence was passed, while his soul was yet warm with the glow of excited feeling, he wrote a letter to his wife, which, as we read it now, seems to have been dictated by the spirit of prophecy "Yesterday," he says, "the greatest question was decided that ever was debated in America; and greater, perhaps, never was or will be decided among men A resolution was passed without one dissenting colony, 'that these United States are, and of right ought to be, free and independent states' The day is passed The Fourth of July, 1776, will be a memorable epoch in the history of America I am apt to believe it will be celebrated by succeeding generations as the great anniversary festival It ought to be commemorated as the day of deliverance by solemn acts of devotion to Almighty God. It ought to be solemnized with pomp, shows games, sports, guns, bells, bonfires and illuminations from one end of the continent to the other, from this time forward forever You will think me transported with enthusiasm, but I am not I am well aware of the toil and blood and treasure that it will cost to maintain this declaration and support and defend these States, yet, through all the gloom I can see the rays of light and glory I can see that the end is worth more than

triumph,

although you and I may rue, which I hope we shall not "

In November, 1777, Mr Adams was appointed a delegate to France, and to co-operate with Benjamin Franklin and Arthur Lee, who were then in Paris, in the endeavor to obtain assistance in arms and money from the French government This was a severe trial to his patriotism, as it separated him from his home, compelled him to cross the ocean in winter, and exposed him to great peril of capture by the British cruisers, who were seeking him He left France June 17, 1779 In September of the same year he was again chosen to go to Paris, and there hold himself in readiness to negotiate a treaty of peace and of commerce with Great Britain, as soon as the British cabinet might be found willing to listen to such proposals He sailed for France in November, and from there he went to Holland, where he negotiated important loans and formed important commercial treaties

Finally, a treaty of peace with England was signed, January 21, 1783 The re-action from the excitement, toil and anxiety through which Mr Adams had passed threw him into a fever After suffering from a continued fever and becoming feeble and emaciated, he was advised to go to England to drink the waters of Bath. While in England, still drooping and desponding, he received dispatches from his own government urging the necessity of his going to Amsterdam to negotiate another loan It was winter, his health was delicate, yet he immediately set out, and through storm, on sea, on horseback and foot, he made the trip

February 24, 1785, Congress appointed Mr Adams envoy to the Court of St James Here he met face to face the King of England, who had so long regarded him as a traitor As England did not condescend to appoint a minister to the United States, and as Mr. Adams felt that he was accomplishing but little, he sought permission to return to his own country, where he arrived in June, 1788

When '
John Ad
services a

President Again, at the second election of Washington as President, Adams was chosen Vice-President In 1796, Washington retired from public life, and Mr Adams was elected President, though not without much opposition Serving in this office four years, he was succeeded by Mr Jefferson, his opponent in politics

While Mr Adams was Vice-President the great French Revolution shook the continent of Europe, and it was upon this point that he was at issue with the majority of his countrymen, led by Mr Jefferson Mr Adams felt no sympathy with the French people in their struggle, for he had no confidence in their power of self-government, and he utterly abhorred the class of atheist philosophers who, he claimed, caused it On the other hand, Jefferson's sympathies were strongly enlisted in behalf of the French people. Hence originated the alienation between these distinguished men, and the two powerful parties were thus soon organized, with Adams at the head of the one whose sympathies were with England, and Jefferson leading the other in sympathy with France

The Fourth of July, 1826, which completed the half-century since the signing of the Declaration of Independence, arrived, and there were but three of the signers of that immortal instrument left upon the earth to hail its morning light. And, as it is well known, on that day two of these finished their earthly pilgrimage, a coincidence so remarkable as to seem miraculous For a few days before Mr Adams had been rapidly failing, and on the morning of the Fourth he found himself too weak to rise from his bed On being requested to name a toast for the customary celebration of the day, he exclaimed "Independence forever!" When the day was ushered in by the ringing of bells and the firing of cannons, he was asked by one of his attendants if he knew what day it was? He replied, "O yes, it is the glorious Fourth of July—God bless it God bless you all!" In the course of the day he said "It is a great and glorious

ed were, "Jeffe.
at one o'clock,
ls of his God

Th: Jefferson

THOMAS JEFFERSON.

THOMAS JEFFERSON was born April 2, 1743, at Shadwell, Albemarle County, Va. His parents were Peter and Jane (Randolph) Jefferson, the former a native of Wales, and the latter born in London. To them were born six daughters and two sons, of whom Thomas was the elder. When fourteen years of age his father died. He received a most liberal education, having been kept diligently at school from the time he was five years of age. In 1760 he entered William and Mary College. Williamsburg was then the seat of the Colonial court, and it was the abode of fashion and splendor. Young Jefferson, who was then seventeen years old, lived somewhat expensively, keeping fine horses, and going much into gay society; yet he was earnestly devoted to his studies, and irreproachable in his morals. In the second year of his college course, moved by some unexplained impulse, he discarded his old companions and pursuits, and often devoted fifteen hours a day to hard study. He thus attained very high intellectual culture, and a like excellence in philosophy and the languages.

Immediately upon leaving college he began the study of law. For the short time he continued in the practice of his profession he rose rapidly, and distinguished himself by his energy and acuteness as a lawyer. But the times called for greater action. The policy of England had awakened the spirit of resistance in the American Colonies, and the enlarged views which Jefferson had ever entertained soon led him into active political life. In 1769 he was chosen a member of the Virginia House ... ried Mrs. Martha Skelton, a very beautiful, wealthy, and highly accomplished young widow.

In 1775 he was sent to the Colonial Congress, where, though a silent member, his abilities as a writer and a reasoner soon become known, and he was placed upon a number of important committees, and was chairman of the one appointed for the drawing up of a declaration of independence. This committee consisted of Thomas Jefferson, John Adams, Benjamin Franklin, Roger Sherman and Robert R. Livingston. Jefferson, as chairman, was appointed to draw up the paper. Franklin and Adams suggested a few verbal changes before it was submitted to Congress. On June 28, a few slight changes were made in it by Congress, and it was passed and signed July 4, 1776.

In 1779 Mr. Jefferson was elected successor to Patrick Henry as Governor of Virginia. At one time the British officer Tarleton sent a secret expedition to Monticello to capture the Governor. Scarcely five minutes elapsed after the hurried escape of Mr. Jefferson and his family ere his mansion was in possession of the British troops. His wife's health, never very good, was much injured by this excitement, and in the summer of 1782 she died.

Mr. Jefferson was elected to Congress in 1783. Two years later he was appointed Minister Plenipotentiary to France. Returning to the United States in September, 1789, he became Secretary of State in Washington's cabinet. This position he resigned January 1, 1794. In 1797, he was chosen Vice-President, and four years later was ... ith Aaron

Burr as Vice-President In 1804 he was re-elected with wonderful unanimity, George Clinton being elected Vice-President

The early part of Mr Jefferson's second administration was disturbed by an event which threatened the tranquillity and peace of the Union, this was the conspiracy of Aaron Burr Defeated in the late election to the Vice-Presidency, and led on by an unprincipled ambition, this extraordinary man formed the plan of a military expedition into the Spanish territories on our south-western frontier, for the purpose of forming there a new republic. This was generally supposed to have been a mere pretext, and although it has not been generally known what his real plans were, there is no doubt that they were of a far more dangerous character.

In 1809, at the expiration of the second term for which Mr. Jefferson had been elected, he determined to retire from political life For a period of nearly forty years he had been continually before the public, and all that time had been employed in offices of the greatest trust and responsibility. Having thus devoted the best part of his life to the service of his country, he now felt desirous of that rest which his declining years required, and upon the organization of the new administration, in March, 1809, he bade farewell forever to public life and retired to Monticello, his famous country home, which, next to Mt Vernon, was the most distinguished residence in the land

The Fourth of July, 1826, being the fiftieth anniversary of the Declaration of American Independence, great preparations were made in every part of the Union for its celebration as the nation's jubilee, and the citizens of Washington, to add to the solemnity of the occasion, invited Mr Jefferson, as the framer and one of the few surviving signers of the Declaration, to participate in their festivities But an illness, which had been of several weeks' duration and had been continually increasing, compelled him to decline the invitation

On the 2d of July the disease under which he was laboring left him but in such a reduced state that [illegible]
hope of h[illegible] perfectly sensible that his last hour was at hand. On the next day, which was Monday, he asked of those around him the day of the month, and on being told it was the 3d of July, he expressed the earnest wish that he might be permitted to breathe the air of the fiftieth anniversary. His prayer was heard—that day whose dawn was hailed with such rapture through our land burst upon his eyes, and then they were closed forever And what a noble consummation of a noble life! To die on that day—the birthday of a nation—the day which his own name and his own act had rendered glorious, to die amidst the rejoicings and festivities of a whole nation, who looked up to him as the author, under God, of their greatest blessings, was all that was wanting to fill up the record of his life

Almost at the same hour of his death, the kindred spirit of the venerable Adams, as if to bear him company, left the scene of his earthly honors. Hand in hand they had stood forth, the champions of freedom; hand in hand, during the dark and desperate struggle of the Revolution, they had cheered and animated their desponding countrymen; for half a century they had labored together for the good of the country, and now hand in hand they departed In their lives they had been united in the same great cause of liberty, and in their deaths they were not divided

In person Mr Jefferson was tall and thin, rather above six feet in height, but well formed; his eyes were light, his hair, originally red, in after life became white and silvery, his complexion was fair, his forehead broad, and his whole countenance intelligent and thoughtful. He possessed great fortitude of mind as well as personal courage, and his command of temper was such that his oldest and most intimate friends never recollected to have seen him in a passion His manners, though dignified, were simple and unaffected, and his hospitality was so unbounded that all found at his house a ready welcome In conversation he was fluent, eloquent and enthusiastic, and his language was remarkably pure and correct He was a finished classical scholar and in his writ-[illegible] which he formed [illegible] antiquity

James Madison

JAMES MADISON.

JAMES MADISON, "Father of the Constitution," and fourth President of the United States, was born March 16, 1757, and died at his home in Virginia June 28, 1836. The name of James Madison is inseparably connected with most of the important events in that heroic period of our country during which the foundations of this great republic were laid. He was the last of the founders of the Constitution of the United States to be called to his eternal reward.

The Madison family were among the early emigrants to the New World, landing upon the shores of the Chesapeake but fifteen years after the settlement of Jamestown. The father of James Madison was an opulent planter, residing upon a very fine estate called Montpelier, in Orange County, Va. It was but twenty-five miles from the home of Jefferson at Monticello, and the closest personal and political attachment existed between these illustrious men from their early youth until death.

The early education of Mr. Madison was conducted mostly at home under a private tutor. At the age of eighteen he was sent to Princeton College, in New Jersey. Here he applied himself to study with the most imprudent zeal, allowing himself for months but three hours' sleep out of the twenty-four. His health thus became so seriously impaired that he never recovered any vigor of constitution. He graduated in 1771, with a feeble body, but with a character of utmost purity, and a mind highly disciplined and richly stored with learning, which embellished and gave efficiency to his subsequent career.

Returning to Virginia, he commenced the study of law and a course of extensive and systematic reading. This educational course, the spirit of the times in which he lived, and the society with which he associated, all combined to inspire him with a strong love of liberty, and to train him for his life work as [illegible]

In the spring [illegible]

age, he was elected a member of the Virginia Convention to frame the constitution of the State. The next year (1777), he was a candidate for the General Assembly. He refused to treat the whisky-loving voters, and consequently lost his election, but those who had witnessed the talent, energy and public spirit of the modest young man enlisted themselves in his behalf, and he was appointed to the Executive Council.

Both Patrick Henry and Thomas Jefferson were Governors of Virginia while Mr. Madison remained member of the Council, and their appreciation of his intellectual, social and moral worth contributed not a little to his subsequent eminence. In the year 1780 he was elected a member of the Continental Congress. Here he met the most illustrious men in our land, and he was immediately assigned to one of the most conspicuous positions among them. For three years he continued in Congress, one of its most active and influential members. In 1784, his term having expired, he was elected a member of the Virginia Legislature.

No man felt more deeply than Mr. Madison the utter inefficiency of the old confederacy, with no national government, and no power to form treaties which would be binding, or to enforce law. There was not any State more prominent than Virginia in the declaration that an efficient national government must be formed. In January, 1786, Mr. Madison carried a resolution through the General Assembly of Virginia, inviting the other States to appoint commissioners to meet in convention at Annapolis to discuss this subject. Five States only were represented. The convention, however, issued another call, drawn up by Mr. Madison, urging all the States to send their delegates to Philadelphia in May, 1787, to draft a Constitution for the United States, to take the place of the Confederate League. The delegates [illegible] State but [illegible] Washing ton was chosen president of the convention, and the present Constitution of the United States was then and there formed There was, perhaps, no mind and no pen more active in framing this immortal document than the mind and the pen of James Madison

The Constitution, adopted by a vote of eighty-one to seventy-nine, was to be presented to the several States for acceptance But grave solicitude was felt Should it be rejected, we should be left but a conglomeration of independent States, with but little power at home and little respect abroad Mr Madison was elected by the convention to draw up an address to the people of the United States, expounding the principles of the Constitution, and urging its adoption There was great opposition to it at first, but at length it triumphed over all, and went into effect in 1789

Mr Madison was elected to the House of Representatives in the first Congress, and soon became the avowed leader of the Republican party While in New York attending Congress, he met Mrs Todd, a young widow of remarkable power of fascination, whom he married She was in person and character queenly, and probaby no lady has thus far occupied so prominent a position in the very peculiar society which has constituted our republican court as did Mrs Madison

Mr Madison served as Secretary of State under Jefferson, and at the close of his administration was chosen President At this time the encroachments of England had brought us to the verge of war British orders in council destroyed our commerce, and our flag was exposed to constant insult. Mr Madison was a man of peace Scholarly in his taste, retiring in his disposition, war had no charms for him But the meekest spirit can be roused It makes one's blood boil, even now, to think of an American ship brought to upon the ocean by the guns of an English cruiser A young lieutenant steps on board and orders the crew to be paraded before him With great nonchalance he selects any number whom he may please to designate as British subjects, orders them down the sl[illegible] him on the gun[illegible] compulsion [illegible] of search and impressment no efforts of our Government could induce the British cabinet to relinquish

On the 18th of June, 1812, President Madison gave his approval to an act of Congress declaring war against Great Britain Notwithstanding the bitter hostility of the Federal party to the war, the country in general approved, and Mr Madison, on the 4th of March, 1813, was re-elected by a large majority, and entered upon his second term of office This is not the place to describe the various adventures of this war on the land and on the water Our infant navy then laid the foundations of its renown in grappling with the most formidable power which ever swept the seas The contest commenced in earnest by the appearance of a British fleet, early in February, 1813, in Chesapeake Bay, declaring nearly the whole coast of the United States under blockade

The Emperor of Russia offered his services as mediator America accepted; England refused A British force of five thousand men landed on the banks of the Patuxet River, near its entrance into Chesapeake Bay, and marched rapidly, by way of Bladensburg, upon Washington

The straggling little city of Washington was thrown into consternation The cannon of the brief conflict at Bladensburg echoed through the streets of the metropolis The whole population fled from the city The President, leaving Mrs Madison in the White House, with her carriage drawn up at the door to await his speedy return, hurried to meet the officers in a council of war He met our troops utterly routed, and he could not go back without danger of being captured But few hours elapsed ere the Presidential Mansion, the Capitol, and all the public buildings in Washington were in flames

The war closed after two years of fighting, and on February 13, 1815, the treaty of peace was signed at Ghent On the 4th of March, 1817, his second term of office expired, and he resigned the Presidential chair to his friend, James Monroe He retired to his beautiful home at Montpelier, and [illegible] days On June 28, [illegible] e years, he fell asleep [illegible] ed July 12, 1849

James Monroe

JAMES MONROE.

JAMES MONROE, the fifth President of the United States, was born in Westmoreland County, Va., April 28, 1758. His early life was passed at the place of his nativity. His ancestors had for many years resided in the province in which he was born. When he was seventeen years old, and in process of completing his education at William and Mary College, the Colonial Congress, assembled at Philadelphia to deliberate upon the unjust and manifold oppressions of Great Britain, declared the separation of the Colonies, and promulgated the Declaration of Independence. Had he been born ten years before, it is highly probable that he would have been one of the signers of that celebrated instrument. At this time he left school and enlisted among the patriots.

He joined the army when everything looked hopeless and gloomy. The number of deserters increased from day to day. The invading armies came pouring in, and the Tories not only favored the cause of the mother country, but disheartened the new recruits, who were sufficiently terrified at the prospect of contending with an enemy whom they had been taught to deem invincible. To such brave spirits as James Monroe, who went right onward undismayed through difficulty and danger, the United States owe their political emancipation. The young cadet joined the ranks and espoused the cause of his injured country, with a firm determination to live or die in her strife for liberty. Firmly, yet sadly, he shared in the melancholy retreat from Harlem Heights and White Plains, and accompanied the dispirited army as it fled before its foes through New Jersey. In four months after the Declaration of Independence, the patriots had been beaten in seven battles. At the battle of Trenton he led the vanguard, and in the act of charging upon the enemy he received a w

As a reward for his bravery, Mr. Monroe was promoted to be captain of infantry, and, having recovered from his wounds, he rejoined the army. He, however, receded from the line of promotion by becoming an officer on the staff of Lord Sterling. During the campaigns of 1777 and 1778, in the actions of Brandywine, Germantown and Monmouth, he continued aide-de-camp, but becoming desirous to regain his position in the army, he exerted himself to collect a regiment for the Virginia line. This scheme failed, owing to the exhausted condition of the State. Upon this failure he entered the office of Mr. Jefferson, at that period Governor, and pursued with considerable ardor the study of common law. He did not, however, entirely lay aside the knapsack for the green bag, but on the invasion of the enemy served as a volunteer during the two years of his legal pursuits.

In 1782 he was elected from King George County a member of the Legislature of Virginia, and by that body he was elevated to a seat in the Executive Council. He was thus honored with the confidence of his fellow-citizens at twenty-three years of age, and having at this early period displayed some of that ability and aptitude for legislation which were afterward employed with unremitting energy for the public good, he was in the succeeding year chosen a member of the Congress of the United States.

Deeply as Mr. Monroe felt the imperfections of the old Confederacy, he was opposed to the new Constitution, thinking, with many others of the Republican party, that it gave too much power to the Central Government, and not enough to the individual States. Still he retained the esteem of his friends who were its warm supporters and who, notwithstanding his opposition, secured its adoption. In 1789 he became a member of the

he held for

four years Every month the line of distinction between the two great parties which divided the nation, the Federal and the Republican, was growing more distinct The differences which now separated them lay in the fact that the Republican party was in sympathy with France, and also in favor of such a strict construction of the Constitution as to give the Central Government as little power, and the State Governments as much power, as the Constitution would warrant, while the Federalists sympathized with England, and were in favor of a liberal construction of the Constitution, which would give as much power to the Central Government as that document could possibly authorize

Washington was then President England had espoused the cause of the Bourbons against the principles of the French Revolution All Europe was drawn into the conflict. We were feeble and far away Washington issued a proclamation of neutrality between these contending powers France had helped us in the struggles for our liberties All the despotisms of Europe were now combined to prevent the French from escaping from a tyranny a thousand-fold worse than that which we had endured Col Monroe, more magnanimous than prudent, was anxious that, at whatever hazard, we should help our old allies in their extremity It was the impulse of a generous and noble nature, and Washington, who could appreciate such a character, showed his calm, serene, almost divine, greatness, by appointing that very James Monroe who was denouncing the policy of the Government, as the minister of that Government to the Republic of France Mr Monroe was welcomed by the National Convention in France with the most enthusiastic demonstration

Shortly after his return to this country, Mr Monroe was elected Governor of Virginia, and held the office for three years He was again sent to France to co-operate with Chancellor Livingston in obtaining the vast territory then known as the province of Louisiana, which France had but shortly [illegible] The united efforts [illegible] tively small s[illegible] entire territory of Orleans and district of Louisiana were added to the United States This was probably the largest transfer of real estate which was ever made in all the history of the world

From France Mr Monroe went to England to obtain from that country some recognition of our rights as neutrals, and to remonstrate against those odious impressments of our seamen But England was unrelenting He again returned to England on the same mission, but could receive no redress He returned to his home and was again chosen Governor of Virginia This he soon resigned to accept the position of Secretary of State under Madison While in this office war with England was declared, the Secretary of War resigned, and during these trying times the duties of the War Department were also put upon him He was truly the armor-bearer of President Madison, and the most efficient business man in his cabinet Upon the return of peace he resigned the Department of War, but continued in the office of Secretary of State until the expiration of Mr Madison's administration. At the election held the previous autumn, Mr Monroe himself had been chosen President with but little opposition, and upon March 4, 1817, he was inaugurated Four years later he was elected for a second term

Among the important measures of his Presidency were the cession of Florida to the United States, the Missouri Compromise, and the famous "Monroe doctrine" This doctrine was enunciated by him in 1823, and was as follows "That we should consider any attempt on the part of European powers to extend their system to any portion of this hemisphere as dangerous to our peace and safety," and that "we could not view any interposition for the purpose of oppressing or controlling American governments or provinces in any other light than as a manifestation by European powers of an unfriendly disposition toward the United States"

At the end of his second term, Mr Monroe retired to his home in Virginia, where he lived un[illegible]rk to live with [illegible]ed, on the 4th [illegible]

J. Q. Adams

JOHN QUINCY ADAMS.

JOHN QUINCY ADAMS, the sixth President of the United States, was born in the rural home of his honored father, John Adams in Quincy, Mass, on the 11th of July, 1767 His mother, a woman of exalted worth, watched over his childhood during the almost constant absence of his father When but eight years of age, he stood with his mother on an eminence, listening to the booming of the great battle on Bunker's Hill, and gazing out upon the smoke and flames billowing up from the conflagration of Charlestown

When but eleven years old he took a tearful adieu of his mother, to sail with his father for Europe, through a fleet of hostile British cruisers The bright, animated boy spent a year and a-half in Paris, where his father was associated with Franklin and Lee as Minister Plenipotentiary His intelligence attracted the notice of these distinguished men, and he received from them flattering marks of attention

John Adams had scarcely returned to this country, in 1779, ere he was again sent abroad Again John Quincy accompanied his father At Paris he applied himself to study with great diligence for six months, and then accompanied his father to Holland, where he entered first a school in Amsterdam, then the University at Leyden About a year from this time, in 1781, when the manly boy was but fourteen years of age, he was selected by Mr Dana, our Minister to the Russian court, as his private secretary

In this school of incessant labor and of ennobling culture he spent fourteen months, and then returned to Holland, through Sweden, Denmark, Hamburg and Bremen This long journey he took alone in the winter, when in his sixteenth year Again he resumed his studies, under a private tutor, at The Hague Then, in the spring of 1782 he accompanied his father to Paris, traveling leisurely, and forming acquaintances with the most distinguis[illegible] ing architectural remains, galleries of paintings and all renowned works of art At Paris he again became associated with the most illustrious men of all lands in the contemplation of the loftiest temporal themes which can engross the human mind After a short visit to England he returned to Paris, and consecrated all his energies to study until May, 1785, when he returned to America to finish his education

Upon leaving Harvard College at the age of twenty, he studied law for three years In June, 1794 being then but twenty-seven years of age, he was appointed by Washington Resident Minister at the Netherlands Sailing from Boston in July, he reached London in October, where he was immediately admitted to the deliberations of Messrs Jay & Pinckney, assisting them in negotiating a commercial treaty with Great Britain After thus spending a fortnight in London, he proceeded to The Hague

In July, 1797, he left The Hague to go to Portugal as Minister Plenipotentiary. On his way to Portugal upon arriving in London, he met with despatches directing him to the court of Berlin, but requesting him to remain in London until he should receive his instructions While waiting he was married to an American lady, to whom he had been previously engaged—Miss Louisa Catherine Johnson, a daughter of Joshua Johnson, American Consul in London, and a lady endowed with that beauty and those accomplishments which eminently fitted her to move in the elevated sphere for which she was destined He reached Berlin with his wife in November 1707, where he remained until July, 1709 when, having fulfilled all the purposes of his mission, he solicited his recall

Soon after his return, in 1802 he was chosen to the Senate of Massachusetts from Boston and then was elected Senator of the United States for six years, from the 4th of March, 1803 His rep[illegible] [illegible]ence placed him immediately among the most prominent and influential members of that body

In 1809, Madison succeeded Jefferson in the Presidential chair, and he immediately nominated John Quincy Adams Minister to St Petersburgh Resigning his professorship in Harvard College, he embarked at Boston in August, 1809

While in Russia, Mr Adams was an intense student. He devoted his attention to the language and history of Russia, to the Chinese trade, to the European system of weights, measures and coins, to the climate and astronomical observations, while he kept up a familiar acquaintance with the Greek and Latin classics In all the universities of Europe, a more accomplished scholar could scarcely be found All through life the Bible constituted an important part of his studies It was his rule to read five chapters every day

On the 4th of March, 1817, Mr Monroe took the Presidential chair, and immediately appointed Mr Adams Secretary of State Taking leave of his numerous friends in public and private life in Europe, he sailed in June, 1819, for the United States On the 18th of August, he again crossed the threshold of his home in Quincy. During the eight years of Mr Monroe's administration, Mr Adams continued Secretary of State

Some time before the close of Mr Monroe's second term of office, new candidates began to be presented for the Presidency The friends of Mr. Adams brought forward his name It was an exciting campaign, and party spirit was never more bitter Two hundred and sixty electoral votes were cast Andrew Jackson received ninety-nine, John Quincy Adams eighty-four, William H Crawford forty-one, and Henry Clay thirty-seven As there was no choice by the people, the question went to the House of Representatives Mr Clay gave the vote of Kentucky to Mr Adams, and he was elected

The friends of all the disappointed candidates now combined in a venomous and persistent assault upon Mr Adams There is nothing more disgraceful [illegible] than the abuse w[illegible] uninterrupted stream upon [illegible] and [illegible] triotic man. There never was an administration more pure in principles, more conscientiously devoted to the best interests of the country, than that of John Quincy Adams, and never, perhaps, was there an administration more unscrupulously and outrageously assailed

On the 4th of March, 1829, Mr Adams retired from the Presidency, and was succeeded by Andrew Jackson John C Calhoun was elected Vice-President The slavery question now began to assume portentous magnitude Mr Adams returned to Quincy and to his studies, which he pursued with unabated zeal But he was not long permitted to remain in retirement In November, 1830, he was elected Representative in Congress For seventeen years, or until his death, he occupied the post as Representative, towering above all his peers, ever ready to do brave battle for freedom, and winning the title of "the Old Man Eloquent" Upon taking his seat in the House, he announced that he should hold himself bound to no party Probably there never was a member more devoted to his duties He was usually the first in his place in the morning, and the last to leave his seat in the evening Not a measure could be brought forward and escape his scrutiny The battle which Mr Adams fought, almost singly, against the pro-slavery party in the Government was sublime in its moral daring and heroism For persisting in presenting petitions for the abolition of slavery, he was threatened with indictment by the grand jury, with expulsion from the House, with assassination, but no threats could intimidate him, and his final triumph was complete

On the 21st of February, 1848, he rose on the floor of Congress with a paper in his hand, to address the speaker Suddenly he fell, again stricken by paralysis, and was caught in the arms of those around him For a time he was senseless, as he was conveyed to the sofa in the rotunda With reviving consciousness, he opened his eyes, looked calmly around and said "This is the end of earth," then after a moment's pause he added "I am content" These were the last words of the "Old Man Eloquent"

Andrew Jackson

ANDREW JACKSON.

ANDREW JACKSON, the seventh President of the United States, was born in Waxhaw settlement, N C, March 15, 1767, a few days after his father's death His parents were poor emigrants from Ireland, and took up their abode in Waxhaw settlement, where they lived in deepest poverty

Andrew, or Andy, as he was universally called, grew up a very rough, rude, turbulent boy His features were coarse, his form ungainly, and there was but very little in his character made visible which was attractive.

When only thirteen years old he joined the volunteers of Carolina against the British invasion In 1781, he and his brother Robert were captured and imprisoned for a time at Camden A British officer ordered him to brush his mud-spattered boots "I am a prisoner of war, not your servant," was the reply of the dauntless boy

Andrew supported himself in various ways, such as working at the saddler's trade, teaching school, and clerking in a general store, until 1784, when he entered a law office at Salisbury, N C He, however, gave more attention to the wild amusements of the times than to his studies In 1788, he was appointed solicitor for the Western District of North Carolina, of which Tennessee was then a part This involved many long journeys amid dangers of every kind, but Andrew Jackson never knew fear, and the Indians had no desire to repeat a skirmish with "Sharp Knife"

In 1791, Mr. Jackson was married to a woman who supposed herself divorced from her former husband Great was the surprise of both parties, two years later, to find that the conditions of the divorce had just been definitely settled by the first husband The marriage ceremony was performed a second time, but the occurrence was often used by his enemies to bring Mr Jackson into disfavor

In January, 1796, the Territory of Tennessee then containing nearly eighty thousand inhabitants, the people met in convention at Knoxville to frame a constitution Five were sent from each of the eleven counties Andrew Jackson was one of the delegates The new State was entitled to but one member in the National House of Representatives. Andrew Jackson was chosen that member Mounting his horse, he rode to Philadelphia, where Congress then held its sessions, a distance of about eight hundred miles

Jackson was an earnest advocate of the Democratic party, and Jefferson was his idol He admired Bonaparte, loved France, and hated England As Mr Jackson took his seat, Gen Washington, whose second term of office was then expiring, delivered his last speech to Congress. A committee drew up a complimentary address in reply Andrew Jackson did not approve of the address, and was one of the twelve who voted against it He was not willing to say that Gen Washington's administration had been "wise firm and patriotic"

Mr Jackson was elected to the United States Senate in 1797, but soon resigned and returned home Soon after he was chosen Judge of the Supreme Court of his State, which position he held for six years

When the War of 1812 with Great Britain commenced, Madison occupied the Presidential chair Aaron Burr sent word to the President that there was an unknown man in the West, Andrew Jackson, who would do credit to a commission if one were conferred upon him Just at that time Gen Jackson offered his services and those of twenty five hundred volunteers His offer was accepted, and the troops were assembled at Nashville

As the British were hourly expected to make an attack upon New Orleans where Gen Wil [illegible] ered to descend the river with fifteen hundred troops to aid Wilkinson The expedition reached Natchez, and after a delay of several weeks there without accomplishing anything, the men were ordered back to their homes But the energy Gen Jackson had displayed, and his entire devotion to the comfort of his soldiers, won for him golden opinions, and he became the most popular man in the State It was in this expedition that his toughness gave him the nickname of "Old Hickory"

Soon after this, while attempting to horsewhip Col Thomas Benton for a remark that gentleman made about his taking part as second in a duel in which a younger brother of Benton's was engaged, he received two severe pistol wounds While he was lingering upon a bed of suffering, news came that the Indians, who had combined under Tecumseh from Florida to the Lakes to exterminate the white settlers, were committing the most awful ravages Decisive action became necessary Gen Jackson, with his fractured bone just beginning to heal, his arm in a sling, and unable to mount his horse without assistance, gave his amazing energies to the raising of an army to rendezvous at Fayettesville, Ala

The Creek Indians had established a strong fort on one of the bends of the Tallapoosa River, near the center of Alabama, about fifty miles below Ft Strother With an army of two thousand men, Gen Jackson traversed the pathless wilderness in a march of eleven days. He reached their fort, called Tohopeka or Horse-shoe, on the 27th of March, 1814 The bend of the river enclosed nearly one hundred acres of tangled forest and wild ravine Across the narrow neck the Indians had constructed a formidable breastwork of logs and brush Here nine hundred warriors, with an ample supply of arms, were assembled

The fort was stormed The fight was utterly desperate Not an Indian would accept quarter When bleeding and dying, they would fight those who endeavored to spare their lives From ten in the morning until dark the battle raged The carnage wa[illegible] themselves [illegible] lets struck t[illegible] every one of the nine hundred warriors was [illegible] killed A few, probably, in the night swam the river and escaped This ended the war.

This closing of the Creek War enabled us to concentrate all our militia upon the British who were the allies of the Indians No man of less resolute will than Gen Jackson could have conducted this Indian campaign to so successful an issue Immediately he was appointed Major-General

Late in August, with an army of two thousand men on a rushing march, Gen Jackson went to Mobile A British fleet went from Pensacola, landed a force upon the beach, anchored near the little fort, and from both ship and shore commenced a furious assault The battle was long and doubtful At length one of the ships was blown up and the rest retired

Garrisoning Mobile, where he had taken his little army, he moved his troops to New Orleans, and the battle of New Orleans, which soon ensued, was in reality a very arduous campaign This won for Gen Jackson an imperishable name Here his troops, which numbered about four thousand men, won a signal victory over the British army of about nine thousand His loss was but thirteen, while the loss of the British was twenty-six hundred.

The name of Gen Jackson soon began to be mentioned in connection with the Presidency, but in 1824 he was defeated by Mr Adams He was, however, successful in the election of 1828, and was re-elected for a second term in 1832 In 1829, just before he assumed the reins of government, he met with the most terrible affliction of his life in the death of his wife, whom he had loved with a devotion which has perhaps never been surpassed. From the shock of her death he never recovered

His administration was one of the most memorable in the annals of our country—applauded by one party, condemned by the other No man had more bitter enemies or warmer friends At the expiration of his two terms of office he retired [illegible] ne 8, 1845 The [illegible] re those of a de-

M Van Buren

MARTIN VAN BUREN.

MARTIN VAN BUREN, the eighth President of the United States, was born at Kinderhook, N. Y., December 5, 1782. He died at the same place, July 24, 1862. His body rests in the cemetery at Kinderhook. Above it is a plain granite shaft, fifteen feet high, bearing a simple inscription about half-way up on one face. The lot is unfenced, unbordered or unbounded by shrub or flower.

There is but little in the life of Martin Van Buren of romantic interest. He fought no battles, engaged in no wild adventures. Though his life was stormy in political and intellectual conflicts, and he gained many signal victories, his days passed uneventful in those incidents which give zest to biography. His ancestors, as his name indicates, were of Dutch origin, and were among the earliest emigrants from Holland to the banks of the Hudson. His father was a farmer, residing in the old town of Kinderhook. His mother, also of Dutch lineage, was a woman of superior intelligence and exemplary piety.

He was decidedly a precocious boy, developing unusual activity, vigor and strength of mind. At the age of fourteen, he had finished his academic studies in his native village, and commenced the study of law. As he had not a collegiate education, seven years of study in a law-office were required of him before he could be admitted to the Bar. Inspired with a lofty ambition, and conscious of his powers, he pursued his studies with indefatigable industry. After spending six years in an office in his native village, he went to the city of New York, and prosecuted his studies for the seventh year.

In 1803, Mr. [illegible] of age, commenced the practice of law in his native village. The great conflict between the Federal and Republican parties was then at its height. Mr. Van Buren was from the beginning a politician. He had, perhaps, imbibed that spirit while listening to the many discussions which had been carried on in his father's hotel. He was in cordial sympathy with Jefferson, and earnestly and eloquently espoused the cause of State Rights, though at that time the Federal party held the supremacy both in his town and State.

His success and increasing reputation led him after six years of practice to remove to Hudson, the county seat of his county. Here he spent seven years, constantly gaining strength by contending in the courts with some of the ablest men who have adorned the Bar of his State.

Just before leaving Kinderhook for Hudson, Mr. Van Buren married a lady alike distinguished for beauty and accomplishments. After twelve short years she sank into the grave, a victim of consumption, leaving her husband and four sons to weep over her loss. For twenty-five years, Mr. Van Buren was an earnest, successful, assiduous lawyer. The record of those years is barren in items of public interest. In 1812, when thirty years of age, he was chosen to the State Senate, and gave his strenuous support to Mr. Madison's administration. In 1815, he was appointed Attorney-General, and the next year moved to Albany, the capital of the State.

While he was acknowledged as one of the most prominent leaders of the Democratic party, he had the moral courage to avow that true democracy did [illegible] which admit [illegible] to the right [illegible] of governing the State In true consistency with his democratic principles, he contended that, while the path leading to the privilege of voting should be open to every man without distinction, no one should be invested with that sacred prerogative unless he were in some degree qualified for it by intelligence, virtue, and some property interests in the welfare of the State

In 1821 he was elected a member of the United States Senate, and in the same year he took a seat in the convention to revise the Constitution of his native State His course in this convention secured the approval of men of all parties No one could doubt the singleness of his endeavors to promote the interests of all classes in the community In the Senate of the United States, he rose at once to a conspicuous position as an active and useful legislator

In 1827, John Quincy Adams being then in the Presidential chair, Mr Van Buren was re-elected to the Senate. He had been from the beginning a determined opposer of the administration, adopting the "State Rights" view in opposition to what was deemed the Federal proclivities of Mr Adams

Soon after this, in 1828, he was chosen Governor of the State of New York, and accordingly resigned his seat in the Senate Probably no one in the United States contributed so much towards ejecting John Q Adams from the Presidential chair, and placing in it Andrew Jackson, as did Martin Van Buren Whether entitled to the reputation or not, he certainly was regarded throughout the United States as one of the most skillful, sagacious and cunning of politicians It was supposed that no one knew so well as he how to touch the secret springs of action, how to pull all the wires to put his machinery in motion, and how to organize a political army which would secretly and stealthily accomplish the most gigantic results By these powers it is said that he outwitted Mr Adams, Mr Clay, and Mr Webster, and secured results which ew then thought could be accomplished

When Andrew Jackson was elected President he appointed Mr Van Buren Secretary of State This position [illegible] mediately app[illegible] he went the sa[illegible] The Senate [illegible] when it met, refused to ratify the nomination, and he returned home, apparently untroubled Later he was nominated Vice-President in the place of Calhoun, at the re-election of President Jackson, and with smiles for all and frowns for none, he took his place at the head of that Senate which had refused to confirm his nomination as ambassador

His rejection by the Senate roused all the zeal of President Jackson in behalf of his repudiated favorite, and this, probably, more than any other cause secured his elevation to the chair of the Chief Executive. On the 20th of May, 1836, Mr Van Buren received the Democratic nomination to succeed Gen Jackson as President of the United States He was elected by a handsome majority, to the delight of the retiring President "Leaving New York out of the canvass," says Mr. Parton, "the election of Mr Van Buren to the Presidency was as much the act of Gen Jackson as though the Constitution had conferred upon him the power to appoint a successor"

His administration was filled with exciting events The insurrection in Canada, which threatened to involve this country in war with England, the agitation of the slavery question, and finally the great commercial panic which spread over the country, all were trials of his wisdom The financial distress was attributed to the management of the Democratic party, and brought the President into such disfavor that he failed of re-election, and on the 4th of March, 1841, he retired from the presidency

With the exception of being nominated for the Presidency by the "Free Soil" Democrats in 1848, Mr Van Buren lived quietly upon his estate until his death He had ever been a prudent man, of frugal habits, and, living within his income, had now fortunately a competence for his declining years From his fine estate at Lindenwald, he still exerted a powerful influence upon the politics of the country From this time until his death, on the 24th of July, 1862, at the age of eighty years, he resided at Lindenwald, a gentleman of leisure, of culture and wealth, enjoying in a [illegible] appiness than [illegible] stormy scenes

W. H. Harrison

WILLIAM HENRY HARRISON.

WILLIAM HENRY HARRISON, the ninth President of the United States, was born at Berkeley, Va., February 9, 1773. His father, Benjamin Harrison, was in comparatively opulent circumstances, and was one of the most distinguished men of his day. He was an intimate friend of George Washington, was early elected a member of the Continental Congress, and was conspicuous among the patriots of Virginia in resisting the encroachments of the British crown. In the celebrated Congress of 1775, Benjamin Harrison and John Hancock were both candidates for the office of Speaker.

Mr. Harrison was subsequently chosen Governor of Virginia, and was twice re-elected. His son William Henry, of course, enjoyed in childhood all the advantages which wealth and intellectual and cultivated society could give. Having received a thorough common-school education, he entered Hampden Sidney College, where he graduated with honor soon after the death of his father. He then repaired to Philadelphia to study medicine under the instructions of Dr. Rush and the guardianship of Robert Morris, both of whom were, with his father, signers of the Declaration of Independence.

Upon the outbreak of the Indian troubles, and notwithstanding the remonstrances of his friends, he abandoned his medical studies and entered the army, having obtained a commission as Ensign from President Washington. He was then but nineteen years old. From that time he passed gradually upward in rank until he became aide to Gen. Wayne, after whose death he resigned his commission. He was then appointed Secretary of the Northwestern Territory. This Territory was then en[titled to a delegate in Con]gress, and Harrison was chosen to fill that position. In the spring of 1800 the Northwestern Territory was divided by Congress into two portions. The eastern portion, comprising the region now embraced in the State of Ohio, was called "The Territory northwest of the Ohio." The western portion, which included what is now called Indiana, Illinois and Wisconsin, was called "the Indiana Territory." William Henry Harrison, then twenty-seven years of age, was appointed by John Adams Governor of the Indiana Territory, and immediately after also Governor of Upper Louisiana. He was thus ruler over almost as extensive a realm as any sovereign upon the globe. He was Superintendent of Indian Affairs, and was invested with powers nearly dictatorial over the then rapidly increasing white population. The ability and fidelity with which he discharged these responsible duties may be inferred from the fact that he was four times appointed to this office—first by John Adams, twice by Thomas Jefferson, and afterwards by President Madison.

When he began his administration there were but three white settlements in that almost boundless region, now crowded with cities and resounding with all the tumult of wealth and traffic. One of these settlements was on the Ohio, nearly opposite Louisville; one at Vincennes, on the Wabash, and the third was a French settlement.

The vast wilderness over which Gov. Harrison reigned was filled with many tribes of Indians. About the year 1806, two extraordinary men, twin brothers of the Shawnee tribe, rose among them. One of these was called Tecumseh, or "the Crouching Panther;" the other Olliwacheca, or "the Prophet." Tecumseh was not ... great sagac ity, far-reaching foresight and indomitable perseverance in any enterprise in which he might engage His brother, the Prophet, was an orator, who could sway the feelings of the untutored Indians as the gale tossed the tree-tops beneath which they dwelt With an enthusiasm unsurpassed by Peter the Hermit rousing Europe to the crusades, he went from tribe to tribe, assuming that he was specially sent by the Great Spirit

Gov Harrison made many attempts to conciliate the Indians, but at last war came, and at Tippecanoe the Indians were routed with great slaughter October 28, 1812, his army began its march When near the Prophet's town, three Indians of rank made their appearance and inquired why Gov Harrison was approaching them in so hostile an attitude After a short conference, arrangements were made for a meeting the next day to agree upon terms of peace

But Gov Harrison was too well acquainted with the Indian character to be deceived by such protestations Selecting a favorable spot for his night's encampment, he took every precaution against surprise His troops were posted in a hollow square and slept upon their arms The wakeful Governor, between three and four o'clock in the morning, had risen, and was sitting in conversation with his aides by the embers of a waning fire It was a chill, cloudy morning, with a drizzling rain In the darkness, the Indians had crept as near as possible, and just then, with a savage yell, rushed, with all the desperation which superstition and passion most highly inflamed could give, upon the left flank of the little army The savages had been amply provided with guns and ammunition by the English, and their war-whoop was accompanied by a shower of bullets

The camp-fires were instantly extinguished, as the light aided the Indians in their aim, and Gen Harrison's troops stood as immovable as the rocks around them until day dawned, when they made a simultaneous charge with the bayonet and swept everything before them, completely routing the [illegible]

Gov Ha[illegible]
to the utmo[illegible]

Canadas, were of themselves a very formidable force, but with their savage allies rushing like wolves from the forest, burning, plundering, scalping, torturing, the wide frontier was plunged into a state of consternation which even the most vivid imagination can but faintly conceive Gen. Hull had made an ignominious surrender of his forces at Detroit Under these despairing circumstances, Gov. Harrison was appointed by President Madison Commander-in-Chief of the Northwestern Army, with orders to retake Detroit and to protect the frontiers It would be difficult to place a man in a situation demanding more energy, sagacity and courage, but he was found equal to the position, and nobly and triumphantly did he meet all the responsibilities

In 1816, Gen Harrison was chosen a member of the National House of Representatives, to represent the District of Ohio In Congress he proved an active member, and whenever he spoke it was with a force of reason and power of eloquence which arrested the attention of all the members

In 1819, Harrison was elected to the Senate of Ohio, and in 1824, as one of the Presidential Electors of that State, he gave his vote for Henry Clay The same year he was chosen to the United States Senate In 1836 his friends brought him forward as a candidate for the Presidency against Van Buren, but he was defeated At the close of Mr. Van Buren's term, he was re-nominated by his party, and Mr Harrison was unanimously nominated by the Whigs, with John Tyler for the Vice-Presidency The contest was very animated Gen Jackson gave all his influence to prevent Harrison's election, but his triumph was signal

The cabinet which he formed, with Daniel Webster at its head as Secretary of State, was one of the most brilliant with which any President had ever been surrounded Never were the prospects of an administration more flattering, or the hopes of the country more sanguine In the midst of these bright and joyous prospects, Gen Harrison was seized by a pleurisy-fever, and after a few [illegible] the 4th of April, [illegible] tion as President [illegible]

John Tyler

JOHN TYLER.

JOHN TYLER, the tenth President of the United States, and was born in Charles City County, Va., March 29, 1790. He was the favored child of affluence and high social position. At the early age of twelve, John entered William and Mary College, and graduated with much honor when but seventeen years old. After graduating, he devoted himself with great assiduity to the study of law, partly with his father and partly with Edmund Randolph, one of the most distinguished lawyers of Virginia.

At nineteen years of age, he commenced the practice of law. His success was rapid and astonishing. It is said that three months had not elapsed ere there was scarcely a case on the docket of the court in which he was not retained. When but twenty-one years of age, he was almost unanimously elected to a seat in the State Legislature. He connected himself with the Democratic party, and warmly advocated the measures of Jefferson and Madison. For five successive years he was elected to the Legislature, receiving nearly the unanimous vote of his county.

When but twenty-six years of age, he was elected a Member of Congress. Here he acted earnestly and ably with the Democratic party, opposing a national bank, internal improvements by the General Government, and a protective tariff, advocating a strict construction of the Constitution and the most careful vigilance over State rights. His labors in Congress were so arduous that before the close of his second term he found it necessary to resign and retire to his estate in Charles City County to recruit his health. He, however, soon after consented to take his seat in the State Legislature, where his influence was powerful in promoting public works of great utility. With a reputation thus constantly increasing, he was chosen by a very large majority of votes Governor of his native State. His administration was a signally successful one, and his popularity secu[illegible]

John Randolph, a brilliant, erratic, half-crazed man, then represented Virginia in the Senate of the United States. A portion of the Democratic party was displeased with Mr. Randolph's wayward course, and brought forward John Tyler as his opponent, considering him the only man in Virginia of sufficient popularity to succeed against the renowned orator of Roanoke. Mr. Tyler was the victor.

In accordance with his professions, upon taking his seat in the Senate, he joined the ranks of the opposition. He opposed the tariff, and spoke against and voted against the bank as unconstitutional; he strenuously opposed all restrictions upon slavery, resisting all projects of internal improvements by the General Government, and avowed his sympathy with Mr. Calhoun's view of nullification; he declared that Gen. Jackson, by his opposition to the nullifiers, had abandoned the principles of the Democratic party. Such was Mr. Tyler's record in Congress—a record in perfect accordance with the principles which he had always avowed.

Returning to Virginia, he resumed the practice of his profession. There was a split in the Democratic party. His friends still regarded him as a true Jeffersonian, gave him a dinner, and showered compliments upon him. He had now attained the age of forty-six, and his career had been very brilliant. In consequence of his devotion to public business, his private affairs had fallen into some disorder, and it was not without satisfaction that he resumed the practice of law, and devoted himself to the cultivation of his plantation. Soon after this he removed to Williamsburg, for the better education of his children, and he again took his seat in the Legislature of Virginia.

By the southern Whigs he was sent to the national convention at Harrisburg in 1839 to nominate a President. The majority of votes were given to Gen. Harrison, a genuine Whig, much [illegible] hich wished for Henry Clay. To conciliate the southern Whigs and to secure their vote, the convention then nominated John Tyler for Vice-President. It was well known that he was not in sympathy with the Whig party in the North, but the Vice-President has very little power in the Government, his main and almost only duty being to preside over the meetings of the Senate. Thus it happened that a Whig President and, in reality, a Democratic Vice-President were chosen.

In 1841 Mr. Tyler was inaugurated Vice-President of the United States. In one short month from that time, President Harrison died, and Mr. Tyler thus found himself, to his own surprise and that of the whole nation, an occupant of the Presidential chair. Hastening from Williamsburg to Washington, on the 6th of April he was inaugurated to the high and responsible office. He was placed in a position of exceeding delicacy and difficulty. All his long life he had been opposed to the main principles of the party which had brought him into power. He had ever been a consistent honest man, with an unblemished record. Gen. Harrison had selected a Whig cabinet. Should he retain them, and thus surround himself with counselors whose views were antagonistic to his own? or, on the other hand, should he turn against the party which had elected him, and select a cabinet in harmony with himself, and which would oppose all those views which the Whigs deemed essential to the public welfare? This was his fearful dilemma. He invited the cabinet which President Harrison had selected to retain their seats, and recommended a day of fasting and prayer, that God would guide and bless us.

The Whigs carried through Congress a bill for the incorporation of a fiscal bank of the United States. The President, after ten days' delay, returned it with his veto. He suggested, however, that he would approve of a bill drawn up upon such a plan as he proposed. Such a bill was accordingly prepared, and privately submitted to him. He gave it his approval. It was passed without alt[illegible]
veto. He[illegible]
said that M[illegible]
[illegible]ure by a published letter from the Hon. John M. Botts, a distinguished Virginia Whig, who severely touched the pride of the President.

The opposition now exultingly received the President into their arms. The party which elected him denounced him bitterly. All the members of his cabinet, excepting Mr. Webster, resigned. The Whigs of Congress, both the Senate and the House, held a meeting and issued an address to the people of the United States, proclaiming that all political alliance between the Whigs and President Tyler was at an end.

Still the President attempted to conciliate. He appointed a new cabinet of distinguished Whigs and Conservatives carefully leaving out all strong party men. Mr. Webster soon found it necessary to resign, forced out by the pressure of his Whig friends. Thus the four years of Mr. Tyler's unfortunate administration passed sadly away. No one was satisfied. The land was filled with murmurs and vituperation. Whigs and Democrats alike assailed him. More and more, however, he brought himself into sympathy with his old friends, the Democrats, until at the close of his term he gave his whole influence to the support of Mr. Polk, the Democratic candidate for his successor.

On the 4th of March, 1845, President Tyler retired from the harassments of office, to the regret of neither party, and probably to his own unspeakable relief. The remainder of his days were passed mainly in the retirement of his beautiful home—Sherwood Forest, Charles City County, Va. His first wife, Miss Letitia Christian, died in Washington in 1842, and in June, 1844, he was again married, at New York, to Miss Julia Gardiner, a young lady of many personal and intellectual accomplishments.

When the great Rebellion rose, which the State Rights and nullifying doctrines of John C. Calhoun had inaugurated, President Tyler renounced his allegiance to the United States, and joined the Confederates. He was chosen a member of their Congress, and while engaged in [illegible]orce of arms, the [illegible]once presided, he

James K. Polk

JAMES K. POLK.

JAMES K POLK, the eleventh President of the United States, was born in Mecklenburgh County, N C, November 2, 1795. His parents were Samuel and Jane (Knox) Polk, the former a son of Col Thomas Polk, who located at the above place, as one of the first pioneers, in 1735 In 1806, with his wife and children, and soon after followed by most of the members of the Polk family, Samuel Polk emigrated some two or three hundred miles farther west, to the rich valley of the Duck River Here, in the midst of the wilderness, in a region which was subsequently called Maury County, they erected their log huts and established their homes In the hard toil of a new farm in the wilderness, James K Polk spent the early years of his childhood and youth His father, adding the pursuit of a surveyor to that of a farmer, gradually increased in wealth, until he became one of the leading men of the region His mother was a superior woman, of strong common sense and earnest piety

Very early in life James developed a taste for reading, and expressed the strongest desire to obtain a liberal education His mother's training had made him methodical in his habits, had taught him punctuality and industry, and had inspired him with lofty principles of morality His health was frail, and his father, fearing that he might not be able to endure a sedentary life, got a situation for him behind the counter, hoping to fit him for commercial pursuits

This was to James a bitter disappointment He had no taste for these duties, and his daily tasks were irksome in the extreme He remained in this uncongenial occupation but a few weeks, when, at his earnest solicitation, his father removed him and made arrangements for him to prosecute his studies Soon after he sent him to Murfreesboro Academy With ardor which could scarcely be surp studies, and in less than two and a-half years, in the autumn of 1815, entered the sophomore class in the University of North Carolina, at Chapel Hill Here he was one of the most exemplary of scholars, punctual in every exercise, never allowing himself to be absent from a recitation or a religious service

Mr Polk graduated in 1818, with the highest honors, being deemed the best scholar of his class, both in mathematics and the classics He was then twenty-three years of age His health was at this time much impaired by the assiduity with which he had prosecuted his studies After a short season of relaxation, he went to Nashville, and entered the office of Felix Grundy, to study law Here Mr Polk renewed his acquaintance with Andrew Jackson, who resided on his plantation, the "Hermitage," but a few miles from Nashville They had probably been slightly acquainted before

Mr Polk s father was a Jeffersonian Republican and James K adhered to the same political faith He was a popular public speaker, and was constantly called upon to address the meetings of his party friends His skill as a speaker was such that he was popularly called the Napoleon of the stump He was a man of unblemished morals, genial and courteous in his bearing and with that sympathetic nature in the joys and griefs of others which gave him hosts of friends In 1823 he was elected to the Legislature of Tennessee, and gave his strong influence toward the election of his friend, Mr Jackson, to the Presidency of the United States

In January, 1824, Mr Polk married Miss Sarah Childress, of Rutherford County, Tenn His bride was altogether worthy of him a lady of beauty and culture In the fall of 1825 Mr Polk was chosen a member of Congress, and the satis

be inferred

from the fact, that for fourteen successive years, or until 1839, he was continued in that office He then voluntarily withdrew, only that he might accept the Gubernatorial chair of Tennessee In Congress he was a laborious member, a frequent and a popular speaker He was always in his seat, always courteous, and whenever he spoke it was always to the point, without any ambitious rhetorical display

During five sessions of Congress Mr Polk was Speaker of the House Strong passions were roused and stormy scenes were witnessed, but he performed his arduous duties to a very general satisfaction, and a unanimous vote of thanks to him was passed by the House as he withdrew on the 4th of March, 1839

In accordance with Southern usage, Mr Polk, as a candidate for Governor, canvassed the State He was elected by a large majority, and on October 14, 1839, took the oath of office at Nashville In 1841 his term of office expired, and he was again the candidate of the Democratic party, but was defeated

On the 4th of March, 1845, Mr Polk was inaugurated President of the United States The verdict of the country in favor of the annexation of Texas exerted its influence upon Congress, and the last act of the administration of President Tyler was to affix his signature to a joint resolution of Congress, passed on the 3d of March, approving of the annexation of Texas to the Union As Mexico still claimed Texas as one of her provinces, the Mexican Minister, Almonte, immediately demanded his passports and left the country, declaring the act of the annexation to be an act hostile to Mexico

In his first message, President Polk urged that Texas should immediately, by act of Congress, be received into the Union on the same footing with the other States In the mean time, Gen Taylor was sent with an army into Texas to hold the country He was first sent to Nueces, which the Mexicans said was the western boundary of Texas Then he was sent nearly two hundred miles further west, to the Rio Grande, where he erected batteries which commanded the Mexican city of Matamoras which was situated on the western banks The anticipated collision soon took place, and war was declared against Mexico by President Polk The war was pushed forward by his administration with great vigor Gen. Taylor, whose army was first called one of "observation," then of "occupation," then of "invasion," was sent forward to Monterey The feeble Mexicans in every encounter were hopelessly slaughtered. The day of judgment alone can reveal the misery which this war caused It was by the ingenuity of Mr. Polk's administration that the war was brought on

"To the victors belong the spoils" Mexico was prostrate before us Her capital was in our hands We now consented to peace upon the condition that Mexico should surrender to us, in addition to Texas, all of New Mexico, and all of Upper and Lower California This new demand embraced, exclusive of Texas, eight hundred thousand square miles This was an extent of territory equal to nine States of the size of New York Thus slavery was securing eighteen majestic States to be added to the Union There were some Americans who thought it all right, there were others who thought it all wrong In the prosecution of this war we expended twenty thousand lives and more than $100,000,000 Of this money $15,000,000 were paid to Mexico

On the 3d of March, 1849, Mr Polk retired from office, having served one term The next day was Sunday On the 5th, Gen Taylor was inaugurated as his successor. Mr Polk rode to the Capitol in the same carriage with Gen Taylor, and the same evening, with Mrs Polk, he commenced his return to Tennessee He was then but fifty-four years of age He had always been strictly temperate in all his habits, and his health was good With an ample fortune, a choice library, a cultivated mind, and domestic ties of the dearest nature, it seemed as though long years of tranquillity and happiness were before him. But the cholera—that fearful scourge—was then sweeping up the Valley of the Mississippi, and he contracted the disease, dying on the 15th of June, 1849, in the fifty-fourth year of his age, greatly mourned by his countrymen

Zachary Taylor

ZACHARY TAYLOR.

ZACHARY TAYLOR, twelfth President of the United States, was born on the 24th of November, 1784, in Orange County, Va His father, Col Taylor, was a Virginian of note, and a distinguished patriot and soldier of the Revolution When Zachary was an infant, his father, with his wife and two children, emigrated to Kentucky, where he settled in the pathless wilderness, a few miles from Louisville In this frontier home, away from civilization and all its refinements, young Zachary could enjoy but few social and educational advantages When six years of age he attended a common school, and was then regarded as a bright, active boy, rather remarkable for bluntness and decision of character He was strong, fearless and self-reliant, and manifested a strong desire to enter the army to fight the Indians, who were ravaging the frontiers There is little to be recorded of the uneventful years of his childhood on his father's large but lonely plantation

In 1808, his father succeeded in obtaining for him a commission as Lieutenant in the United States army, and he joined the troops which were stationed at New Orleans under Gen Wilkinson Soon after this he married Miss Margaret Smith, a young lady from one of the first families of Maryland

Immediately after the declaration of war with England, in 1812, Capt Taylor (for he had then been promoted to that rank) was put in command of Ft Harrison, on the Wabash, about fifty miles above Vincennes This fort had been built in the wilderness by Gen Harrison, on his march to Tippecanoe. It was one of the first points of attack by the Indians, led by Tecumseh Its garrison consisted of a broken company of infantry, numbering fifty men, many of whom were sick

Early in the autumn of 1812, the Indians, stealthily, and i-

fort Their approach was first indicated by the murder of two soldiers just outside of the stockade Capt Taylor made every possible preparation to meet the anticipated assault On the 4th of September, a band of forty painted and plumed savages came to the fort, waving a white flag, and informed Capt Taylor that in the morning their chief would come to have a talk with him. It was evident that their object was merely to ascertain the state of things at the fort, and Capt. Taylor, well versed in the wiles of the savages, kept them at a distance

The sun went down, the savages disappeared, the garrison slept upon their arms One hour before midnight the war-whoop burst from a thousand lips in the forest around, followed by the discharge of musketry and the rush of the foe Every man, sick and well, sprang to his post Every man knew that defeat was not merely death, but, in the case of capture death by the most agonizing and prolonged torture No pen can describe, no imagination can conceive, the scenes which ensued The savages succeeded in setting fire to one of the block-houses Until six o'clock in the morning this awful conflict continued, when the savages, baffled at every point and gnashing their teeth with rage, retired Capt. Taylor, for this gallant defense, was promoted to the rank of Major by brevet

Until the close of the war, Maj Taylor was placed in such situations that he saw but little more of active service He was sent far away into the depths of the wilderness to Ft. Crawford, on Fox River, which empties into Green Bay Here there was little to be done but to wear away the tedious hours as one best could There were no books, no society, no intellectual stimulus Thus with him the uneventful years rolled on Gradually he rose to the rank of

which resulted in the capture of that renowned chieftain, Col Taylor took a subordinate, but a brave and efficient, part

For twenty-four years Col Taylor was engaged in the defense of the frontiers, in scenes so remote, and in employments so obscure, that his name was unknown beyond the limits of his own immediate acquaintance In the year 1836, he was sent to Florida to compel the Seminole Indians to vacate that region, and retire beyond the Mississippi, as their chiefs by treaty had promised they should do The services rendered here secured for Col Taylor the high appreciation of the Government, and as a reward he was elevated to the high rank of Brigadier-General by brevet, and soon after, in May, 1838, was appointed to the chief command of the United States troops in Florida

After two years of wearisome employment amidst the everglades of the Peninsula, Gen Taylor obtained, at his own request, a change of command, and was stationed over the Department of the Southwest This field embraced Louisiana, Mississippi, Alabama and Georgia Establishing his headquarters at Ft Jessup, in Louisiana, he removed his family to a plantation which he purchased near Baton Rouge Here he remained for five years, buried, as it were, from the world, but faithfully discharging every duty imposed upon him

In 1846, Gen Taylor was sent to guard the land between the Nueces and Rio Grande, the latter river being the boundary of Texas, which was then claimed by the United States Soon the war with Mexico was brought on, and at Palo Alto and Resaca de la Palma, Gen Taylor won brilliant victories over the Mexicans The rank of Major-General by brevet was then conferred upon Gen Taylor, and his name was received with enthusiasm almost everywhere in the nation Then came the battles of Monterey and Buena Vista, in which he won signal victories over forces much larger than he commanded

The tidings of the brilliant victory of Buena Vista spread [illegible] over the country [illegible] Gen Taylor was on every one's lips [illegible] Wh[illegible] to take advantage of this wonderful popularity in bringing forward the unpolished, unlettered, honest soldier as their candidate for the Presidency Gen Taylor was astonished at the announcement, and for a time would not listen to it, declaring that he was not at all qualified for such an office So little interest had he taken in politics, that for forty years he had not cast a vote It was not without chagrin that several distinguished statesmen, who had been long years in the public service, found their claims set aside in behalf of one whose name had never been heard of, save in connection with Palo Alto, Resaca de la Palma, Monterey and Buena Vista It is said that Daniel Webster, in his haste, remarked, "It is a nomination not fit to be made"

Gen Taylor was not an eloquent speaker nor a fine writer His friends took possession of him, and prepared such few communications as it was needful should be presented to the public The popularity of the successful warrior swept the land He was triumphantly elected over two opposing candidates,—Gen Cass and Ex-President Martin Van Buren' Though he selected an excellent cabinet, the good old man found himself in a very uncongenial position, and was at times sorely perplexed and harassed His mental sufferings were very severe, and probably tended to hasten his death The pro-slavery party was pushing its claims with tireless energy, expeditions were fitting out to capture Cuba, California was pleading for admission to the Union, while slavery stood at the door to bar her out Gen Taylor found the political conflicts in Washington to be far more trying to the nerves than battles with Mexicans or Indians

In the midst of all these troubles, Gen. Taylor, after he had occupied the Presidential chair but little over a year, took cold, and after a brief sickness of but little over five days, died, on the 9th of July, 1850 His last words were "I am not afraid to die I am ready I have endeavored to do my duty" He died universally respected and beloved An honest, unpretending man [illegible] ing in the affection [illegible] the Nation bitterly lamented his death

Millard Fillmore

MILLARD FILLMORE.

MILLARD FILLMORE, thirteenth President of the United States, was born at Summer Hill, Cayuga County, N. Y., on the 7th of January, 1800. His father was a farmer, and, owing to misfortune, in humble circumstances. Of his mother, the daughter of Dr. Abiathar Millard, of Pittsfield, Mass., it has been said that she possessed an intellect of a high order, united with much personal loveliness, sweetness of disposition, graceful manners and exquisite sensibilities. She died in 1831, having lived to see her son a young man of distinguished promise, though she was not permitted to witness the high dignity which he finally attained.

In consequence of the secluded home and limited means of his father, Millard enjoyed but slender advantages for education in his early years. The common schools, which he occasionally attended, were very imperfect institutions, and books were scarce and expensive. There was nothing then in his character to indicate the brilliant career upon which he was about to enter. He was a plain farmer's boy—intelligent, good-looking, kind hearted. The sacred influences of home had taught him to revere the Bible, and had laid the foundations of an upright character. When fourteen years of age, his father sent him some hundred miles from home to the then wilds of Livingston County, to learn the trade of a clothier. Near the mill there was a small village, where some enterprising man had commenced the collection of a village library. This proved an inestimable blessing to young Fillmore. His evenings were spent in reading. Soon every leisure moment was occupied with books. His thirst for knowledge became insatiate, and the selections which he made were continually more elevating and instructive. [illegible] oratory, and tl [illegible] in his heart a desire to be something more than a mere worker with his hands.

The young clothier had now attained the age of nineteen years, and was of fine personal appearance and of gentlemanly demeanor. It so happened that there was a gentleman in the neighborhood of ample pecuniary means and of benevolence,—Judge Walter Wood,—who was struck with the prepossessing appearance of young Fillmore. He made his acquaintance, and was so much impressed with his ability and attainments that he advised him to abandon his trade and devote himself to the study of the law. The young man replied that he had no means of his own, no friends to help him, and that his previous education had been very imperfect. But Judge Wood had so much confidence in him that he kindly offered to take him into his own office, and to lend him such money as he needed. Most gratefully the generous offer was accepted.

There is in many minds a strange delusion about a collegiate education. A young man is supposed to be liberally educated if he has graduated at some college. But many a boy who loiters through university halls and then enters a law office is by no means as well prepared to prosecute his legal studies as was Millard Fillmore when he graduated at the clothing mill at the end of four years of manual labor, during which every leisure moment had been devoted to intense mental culture.

In 1823, when twenty-three years of age, he was admitted to the Court of Common Pleas. He then went to the village of Aurora, and commenced the practice of law. In this secluded, quiet region, his practice, of course, was limited, and there was no opportunity for a sudden rise in fortune or in fame. Here, in 1826, he married a [illegible] capable of adorning any station she might be called to fill,—Miss Abigail Powers

His elevation of character, his untiring industry, his legal acquirements, and his skill as an advocate, gradually attracted attention, and he was invited to enter into partnership, under highly advantageous circumstances, with an elder member of the Bar in Buffalo Just before removing to Buffalo, in 1829, he took his seat in the House of Assembly of the State of New York, as a Representative from Erie County Though he had never taken a very active part in politics, his vote and sympathies were with the Whig party The State was then Democratic, and he found himself in a helpless minority in the Legislature, still the testimony comes from all parties that his courtesy, ability and integrity won, to a very unusual degree, the respect of his associates

In the autumn of 1832, he was elected to a seat in the United States Congress He entered that troubled arena in the most tumultuous hours of our national history, when the great conflict respecting the national bank and the removal of the deposits was raging

His term of two years closed, and he returned to his profession, which he pursued with increasing reputation and success After a lapse of two years he again became a candidate for Congress, was re-elected, and took his seat in 1837 His past experience as a Representative gave him strength and confidence The first term of service in Congress to any man can be but little more than an introduction He was now prepared for active duty. All his energies were brought to bear upon the public good Every measure received his impress.

Mr Fillmore was now a man of wide repute, and his popularity filled the State In the year 1847, when he had attained the age of forty-seven years, he was elected Comptroller of the State His labors at the Bar, in the Legislature, in Congress and as Comptroller, had given him very considerable fame The Whigs were casting about to find suitable candidates for President and Vi[illegible] tion Far a[illegible] the Ri[illegible] there was a [illegible] one or two successful battles with the Mexicans, which had caused his name to be proclaimed in trumpet-tones all over the land as a candidate for the presidency But it was necessary to associate with him on the same ticket some man of reputation as a statesman

Under the influence of these considerations, the names of Zachary Taylor and Millard Fillmore became the rallying-cry of the Whigs, as their candidates for President and Vice-President The Whig ticket was signally triumphant On the 4th of March, 1849, Gen Taylor was inaugurated President, and Millard Fillmore Vice-President, of the United States

On the 9th of July, 1850, President Taylor, about one year and four months after his inauguration, was suddenly taken sick and died By the Constitution, Vice-President Fillmore thus became President He appointed a very able cabinet, of which the illustrious Daniel Webster was Secretary of State, nevertheless, he had serious difficulties to contend with, since the opposition had a majority in both Houses He did all in his power to conciliate the South, but the pro-slavery party in the South felt the inadequacy of all measures of transient conciliation The population of the free States was so rapidly increasing over that of the slave States, that it was inevitable that the power of the Government should soon pass into the hands of the free States The famous compromise measures were adopted under Mr Fillmore's administration, and the Japan expedition was sent out On the 4th of March, 1853, he, having served one term, retired.

In 1856, Mr. Fillmore was nominated for the Presidency by the "Know-Nothing" party, but was beaten by Mr Buchanan. After that Mr Fillmore lived in retirement During the terrible conflict of civil war, he was mostly silent It was generally supposed that his sympathies were rather with those who were endeavoring to overthrow our institutions President Fillmore kept aloof from the conflict, without any cordial words of cheer to one party or the other He was thus [illegible] a ripe old age, and [illegible] 8, 1874

Franklin Pierce

FRANKLIN PIERCE.

FRANKLIN PIERCE, the fourteenth President of the United States, was born in Hillsborough, N. H., November 23, 1804. His father was a Revolutionary soldier, who with his own strong arm hewed out a home in the wilderness. He was a man of inflexible integrity, of strong, though uncultivated, mind, and was an uncompromising Democrat. The mother of Franklin Pierce was all that a son could desire—an intelligent, prudent, affectionate, Christian woman.

Franklin, who was the sixth of eight children, was a remarkably bright and handsome boy, generous, warm-hearted and brave. He won alike the love of old and young. The boys on the play-ground loved him. His teachers loved him. The neighbors looked upon him with pride and affection. He was by instinct a gentleman, always speaking kind words, and doing kind deeds, with a peculiar, unstudied tact which taught him what was agreeable. Without developing any precocity of genius, or any unnatural devotion to books, he was a good scholar, and in body and mind a finely developed boy.

When sixteen years of age, in the year 1820, he entered Bowdoin College, at Brunswick, Me. He was one of the most popular young men in the college. The purity of his moral character, the unvarying courtesy of his demeanor, his rank as a scholar, and genial nature, rendered him a universal favorite. There was something peculiarly winning in his address, and it was evidently not in the slightest degree studied—it was the simple outgushing of his own magnanimous and loving nature.

Upon graduating, in the year 1824, Franklin Pierce commenced the study of law in the office of Judge Wood

lawyers of the State, and a man of great private worth. The eminent social qualities of the young lawyer, his father's prominence as a public man, and the brilliant political career into which Judge Woodbury was entering, all tended to entice Mr. Pierce into the fascinating yet perilous path of political life. With all the ardor of his nature he espoused the cause of Gen. Jackson for the Presidency. He commenced the practice of law in Hillsborough, and was soon elected to represent the town in the State Legislature. Here he served for four years. The last two years he was chosen Speaker of the House by a very large vote.

In 1833, at the age of twenty-nine, he was elected a member of Congress. In 1837, being then but thirty-three years old, he was elected to the Senate, taking his seat just as Mr. Van Buren commenced his administration. He was the youngest member in the Senate. In the year 1834 he married Miss Jane Means Appleton, a lady of rare beauty and accomplishments, and one admirably fitted to adorn every station with which her husband was honored. Of the three sons who were born to them, all now sleep with their parents in the grave.

In the year 1838, Mr. Pierce, with growing fame and increasing business as a lawyer, took up his residence in Concord, the capital of New Hampshire. President Polk, upon his accession to office, appointed Mr. Pierce Attorney-General of the United States, but the offer was declined in consequence of numerous professional engagements at home, and the precarious state of Mrs. Pierce's health. He also, about the same time, declined the nomination for Governor by the

exico called

Mr Pierce into the army Receiving the appointment of Brigadier-General, he embarked with a portion of his troops at Newport, R I., on the 27th of May, 1847. He took an important part in this war, proving himself a brave and true soldier

When Gen Pierce reached his home in his native State, he was received enthusiastically by the advocates of the Mexican War, and coldly by his opponents He resumed the practice of his profession, very frequently taking an active part in political questions, giving his cordial support to the pro-slavery wing of the Democratic party The compromise measures met cordially with his approval, and he strenuously advocated the enforcement of the infamous Fugitive Slave Law, which so shocked the religious sensibilities of the North He thus became distinguished as a "Northern man with Southern principles" The strong partisans of slavery in the South consequently regarded him as a man whom they could safely trust in office to carry out their plans

On the 12th of June, 1852, the Democratic convention met in Baltimore to nominate a candidate for the Presidency For four days they continued in session, and in thirty-five ballotings no one had obtained a two-thirds vote Not a vote thus far had been thrown for Gen Pierce Then the Virginia delegation brought forward his name There were fourteen more ballotings, during which Gen Pierce constantly gained strength, until, at the forty-ninth ballot, he received two hundred and eighty-two votes, and all other candidates eleven Gen Winfield Scott was the Whig candidate Gen Pierce was chosen with great unanimity Only four States—Vermont, Massachusetts, Kentucky and Tennessee—cast their electoral votes against him. Gen Franklin Pierce was therefore inaugurated President of the United States on the 4th of March, 1853

His administration proved one of the most stormy our country had ever experienced The controversy between slavery and freedom was then approach[illegible] culminating point It became eviden[illegible] conflict bet[illegible] could not long [illegible]

President Pierce, during the whole of his administration, did everything he could to conciliate the South, but it was all in vain The conflict every year grew more violent, and threats of the dissolution of the Union were borne to the North on every Southern breeze

Such was the condition of affairs when President Pierce approached the close of his four-years term of office The North had become thoroughly alienated from him The anti-slavery sentiment, goaded by great outrages, had been rapidly increasing, all the intellectual ability and social worth of President Pierce were forgotten in deep reprehension of his administrative acts The slaveholders of the South also, unmindful of the fidelity with which he had advocated those measures of Government which they approved, and perhaps feeling that he had rendered himself so unpopular as no longer to be able to acceptably serve them, ungratefully dropped him, and nominated James Buchanan to succeed him

On the 4th of March, 1857, President Pierce returned to his home in Concord His three children were all dead, his last surviving child having been killed before his eyes in a railroad accident and his wife, one of the most estimable and accomplished of ladies, was rapidly sinking in consumption The hour of dreadful gloom soon came, and he was left alone in the world without wife or child

When the terrible Rebellion burst forth which divided our country into two parties, and two only, Mr Pierce remained steadfast in the principles which he had always cherished, and gave his sympathies to that pro-slavery party with which he had ever been allied He declined to do anything, either by voice or pen, to strengthen the hand of the National Government He continued to reside in Concord until the time of his death, which occurred in October, 1869 He was one of the most genial and social of men an honored communicant of the Episcopal Church, and one of the kindest of neighbors Generous to a fault, he contributed liberally toward the alleviation [illegible] d many of his [illegible] l by his maternal

James Buchanan

JAMES BUCHANAN.

JAMES BUCHANAN, the fifteenth President of the United States, was born in a small frontier town, at the foot of the eastern ridge of the Alleghanies, in Franklin County, Pa., on the 23d of April, 1791. The place where the humble cabin home stood was called Stony Batter. His father was a native of the north of Ireland, who had emigrated in 1783, with little property save his own strong arms. Five years afterward he married Elizabeth Spear, the daughter of a respectable farmer, and, with his young bride, plunged into the wilderness, staked his claim, reared his log hut, opened a clearing with his axe, and settled down there to perform his obscure part in the drama of life. When James was eight years of age, his father removed to the village of Mercersburg, where his son was placed at school, and commenced a course of study in English, Latin and Greek. His progress was rapid, and at the age of fourteen he entered Dickinson College, at Carlisle. Here he developed remarkable talent, and took his stand among the first scholars in the institution.

In the year [illegible] he graduated with the highest honors of his class. He was then eighteen years of age, tall and graceful, vigorous in health, fond of athletic sports, an unerring shot, and enlivened with an exuberant flow of animal spirits. He immediately commenced the study of law in the city of Lancaster, and was admitted to the Bar in 1812, when he was but twenty-one years of age.

In 1820, he reluctantly consented to run as a candidate for Congress. He was elected, and for ten years he remained a member of the Lower House. During the vacations of Congress he occasionally tried some important case. In 1831 he retired altogether from the toils of his profession, having acquired an ample fortune.

Gen. Jackson, upon his elevation to the Presidency, appointed Mr. Buchanan Minister to Russia. The duties of his mission he performed with ability, and gave satisfaction to all parties. Upon his return, in 1833, he was elected to a seat in the United States Senate. He there met as his associates Webster, Clay, Wright and Calhoun. He advocated the measures proposed by President Jackson, of making reprisals against France to enforce the payment of our claims against that country, and defended the course of the President in his unprecedented and wholesale removal from office of those who were not the supporters of his administration. Upon this question he was brought into direct collision with Henry Clay. He also, with voice and vote, advocated expunging from the journal of the Senate the vote of censure against Gen. Jackson for removing the deposits. Earnestly he opposed the abolition of slavery in the District of Columbia, and urged the prohibition of the circulation of anti-slavery documents by the United States mails. As to petitions on the subject of slavery, he advocated that they should be respectfully received, and that the reply should be returned that Congress had no power to legislate upon the subject. "Congress," said he, "might as well undertake to interfere with slavery under a foreign government as in any of the States where it now exists."

Upon Mr. Polk's accession to the Presidency, Mr. Buchanan became Secretary of State, and as such, took his share of the responsibility in the conduct of the Mexican War. Mr. Polk assumed that crossing the Nueces by the American troops into the disputed territory was not wrong, but for the Mexicans to cross the Rio Grande into Texas was a declaration of war. No candid man can read with pleasure the account of the course our Government pursued in that movement.

Mr. Buchanan identified himself thoroughly with the party devoted to the perpetuation and extension of slavery, and brought all the energies of his mind to bear against the Wilmot Proviso. He gave his cordial approval to the compromise measures of 1850, which included the Fugitive Slave Law. Mr. Pierce, upon his election to the Presidency, honored Mr. Buchanan with the mission to England.

In the year 1856, a national Democratic Convention nominated Mr. Buchanan for the Presidency. The political conflict was one of the most severe in which our country has ever engaged. All the friends of slavery were on one side, all the advocates of its restriction and final abolition on the other. Mr. Fremont, the candidate of the enemies of slavery, received one hundred and fourteen electoral votes. Mr. Buchanan received one hundred and seventy-four, and was elected. The popular vote stood 1,340,618 for Fremont, 1,224,750 for Buchanan. On March 4, 1857, the latter was inaugurated.

Mr. Buchanan was far advanced in life. Only four years were wanting to fill up his three-score years and ten. His own friends, those with whom he had been allied in political principles and action for years, were seeking the destruction of the Government, that they might rear upon the ruins of our free institutions a nation whose corner-stone should be human slavery. In this emergency, Mr. Buchanan was hopelessly bewildered. He could not, with his long-avowed principles, consistently oppose the State Rights party in their assumptions. As President of the United States, bound by his oath faithfully to administer the laws, he could not, without perjury of the grossest kind, unite with those endeavoring to overthrow the Republic. He therefore did not[illegible].

The opponents of Mr. Bu[illegible] tion nominated Abraham Lincoln as their standard-bearer in the next Presidential canvass. The pro-slavery party declared that if he were elected and the control of the Government were thus taken from their hands, they would secede from the Union, taking with them as they retired the National Capitol at Washington and the lion's share of the territory of the United States.

As the storm increased in violence, the slave-holders claiming the right to secede, and Mr. Buchanan avowing that Congress had no power to prevent it, one of the most pitiable exhibitions of governmental imbecility was exhibited that the world has ever seen. He declared that Congress had no power to enforce its laws in any State which had withdrawn, or which was attempting to withdraw, from the Union. This was not the doctrine of Andrew Jackson, when, with his hand upon his sword-hilt, he exclaimed "The Union must and shall be preserved!"

South Carolina seceded in December, 1860, nearly three months before the inauguration of President Lincoln. Mr. Buchanan looked on in listless despair. The rebel flag was raised in Charleston, Ft. Sumter was besieged, our forts, navy-yards and arsenals were seized; our depots of military stores were plundered, and our custom-houses and post-offices were appropriated by the rebels.

The energy of the rebels and the imbecility of our Executive were alike marvelous. The nation looked on in agony, waiting for the slow weeks to glide away and close the administration, so terrible in its weakness. At length the long-looked-for hour of deliverance came, when Abraham Lincoln was to receive the scepter.

The administration of President Buchanan was certainly the most calamitous our country has experienced. His best friends can not recall it with pleasure. And still more deplorable it is for his fame, that in that dreadful conflict which rolled its billows of flame and blood over our whole land, no word came from his lips to indicate his wish that our country's banner should triumph over the flag of the Rebellion. He died at his W[illegible]

Your friend as ever
A. Lincoln

ABRAHAM LINCOLN.

ABRAHAM LINCOLN, the sixteenth President of the United States, was born in Hardin County, Ky., February 12, 1809. About the year 1780, a man by the name of Abraham Lincoln left Virginia with his family and moved into the then wilds of Kentucky. Only two years after this emigration, and while still a young man, he was working one day in a field, when an Indian stealthily approached and killed him. His widow was left in extreme poverty with five little children, three boys and two girls. Thomas, the youngest of the boys, and the father of President Abraham Lincoln, was four years of age at his father's death.

When twenty-eight years old, Thomas Lincoln built a log cabin, and married Nancy Hanks, the daughter of another family of poor Kentucky emigrants, who had also come from Virginia. Their second child was Abraham Lincoln, the subject of this sketch. The mother of Abraham was a noble woman, gentle, loving, pensive, created to adorn a palace, but doomed to toil and pine, and die in a hovel. "All that I am, or hope to be," exclaimed the grateful son, "I owe to my angel-mother." When he was eight years of age, his father sold his cabin and small farm and moved to Indiana, where two years later his mother died.

As the years rolled on, the lot of this lowly family was the usual lot of humanity. There were joys and griefs, weddings and funerals. Abraham's sister Sarah, to whom he was tenderly attached, was married when a child of but fourteen years of age, and soon died. The family was gradually scattered, and Thomas Lincoln sold out his squatter's claim in 1830, and emigrated to Macon County, Ill.

Abraham Lincoln was then twenty-one years of age. With vigorous hands he aided his father in rearing another log cabin, and worked quite diligently at this until he saw the family comfortably settled, and their small lot of enclosed prairie planted [illegible] his father his intention to leave home, and to go out into the world and seek his fortune. Little did he or his friends imagine how brilliant that fortune was to be. He saw the value of education and was intensely earnest to improve his mind to the utmost of his power. Religion he revered. His morals were pure, and he was uncontaminated by a single vice.

Young Abraham worked for a time as a hired laborer among the farmers. Then he went to Springfield, where he was employed in building a large flat-boat. In this he took a herd of swine, floated them down the Sangamon to Illinois, and thence by the Mississippi to New Orleans. Whatever Abraham Lincoln undertook he performed so faithfully as to give great satisfaction to his employers. In this adventure the latter were so well pleased, that upon his return they placed a store and mill under his care.

In 1832, at the outbreak of the Black Hawk War, he enlisted and was chosen Captain of a company. He returned to Sangamon County, and, although only twenty-three years of age, was a candidate for the Legislature, but was defeated. He soon after received from Andrew Jackson the appointment of Postmaster of New Salem. His only post-office was his hat. All the letters he received he carried there, ready to deliver to those he chanced to meet. He studied surveying, and soon made this his business. In 1834 he again became a candidate for the Legislature and was elected. Mr. Stuart, of Springfield, advised him to study law. He walked from New Salem to Springfield, borrowed of Mr. Stuart a load of books, carried them back, and began his legal studies. When the Legislature assembled, he trudged on foot with his pack on his back one hundred miles to Vandalia, then the capital. In 1836 he was re-elected to the Legislature. Here it was he first met Stephen A. Douglas. In 183[illegible] he removed to Springfield and began the practice [illegible] as so great that he was soon engaged in almost every noted case in the circuit.

In 1854 the great discussion began between Mr. Lincoln and Mr. Douglas on the slavery question. In the organization of the Republican party in Illinois, in 1856, he took an active part, and at once became one of the leaders in that party. Mr. Lincoln's speeches in opposition to Senator Douglas in the contest in 1858 for a seat in the Senate, form a most notable part of his history. The issue was on the slavery question, and he took the broad ground of the Declaration of Independence, that all men are created equal. Mr. Lincoln was defeated in this contest, but won a far higher prize.

The great Republican Convention met at Chicago on the 16th of June, 1860. The delegates and strangers who crowded the city amounted to twenty-five thousand. An immense building called "The Wigwam," was reared to accommodate the convention. There were eleven candidates for whom votes were thrown. William H. Seward, a man whose fame as a statesman had long filled the land, was the most prominent. It was generally supposed he would be the nominee. Abraham Lincoln, however, received the nomination on the third ballot.

Election day came, and Mr. Lincoln received one hundred and eighty electoral votes out of two hundred and three cast, and was, therefore, constitutionally elected President of the United States. The tirade of abuse that was poured upon this good and merciful man, especially by the slaveholders, was greater than upon any other man ever elected to this high position. In February, 1861, Mr. Lincoln started for Washington, stopping in all the large cities on his way, making speeches. The whole journey was fraught with much danger. Many of the Southern States had already seceded, and several attempts at assassination were afterward brought to light. A gang in Baltimore had arranged upon his arrival to "get up a row," and in the confusion to make sure of his death with revolvers and hand-grenades. A detective unravelled the plot. A secret and special [illegible] Harrisburg [illegible] hour of the night. The train started at half-past ten, and to prevent any possible communication on the part of the Secessionists with their Confederate gang in Baltimore, as soon as the train had started the telegraph-wires were cut. Mr. Lincoln reached Washington in safety and was inaugurated, although great anxiety was felt by all loyal people.

In the selection of his cabinet Mr. Lincoln gave to Mr. Seward the Department of State, and to other prominent opponents before the convention he gave important positions, but during no other administration had the duties devolving upon the President been so manifold, and the responsibilities so great, as those which fell to his lot. Knowing this and feeling his own weakness and inability to meet, and in his own strength to cope with, the difficulties, he learned early to seek Divine wisdom and guidance in determining his plans, and Divine comfort in all his trials, both personal and national. Contrary to his own estimate of himself, Mr. Lincoln was one of the most courageous of men. He went directly into the rebel capital just as the retreating foe was leaving, with no guard but a few sailors. From the time he had left Springfield, in 1861, however, plans had been made for his assassination, and he at last fell a victim to one of them. April 14, 1865, he, with Gen. Grant, was urgently invited to attend Ford's Theatre. It was announced that they would be present. Gen. Grant, however, left the city. President Lincoln, feeling with his characteristic kindliness of heart, that it would be a disappointment if he should fail them, very reluctantly consented to go. While listening to the play, an actor by the name of John Wilkes Booth entered the box where the President and family were seated, and fired a bullet into his brain. He died the next morning at seven o'clock.

Never before in the history of the world was a nation plunged into such deep grief by the death of its ruler. Strong men met in the streets and wept in speechless anguish. His was a life which will fitly become a model. His name as the [illegible] with that of Wash- [illegible]

Andrew Johnson

ANDREW JOHNSON.

ANDREW JOHNSON, seventeenth President of the United States. The early life of Andrew Johnson contains but the record of poverty, destitution and friendlessness. He was born December 29, 1808, in Raleigh, N. C. His parents, belonging to the class of "poor whites" of the South, were in such circumstances that they could not confer even the slightest advantages of education upon their child. When Andrew was five years of age, his father accidentally lost his life, while heroically endeavoring to save a friend from drowning. Until ten years of age, Andrew was a ragged boy about the streets, supported by the labor of his mother, who obtained her living with her own hands.

He then, having never attended a school one day, and being unable either to read or write, was apprenticed to a tailor in his native town. A gentleman was in the habit of going to the tailor's shop occasionally, and reading to the boys at work there. He often read from the speeches of distinguished British statesmen. Andrew, who was endowed with a mind of more than ordinary ability, became much interested in these speeches; his ambition was roused, and he was inspired with a strong desire to learn to read.

He accordingly applied himself to the alphabet, and with the assistance of some of his fellow-workmen learned his letters. He then called upon the gentleman to borrow the book of speeches. The owner, pleased with his zeal, not only gave him the book, but assisted him in learning to combine the letters into words. Under such difficulties he pressed onward laboriously, spending usually ten or twelve hours at work in the shop, and then robbing himself of rest and recreation to devote such time as he could to reading.

He went to Ten

Greenville, where he married a young lady who possessed some education. Under her instructions he learned to write and cipher. He became prominent in the village debating society, and a favorite with the students of Greenville College. In 1828, he organized a working man's party, which elected him Alderman, and in 1830 elected him Mayor, which position he held three years.

He now began to take a lively interest in political affairs, identifying himself with the working-class, to which he belonged. In 1835, he was elected a member of the House of Representatives of Tennessee. He was then just twenty-seven years of age. He became a very active member of the Legislature, gave his support to the Democratic party, and in 1840 "stumped the State," advocating Martin Van Buren's claims to the Presidency, in opposition to those of Gen. Harrison. In this campaign he acquired much readiness as a speaker, and extended and increased his reputation.

In 1841, he was elected State Senator; in 1843, he was elected a Member of Congress, and by successive elections held that important post for ten years. In 1853, he was elected Governor of Tennessee, and was re-elected in 1855. In all these responsible positions, he discharged his duties with distinguished ability, and proved himself the warm friend of the working classes. In 1857, Mr. Johnson was elected United States Senator.

Years before, in 1845, he had warmly advocated the annexation of Texas, stating, however, as his reason, that he thought this annexation would probably prove "to be the gateway out of which the sable sons of Africa are to pass from bondage to freedom, and become merged in a population congenial to themselves." In 1850, he also sup

to essen

tial features of which were, that the white people of the Territories should be permitted to decide for themselves whether they would enslave the colored people or not, and that the free States of the North should return to the South persons who attempted to escape from slavery.

Mr. Johnson was never ashamed of his lowly origin; on the contrary, he often took pride in avowing that he owed his distinction to his own exertions. "Sir," said he on the floor of the Senate, "I do not forget that I am a mechanic, neither do I forget that Adam was a tailor and sewed fig-leaves, and that our Savior was the son of a carpenter."

In the Charleston-Baltimore convention of 1860, he was the choice of the Tennessee Democrats for the Presidency. In 1861, when the purpose of the Southern Democracy became apparent, he took a decided stand in favor of the Union, and held that "slavery must be held subordinate to the Union at whatever cost." He returned to Tennessee, and repeatedly imperiled his own life to protect the Unionists of that State. Tennessee having seceded from the Union, President Lincoln, on March 4, 1862, appointed him Military Governor of the State, and he established the most stringent military rule. His numerous proclamations attracted wide attention. In 1864, he was elected Vice-President of the United States, and upon the death of Mr. Lincoln, April 15, 1865, became President. In a speech two days later he said, "The American people must be taught, if they do not already feel, that treason is a crime and must be punished, that the Government will not always bear with its enemies, that it is strong not only to protect, but to punish. * * The people must understand that it (treason) is the blackest of crimes, and will surely be punished." Yet his whole administration, the history of which is so well known, was in utter inconsistency with, and in the most violent opposition to, the principles laid down in that speech.

In his loose policy of reconstruction and general amnesty, he was opposed by Congress, and he characteri[illegible] lawlessly d[illegible] most. In [illegible]

"High crimes and misdemeanors," the principal of which was the removal of Secretary Stanton in violation of the Tenure of Office Act, articles of impeachment were preferred against him, and the trial began March 23.

It was very tedious, continuing for nearly three months. A test article of the impeachment was at length submitted to the court for its action. It was certain that as the court voted upon that article so would it vote upon all. Thirty-four voices pronounced the President guilty. As a two-thirds vote was necessary to his condemnation, he was pronounced acquitted, notwithstanding the great majority against him. The change of one vote from the *not guilty* side would have sustained the impeachment.

The President, for the remainder of his term, was but little regarded. He continued, though impotently, his conflict with Congress. His own party did not think it expedient to renominate him for the Presidency. The Nation rallied with enthusiasm, unparalleled since the days of Washington, around the name of Gen. Grant. Andrew Johnson was forgotten. The bullet of the assassin introduced him to the President's chair. Notwithstanding this, never was there presented to a man a better opportunity to immortalize his name, and to win the gratitude of a nation. He failed utterly. He retired to his home in Greenville, Tenn., taking no very active part in politics until 1875. On January 26, after an exciting struggle, he was chosen by the Legislature of Tennessee United States Senator in the Forty-fourth Congress, and took his seat in that body, at the special session convened by President Grant, on the 5th of March. On the 27th of July, 1875, the ex-President made a visit to his daughter's home, near Carter Station, Tenn. When he started on his journey, he was apparently in his usual vigorous health, but on reaching the residence of his child the following day, he was stricken with paralysis which rendered him unconscious. He rallied occasionally, but finally passed away at 2 A. M., July 31, aged sixty-seven years. His funeral was [illegible] of August, with [illegible]

U. S. Grant

ULYSSES S. GRANT.

ULYSSES S GRANT, the eighteenth President of the United States, was born on the 29th of April, 1822, of Christian parents, in a humble home at Point Pleasant, on the banks of the Ohio Shortly after, his father moved to Georgetown, Brown County, Ohio In this remote frontier hamlet, Ulysses received a common-school education At the age of seventeen, in the year 1839, he entered the Military Academy at West Point. Here he was regarded as a solid, sensible young man, of fair ability, and of sturdy, honest character He took respectable rank as a scholar In June, 1843, he graduated about the middle in his class, and was sent as Lieutenant of Infantry to one of the distant military posts in the Missouri Territory Two years he passed in these dreary solitudes, watching the vagabond Indians

The war with Mexico came Lieut Grant was sent with his regiment to Corpus Christi His first battle was at Palo Alto There was no chance here for the exhibition of either skill or heroism, nor at Resaca de la Palma, his second battle. At the battle of Monterey, his third engagement, it is said that he performed a signal service of daring and skillful horsemanship

At the close of the Mexican War Capt Grant returned with his regiment to New York, and was again sent to one of the military posts on the frontier The discovery of gold in California causing an immense tide of emigration to flow to the Pacific shores, Capt Grant was sent with a battalion to Ft Dallas, in Oregon, for the protection of the interests of the immigrants But life was wearisome in those wilds and he resigned his commission and returned to the States Having married he entered upon the cultivation of a small farm near St

skill as a farmer, and finding his toil not remunerative, he turned to mercantile life, entering into the leather business, with a younger brother at Galena, Ill This was in the year 1860 As the tidings of the rebels firing on Ft Sumter reached the ears of Capt Grant in his counting-room, he said "Uncle Sam has educated me for the army, though I have served him through one war, I do not feel that I have yet repaid the debt I am still ready to discharge my obligations I shall therefore buckle on my sword and see Uncle Sam through this war too"

He went into the streets, raised a company of volunteers, and led them as their Captain to Springfield, the capital of the State, where their services were offered to Gov Yates The Governor, impressed by the zeal and straightforward executive ability of Capt Grant, gave him a desk in his office to assist in the volunteer organization that was being formed in the State in behalf of the Government On the 15th of June, 1861, Capt Grant received a commission as Colonel of the Twenty first Regiment of Illinois Volunteers His merits as a West Point graduate, who had served for fifteen years in the regular army were such that he was soon promoted to the rank of Brigadier-General, and was placed in command at Cairo The rebels raised their banner at Paducah, near the mouth of the Tennessee River Scarcely had its folds appeared in the breeze ere Gen Grant was there The rebels fled, their banner fell, and the Stars and Stripes were unfurled in its stead

He entered the service with great determination and immediately began active duty This was the beginning, and until the surrender of

ie enemy

with great vigor and effectiveness. At Belmont, a few days later, he surprised and routed the rebels, then at Ft. Henry won another victory. Then came the brilliant fight at Ft. Donelson. The nation was electrified by the victory, and the brave leader of the boys in blue was immediately made a Major-General, and the military district of Tennessee was assigned to him.

Like all great captains, Gen. Grant knew well how to secure the results of victory. He immediately pushed on to the enemies' lines. Then came the terrible battles of Pittsburg Landing, Corinth, and the siege of Vicksburg, where Gen. Pemberton made an unconditional surrender of the city with over thirty thousand men and one hundred and seventy-two cannon. The fall of Vicksburg was by far the most severe blow which the rebels had thus far encountered, and opened up the Mississippi from Cairo to the Gulf.

Gen. Grant was next ordered to co-operate with Gen. Banks in a movement upon Texas, and proceeded to New Orleans, where he was thrown from his horse, and received severe injuries, from which he was laid up for months. He then rushed to the aid of Gens. Rosecrans and Thomas at Chattanooga, and by a wonderful series of strategic and technical measures put the Union army in fighting condition. Then followed the bloody battles at Chattanooga, Lookout Mountain and Missionary Ridge, in which the rebels were routed with great loss. This won for him unbounded praise in the North. On the 4th of February, 1864, Congress revived the grade of lieutenant-general, and the rank was conferred on Gen. Grant. He repaired to Washington to receive his credentials and enter upon the duties of his new office.

Gen. Grant decided as soon as he took charge of the army to concentrate the widely-dispersed National troops for an attack upon Richmond, the nominal capital of the rebellion, and endeavor there to destroy the rebel armies which would be promptly assembled from all quarters for its defense. The whole continent seemed to tremble under the [illegible]
to the deci[illegible]
ed with t[illegible]

with closely-packed thousands. His plans were comprehensive, and involved a series of campaigns, which were executed with remarkable energy and ability, and were consummated at the surrender of Lee, April 9, 1865.

The war was ended. The Union was saved. The almost unanimous voice of the nation declared Gen. Grant to be the most prominent instrument in its salvation. The eminent services he had thus rendered the country brought him conspicuously forward as the Republican candidate for the Presidential chair.

At the Republican Convention held at Chicago, May 21, 1868, he was unanimously nominated for the Presidency, and at the autumn election received a majority of the popular vote, and two hundred and fourteen out of two hundred and ninety-four electoral votes.

The National Convention of the Republican party, which met at Philadelphia on the 5th of June, 1872, placed Gen. Grant in nomination for a second term by a unanimous vote. The selection was emphatically indorsed by the people five months later, two hundred and ninety-two electoral votes being cast for him.

Soon after the close of his second term, Gen. Grant started upon his famous trip around the world. He visited almost every country of the civilized world, and was everywhere received with such ovations and demonstrations of respect and honor, private as well as public and official, as were never before bestowed upon any citizen of the United States.

He was the most prominent candidate before the Republican National Convention in 1880 for a renomination for President. He went to New York and embarked in the brokerage business under the firm name of Grant & Ward. The latter proved a villain, wrecked Grant's fortune, and for larceny was sent to the penitentiary. The General was attacked with cancer in the throat, but suffered in his stoic-like manner, never complaining. He was re-instated as General of the Army, and retired by Congress. The cancer [illegible] nd July 23, 1885
[illegible] ver the death of
[illegible]

Sincerely
R. B. Hayes

RUTHERFORD B. HAYES.

RUTHERFORD B. HAYES, the nineteenth President of the United States, was born in Delaware, Ohio, October 4, 1822, almost three months after the death of his father, Rutherford Hayes. His ancestry on both the paternal and maternal sides was of the most honorable character. It can be traced, it is said, as far back as 1280, when Hayes and Rutherford were two Scottish chieftains, fighting side by side with Baliol, William Wallace and Robert Bruce. Both families belonged to the nobility, owned extensive estates, and had a large following. Misfortune overtaking the family, George Hayes left Scotland in 1680, and settled in Windsor, Conn. His son George was born in Windsor, and remained there during his life. Daniel Hayes, son of the latter, married Sarah Lee, and lived from the time of his marriage until his death in Simsbury, Conn. Ezekiel, son of Daniel, was born in 1724, and was a manufacturer of scythes at Bradford, Conn. Rutherford Hayes, son of Ezekiel and grandfather of President Hayes, was born in New Haven, in August, 1756. He was a farmer, blacksmith and tavern-keeper. He emigrated to Vermont at an unknown date, settling in Brattleboro, where he established a hotel. Here his son, Rutherford Hayes, the father of President Hayes, was born. He was married, in September, 1813, to Sophia Birchard, of Wilmington, Vt., whose ancestors emigrated thither from Connecticut, they having been among the wealthiest and best families of Norwich. Her ancestry on the male side is traced back to 1635, to John Birchard, one of the principal founders of Norwich. Both of her grandfathers were soldiers in the Revolutionary War.

The father of President Hayes was an industrious, frugal, yet [illegible] mechanical turn of mind, and could mend a plow, knit a stocking, or do almost anything else that he chose to undertake. He was a member of the church, active in all the benevolent enterprises of the town, and conducted his business on Christian principles. After the close of the War of 1812, for reasons inexplicable to his neighbors, he resolved to emigrate to Ohio.

The journey from Vermont to Ohio in that day, when there were no canals, steamers, or railways, was a very serious affair. A tour of inspection was first made, occupying four months. Mr. Hayes decided to move to Delaware, where the family arrived in 1817. He died July 22, 1822, a victim of malarial fever, less than three months before the birth of the son of whom we write. Mrs. Hayes, in her sore bereavement, found the support she so much needed in her brother Sardis, who had been a member of the household from the day of its departure from Vermont, and in an orphan girl, whom she had adopted some time before as an act of charity.

Rutherford was seven years old before he went to school. His education, however, was not neglected. He probably learned as much from his mother and sister as he would have done at school. His sports were almost wholly within doors, his playmates being his sister and her associates. These circumstances tended, no doubt, to foster that gentleness of disposition and that delicate consideration for the feelings of others which were marked traits of his character.

His uncle, Sardis Birchard, took the deepest interest in his education, and as the boy's health had improved, and he was making good progress in his studies, he proposed to send him to college. [illegible] or at home, but he was afterwards sent for one year to a professor in the Wesleyan University in Middletown, Conn He entered Kenyon College in 1838, at the age of sixteen, and was graduated at the head of his class in 1842

Immediately after his graduation he began the study of law in the office of Thomas Sparrow, Esq, in Columbus Finding his opportunities for study in Columbus somewhat limited, he determined to enter the Law School at Cambridge, Mass, where he remained two years

In 1845, after graduating at the Law School, he was admitted to the Bar at Marietta, Ohio, and shortly afterward went into practice as an attorney-at-law with Ralph P Buckland, of Fremont Here he remained three years, acquiring but a limited practice, and apparently unambitious of distinction in his profession

In 1849 he moved to Cincinnati, where his ambition found a new stimulus For several years, however, his progress was slow. Two events occurring at this period had a powerful influence upon his subsequent life One of these was his marriage with Miss Lucy Ware Webb, daughter of Dr James Webb, of Chillicothe, the other was his introduction to the Cincinnati Literary Club, a body embracing among its members such men as Chief Justice Salmon P Chase, Gen John Pope, Gov. Edward F Noyes, and many others hardly less distinguished in after life. The marriage was a fortunate one in every respect, as everybody knows. Not one of all the wives of our Presidents was more universally admired, reverenced and beloved than was Mrs Hayes, and no one did more than she to reflect honor upon American womanhood The Literary Club brought Mr Hayes into constant association with young men of high character and noble aims, and lured him to display the qualities so long hidden by his bashfulness and modesty

In 1856 he was nominated to the office of Judge of the Court of Common Pleas, but he declined to accept the nomination Two years later, the office of City Solicitor becoming vacant, the City Council el [illegible]

In 1861 [illegible] at the zenith [illegible] the Bar was among the first But the news of the attack on Ft Sumter found him eager to take up arms for the defense of his country

His military record was bright and illustrious In October, 1861, he was made Lieutenant-Colonel, and in August, 1862, promoted Colonel of the Seventy-ninth Ohio Regiment, but he refused to leave his old comrades and go among strangers Subsequently, however, he was made Colonel of his old regiment At the battle of South Mountain he received a wound, and while faint and bleeding displayed courage and fortitude that won admiration from all

Col Hayes was detached from his regiment, after his recovery, to act as Brigadier-General, and placed in command of the celebrated Kanawha division, and for gallant and meritorious services in the battles of Winchester, Fisher's Hill and Cedar Creek, he was promoted Brigadier-General He was also breveted Major-General, "for gallant and distinguished services during the campaigns of 1864 in West Virginia " In the course of his arduous services, four horses were shot from under him, and he was wounded four times

In 1864, Gen Hayes was elected to Congress from the Second Ohio District, which had long been Democratic He was not present during the campaign, and after the election was importuned to resign his commission in the army, but he finally declared, "I shall never come to Washington until I can come by way of Richmond " He was re-elected in 1866

In 1867, Gen Hayes was elected Governor of Ohio, over Hon Allen G Thurman, a popular Democrat, and in 1869 was re-elected over George H Pendleton He was elected Governor for the third term in 1875

In 1876 he was the standard-bearer of the Republican party in the Presidential contest, and after a hard, long contest was chosen President, and was inaugurated Monday, March 5, 1877. He served his full term, not, however, with satisfaction to his party but his administration was an average one The remaining years of his life [illegible] home, where he [illegible]

J. A. Garfield

JAMES A. GARFIELD.

JAMES A GARFIELD, twentieth President of the United States, was born November 19, 1831, in the woods of Orange, Cuyahoga County, Ohio His parents were Abram and Eliza (Ballou) Garfield, both of New England ancestry, and from families well known in the early history of that section of our country, but who had moved to the Western Reserve, in Ohio, early in its settlement

The house in which James A was born was not unlike the houses of poor Ohio farmers of that day. It was about 20 x 30 feet, built of logs, with the spaces between the logs filled with clay His father was a hard-working farmer, and he soon had his fields cleared, an orchard planted, and a log barn built The household comprised the father and mother and their four children, Mehetabel, Thomas, Mary and James In May, 1823, the father died from a cold contracted in helping to put out a forest fire At this time James was about eighteen months old, and Thomas about ten years old No one, perhaps, can tell how much James was indebted to his brother's toil and self-sacrifice during the twenty years succeeding his father's death He now lives in Michigan, and the two sisters live in Solon, Ohio, near their birthplace

The early educational advantages young Garfield enjoyed were very limited, yet he made the most of them He labored at farm work for others, did carpenter work, chopped wood, or did anything that would bring in a few dollars to aid his widowed mother in her struggles to keep the little family together Nor was Gen Garfield ever ashamed of his origin, and he never forgot the friends of his struggling childhood, youth and manhood, neither did they ever forget him When in the highest seats of honor, the humblest friend of his boyhood was as kindly greeted as ever. The poorest laborer was sure of the sympathy of one w [illegible]

want and the sweetness of bread earned by the sweat of the brow He was ever the simple, plain, modest gentleman

The highest ambition of young Garfield until he was about sixteen years old was to be captain of a vessel on Lake Erie He was anxious to go aboard a vessel, but this his mother strongly opposed She finally consented to his going to Cleveland, with the understanding, however, that he should try to obtain some other kind of employment. He walked all the way to Cleveland This was his first visit to the city After making many applications for work, and trying to get aboard a lake vessel and not meeting with success, he engaged as a driver for his cousin, Amos Letcher, on the Ohio & Pennsylvania Canal He remained at this work but a short time, when he went home, and attended the seminary at Chester for about three years He then entered Hiram and the Eclectic Institute, teaching a few terms of school in the mean time, and doing other work This school was started by the Disciples of Christ in 1850, of which body he was then a member He became janitor and bell-ringer in order to help pay his way He then became both teacher and pupil Soon "exhausting Hiram," and needing a higher education, in the fall of 1854 he entered Williams College, from which he graduated in 1856, taking one of the highest honors of his class He afterwards returned to Hiram College as its President As above stated, he early united with the Christian, or Disciples, Church at Hiram, and was ever after a devoted, zealous member, often preaching in its pulpit and places where he happened to be

Mr. Garfield was united in marriage, November 11, 1858, with Miss Lucretia Rudolph, who proved herself worthy as the wife of one whom all the world loved To them were born seven children, five of whom are still living, four boys [illegible]

Mr Garfield made his first political speeches in 1856, in Hiram and the neighboring villages, and three years later he began to speak at county mass-meetings, and became the favorite speaker wherever he was During this year he was elected to the Ohio Senate He also began to study law at Cleveland, and in 1861 was admitted to the Bar The great Rebellion broke out in the early part of this year, and Mr Garfield at once resolved to fight as he had talked, and enlisted to defend the Old Flag He received his commission as Lieutenant-Colonel of the Forty-second Regiment of Ohio Infantry August 14, 1861 He was immediately put into active service, and before he had ever seen a gun fired in action, was placed in command of four regiments of infantry and eight companies of cavalry, charged with the work of driving out of his native State the able rebel officer, Humphrey Marshall, of Kentucky This work was bravely and speedily accomplished, although against great odds, and President Lincoln commissioned him Brigadier-General, January 10, 1862; and "as he had been the youngest man in the Ohio Senate two years before, so now he was the youngest General in the army " He was with Gen Buell's army at Shiloh, in its operations around Corinth and its march through Alabama He was then detailed as a member of the general court martial for the trial of Gen Fitz-John Porter He was next ordered to report to Gen Rosecrans, and was assigned to the "Chief of Staff" The military history of Gen Garfield closed with his brilliant services at Chickamauga, where he won the rank of Major-General

Without an effort on his part, Gen Garfield was elected to Congress in the fall of 1862, from the Nineteenth District of Ohio This section of Ohio had been represented in Congress for sixty years mainly by two men—Elisha Whittlesey and Joshua R Giddings It was not without a struggle that he resigned his place in the army At the time he entered Congress he was the youngest member in that body There he remained by successive re-elections until he was elected President, in 18 [illegible] Hoar says [illegible] think of [illegible] Congress, or discussed before a tribunal of the American people, in regard to which you will not find, if you wish instruction, the argument on one side stated, in almost every instance better than by anybody else, in some speech made in the House of Representatives or on the hustings by Mr Garfield "

Upon January 14, 1880, Gen Garfield was elected to the United States Senate, and on the 8th of June, of the same year, was nominated as the candidate of his party for President at the great Chicago Convention He was elected in the following November, and on March 4, 1881, was inaugurated Probably no administration ever opened its existence under brighter auspices than that of President Garfield, and every day it grew in favor with the people By the 1st of July he had completed all the initiatory and preliminary work of his administration, and was preparing to leave the city to meet his friends at Williams College While on his way and at the depot, in company with Secretary Blaine, a man stepped behind him, drew a revolver, and fired directly at his back. The President tottered and fell, and as he did so the assassin fired a second shot, the bullet cutting the left coat sleeve of his victim, but inflicting no further injury It has been very truthfully said that this was "the shot that was heard around the world." Never before in the history of the nation had anything occurred which so nearly froze the blood of the people for the moment as this awful deed He was smitten on the brightest, gladdest day of all his life, at the summit of his power and hope For eighty days, all during the hot months of July and August, he lingered and suffered He, however, remained master of himself till the last, and by his magnificent bearing taught the country and the world one of the noblest of human lessons—how to live grandly in the very clutch of death Great in life, he was surpassingly great in death He passed serenely away September 19, 1883, at Elberon, N J, on the very bank of the ocean, where he had been taken shortly be- [illegible] eath, as it rarely [illegible] f any other great [illegible]

CHESTER A. ARTHUR.

CHESTER A ARTHUR, twenty-first President of the United States, was born in Franklin County, Vt, on the 5th day of October, 1830, and was the eldest of a family of two sons and five daughters His father was the Rev. Dr William Arthur, a Baptist clergyman, who emigrated to this country from County Antrim, Ireland, in his eighteenth year, and died in 1875, in Newtonville, near Albany, after a long and successful ministry

Young Arthur was educated at Union College, Schenectady, where he excelled in all his studies After his graduation he taught school in Vermont for two years, and at the expiration of that time came to New York, with $500 in his pocket, and entered the office of ex-Judge E D Culver as a student After being admitted to the Bar, he formed a partnership with his intimate friend and room-mate, Henry D Gardiner, with the intention of practicing in the West, and for three months they roamed about in the Western States in search of an eligible site, but in the end returned to New York, where they hung out their shingle, and entered upon a successful career almost from the start Gen Arthur soon after married the daughter of Lieut Herndon, of the United States Navy, who was lost at sea Congress voted a gold medal to his widow in recognition of the bravery he displayed on that occasion Mrs Arthur died shortly before Mr Arthur's nomination to the Vice-Presidency, leaving two children.

Gen Arthur obtained considerable legal celebrity in his first great case, the famous Lemmon suit, brought to recover possession of eight slaves who had been declared free by Judge Paine, of the Superior Court [illegible] 1852 that Jonathan Lemmon, of Virginia, went to New York with his slaves, intending to ship them to Texas, when they were discovered and freed The Judge decided that they could not be held by the owner under the Fugitive Slave Law A howl of rage went up from the South, and the Virginia Legislature authorized the Attorney-General of that State to assist in an appeal William M. Evarts and Chester A Arthur were employed to represent the people, and they won their case, which then went to the Supreme Court of the United States Charles O'Conor here espoused the cause of the slaveholders, but he, too, was beaten by Messrs Evarts and Arthur, and a long step was taken toward the emancipation of the black race

Another great service was rendered by Gen Arthur in the same cause in 1856 Lizzie Jennings, a respectable colored woman, was put off a Fourth Avenue car with violence after she had paid her fare Gen Arthur sued on her behalf and secured a verdict of $500 damages The next day the company issued an order to admit colored persons to ride on their cars, and the other car companies quickly followed their example Before that the Sixth Avenue Company ran a few special cars for colored persons, and the other lines refused to let them ride at all

Gen Arthur was a delegate to the convention at Saratoga that founded the Republican party. Previous to the war he was Judge-Advocate of the Second Brigade of the State of New York, and Gov Morgan, of that State appointed him Engineer-in-Chief of his staff In 1861, he was made Inspector-General, and soon afterward became Quartermaster-General In each of these [illegible] the Government during the war At the end of Gov Morgan's term he resumed the practice of law, forming a partnership with Mr Ransom, and then Mr Phelps, the District Attorney of New York, was added to the firm The legal practice of this well-known firm was very large and lucrative, as each of the gentlemen composing it was an able lawyer, and possessed a splendid local reputation, if not, indeed, one of national extent

Mr Arthur always took a leading part in State and city politics He was appointed Collector of the Port of New York by President Grant, November 21, 1872, to succeed Thomas Murphy, and he held the office until July 20, 1878, when he was succeeded by Collector Merritt

Mr Arthur was nominated on the Presidential ticket, with Gen James A Garfield, at the famous National Republican Convention held at Chicago in June, 1880 This was perhaps the greatest political convention that ever assembled on the continent It was composed of the leading politicians of the Republican party, all able men, and each stood firm and fought vigorously and with signal tenacity for his respective candidate that was before the convention for the nomination Finally Gen Garfield received the nomination for President, and Gen Arthur for Vice-President The campaign which followed was one of the most animated known in the history of our country Gen Hancock, the standard-bearer of the Democratic party, was a popular man, and his party made a valiant fight for his election

Finally the election came, and the country's choice was Garfield and Arthur They were inaugurated March 4, 1881, as President and Vice-President. A few months only had passed ere the newly-chosen President was the victim of the assassin's bullet Then came terrible weeks of suffering—those moments of anxious suspense, when the hearts of all civilized nations were throbbing in unison, longing for the recovery of the noble, the good President The remarkable patience that he manifested during those hours and weeks, [illegible] suffering m[illegible] upon to endure, was [illegible] certainly godlike During all this period of deepest anxiety Mr Arthur's every move was watched, and, be it said to his credit, that his every action displayed only an earnest desire that the suffering Garfield might recover to serve the remainder of the term he had so auspiciously begun Not a selfish feeling was manifested in deed or look of this man, even though the most honored position in the world was at any moment likely to fall to him

At last God in his mercy relieved President Garfield from further suffering, and the world, as never before in its history over the death of any other man, wept at his bier. Then it became the duty of the Vice-President to assume the responsibilities of the high office, and he took the oath in New York, September 20, 1881 The position was an embarrassing one to him, made doubly so from the fact that all eyes were on him, anxious to know what he would do, what policy he would pursue, and whom he would select as advisers The duties of the office had been greatly neglected during the President's long illness, and many important measures were to be immediately decided by him; and to still further embarass him he did not fail to realize under what circumstances he became President, and knew the feelings of many on this point Under these trying circumstances, President Arthur took the reins of the Government in his own hands, and, as embarrassing as was the condition of affairs, he happily surprised the nation, acting so wisely that but few criticized his administration He served the nation well and faithfully until the close of his administration, March 4, 1885, and was a popular candidate before his party for a second term His name was ably presented before the convention at Chicago, and was received with great favor, and doubtless but for the personal popularity of one of the opposing candidates, he would have been selected as the standard-bearer of his party for another campaign He retired to private life, carrying with him the best wishes of the American people, whom he had served in a manner satisfac[illegible] himself. One [illegible] al rest

Grover Cleveland

STEPHEN GROVER CLEVELAND.

STEPHEN GROVER CLEVELAND, the twenty-second President of the United States, was born in 1837 in the obscure town of Caldwell, Essex County, N J, and in a little two-and-a-half-story white house, which is still standing to characteristically mark the humble birthplace of one of America's great men, in striking contrast with the Old World, where all men high in office must be high in origin and born in the cradle of wealth When the subject of this sketch was three years of age, his father, who was a Presbyterian minister with a large family and a small salary, moved, by way of the Hudson River and Erie Canal, to Fayetteville, N Y, in search of an increased income and a larger field of work Fayetteville was then the most straggling of country villages, about five miles from Pompey Hill, where Governor Seymour was born

At the last-mentioned place young Grover commenced going to school in the good, old-fashioned way, and presumably distinguished himself after the manner of all village boys—in doing the things he ought not to do Such is the distinguishing trait of all geniuses and independent thinkers When he arrived at the age of fourteen years, he had outgrown the capacity of the village school, and expressed a most emphatic desire to be sent to an academy To this his father decidedly objected Academies in those days cost money, besides, his father wanted him to become self-supporting by the quickest possible means, and this at that time in Fayetteville seemed to be a position in a country store, where his father and t

considerable influence Grover was to be paid $50 for his services the first year, and if he proved trustworthy he was to receive $100 the second year Here the lad commenced his career as salesman, and in two years he had earned so good a reputation for trustworthiness that his employers desired to retain him for an indefinite length of time

But instead of remaining with this firm in Fayetteville, he went with the family in their removal to Clinton, where he had an opportunity of attending a High School Here he industriously pursued his studies until the family removed with him to a point on Black River known as the "Holland Patent," a village of five or six hundred people, fifteen miles north of Utica, N Y At this place his father died, after preaching but three Sundays This event broke up the family, and Grover set out for New York City to accept, at a small salary, the position of under-teacher in an asylum for the blind He taught faithfully for two years, and although he obtained a good reputation in this capacity, he concluded that teaching was not his calling in life, and, reversing the traditional order, he left the city to seek his fortune, instead of going to the city He first thought of Cleveland, Ohio, as there was some charm in that name for him, but before proceeding to that place he went to Buffalo to ask advice of his uncle, Lewis F Allan, a noted stock-breeder of that place The latter did not speak enthusiastically. "What is it you want to do, my boy?" he asked "Well, sir, I want to study law," was the reply "Good gracious!" remarked

? Whatever

put that into your head? How much money have you got?" "Well, sir, to tell the truth, I haven't got any."

After a long consultation, his uncle offered him a place temporarily as assistant herd-keeper, at $50 a year, while he could look around One day soon afterward he boldly walked into the office of Rogers, Bowen & Rogers, of Buffalo, and told them what he wanted A number of young men were already engaged in the office, but Grover's persistency won, and he was finally permitted to come as an office boy and have the use of the law library, receiving as wages the sum of $3 or $4 a week Out of this he had to pay for his board and washing The walk to and from his uncle's was a long and rugged one, and although the first winter was a memorably severe one, his shoes were out of repair, and as for his overcoat he had none, yet he was, nevertheless, prompt and regular On the first day of his service there, his senior employer threw down a copy of Blackstone before him, with a bang that made the dust fly, saying "That's where they all begin" A titter ran around the little circle of clerks and students, as they thought that was enough to scare young Grover out of his plans, but in due time he mastered that cumbersome volume Then, as ever afterward, however, Mr Cleveland exhibited a talent for executiveness rather than for chasing principles through all their metaphysical possibilities "Let us quit talking and go and do it," was practically his motto

The first public office to which Mr Cleveland was elected was that of Sheriff of Erie County, N Y, in which Buffalo is situated, and in such capacity it fell to his duty to inflict capital punishment upon two criminals In 1881 he was elected Mayor of the City of Buffalo, on the Democratic ticket, with especial reference to bringing about certain reforms in the administration of the municipal affairs of that city In this office, as well as in that of Sheriff, his performance of duty has generally been considered fair, with possibly a few exceptions, which were ferreted out and ma[illegible] paign As [illegible] plain language in a veto mess[illegible] an iniquitous street-cleaning contract "This is a time for plain speech, and my objection to your action shall be plainly stated I regard it as the culmination of a most bare-faced, impudent and shameless scheme to betray the interests of the people and to worse than squander the people's money" The New York *Sun* afterward very highly commended Mr Cleveland's administration as Mayor of Buffalo, and thereupon recommended him for Governor of the Empire State To the latter office he was elected in 1882, and his administration of the affairs of State was generally satisfactory The mistakes he made, if any, were made very public throughout the nation after he was nominated for President of the United States For this high office he was nominated July 11, 1884, by the National Democratic Convention at Chicago, when other competitors were Thomas F Bayard, Roswell P. Flower, Thomas A Hendricks, Benjamin F Butler, Allen G Thurman, etc, and he was elected by the people, by a majority of about a thousand, over the brilliant and long-tried Republican statesman, James G Blaine President Cleveland resigned his office as Governor of New York in January, 1885, in order to prepare for his duties as the Chief Executive of the United States, in which capacity his term commenced at noon on the 4th of March, 1885

The silver question precipitated a controversy between those who were in favor of the continuance of silver coinage and those who were opposed, Mr Cleveland answering for the latter, even before his inauguration

On June 2, 1886, President Cleveland married Frances, daughter of his deceased friend and partner, Oscar Folsom, of the Buffalo Bar. Their union has been blessed by the birth of two daughters In the campaign of 1888, President Cleveland was renominated by his party, but the Republican candidate, Gen. Benjamin Harrison, was victorious In the nominations of 1892 these two candidates for the highest position in the gift of the people were again pitted against [illegible]ction President Cleve[illegible] overwhelming majorit[illegible]

Benj. Harrison

BENJAMIN HARRISON.

BENJAMIN HARRISON, the twenty-third President, is the descendant of one of the historical families of this country The first known head of the family was Maj -Gen Harrison, one of Oliver Cromwell's trusted followers and fighters In the zenith of Cromwell's power it became the duty of this Harrison to participate in the trial of Charles I , and afterward to sign the death warrant of the king He subsequently paid for this with his life, being hung October 13, 1660 His descendants came to America, and the next of the family that appears in history is Benjamin Harrison, of Virginia, great-grandfather of the subject of this sketch and after whom he was named. Benjamin Harrison was a member of the Continental Congress during the years 1774, 1775 and 1776, and was one of the original signers of the Declaration of Independence He was three times elected Governor of Virginia

Gen William Henry Harrison, the son of the distinguished patriot of the Revolution, after a successful career as a soldier during the War of 1812, and with a clean record as Governor of the Northwestern Territory, was elected President of the United States in 1840 His career was cut short by death within one month after his inauguration

President Ha

Hamilton County, Ohio, August 20, 1833 His life up to the time of his graduation from Miami University, at Oxford, Ohio, was the uneventful one of a country lad of a family of small means His father was able to give him a good education, and nothing more He became engaged while at college to the daughter of Dr Scott, Principal of a female school at Oxford After graduating, he determined to enter upon the study of law. He went to Cincinnati and there read law for two years At the expiration of that time young Harrison received the only inheritance of his life—his aunt, dying, left him a lot valued at $800. He regarded this legacy as a fortune, and decided to get married at once, take this money and go to some Eastern town and begin the practice of law He sold his lot, and, with the money in his pocket, he started out with his young wife to fight for a place in the world He decided to go to Indianapolis, which was even at that time a town of promise He met with slight encouragement at first, making scarcely anything the first year He worked diligently, applying himself closely to his calling, built up an extensive practice and took a leading rank in the legal profession

In 1860, Mr Harrison was nominated for the position of Supreme Court Reporter, and then be-

i He canvassed the State thoroughly, and was elected by a handsome majority In 1862 he raised the Seventeenth Indiana Infantry, and was chosen its Colonel His regiment was composed of the rawest material, but Col Harrison employed all his time at first in mastering military tactics and drilling his men, and when he came to move toward the East with Sherman, his regiment was one of the best drilled and organized in the army At Resaca he especially distinguished himself, and for his bravery at Peachtree Creek he was made a Brigadier-General, Gen Hooker speaking of him in the most complimentary terms

During the absence of Gen Harrison in the field, the Supreme Court declared the office of Supreme Court Reporter vacant, and another person was elected to the position From the time of leaving Indiana with his regiment until the fall of 1864 he had taken no leave of absence, but having been nominated that year for the same office, he got a thirty-day leave of absence, and during that time made a brilliant canvass of the State, and was elected for another term He then started to rejoin Sherman, but on the way was stricken down with scarlet fever, and after a most trying attack made his way to the front in time to participate in the closing incidents of the war

In 1868 Gen Harrison declined a re-election as Reporter, and resumed the practice of law In 1876 he was a candidate for Governor Although defeated, the brilliant campaign he made won for him a national reputation, and he was much sought after, especially in the East, to make speeches In 1880, as usual, he took an active part in the campaign, and was elected to the United States Senate Here he served for six years, and was known as one of the ablest men, best lawyers and strongest debaters in that body With the expiration of his senatorial term he returned to the practice of his profession, becoming the head of one of the strongest firms in the State.

The political campaign of 1888 was one of the most memorable in the history of our country The convention which assembled in Chicago in June and named Mr Harrison [illegible] the chief [illegible] and-ard-bearer of the Republican party was [illegible] in every particular and in the [illegible] at-titude it assumed upon the vital questions of the day, chief among which was the tariff, awoke a deep interest in the campaign throughout the nation Shortly after the nomination, delegations began to visit Mr Harrison at Indianapolis, his home This movement became popular, and from all sections of the country societies, clubs and delegations journeyed thither to pay their respects to the distinguished statesman

Mr Harrison spoke daily all through the summer and autumn to these visiting delegations, and so varied, masterly, and eloquent were his speeches that they at once placed him in the foremost rank of American orators and statesmen. Elected by a handsome majority, he served his country faithfully and well, and in 1892 was nominated for re-election, but the people demanded a change and he was defeated by his predecessor in office, Grover Cleveland

On account of his eloquence as a speaker and his power as a debater, Gen Harrison was called upon at an early age to take part in the discussion of the great questions that then began to agitate the country He was an uncompromising anti-slavery man, and was matched against some of the most eminent Democratic speakers of his State No man who felt the touch of his blade desired to be pitted with him again With all his eloquence as an orator he never spoke for oratorical effect, but his words always went like bullets to the mark. He is purely American in his ideas, and is a splendid type of the American statesman Gifted with quick perception, a logical mind and a ready tongue, he is one of the most distinguished impromptu speakers in the nation Many of these speeches sparkled with the rarest eloquence and contained arguments of great weight, and many of his terse statements have already become aphorisms Original in thought, precise in logic, terse in statement, yet withal faultless in eloquence, he is recognized as the sound statesman and brilliant orator of the day During the last days of his administration President Harrison suffered an irreparable loss in the death of his devoted wife, [illegible] (Scott) Harrison, a lady of [illegible] charms and virtue [illegible] Th[illegible] two children

WINONA COUNTY,

MINNESOTA.

INTRODUCTORY.

THE time has arrived when it becomes the duty of the people of this county to perpetuate the names of their pioneers, to furnish a record of their early settlement, and relate the story of their progress. The civilization of our day, the enlightenment of the age and the duty that men of the present time owe to their ancestors, to themselves and to their posterity, demand that a record of their lives and deeds should be made. In biographical history is found a power to instruct man by precedent, to enliven the mental faculties, and to waft down the river of time a safe vessel in which the names and actions of the people who contributed to raise this country from its primitive state may be preserved. Surely and rapidly the great and aged men, who in their prime entered the wilderness and claimed the virgin soil as their heritage, are passing to their graves. The number remaining who can relate the incidents of the first days of settlement is becoming small indeed, so that an actual necessity exists for the collection and preservation of events without delay, before all the early settlers are cut down by the scythe of Time.

To be forgotten has been the great dread of mankind from remotest ages. All will be forgotten soon enough, in spite of their best works and the most earnest efforts of their friends to perserve the memory of their lives. The means employed to prevent oblivion and to perpetuate their memory has been in proportion to the amount of intelligence they possessed. The pyramids of Egypt were built to perpetuate the names and deeds of their great rulers. The exhumations made by

buried Memphis i

to perpetuate the memory of their achievements The erection of the great obelisks were for the same purpose. Coming down to a later period, we find the Greeks and Romans erecting mausoleums and monuments, and carving out statues to chronicle their great achievements and carry them down the ages. It is also evident that the Mound-builders, in piling up their great mounds of earth, had but this idea—to leave something to show that they had lived. All these works, though many of them costly in the extreme, give but a faint idea of the lives and characters of those whose memory they were intended to perpetuate, and scarcely anything of the masses of the people that then lived. The great pyramids and some of the obelisks remain objects only of curiosity; the mausoleums, monuments and statues are crumbling into dust.

It was left to modern ages to establish an intelligent, undecaying, immutable method of perpetuating a full history—immutable in that it is almost unlimited in extent and perpetual in its action; and this is through the art of printing.

To the present generation, however, we are indebted for the introduction of the admirable system of local biography By this system every man, though he has not achieved what the world calls greatness, has the means to perpetuate his life, his history, through the coming ages.

The scythe of Time cuts down all; nothing of the physical man is left. The monument which his children or friends may erect to his memory in the cemetery will crumble into dust and pass away; but his life, his achievements, the work he has accomplished, which otherwise would be forgotten, is perpetuated by a record of this kind.

To preserve the lineaments of our companions we engrave their portraits, for the same reason we collect the attainable facts of their history. Nor do we think it necessary, as we speak only truth of them, to wait until they are dead, or until those who know them are gone: to do this we are ashamed only to

those lives

John Arnot Mathews.

JOHN ARNOT MATHEWS, a real-estate and loan agent, who is doing a successful business in Winona, where he has carried on operations since 1855, is a son of Henry H. Mathews, who was born near Elmira, N. Y. The grandfather, Col. Selah Mathews, with several brothers, removed from Orange County to Tioga (now Chemung) County, N. Y., about 1790. The original American ancestor was closely connected by marriage with Governor Fletcher, and in an early day in Colonial history came with him to this country. Colonel Mathews was a Federalist of the old school, and stood at the head of local affairs in Tioga County for many years. His brother, Gen. Vincent Mathews, who died in Rochester, N. Y., in 1847, held the office of District Attorney for the Western District for many years, and served both in the State Legislature and the State Senate, and in the Congress of the United States. For forty years he was recognized as the most prominent lawyer at the Elmira Bar. General Mathews left Elmira for Bath, where he resided for a short time, and then removed to Rochester, N. Y., where at a ly lamented. His portrait now graces the court-rooms in Rochester and Canandaigua, N. Y.

When a young man, in 1819, Henry H. Mathews entered the store of John Arnot, of Elmira, N. Y., and soon after married Isabella Arnot, a sister of his employer and a native of Perthshire, Scotland, who came to America about 1803. He then engaged in merchandising at Painted Post with Mr. Arnot, and while there residing filled many responsible positions. Subsequently he returned to Elmira, and was made its Postmaster by Gen. Zachary Taylor, a position which he filled for several years.

John Arnot Mathews, one of Winona's representative business men, was born in Elmira, N. Y., April 6, 1824, and is the eldest in a family of nine children, eight of whom grew to mature years, while five are yet living and are residents of Minnesota. His boyhood days were passed in his native city and at Painted Post, and he became familiar with business men and methods in his father's mercantile establishment. At the age of nineteen he returned to Elmira, where he attended until 1845.

He then removed to Tioga, Pa., where he became clerk in the store of B. C. Wickham & Co., with whom he continued two years. In company with two other young men he then bought out the store, and carried on an extensive and successful business until 1853.

The following year Mr. Mathews sought a home in the West. He stopped for a time at McGregor, Iowa, visited many points in the northeastern part of that state, and explored the pine woods of Wisconsin with a view to engaging in the lumber business. A land-office was then at Stevens' Point, Wis., and he became attracted by the opportunities offered for dealing in land-warrants and locating them on time to actual settlers. There was also a land-office at Brownsville, Minn., and from that place he started out on an exploring tour. While at Chatfield, Minn., he heard parties from Winona speaking of the town, and resolved to come to this place after his return to McGregor. On a small stern-wheel steamer he came up the Mississippi, reaching his destination in July, 1854. Not being favorably impressed with the location, he took the next steamer for Red Wing, Minn., where there was also a land-office, and then visited Dodge and other counties in Minnesota, after which he returned to McGregor, Iowa. In the succeeding autumn he returned to Tioga, Pa., but had determined that he would locate at McGregor, Red Wing or Winona. The land-office was located at the last-named place in the spring of 1855, and in the autumn Mr. Mathews opened here his real-estate and loan office.

On the 9th of October of that year Mr. Mathews was united in marriage with Miss Ellen B. Bush, a native of Tioga, Pa., and a daughter of A. C. Bush, of that place. Their wedding was celebrated in Tioga, and they at once started for Winona, arriving here in time for the land sales in the latter part of October. Mr. Mathews began to buy and sell land-warrants, to locate lands and loan money. For a year he spent half of each day in a land-office, and continued this business until the removal of the office to Faribault. He has now been engaged in loaning money for nearly forty years. He loans on real-estate security and makes a specialty of farm loans. He has done a good business and has ever had the confidence and trust, as well as the high regard, of those with whom he has been brought in contact.

Mr. and Mrs. Mathews have no children of their own, but have reared two of his brother Henry's children: Jennie C., now the wife of E. S. Gregory; and Isabella A., wife of E. J. Chamberlain. Mr. Mathews has always been a supporter of the Democracy. He has never cared to become prominent in the councils of his party, but believes in and upholds its principles. For four terms he held the office of Mayor of the city, and took a decided stand against the city issuing bonds for the assistance of the railroads; and even when a stockholder and one of the Directors of the Winona & South-western Railroad and Mayor of the city he was true to this belief. He has always taken a warm interest in everything pertaining to the advancement of Winona, and is public spirited and progressive. For almost forty years he has been identified with the history of this community, and his worth is recognized by his fellow-townsmen. He is one of the most popular citizens of Winona, is a safe and substantial business man, a true friend, and has the confidence of the people in an unusual degree.

William W. Caine.

WILLIAM W. CAINE, who resides on section 11 Wiscoy Township, has to some extent passed an eventful life. He has lived as a pioneer, and during the Civil War was numbered among the boys in blue who defended the Union against the rebellion of the South. He comes from the old Bay State, his birth having occurred in Boston, Mass., on the 22d of August, 1837. His father, Thomas Caine, was a native of the Isle of Man, and the family is of English origin. He married Miss Mary Callister, and to them were born seven children. Thomas, who is a carpenter, resides in Hingham, Mass. Mary died January 17, 1868. John enlisted in the regular army in 1859, became a member of the Seventh United States Infantry, and was one of the heroes who fell at the hard-fought battle of Gettysburg, on the 3d of July, 1863. His remains were interred on the battlefield. Margaret died October 15, 1857. Abigail is the wife of John Jeffries, an iron-molder of Hingham, Mass. William W. is the next younger. Robert enlisted as a private of Company D, Third Wisconsin Infantry, April 25, 1861, and was wounded by a minie ball at the battle of Chancellorsville, but continued in the service until after the close of the war. He now resides in Dodge County, Wis.

William W. Caine began his education in the public schools of Boston, and when twelve years of age went on board a ship, where he remained two years. In 1852 we find him in the Mississippi Valley, the journey westward having been made by way of the l

resident of Chester, Dodge County, Wis., and began working as a farm hand by the month, thus serving until 1855, when with ox-teams he made an overland trip to Kansas, settling in Anderson County. There he pre-empted one hundred and sixty acres of land, but was driven away from his home by border ruffians. During his stay there he served as a scout, and once was shot with a double-barrelled gun, the charge being imbedded in his foot.

Returning to Dodge County, Mr. Caine then continued to work as a farm hand until, feeling that his country needed his services, he responded to the President's call for volunteers to serve three years. He joined Company D, Third Wisconsin Infantry, August 21, 1861, and was mustered into the service at Waupun, Wis. The first engagement in which he participated was at Cedar Mountain, after which he took part in the battles of Antietam, Chancellorsville, Beverly Ford and Gettysburg. He then went to New York City with his regiment in order to quell the riots there, and remained in the city for about a month. The troops then returned to Virginia, followed Lee across the river and proceeded to Lookout Mountain, where a battle occurred. Mr. Caine also participated in the engagements at Buzzard's Roost, Resaca, Dallas, Pine Mountain, Kenesaw Mountain and the Atlanta campaign, then went with Sherman on the march to the sea and through the Carolinas. The last engagement in which he participated was at Bentonville, N. C. At the battle

d and has

caused a partial loss of his hearing. He was wounded by a piece of shell at the battle of Dallas. At Kingston, Ga., he was promoted to the rank of Corporal, and at Louisville, Ky., he was mustered out, while at Madison, Wis., on the 26th of August, 1865, he received an honorable discharge.

Mr. Caine, when his country no longer needed his services, returned to his home in Dodge County, Wis., and there engaged in farming until October, 1865, when he came to Winona County, and settled upon the farm which has since been his home. It comprises eighty acres of good land on section 14, Wiscoy Township, and he carries on general farming with good success, his place being under a high state of cultivation and well improved.

On the 2d of September, 1860, Mr. Caine wedded Miss Mary Cowell. They have five children, namely: Mary E., wife of Thomas O'Brian, a farmer, residing in Wilson Township; Belbert, an agriculturist living in Wiscoy Township; Elsie, wife of Fred Harvey, a farmer of Wiscoy Township; and Alice and Annie, at home. Mr. Caine has always been a supporter of the Republican party, and is now serving as Assessor of his township, a position he has filled for twelve years. He is also School Clerk. Socially he is connected with the Grand Army of the Republic and with the Odd Fellows' lodge. His life has been well and worthily spent, and all who know him hold him in high regard.

William Watts.

WILLIAM WATTS, who follows farming and stock-raising on section 16, Saratoga Township, was born in County Sligo, Ireland, in November, 1841, and is a son of Henry and Rachel (Londey) Watts, whose family numbered five children, three sons and two daughters. With his brothers and sisters William was reared on the home farm, the duties of which were soon made familiar to him, for he early began work in the fields. He received no special school privileges, in fact he is largely self-educated, but he possesses an observing eye and retentive memory and has become well informed.

Mr. Watts started out in life for himself at the age of twenty-one, and secured a position as foreman on a lar[illegible] he had char[illegible] 1868 he bade adieu to his friends and home in the Emerald Isle and sailed for the New World, landing in New York City, but he did not seek a residence in the Empire State. Instead he came at once to Minnesota, and located in Saratoga Township, Winona County. Here for six years he was employed as a farm hand by the month, and at the expiration of that period he had $1,378 due him. During four years he was never absent from his work for a single day.

With the capital he had acquired through earnest and untiring labor, through perseverance and good management, Mr. Watts then purchased a farm of one hundred and twenty acres on section 7, Saratoga Township, of partially improved land. He [illegible]pment and culti[illegible] it his home, after which he sold out and purchased the farm which is now his place of residence It comprises two hundred acres of rich and arable land, which yields to him a golden tribute in return for the care and labor he bestows upon it. He has also been very successful as a stock-raiser, and makes a specialty of the breeding of Poland-China hogs, in consequence of which the farm is known as the Poland-China Stock Farm. All of the improvements thereon are the work of Mr Watts, who is an industrious and enterprising man, devoted to his business interests and his family. He has worked his way upward from an humble position to one of affluence, and though he has met with obstacles and difficulties in his path, he has overcome these by determined effort and good management He well deserves great credit for his success

In 1876 Mr Watts wedded Miss Mary J McKeowen They have seven children Rachel M, Annie M Mary J Henry W, Florence. Maggie and Samuel C Mr Watts has never aspired to office, and votes with the Populist party He is a member of the Episcopal Church, and takes an active interest in everything pertaining to the welfare of the community.

Cyrus Crosgrove.

CYRUS CROSGROVE, who occupies a leading position in business circles, and is recognized as one of the representative citizens of Winona is now engaged in the wholesale and retail harness trade This enterprise is one of the centers of industry in the city, and at its head is a young man whose progressive spirit and indomitable energy will win him success in whatever he undertakes He is numbered among Winona's native sons, his birth having here occurred on the 26th of October 1862, and he is the eldest in a family of four children, whose parents were Robert and Mary (Sinclair) Crosgrove Sylvia, the second, is now the wife of I. E Whiting, of St. Charles, Mildred is the wife of A D Palmer, of Austin, Minn, and Frederick, the youngest, is still at home. The father of this family was born in Ireland, and d

America by his parents, who settled in New York, where he was reared to manhood on a farm In the spring of 1856 he came to Winona, having made the journey on foot from Milwaukee. Here he entered land from the Government, near the county seat, and at once began its development and cultivation which he carried on in connection with his trade of harness-making for some time In 1870 he opened a retail harness store which he conducted up to the time of his death, becoming the leader in this line in the city. He was a very energetic man who carried forward to a successful completion whatever he undertook He met obstacles and difficulties in his path, but these he overcame by a determined effort and steadily worked his way upward to prosperity. He was called to the home beyond in January,

His wife, a

native of Maine, is still residing in Winona. She is a daughter of C. B. Sinclair, one of the honored pioneers and representative citizens of this county.

No event of special importance occurred during the childhood and youth of Cyrus Crosgrove. He remained at home and attended the common schools, the State Normal and a business college until twenty years of age, thus acquiring an excellent education, which has well fitted him for the practical duties of life. During that time he also learned the harness-maker's trade in his father's shop. He then went to Estelline, S. Dak., where he established a retail harness shop, and during the next ten years conducted three shops at different points. Upon his father's death he returned to Winona and took charge of the harness business which had been established years before, and which he yet carries on. He has a full and complete stock of harness, his store being the largest of the kind in southern Minnesota. For years his trade has constantly increased, until it has now assumed extensive proportions.

On the 1st of July, 1890, Mr. Crosgrove was joined in wedlock with Miss Mary Belle Clarke, a daughter of Doran Clarke, one of the pioneer settlers of this city. Two children bless this union, Ellen and Robert. Mr. Crosgrove, who votes with the Democracy, warmly advocates its principles, and served as State Representative while in South Dakota in 1888. He was also Mayor of the town in which he lived, and was a prominent and influential citizen, who had the confidence and respect of a wide circle of friends and acquaintances. He now holds membership with Winona Lodge No. 18, A. F. & A. M. One of the leading and wide-awake young business men of Winona, he is popular in social circles, where his pleasant and genial manner makes him a great favorite. Were all her native sons like Mr. Crosgrove, Winona would be a model city.

Leonard Knapp.

LEONARD KNAPP, of St. Charles, who for many years was extensively engaged in farming and stock-raising, but is now practically living a retired life, is one of the well known and highly respected citizens of Winona County. A native of New York, he was born in Harrisburg Township, Lewis County, on the 17th of February, 1825. The family was founded in New England during Colonial days, and the grandfather, Wright Knapp, was probably a native of Connecticut. German Knapp, the father of Leonard, was bo[...]

and having [...]

Catherine Elliott, a native of Dutchess County, N. Y., and a daughter of Richard Elliott, who was born in Ireland, and died when Catherine was eight years of age. German Knapp was called to the home beyond in his seventy-sixth year.

The gentleman whose name heads this notice was reared on the old home farm until his twenty-third year, when he left the parental roof with the intention of trying his fortune in the West. In 1847 he emigrated to Wisconsin, settling in Le Roy, Dodge County, where he secured Government land [...]

[...]og house, with a

[...] in the midst of

the timber and three miles from a neighbor. There he continued to live for seven years before his marriage. On the 2d of April, 1851, in his thirtieth year, he wedded Miss Sarah Thompson, and the next month came to Minnesota, reaching Dover Township, Olmsted County, on the 27th of May. The previous winter he had visited this place in company with George Clark, the pioneer resident of Winona. He selected land on section 26, Dover Township, then known as Township 106, Range 11 west. He was the first actual settler in Dover Township, and there were not more than five or six families in Olmsted County. William Potter and Ben Bear and a few residents in Eyota Township comprised the inhabitants of the county. In July of that year Rochester obtained its first permanent settlers, John and George Head. Mr. Knapp had for a neighbor Lewis H. Springer, of St. Charles, who had come to the county in 1853 and erected a log house near the site of the village, in which he carried on a hotel. William Davison lived in St. Charles Township, two miles north of the town, and there were but two settlers on the prairie east of Mr. Knapp's home. Our subject sought for a stock farm where he could have both water and timber, and found the land he desired in what is now Olmsted, but was then a part of Fillmore County. He had twenty-one head of cattle, and his possessions altogether were valued at about $1,000. Mr. Knapp lived in his tent until the latter part of July, when he built a log cabin, covering it with hay. He turned his attention to stock-growing, and in 1861 sold his original farm and purchased an adjoining tract, on which he lived until 1892. He made a specialty of the breeding of cattle and sheep, and brought the first Shorthorn bull into the county. The boundaries of the home farm he extended until it comprised two hundred and forty acres, and he also purchased other land, but disposed of the greater part of this on coming to St. Charles.

In 1864 Mr. Knapp was called upon to mourn the loss of his wife, who died on the 24th of March. They had three children, but the eldest died at the age of two years. Kate is now the wife of Horace M. Sherman, of [illegible]
is a farmer of [illegible]

married in Rochester, January 18, 1867, his second union being with Mrs. Lucretia (Harris) Groom. She died November 16, 1880, leaving a son, George L., now in Colorado. On the 1st of February, 1884, Mr. Knapp married Mrs. Martha J. Waterman, widow of Elliston C. Waterman, of Wabasha County. She was born in Guilford, Windham County, Vt., July 15, 1833, and was a daughter of David and Abigail (Marsh) Houghton, who came to Minnesota in 1870, and spent their last days in Wabasha County. She was married in Dodge County, Wis., October 16, 1851, to William D. Woodward, of New Hampshire, and the same fall came to Minnesota, locating in Quincy Township, in the extreme northeast corner of Olmsted County. It was a timber claim, and Mr. Woodward and Mr. Wetmore started a sawmill, the machinery for which had been brought from Massachusetts by the former. He soon sold out and not long after settled on a farm in Wabasha County, where he died in 1871. Three years later Mrs. Woodward became the wife of Mr. Waterman, and made her home in Wabasha County until his death. Her son had settled on a farm, and she removed to Elgin, where she lived until becoming the wife of Mr. Knapp. By her first marriage she had four sons and one daughter: William Henry, who now operates the farm; David Otto, of Spokane, Wash.; Mary Ella, who died January 21, 1883, at the age of twenty years; Everett Ellsworth, of Nevada; and Albert Alvin, of Clark County, S. Dak.

Since 1892 Mr. Knapp has lived in St. Charles. His home is located on a six-acre tract of land and is a valuable and desirable property. His possessions have all been acquired through his own efforts, and he may truly be called a self-made man. His business career has been one of success, and he is now numbered among the substantial citizens of Winona County. When starting out in life for himself amid the wilderness of Wisconsin, having no near companions, he devoted a good deal of time to close study of a Bible which his mother had given him on leaving home. He first read it with interest, then studied and familiarized himself [illegible] nt text in it,
[illegible] nts and that

the record of important events was often given in contradictory ways. He would often read until one or two o'clock in the morning, and made a thorough study of the book, but after a time felt that he could not accept its statements and became an infidel. This was before he had ever read Paine, Voltaire or other infidel writers. He is a man strong in argument and takes great delight in the same. In politics he is not strictly partisan, but usually votes with the Democracy.

James Chambers.

JAMES CHAMBERS has been one of the esteemed citizens and leading agriculturists of this county for about thirty years. He is a veteran of the Civil War, and has suffered severely for the Union cause, as he was wounded by a minie-ball, which lodged in the right leg, above the knee, and this resulted in much trouble for the worthy soldier. He enlisted as a private, and when he left the service bore the rank of Corporal.

Mr. Chambers was born in Newburg, Orange County, N. Y., on Christmas Day, 1830, and is the son of Samuel and Jane (McCord) Chambers. They were the parents of six children, among them being William; John, who died in defense of the Old Flag, and Lizzie. John, above mentioned, enlisted as a soldier and was an officer at the time of his death in the One Hundred and Twenty-fourth Regiment of New York Infantry. His death occurred in the city of Washington in 1864, from exposure in the service. He was an exemplary soldier, as the record proves.

The early years of our subject were passed quietly near the beautiful village of Newburg. The boy was tra[illegible] ly familiar [illegible] experience. When seventeen years of age he began to make his own way in the world, entirely through his own efforts. His first employment was as a farm hand, and he continued in this field of labor until 1815, when he went to Michigan. Settling in Oakland County, he continued there to make his home until he was enrolled as a private soldier, in 1861, when he was placed in Company C, Fifth Michigan Cavalry. He was sent to Grand Rapids, thence to Stevensburg, Va., and his first action on the field of battle was near Richmond, under Kilpatrick. Thence he proceeded down the Shenandoah Valley, participating in the Battle of the Wilderness, Spottsylvania and many other engagements of lesser importance. He continued to serve until near the close of the war, being discharged March 10, 1866.

Returning to Michigan, our subject remained in that state until the summer of 1866, when he concluded to try his fortunes farther west, and accordingly came to Winona County. He first located in Pleasant Hill Township, and still owns eighty acres of land on section 21. His place is well [illegible] ubstantial fences, [illegible] and is kept under good cultivation. In his political faith Mr. Chambers is a Democrat, and though not desirous of holding official positions, has served as a member of the Board of Township Supervisors, occupying the post of Chairman. He is a member of the Grand Army of the Republic and can always be relied upon to use his influence in behalf of all worthy enterprises and measures calculated to advance the public good.

June 15, 1866, Mr. Chambers married Miss Amelia S. Cottrelle. One child has been born of their union, Amelia, who is now the wife of William Goss, a leading farmer of this township. The young couple have three children: John W., Homer and Samuel. The Chambers family number many warm friends in the community with which they have been identified for the past three decades, and their hospitable doors are always open for the reception of their numerous acquaintances and well-wishers.

William Hendee.

WILLIAM HENDEE, who has been officially connected with the interests of St. Charles, and has long been recognized as one of its representative citizens, is now living retired. He was born near St. Catharines, Ontario, September 23, 1819, and is a son of Acil and Elizabeth (Mann) Hendee, the former a native of New York, and the latter of Canada. The father was a carpenter by trade. He died when William was a year old, after which his widow became the wife of Amos Dakins. William Hendee then remained with his mother until fourteen years of age, when he chose an uncle as guardian, who bound him out to another uncle on a farm, where he remained for three and a-half years. On the expiration of that period he began working by the day as a farm hand. Six months later he sought a home in the West, hoping thereby to benefit his financial condition. He went to Dundas, Minn., and worked on a farm for one man for sixteen years, his services being employed in the fields during

winter season

ing the first six years of his long engagement he only lost six days, and his faithfulness to his employer's interest won him the confidence and respect of all. He first received $109 per year, and after the first six years he began operating a farm for himself, having from ten to fourteen men under his charge. He worked extremely hard, so that his health almost failed him, and in the spring of 1855 he came to Winona County in company with a blacksmith, John Ellsbury, now of Dover.

Through the influence of Mr. Ellsbury Mr. Hendee returned to this place in the spring and took up a quarter-section of land lying just northeast of St. Charles and adjoining the town. He had about $1,200 in cash, and with this he made a start in his new home. He built a log shanty and at once began to clear and improve his land. In the fall he erected a frame house, 16x22 feet in dimensions, then the best dwelling in St. Charles. Here he entertained all the preachers and business men who came to this place. His time and attention

s, and he suc-

October, 1883,

when he came to the town. He had added to his first purchase of land, and at length disposed of the old homestead by selling it to his son. He was a most energetic and untiring worker, but at length his once strong constitution was forced to give way before the great strain placed upon it, and for the past ten years he has been a constant sufferer from inflammatory rheumatism.

On the 31st of August, 1843, in West Flamboro, Wentworth County, Ontario, Mr. Hendee was married to Miss Mary Cummings, who was born near Hamilton, Canada, on the 1st of March, 1822. For more than a half-century they have traveled life's journey together, sharing with each other in the joys and sorrows, adversity and prosperity which checker the pathway of all, and in 1893 they celebrated the fiftieth anniversary of their marriage by a golden wedding, in which many friends and relatives joined with them in commemorating the day. In their family were eleven children, viz.: Elizabeth, wife of Henry Talbot, of St. Charles; Selina, wife of Frank Sheets, of Lisbon, N. Dak.; Jacob, who owns the old farm near St. Charles; Acil, who is engaged in wagon-making; Orilla, wife of U. S. Usher, of Chicago; Selim, who died in St. Charles at the age of twenty-seven; Priscilla, who became the wife of Casky Coles, of Minneapolis, and died at the age of twenty-two; Cordilla, wife of William Parr, the present City Marshal of St. Charles; Arvilla, the wife of Harry Stone, a sailor, of Minneapolis; Simeon, who makes his home with his parents; and Rosilla, wife of A. J. Aemon, of Grand Rapids, Minn.

Mr. Hendee was reared as a Reformer in Canada, and on coming to the United States joined the ranks of the Republican party, with which he has since affiliated, always supporting its men and measures. He has never been a politician in the sense of actively seeking office, but has served as Assessor and was long the Census-taker. The best interests of the community have ever found in him a friend, and he is recognized as a valued citizen, in whom his friends place the utmost confidence, for all who know him recognize his many excellent traits of character.

H. M. Litchtenstein, M. D.

H. M. LITCHTENSTEIN, M. D., who is actively engaged in the practice of medicine in Winona, was born in Koenigsberg, East Prussia, on the 22d of October, 1866. His grandfather and the ancestors for several generations remote, were members of the medical profession, and a number of them became quite prominent along that line. The Doctor's father, Isidore Litchte[illegible] gaged in acti[illegible] which, however, occurred at the early age of thirty-five years. He was a medical practitioner of note in Koenigsberg, and in his professional capacity also served in the army.

The gentleman whose name heads this sketch was reared in his native land and acquired his literary education in Stuttgart, Germany. He afterwards studied in the Universities of Berlin, Stras[illegible]duated from the [illegible], 1889. Having now fitted himself for the medical profession, he engaged in practice for a year at Wurtemberg, and then received an appointment as physician on the German trans-Atlantic steamers going to the ports of New York and Baltimore and to the West Indies

The year 1891 witnessed the arrival of Dr Lichtenstein in America for the purpose of making a permanent settlement He located in Winona and has since engaged in active practice, meeting with excellent success and gaining a reputation for skill and ability which has brought him a liberal patronage. While in college he was a thorough student and his studies are yet continued to the benefit of those who employ his services. He is a member of the Winona County Medical Society, and is a highly educated man who in this community has won many friends The Doctor's wife was formerly Miss Carolina Claussen, a native of Schleswig-Holstein, Germany They were married in 1890

P. Fitzpatrick.

P FITZPATRICK is a leading member of the Winona County Bar, successfully engaged in practice in the county seat. He is a western man, his birth having occurred in Galena, Ill, on the 17th of March, 1851. In the family of seven children, six of whom are yet living, he is the eldest The others are Anna, now Mrs M. Buck of Lanesboro Minn, Mary, Sarah, wife of John Buck, also of Lanesboro, Margaret and John. The parents of this family were James and Mary (McDonald) Fitzpatrick. The father was born in Ireland in 1813, and came to America during the presidency of General Jackson, being then twenty years of age. For a time he worked at his trade of stonemason in New York, Kentucky and other states, and finally made a permanent location in Galena, Ill This was about 1845 In Galena he married Miss Mary McDonald and there continued to make his home until 1861, when he came to Minnesota, locat[illegible] Fillmore County [illegible] spent his remain[illegible] death occurred in 1881, at the age of sixty-eight years. His wife passed away six years previous being called to her final rest in 1875

P Fitzpatrick spent the first ten years of his life in his native city and then accompanied his parents on their removal to Fillmore County, Minn, where he attended such schools as had then been established, but owing to the undeveloped condition of the country at that time, his early educational privileges were somewhat limited Later, however, he attended the State Normal School of Winona, and was graduated from that institution in the Class of '74 Extensive reading, experience and observation have also added largely to his knowledge and made him a well informed man On his return from Winona he taught school for a time and then entered the State University of Minnesota at Minneapolis, pursuing the regular three-years course, which he completed in 1878 [illegible] Fillmore County, and [illegible]g to change his profession, Mr. Fitzpatrick then entered the law office of Wilson & Gale, one of the leading law firms of the city, and under their instruction read for two years. In April, 1881, he was admitted to the Bar, and since that time has been continuously engaged in active practice in Winona.

On the 4th of September, 1879, Mr. Fitzpatrick was united in marriage with Miss Mary Leahy, of Lanesboro, Minn., daughter of John and Julia (Nolan) Leahy. Mrs. Fitzpatrick died May 29, 1883, leaving two children, Mary, born November 1, 1880, and James, May 25, 1883.

In his political views Mr. Fitzpatrick is a Democrat, and in the fall of 1882 was elected on that ticket to the office of County Attorney, which position he filled for ten consecutive years in a most satisfactory manner, as is shown by his long continued service, which also indicates his personal popularity. At the Bar he is recognized as a lawyer of ability. In argument he is logical and convincing, and his courteous manner and gentlemanly bearing win him the confidence and trust of all with whom he is brought in contact.

N. B. STEVENS.

Norman Bronson Stevens.

NORMAN BRONSON STEVENS, the eldest son of Silas and Selina (Bronson) Stevens, was born at Honesdale, Pa., May 15, 1828. His early life was largely spent in the family home in Lake County, Ill., the family having located there during his childhood. In the spring of 1850, possessed of an uncontrollable desire to travel and see the world, he joined a company bound overland for the gold fields of California. Passing through many vicissitudes and enduring incredible hardships in crossing the plains and Rocky Mountains, the party arrived at Placerville, Cal., July 29, 1850, and at once began mining for gold.

Mr. Stevens remained in California meeting with varying success, until the spring of 1855, when he returned to his home in the East. August 16, 1855, he came to Winona County and settled upon the claim located by his father in 1851 in what is now the city of Winona. He later established a nursery in Burns Valley, and for many years was engaged in the fruit-tree industry. In this line he was u

in the propagation

this climate, very many of the trees now in bearing in the surrounding country having been introduced by him.

In addition to the latter business, in 1862 Mr. Stevens was appointed by the firm of D. M. Osborne & Co. agent for the "Kirby" reaper, and in the development of this business during a series of years he was remarkably successful, carrying off the awards in many severely contested field trials. Having demonstrated his rare ability as a business man Mr. Stevens was, in 1868, called on to take the general agency for the entire Northwest of the "Kirby" reaper, with headquarters at Chicago, and in this wider field he fully maintained his reputation for ability and enterprise. When, in 1873, the D. M. Osborne Company decided to send a man to properly represent their great interests at the Vienna (Austria) Exposition of that year, the choice naturally fell to Mr. Stevens, and he spent the entire summer of that year abroad, exploiting the merits of the "Kirby," and thus becoming widely known among the machine men of

he highest

many field

trials. After so ably discharging the arduous duties devolving upon him abroad, Mr Stevens returned home to Chicago, and feeling the need of rest and recreation, he retired from traveling and spent the following winter in New England

Returning to Chicago Mr. Stevens remained there until the spring of 1876, when he came with his family to Winona. He purchased the residence on the northeast corner of Broadway and La Fayette Streets, where he made his home during the remainder of his life

On the 29th of March, 1879, Alfred Ferry, of Detroit, Mich, a representative of the Royal Arcanum, with Mr. Stevens, organized the Pioneer Council of Winona, the first lodge organized in the state of Minnesota He also received a Deputy Supreme Regent's commission in the district in which the Pioneer Council is located, and was prominent in the work of the order until failing health forced him to abandon it He was a member of the Old Settlers Society and was one of the moving spirits among the early settlers of Winona County

In the fall of 1882 Mr Stevens accepted the position of traveling agent for the L C. Porter Milling Company selling goods and establishing agencies in Canada and the Maritime Provinces, and meeting with excellent success until the winter of 1885, when failing health warned him against further work and he remained at home for years, a sufferer from nervous prostration. During the summer of 1888 he took a trip to California for his health, revisiting many of the scenes of his early trials and privations Returning home in the spring of 1889, he there remained until death ended his sufferings. All that human mind could suggest or hands do was done to alleviate his sufferings during those years. After his life work was accomplished he quietly passed away October 6, 1892

Mr Stevens was a man of characteristics positive in the extreme Whatever he did was done with all his might, and his success in life was due partly to his exceptional energy and a high order of intelligence His love of travel and adventure was strong to a degree, and being a remarkably close observer, with a wonderful recollection of places, dates of events, etc., joined to an exceptional command of language, his many writings are interesting beyond the common. In his description of sights and scenes in both the Old and New World he was particularly happy and these writings are treasured by his family He was for many years a member of the Congregational Church, and contributed liberally to its support

Mr Stevens was married, September 26, 1860, in Lake City, Minn, to Miss Orilla A Howe, a native of Millbury, Worcester County, Mass. She was a member of the noted Howe family of which the well known Julia Ward Howe is also a member. At a reunion of the Howe family at South Framingham, Mass., in 1871, where over five thousand members were present, Julia Ward Howe gave the address of welcome The original ancestors in this country were three brothers descendants of Lord Howe of England who crossed the Atlantic in the "Mayflower," and the branch of the family to which Mrs Stevens belongs settled at Sudbury Mass., and kept the Howe Tavern in that town, made famous in Longfellow's song as the "Wayside Inn"

Mr Stevens daughter by a former marriage, Mary E., is now the wife of Willard S Farrington, of Portland, Oregon, a son of Dr Farrington, formerly of Winona

Almon Sartwell.

ALMON SARTWELL, who carries on general farming on section 28, Warren Township, where he owns a good farm of one hundred and sixty acres, was born on the 29th of December, 1819, in Langdon, N. H., and is a son of Royal and Elvira (Evans) Sartwell. Both parents were of English descent, and the father was a native of the Granite State, while the mother was born in Massachusetts. They had a family of eight children, namely: Phila, wife of Amos Bean, a resident of Vermont; Almon, of this sketch; Maria, who died in 1816; Roswell, who died in 1869; Henry; Eliza, wife of Major Flint, who is a resident of Douglas County, Minn.; Ellen, wife of L. B. Fait, a resident of Douglas County; and Warren, who was drowned. The father served in the War of 1812. He was a wagon-maker by trade and did business in the East until 1855, when with his family he came to Minnesota, where his remaining days were passed. His death occurred August 18, 1862, at the age of seventy-four years, one month and sixteen days, and his wife died June 8, 1872, when seventy-five years of age.

In the usual manner of farmer lads Almon Sartwell was reared. His educational privileges were limited to those afforded by the common schools, which he attended until sixteen years of age. That he is now a well informed man is due to his keen observation, his experience, his reading and retentive memory. When he was only about two years old the family had removed to Vermont, and in 1837 went to Erie County, Pa., where Mr. Sartwell continued to reside until 1839. With a view to trying his fortune on the broad prairies of the West, he then

making the trip

for the railroad center had not then become acquainted with the sound of the engine, and palace cars did not make it possible to reach the West after a few hours' travel from New York.

Mr. Sartwell first located in Chicago, then a small town of little importance, and began work on the canal which was being built from that city to Peru, Ill. A year later he removed to Kane County, where he began work as a carpenter, and was also employed in different mills. His next place of residence was in Galena, Jo Daviess County, where he engaged in farming and made his home until the spring of 1855, when he emigrated further westward, crossing the Mississippi into Minnesota. Winona County was his destination, and he settled on the farm which has since been his home, pre-empting a claim of one hundred and sixty acres on section 28, and eighty acres on section 27, Warren Township. The land was undeveloped prairie and oak openings. In true pioneer style he began life in the West, his first home being a log cabin 12x14 feet, in which was no floor save that made by the earth. There he lived for two years, after which he built a board house. This was replaced in 1868 by his present commodious and comfortable residence. He began farming with ox-teams, and back and forth traveled over the fields until the furrows were turned and crops were planted. Later came the harvests which brought reward for his labors. Farming and stock-raising have been his life work, and in his undertakings he has met with success.

Mr. Sartwell has been twice married. In October, 1852, he wedded Miss Susanna Beall, and they

nely: Fred-

of age, Jasper N., who carries on agricultural pursuits in Warren Township, Lena, who died at the age of eight years, Almon H., deceased, Phila, also deceased, and Susanna B., now residing in Pennsylvania, the wife of Edson Hill. The children who died all passed away in 1863 within a few weeks of one another. On the 7th of November of the same year Mrs. Sartwell was called to her final rest. Mr. Sartwell was again married, in 1865, his second union being with Emily Milligan, by whom he has two children: Addie L., now the wife of Bert Thompson, a resident of Fillmore County, Minn., and Edgar M., who married Miss May Gage, and lives on the old home farm.

Mr. Sartwell exercises his right of franchise in the support of the Republican party, with which he has been identified since its organization. His first Presidential vote was cast for William Henry Harrison. He was among the first Township Supervisors, serving in that office for two terms, was Township Treasurer for about twelve years and was Assessor for the long period of fifteen years. His public duties were discharged with promptness and fidelity, for he is always true to a trust reposed in him, whether public or private. Mr. Sartwell started out in life a poor boy, without wealth or influential friends to aid him in the struggle, and by his own efforts he has risen to a position of affluence. He may truly be called a self-made man.

Hiram C. Wilber.

HIRAM C. WILBER, who wore the blue during the late war, now follows farming and stock-raising on section 33, Warren Township. He was born in Madison County, N. Y., on the 11th of May, 1833. His father, Hiram C. Wilber, Sr., was a native of Rhode Island, and was of English descent. His mother bore the maiden name of Roxy May, and her only child was the subject of this sketch. She died in early life, after which the father married Hannah Nickerson, by whom he had ten children. The members of the family are: Charles, who was born February 8, 1852; Caroline, who is the widow of Herman Stage, and resides with Hiram C.; Roxy J., who died in 1877; Charles H., who is living with his eldest brother; Lucy, who died November 1, 1870; Linus V., who is County Superintendent of the public schools in Winona County, Minn.; Mary, who makes her home with her brother Hiram; Willie A., ... April 1861 ... A ... Wilber household, and Myra J., wife of George Crane, a resident of Fremont, Minn.

The father of this family was born in 1802, and his second marriage was celebrated October 6, 1841. The lady was a native of the Empire State, and was born December 12, 1821. Mr. Wilber was a shoe-maker by trade, and followed that business during his early days, but in later life carried on farming. In 1855 he removed to Wisconsin, settling in Dodge County, where he made his home until 1863, when he came to Winona County, Minn. Here he made his home until his death, which occurred on the 1st of April, 1887, in the eighty-fifth year of his age. While in New York he served as Supervisor and Assessor, and after coming to Minnesota he was again called to public office, being appointed Postmaster in Wyattville in 1865, which position he held until his death. He was a competent and faithful officer, ... hether public or ... ith the Masonic fraternity, and with the Methodist Church When called to the home beyond he was laid to rest in Warren Cemetery, and many friends mourned his loss.

The life of a farmer's boy was that of the youth of Hiram C. Wilber, the subject of this sketch. He early began work in the fields, where he labored through the summer months, while in the winter season his education was acquired He attended the district schools for some time, and later entered an academy where he acquired a good practical knowledge, which has been of much benefit to him in his business career With his parents he removed to Wisconsin, and thence to Minnesota in 1863 He had previously taught school in Wisconsin during the winter of 1855-56, but has practically made farming his life work although he again engaged in school teaching in Hart Township, Winona County, in 1867-68, in Warren Township in 1868-69, and in Fremont Township in 1869-70

During the late war Mr Wilber responded to the country's call for troops, enlisting on the 5th of September 1861, as a member of Company K Eleventh Minnesota Infantry He was mustered into service at Ft Snelling, and was thence sent to Nashville, Tenn, where he was engaged in guarding railroads until the close of the war, when, on the 16th of July, 1865, he was honorably discharged He then at once returned to his home in Winona County, where he has made his home continuously since. For the first two years after his arrival in Minnesota he lived upon a rented farm, and then removed to the farm on which he now resides, an eighty-acre tract on section 33, Warren Township. His time and energies are devoted to general farming and stock-raising and in the management of his business affairs he manifests good executive ability He is enterprising and industrious, and is both public spirited and progressive.

Mr Wilber's duties of citizenship are ever faithfully and promptly performed. He votes with the Republican party, and has held the office of Township Clerk for about fourteen years altogether He is now serving as Chairman of the Town Board of Supervisors, for five years has been Justice of the Peace, and was Notary Public for about fifteen years He has held various school offices, having served both as School Clerk and School Treasurer Socially he is connected with the Masonic order, and also with the Grand Army of the Republic

Michael Nagle.

MICHAEL NAGLE, one of the honored veterans of the late war, now owns and operates a good farm of one hundred and forty-three acres on section 10, Wiscoy Township He is a native of the Emerald Isle, his birth having occurred in County Cork, Ireland, on the 25th of September, 1837

(Fitzgerald) Nagle

three of whom are now deceased Those still living are Mary, Daniel, Michael, William, Luke and John, the last-named being the only one born in America

Michael Nagle spent the first fifteen years of his life on his father's farm in Ireland, and then ac-

to Amer-

d in 1852,

and after a voyage of four weeks and three days' duration landed at New York City. They made a location on the banks of the beautiful Hudson in the Empire State, and there the subject of this sketch grew to manhood. He continued a resident of New York until 1860, when he resolved to try his fortune in the West, hoping thereby to benefit his financial condition. He first located in Michigan, but continued there only a short time, for in the autumn of the same year he came with the family to Winona County. The father purchased a farm of one hundred and sixty acres in Wiscoy Township, and he aided in its cultivation and development until 1864.

On the 27th of August of that year Mr. Nagle responded to the call for troops to aid in crushing out the rebellion, and, donning the blue, was assigned to Company K, Eleventh Minnesota Infantry. He was mustered into service at Ft. Snelling, and during most of the time until the close of the war was engaged in guarding railroads. He received an honorable discharge on the 11th of July, 1865, when the war had ended.

Mr. Nagle then returned to Winona County, where he has since made his home. His farm of one hundred and forty-three acres is under a high state of cultivation, and well improved with good buildings and all modern accessories. He carries on general farming, and his good management in business affairs, combined with perseverance and diligence has placed him in comfortable circumstances.

Mr. Nagle was married, November 22, 1863, to Miss Bridget Hennigan. To them have been born nine children, and the family circle yet remains unbroken. In order of birth they are as follows: Margaret, Mary A., Kate, Bridget, Agnes, Johanna, Sarah, Blanche and Cecil. Mr. Nagle and his family are members of the Catholic Church, and in politics he is affiliated with the Democracy.

D. E. Vance.

D. E. VANCE. There are few professions that exercise a greater influence on mankind than that of the law, and its representatives are usually leading men of the community. Their life calls into action their ability for leadership and their power for influencing the minds of others, and in consequence they become prominent. Mr. Vance belongs to this class of men, and is a well known and highly respected attorney of W[illegible]

Born in [illegible] bury, on the 6th of January, 1811, the subject of this sketch is one of a family of eight children, all of whom are yet living. The parents were Aaron and Lucinda (Tucker) Vance. The eldest child, George L., is now Supervisor of Education in Joliet, Ill. D. E. is the second in order of birth. William A. is now serving as Postmaster of Houston, Minn. Albert N. is a wholesale and retail grocer of Decorah, Iowa. Nancy Jane is the wife [illegible] Nicholas W. is a [illegible] M. is the wife of

Calvin Vance, of Money Creek, Minn.; and Aaron E. is engaged in merchandising in Joliet, Ill. The father of this family, Aaron Vance, Sr., was born October 10, 1812, in Vermont, where he lived until March, 1866, when he emigrated westward, hoping thereby to benefit his financial condition. He took up his residence in Money Creek Township, Houston County, Minn. He was a shoemaker by trade, and followed that business in New England, but after coming West he embarked in farming, which he carried on throughout the remainder of his active business life. Four years ago he came to Winona to spend his last years, and now makes his home in this city. He has reached the age of eighty-two, but is still hale and hearty and bids fair to live for many years to come. For a long time he served as Supervisor of his township, and was a public-spirited and progressive citizen, always interested in everything pertaining to the community in which he made his home and its development.

David Vance, the grandfather of the subject of this sketch, was born in the Green Mountain State, and there spent his entire life. He was the wealthiest man of his town, and was a typical New Englander of the old school. For several years he was a member of the State Legislature, and it was his custom to put a change of linen in a bandanna handkerchief and walk thirty miles to attend the sessions of the General Assembly. For a long time he served as Captain of a militia company, and was recognized as one of the leading spirits of his time.

D. E. Vance lived in the style of most New England boys belonging to the middle classes. Amidst play and work his childhood was passed, and under the parental roof he remained until he had attained his majority. At that time he left home for the seat of war, for he believed that his country needed the services of all its loyal citizens. On the 13th of June, 1862, he joined Company G, of the Ninth Vermont Infantry, and went to the front. He participated in the battles of Winchester and Harper's Ferry, and at the latter place was taken prisoner, but was afterward paroled. Later he spent fifteen months in Chicago, acting as Assistant Commissary for the prisoners, and then rejoi

racks, N. C. Later he was stationed at Newbern, N. C., guarding property, and afterward was in front of Richmond, taking part in the siege of that city from September, 1864, until April, 1865, when Lee surrendered. His was the first regiment of United States infantry that marched into the city after its surrender, and there he remained for two and a-half months.

On the 16th of June, 1865, Mr. Vance was honorably discharged from the service and immediately returned to his home. In December, however, he came West, locating in Chicago, where he remained until August, 1866. During that time he attended Eastman's Commercial College of that city, and then engaged in clerking until the date above mentioned, when he came to Minnesota, locating at Money Creek. Here he taught school until 1877, when he settled in Winona and took up the study of law in the office of Judge Barber. In April, 1878, he was admitted to the Bar, and has since been engaged in active practice. In his profession he has met with marked success, and is now enjoying an extensive patronage.

On the 20th of November, 1879, Mr. Vance wedded Miss Alice Maybury, daughter of C. G. and Rebecca (Cole) Maybury, who had a family of six children. Mr. and Mrs. Vance have a family of four children, Jessie M., Mary A., Albert Elmer and Stanley M., all at home.

The Republican party finds in Mr. Vance a stalwart supporter, and an able advocate of its principles. He has served as a member of the City Council of Winona for several years and labored earnestly for the best interests of the town. Socially he is connected with the Ancient Order of United Workmen, and in 1885 served as Grand Master of the lodge for the then jurisdiction of Minnesota, Dakota and Manitoba. He belongs to the Equitable Aid Union; to Orient Lodge No. 20, A. F. & A. M., of Money Creek, and to John Ball Post, G. A. R. He has three times served as its Commander, and is now serving as Adjutant of the post. His career in business circles has ever been honorable and straightforward. In days of war it was that of a faithful soldier, and in times of peace it is that of a loyal citizen, true to all

J. M. Sheardown.

J M SHEARDOWN, the efficient and popular Clerk of the District Court, was born in Channing County, N Y., on the 10th of January, 1831, and is of English descent His parents, Thomas S and Esther (Grassen) Sheardown were both natives of England. The father, who was a Baptist minister, came to America in 1820, and located first in Tompkins County, N Y The remainder of his days were spent in the Empire State and in northern Pennsylvania His death occurred in Troy, Bradford County, Pa, at the age of eighty-four years Two days previous to his death he had supplied a pulpit His wife long preceded him to the final home, having passed away in 1851 This worthy couple were the parents of twelve children, but only two are now living Henry C, of Tioga County, Pa., and John M The family name is almost extinct there being only four male representatives in America, the two brothers and their nephews Ward B, who is general agent for the Diamond Mill Company, of Duluth, and Thomas W, who is now a physician of Chicago.

J M Sheardown resided in various places in New York until 1857, and acquired his education in Channing and Steuben Counties In 1847 he left home and entered upon his business career as clerk in a [illegible] which [illegible] then Jefferson [illegible] Watkins N. Y. He re-mained there until 1851. In 1852 he began reading law with Mark Crawford, of Havana, N Y., and was admitted to the Bar in Minnesota in 1860 In September, 1857, he came to Winona, where he has since made his home, with the exception of the four years he spent in the army

Upon the breaking out of the war Mr Sheardown, prompted by patriotic impulses, responded to the country's call for troops, and enlisted in Company B, Fifth New York Cavalry He was wounded at the battle of Culpeper Court House, W Va, was there captured and sent to Libby Prison, where he was incarcerated for six weeks, after which he was paroled He took part in the battles of Bristol Station, Warrentown, Gettysburg, Chantilly Winchester, Rude's Hill, Fisher's Hill, Cedar Creek and the campaign in the Shenandoah Valley At length, when his term had expired, he was mustered out and returned to his home in Winona

Soon after, on the 31st of October, 1865 Mr Sheardown was united in marriage with Miss Anna Kemp daughter of John A. and Phœbe (Cook) Kemp Three children have been born of this union Minnie M, Myrtle A, now the wife of P. W Henry, who is connected with the Winona Willow-ware Company, and Mabel L Mrs Sheardown and her daughters are members of the Con-[illegible] daughter was [illegible] School, afterwards engaged in teaching in the public schools of this city for three years, and is now attending the Pratt Art Institute of Brooklyn, N. Y.

After his return from the war Mr. Sheardown took up the practice of law, which he continued until 1872, when he was elected City Justice of the Peace, which office he held until the fall of 1877. In that year he was elected Clerk of the District Court, which position he still fills, covering a period of seventeen consecutive years. His long continuance in office is the result of faithful service. He has manifested the same fidelity to duty as when on Southern battle-fields he followed the Old Flag to victory. He was a valiant soldier and is an honored citizen. He is a member of S. B. Sheardown Post No. 189, G. A. R.; the Ancient Order of United Workmen, the Royal Arcanum and the Northwestern Legion of Honor. He now owns a beautiful farm of one hundred and forty-eight acres, seven miles from Winona, besides his home property and other lots in the city. He has been a resident of Winona for thirty-seven years, and is recognized as one of its most prominent and representative citizens.

John L. Farrar.

JOHN L. FARRAR is a farmer and stock-raiser of Warren Township, residing on section 20, and is an enterprising and progressive citizen, both widely and favorably known throughout the community. A native of New Hampshire, he was born near Laconia, the county seat of Belknap County, on the 19th of May, 1831. The family is of English origin. The paternal grandfather, Indulthan Farrar, was a farmer, and was also one of the heroes of the Revolutionary War, aiding the Colonies in their struggle to throw off the yoke of British tyranny. His son, Indulthan Farrar, Jr., was born in the old Granite State, and carried on agricultural pursuits throughout his entire life. He married Miss Sallie Cate, who was also born in New Hampshire, and they became the parents of nine children: William H., who died in 1882; J. Warren, who is also deceased; Eliza A., deceased, wife of Joseph Sanborn; Sarah J., who became the wife of Dr. L. A. Hill, and has now passed away; who is living on the old homestead in New Hampshire on which his grandfather settled; John L., of this sketch; Mary M., wife of Andrew Doran, a resident of Laconia, N. H., and Martha J., wife of David Turner, who is located in Massachusetts.

John L. Farrar was reared in the state of his nativity, and began his education in the district schools of the neighborhood in which he lived, completing it in the high school of Woonsocket, R. I. He thus obtained a good knowledge of those branches of learning which are of use to a practical business man, and by reading he always keeps himself well informed on matters of general interest. He remained under the parental roof until he had attained his majority, when he started out in life for himself. He began by working in an insane asylum at Concord, N. H., and there served as an attendant of wards for about three years, after which he pursued his studies in the high school, as before mentioned, for two years.

entered a

wholesale grocery store in Providence, R. I., in the capacity of salesman, but did not long continue in that position, for, attracted by the advantages of the West, he resolved to test its opportunities, and came to Minnesota in the autumn of 1855.

Mr. Farrar made the trip westward by rail and water, and at length took up his residence in Warren Township, Winona County, where he pre-empted one hundred and sixty acres of land on section 30. He lived upon that farm long enough to hold the claim, and during the remainder of the year worked as a farm hand in Dane County, Wis., near Blue Mound. He then purchased land in that locality, and continued its cultivation for two years, after which he returned to Minnesota and worked as a farm hand for one year. At length he bought eighty acres of land on section 21, an unimproved tract, to the cultivation and development of which he at once turned his time and attention. Subsequently he removed to his present farm, which comprises two hundred and forty acres of rich land on sections 20 and 29, Warren Township. He also owns twenty acres of timber-land. He carries on general farming and stock-raising, and has a highly improved tract of land, which yields to him a good income.

On the 27th of April, 1858, Mr. Farrar was united in marriage with Miss Calesta J. Cheney' daughter of Stephen A. and Jerusha A. Cheney, and a native of New Hampshire. By their union were born seven children, namely: Orrin L., an agriculturist of Warren Township; Harry C., a graduate of the State Normal and the present efficient County Superintendent of Schools; Mildora F. and Edna, at home; Martha L., who became the wife of Robert E. Brown, and died in 1891; May B. and Alice, who complete the family.

In his political views Mr. Farrar is a Populist. He has been called upon to fill a number of public positions, having served his township as Supervisor (being Chairman of the Board for more than six years), as Township Treasurer for eight years, and also as Township Assessor. In the year 1881 he was elected to the Legislature on the Democratic ticket. He is at present Justice of the Peace, a position which he has filled for more than twenty years with credit to himself and to the entire satisfaction of those concerned. Socially he is connected with the Masonic fraternity. He is ever interested in what pertains to the welfare of the community and its upbuilding, and is recognized as one of the valued citizens of Winona County.

Verrazano Simpson.

VERRAZANO SIMPSON is a worthy representative of the business interests of Winona. He is now engaged in the real-estate and loan business, and in his undertakings is meeting with good success. The record of his life is as follows: A native of New Hampshire he was born in Windham, on the 31st of December, 1832, and is a son of Benjamin F. and Elizabeth (McDermaid) Simpson, who were also natives of Windham. The paternal grandfather, George Simpson, was born in Windham, and was of Scotch-Irish descent, his ancestors having emigrated to this country in 1653. The two hundred and fiftieth anniversary of that event was celebrated by their descendants in 1893. The grandfather was a farmer by occupation, and spent most of his life in his native town, but died at West Rumney, at the very advanced age of ninety-six years. He was married a second time, at the age of eighty-two, and had two children by that union, who are still living. Nine children were born of the first marriage. Mr. Simpson was a genial, pleasant man, fond of joking, and a great lover of music. The maternal grandfather, Archibald McDermaid, was a native of Scotland, and coming to America before the beginning of the nineteenth century, located on a claim fifteen miles south of the White Mountains, where he spent his remaining days. He also devoted his time and attention to agricultural pursuits, and was called to the home beyond at the age of eigh

advanced age of ninety-seven. They belonged to the Scotch-Presbyterian Church.

Dr. Benjamin F. Simpson, father of Verrazano, was a physician and surgeon, who practiced in Windham for a number of years, and then removed to Lowell, Mass., where he died in 1883 at the age of eighty-four. His wife still survives him, and is living in Lowell at the age of ninety-three. Like her husband, she holds membership with the Unitarian Church. In their family there are four children, three sons and a daughter, namely: Olena, Odanathus, Verrazano and Longinus.

Mr. Simpson, whose name heads this chapter, was reared in Lowell, Mass., and acquired his education in its public schools. During his youth he entered his father's drug store and for some years did business as a pharmacist. Later he went from Boston to the East Indies as a sailor, and continued before the mast for three years. In 1853 he emigrated westward, having resolved to try his fortune in the Mississippi Valley, and located first in Dubuque, Iowa, where he made his home until 1855, when he came to Winona, Minn., and purchased a couple of lots, for which he paid $1,800. This was before the Indian title had expired. Upon his land he erected a store building, and was engaged in merchandising until 1857, when he went into the forwarding commission business, and was a steamboat and railroad agent until 1862, representing a number of eastern lines

o Winona

When a road was built to this place and more fully opened up the country to civilization, he embarked in the real-estate business which he has since successfully followed.

On the 20th of November, 1854, Mr. Simpson married Miss Ann, daughter of David and Mary (Ferren) Manahan of Lowell, Mass. Their marriage was blessed with two children, Elizabeth and Edith. The former is now the wife of E. G. Nevins, of Winona, and they have four children, Guy, Edith, Simpson and Blake. Edith is the wife of Ralph Metcalf, and with their daughter, Elizabeth, they make their home in Tacoma, Wash. Mr. Simpson's second wife bore the maiden name of Mary L. Dyer. For his third wife he chose Miss Josephine Harb, daughter of Henry and Catherine (Arnold) Harb. They now have one child, Josephine.

In his political views Mr. Simpson is a Democrat, and was honored with an election to the office of Mayor of Winona on two different occasions, which position he filled with credit to himself and satisfaction to his constituents. He has always taken an active interest in the city's welfare, and has ever borne his part in the work of progress and advancement. He has probably erected more buildings in Winona than any other of its residents, and with the development of the community his name is inseparably connected. He also owns quite an extensive amount of farm land and has a beautiful home. He possesses excellent business and executive ability, is sagacious and far-sighted, and in his undertakings has met a well merited prosperity.

Lafayette Hill.

LAFAYETTE HILL, one of Winona County's self-made men, who now follows farming and stock-raising on sections 27 and 28, Warren Township, is a native of Vermont. He was born March 27, 1828, and is a son of Randall and Jemima (Blanchard) Hill, who were also born in Vermont. Their family numbered eight children, namely: Betsy, Lydia, Rhoda, Randolph T., Frank, Lafayette, Joseph and Sarah.

When Lafayette Hill was a child of two years the family left his native state and removed to Grafton County, N. H., where he grew to manhood on a farm, and in the usual manner of farmer lads the days [illegible] He worked [illegible] the [illegible] months, and in the winter season attended the district schools until sixteen years of age. During the four succeeding years he gave his father the benefit of his services, and when twenty years of age he started out in life for himself, working as a farm hand for $16 per month. For some time he was employed in this capacity and in operating rented land.

As a companion and helpmate on life's journey, Mr. Hill chose Miss Ann M. Chenney, their wedding being celebrated in 1853. They continued to reside in New Hampshire until 1857, when they bade adieu to home and friends in New England and [illegible] Since that time they have [illegible] For three years they lived in Utica Township, and then came to Warren Township, where Mr. Hill purchased a farm of one hundred and twenty acres of wild land. He first erected a small board house, and with characteristic energy began the cultivation of his property, which he transformed into one of the valuable places of the neighborhood. He is a wide-awake and enterprising man, and has made all of the improvements upon his farm, which is now under a high state of cultivation, and supplied with all modern accessories in the way of houses, barns and outbuildings.

To Mr. and Mrs. Hill were born six children, of whom two are now deceased, Annie and Edwin. Those still living are Charley, a resident farmer of Warren Township; Della, wife of Nathan Wood, who is living in Canton, Minn.; Elmer, a farmer in this county, and Frank, who carries on agricultural pursuits in this community. The mother of this family died in 1867, and in 1872 Mr. Hill was united in marriage with Miss Amanda Wood.

Mr. Hill entertains strong temperance principles, and his views are made manifest in his political affiliations, for he votes with the Prohibition party. He has never been a politician in the sense of office-seeking, yet has served as Supervisor, School Director, School Trustee and Pathmaster. He belongs to the Masonic fraternity, and to the Methodist Church, in which he has served as Class Leader. More than a third of a century has passed since he came to Minnesota, and in these years he has ever lived so as to win friends, who hold him in the highest regard, and his enviable position is well merited.

Robert Palmby.

ROBERT PALMBY, who carries on farming on section 14, Wiscoy Township, claims England as his native land. His birth occurred in Cambridgeshire, on the 17th of November, 1832, his parents being Robert and Mary (Wiseman) Palmby. The father was twice married, and by his first union had two children, but Robert was the only child of the second marriage. He was born in the village of Wicken, and acquired his education in the public schools, but his privileges were very limited. He had no special advantages in his youth, and since the age of seventeen years he has been entirely dependent on his own resources, so th[illegible] serves great credit.

At that time he bade adieu to friends and native land and started for America, taking passage on a sailing-vessel, which after a voyage of five weeks and one day reached the harbor of New York. Mr. Palmby landed in the city, but at once took up his residence in Orleans County, near Gaines, where he began working as a farm hand by the month, and also on a canal. He was thus employed for four years, after which he started westward, making a location in Richmond, Ill. There he carried on a farm on shares for one year and later spent one season in La Crosse, Ill. The year 1856 witnessed his arrival in Minnesota, and [illegible] n County [illegible] fe he continued work as a farm hand, and then came to Winona County, where, with the capital he had acquired through his industry and perseverance in former years, he purchased eighty acres of land on section 9, Wiscoy Township.

Mr. Palmby now began life in earnest. His farm was bottom land, and he at once began to clear and improve it. Two years later he traded it for another eighty-acre tract of land in Wiscoy Township, whereon he made his home for three years, when he sold out and purchased the farm on which he now resides. It comprises three hundred and twenty acres of rich land all in one body, and his time and attention are now devoted to general farming and stock-raising. This has been his place of residence since March, 1882, and its neat and thrifty appearance indicates his careful supervision.

During the late war Mr. Palmby manifested his loyalty to his adopted country by enlisting in August, 1864, as a private of Company K, Eleventh Minnesota Infantry. He was mustered into service at Camp Miller, above Ft. Snelling, and then went to Nashville, Tenn., whence he was sent to Gallatin, where he engaged in guarding railroads until the close of the war. He was honorably discharged in June, 1865, and since that time has lived in Winona County.

Mr. Palmby was married in March 1857, the lady of his choice being Miss Catherine E. Skinkle, of Houston County. They have four children: Mary, who has successfully engaged in teaching school for about seven years; Robert Henry, who aids in the operation of the home farm; William, who is now deceased; and Jesse, who completes the family.

Mr. Palmby, his wife and children have many friends in this community, and are held in high regard. The husband and father is connected with the Grand Army of the Republic and in politics is a Republican, but has never sought or desired office, preferring to give his entire time and attention to his business interests. He is a self-educated and self-made man, who by enterprise, industry and perseverance has steadily worked his way upward and by good management has secured a comfortable competence.

Daniel Baker.

DANIEL BAKER, who resides on section 26, Hillsdale Township, where he has a finely improved farm, was born in Allegany County, N. Y., near Rushford, on the 20th of June, 1839. His father, John Baker, was a native of Vermont, and his mother, who bore the maiden name of S[illegible] [illegible] Both grandf[illegible] [illegible] tionary War. Daniel was the youngest in the family of ten children. His parents were early settlers of Allegany County, N. Y., where their respective families had settled soon after the War for Independence. John Baker served in the War of 1812. He was a stonemason by trade but dur[illegible] [illegible]rried on agricult[illegible] [illegible] work along that line and died on the old home farm at the age of ninety-one. In his political views he was a Democrat, unflinching in the support of the party of his choice. His wife reached the age of seventy-eight. Of their ten children seven are yet living, one brother, Benjamin F., being now a resident of Winona County.

Daniel Baker spent the first eighteen years of his life in the state of his nativity and then emigrated westward to Wisconsin, joining his two brothers, who were located in Green Lake County. There he remained until the breaking out of the late war, when, prompted by patriotic impulses, he responded to the country's call for troops, enlisting in Company D, of the Eighth Wisconsin Infantry. This was the famous "Eagle" Regiment. It was organized September 2, 1861, at Fox Lake, by R. C. Murphy, and was mustered in at Camp Randall, Madison, Wis., on the 12th of October. Col. R. C. Murphy was placed in command, and with his regiment of nine hundred and ninety men departed for the seat of war, going direct to St. Louis, Mo., where they were quartered at Benton Barracks. The regiment won its name from the fact that an eagle, "Old Abe," accompanied them through the war, usually perched on the flag-staff. The first active engagement in which the Eagle Regiment participated was near Greenville, Mo., where they met the enemy under Gen. Jeff Thompson, the famous "Swamp Angel" of the Confederacy. They remained in southeastern Missouri during the following winter, mainly engaged in guarding bridges and prisoners. In March, 1862, they left Cairo for field service, and with General Pope in command assisted in capturing six thousand rebels, April 8, 1862, at Island No. 10. General Pope ordered the words "New Madrid and Island No. 10" inscribed on the banner of the Eagle Regiment for gallantry during the campaign. The members of this regiment also actively participated in the campaign of Corinth and did valuable service in capturing vast stores of provisions and many prisoners. They won a reputation for valor on many a battlefield, including Fredericktown, Farmington, Corinth, Iuka, the second battle of Corinth, Jackson and [illegible] Vicksburg. They [illegible]

[illegible] dred miles, and had twenty-nine men killed and one hundred and forty-four wounded, while twenty-one were reported missing.

On the 6th of June, 1864, at Lake Chicot, Mr. Baker was wounded by a gunshot in the left arm. While engaged in skirmishing a minie-ball passed through the forearm into the upper arm, then plunged down to the elbow, where it lodged, and was cut out nine days later, the doctor having failed to locate it before that time. After convalescing Mr. Baker was sent on recruiting service to Madison and then rejoined his regiment in time to participate in the battle of Nashville. He had a most excellent view of that famous battle, being stationed on a bluff which overlooked the entire field. As his arm was disabled and he could not take part in field engagements he served on detached duty. He was in Alabama at the time of Lee's surrender, but the regiment was not at once discharged, being there retained for service for some time after. At length, with his comrades he received an honorable discharge, after four years and three days, and on the 5th of September, after reaching home, was mustered out.

In the autumn of 1865 Mr. Baker purchased land near Elgin, Minn., and the following year was passed in this state, but in 1867 he returned to Wisconsin, where on the 8th of July he was united in marriage with Miss Mary Smith, whose brother had served as his companion in arms during the long struggle to preserve the Union. By this marriage have been born three children, Stella M., Ida Belle and Arthur L.

Mr. Baker at once brought his young wife to Winona, where he began work at the carpenter's trade. He soon secured a small tract of land, but continued to engage in contracting and building for a number of years. About seven years ago he came to his present place of residence pleasantly located seven and a-half miles west of Winona. It comprises two hundred and forty acres of valuable land, lying on the Winona & St. Peter Railway, near Stockton. There he carried on general farming and stock-raising. He first purchased one hundred acres, and four years later bought another [illegible] He has [illegible] ley land, surrounded by beautiful and picturesque hills, and his farm is noted for its fine improvements. There are a pleasant residence, barns and outbuildings, which are models of convenience, and all other modern accessories.

Mr. Baker also takes a commendable interest in public affairs and does all in his power to promote the general welfare and advance the public good. He has served as Township Assessor and Clerk, and in politics has been a stanch Republican since casting his first Presidential vote for Abraham Lincoln in 1860. He has served as delegate to the Congressional Conventions, but has never been an active politician. Socially he is connected with the Grand Army of the Republic. In all the relations of life he is found true and faithful, and in his duties of citizenship manifests the same loyalty that he displayed when on Southern battlefields he followed the Stars and Stripes to victory.

GEN. C. H. BERRY.

Hon. Charles Henry Berry.

HON. CHARLES HENRY BERRY, attorney-at-law of Winona, was born in the town of Westerly, R. I., on the 12th of September, 1823, and comes of an old family of that state, probably of Huguenot origin. The great-grandfather was Samuel Berry, Sr. The grandfather, who also bore the name of Samuel, was born in Rhode Island, and in 1771 served as Justice of the Peace and of the Sessions in the town of Westerly, in the Colony of Rhode Island, under King George III. When the independence of the United States was established he was re-appointed to the same office under the new Government. He was a farmer and owned large landed interests, and was also engaged in the coasting trade. His death occurred May 29, 1811, at the age of sixty-seven years. The maternal grandfather, Henry Stanton, was a native of Stonington, Conn., and there made his home until called to his final rest in October, 1819, at the age of sixty years. He was one of the heroes of the Revolution and was a direct descendant of Thomas Stanton, who embarked for America on the 2d of January, 1635, from London, in th

After a residence

Massachusetts he settled in Hartford, Conn., in 1637, and there married Ann Lord, daughter of Dr. Thomas and Dorothy Lord, of Hartford.

Samuel Foster Berry, father of the General, was in early life a sea-faring man, and engaged in the coasting trade, sailing to ports along the Atlantic. In 1828 he turned his attention to farming and also engaged in milling to some extent. He removed from Rhode Island to New York in October, 1828, and settled at what is now Caton, five miles south of the village of Corning, where his last days were passed. He died in 1865 at the age of seventy-six, and his wife passed away December 19, 1875, at the age of eighty. She bore the maiden name of Lucy Stanton, and like her husband was a native of Rhode Island. In early life she was a member of the Seventh-Day Baptist Church, but after removing to New York joined the Methodist Episcopal Church. Mr. Berry was for a short time engaged in coast defense during the War of 1812 at Groton and other points along the Rhode Island and Connecticut coast. To him and his wife were born four sons and six

et living

rules H.,

Phœbe, wife of John M Wolcott, of Caton, N. Y., Emily, widow of John Ross of Maine, N Y, Eunice, wife of Jonas Griffith, of Elgin, Ill, and Elizabeth F, widow of Hiram Knapp of Goshen, Ind

Charles Henry Berry left Rhode Island with his parents when a child of four years and lived in Caton, N Y, until 1838 During his boyhood he aided in clearing the dense timber from the farm. He acquired his early education in the schools established by law, and in 1838 went to the village of Maine, where he entered a select school carried on by Rev William Gates There he continued until early in 1843, when he entered an academy in Canandaigua, N. Y, from which he was graduated on completing the prescribed course in 1846 Immediately after he began studying law in the office of E G Lapham afterward Senator Lapham, and was admitted to the Bar in 1848, from the office of Alva Worden of Canandaigua

Mr Berry entered upon practice in Corning in 1849, and there continued until 1855, since which time he has been a resident and a prominent legal practitioner of Winona In 1857 he was honored by an election to the office of Attorney-General of Minnesota, and thus served until 1860, the first to hold that office during Minnesota's existence as a state. He was also State Senator in 1874–75, and has from time to time held municipal offices During the first term of President Cleveland's administration he was appointed Associate Justice of the Supreme Court of the territory of Idaho, and his rulings on the Edmunds law, which were carried by appeal to the Supreme Court of the United States, at Washington, and there sustained as well as by the Supreme Court of the territory of Idaho, led to the abandonment of polygamy by the Mormons He has always been a Democrat and was a member of the National Conventions of 1864 and 1872 When slavery existed he was an opponent of that institution

In 1850 Mr Berry married Miss Frances Eliza Hubbell daughter of Philo P and Eliza (Backus) Hubbell the wedding being celebrated in Corning, N Y One child was born of that union, Kate Louise, now the wife of Charles A. Morey, the junior member of Berry & Morey They have four children Jeannette, Charles B, Frances and Bertha L

Mr Berry was made a Mason in the lodge of Painted Post, N Y, in 1852 His wife belongs to the Episcopal Church, and he is a member of the Old Settlers' Association of Winona County He is one of the oldest residents of this place, has been prominently identified with its best interests, educational and otherwise, and is one of its most public-spirited and useful citizens. He was instrumental in the establishment of the State Normal School at this place, and has always taken a lively interest in the public schools and at one time held the office of resident Director He is a gentleman of fine appearance, with a noble and manly bearing, which is in keeping with his honorable and upright character His ability and skill at the Bar have made him widely known in legal circles, and his prominence in politics has gained him many acquaintances, but his best friends are among those who have witnessed his every-day life and have had opportunity to judge of his true nobility

James H. Swindler.

JAMES H. SWINDLER, a farmer of Hillsdale Township, residing on section 35, is numbered among the pioneer settlers of Winona County. He has long witnessed its growth and advancement, and has aided in its progress and development. From the time when it was a frontier settlement he has been familiar with its history; has seen its wild lands transformed into beautiful homes and farms, and has witnessed the organization and growth of towns and villages which had not sprung into existence at the time of his arrival. In all the work of public improvement he has taken an active interest and has ever borne his part.

Mr. Swindler was born near Brownsville, Fayette County, Pa., on the 12th of April, 1829, and comes of English origin. His father, Benjamin F. Swindler, was a native of the Keystone State, and having attained his majority he married Miss Elizabeth Williams, by whom he had a family of ten children, seven sons and three daughters: Henrietta and George W., both now deceased; James H., of this sketch; William, a mason residing in Pacific, Mo.; Ella M., Elizabeth and Thomas, all deceased; Albert, who carries on agricultural pursuits in Iowa; and Samuel and Eli, who have passed away.

The subject of this notice attended the district schools at intervals until about seventeen years of age and acquired a fair business education. He began earning his livelihood at the age of ten, working on a farm for his uncle for his board and clothing. On reaching his majority he commenced work at the plaste

apprenticeship, during which time he received $1.50 per month. His residence in Pennsylvania continued until 1853, when he emigrated westward to St. Louis, Mo., and a few months later went to Keithsburg, Ill., where he made his home until the spring of 1855. In that year, by his arrival in Minnesota, Winona County gained one of its valued citizens. He pre-empted a tract of one hundred and twenty acres of land on section 35, Hillsdale Township, and has since made his home thereon. A log cabin had been built upon the place, but it was otherwise destitute of improvements, and with characteristic energy he began its further development. In course of time he had transformed it into a rich and fertile tract, and the well tilled fields were made to yield him a golden tribute for the care and labor he bestowed upon them. He also extended the boundaries of his farm until it comprised one hundred and fifty-two acres. In connection with farming he also worked at the plasterer's trade until a few years since.

Mr. Swindler was married on the 25th of May, 1851, the lady of his choice being Miss Lydia Dubbleblass, a native of Columbia County, Pa., born December 26, 1830, and a daughter of Jacob and Mary (Everett) Dubbleblass. Six children were born of this marriage, namely: Altha A., wife of Robert R. Richey, general agent of the Chicago & North-western Railroad Company at Omaha, Neb.; Albert, a general merchant and Postmaster of Stockton, Minn.; Vesta E., who resides at home; George, who died on the 5th of January, 1869; Gertrude M., wife of G. S. Blanchard, a farmer re-

, twin sister of Gertrude and wife of F. M. Curtis, who is located in Lewiston. Their eldest daughter, Mrs. Richey, was the first white child born in this neighborhood.

Mr. Swindler votes with the Republican party and is a warm advocate of its principles. He has held the office of Justice of the Peace, has been Chairman of the Town Board of Supervisors, was United States Census Taker in 1880, and has been a member of the School Board for a number of years. The cause of education finds in him a warm friend, and he does all in his power to promote the welfare of the schools. He is a member of the Methodist Church.

Albert Thomas.

ALBERT THOMAS, deceased, was a native of Maine, born near Augusta, on the 24th of February, 1834, and was one of a family of five sons, whose parents were Jacob and Elizabeth (Brown) Thomas. The days of his boyhood and youth were spent upon his father's farm, no event of special importance occurring during that period. He acquired a good business education in the public schools, and at the age of fourteen started out in life for himself. From that time he was dependent on his own resources, and whatever success he achieved in life was due entirely to his own efforts. Between the ages of seventeen and twenty-four years he was employed in teaching in the grammar schools in Maine, and with the capital he had thus acquired he then embarked in the boot and shoe business, establishing a store in Hallowell, Me., where he successfully carried on operations for a period of eight years.

Mr. Thomas then determined to try his fortune in the West, believing that greater prosperity might attend his efforts in this new and rapidly growing section of the country. Accordingly he came to Winona County and settled in Stockton, where during the succeeding winter he engaged in teaching school. In the spring of 1858 he came to Winona, where he was employed as a teacher in the public schools until 1860, when he again went to Stockton and purchased a farm of about two hundred acres. He then carried on general farming in connection with teaching for about eight years. In 1868 he removed to Winona, where he opened an office as a fire and life insurance agent, carrying on that business until his death. He owned considerable real estate in the city and also other property.

On the 6th of June, 1849, Mr. Thomas was united in marriage with Miss Mary D. Churchill, who was born in Parker, Me., and is a daughter of Jabez and Phœbe (Hazelton) Churchill. Five children were born of this union, three sons and two daughters, namely: Lizzie, who died on the 7th of September, 1851; Fred A., who is Register of Deeds of Bottineau County, N. Dak.; Charles F., who makes his home in Minnesota City as joint agent for the Milwaukee & St. Paul and Chicago & North-western Railroads; Walter H., who is engaged in the hardware business in North Dakota, and Alberta M., wife of Joseph Benson, who is engaged in merchandising at Brown's Valley, Minn.

In his political views Mr. Thomas was a Republican, but never sought or desired official distinction, preferring to give his time and attention to his business interests in which he met with good success, so that he was enabled to leave his family in comfortable circumstances. He belonged to the Masonic fraternity, and in religious belief was a Baptist, holding membership with the first church of that denomination organized in Winona. His life was an honorable and upright one, and all who knew him esteemed him highly for his sterling worth and the many excellences of his character. He was called to the home beyond on the 7th of May, 1869, and his remains were interred in Woodlawn Cemetery in Winona. His widow, a most estimable lady, still survives her husband, and is now living in Stockton, where she has a pleasant home and many friends.

John Francis Martin.

JOHN FRANCIS MARTIN has been prominent in the agricultural and official interests of Winona County, and during the late war he was found among the able defenders of his country who responded to the call for troops and valiantly aided in crushing out the rebellion. He now resides on section 9, Pleasant Hill Township, and devotes his time and attention to general farming and stock-raising. The record of his life is as follows.

A native of France, Mr. Martin was born in the city of Vesoul, in 1825, and is a son of John and Annie (Pagt) Martin. They had only two children, John F. and Joseph, who died in 1840. The father was called to his final rest in 1828, after which Mrs. Martin became the wife of John Mosher. By the second marriage were born five children: Eliza, Mary, Christine and Anthony, all deceased, and Lucinda Mary, the wife of Hubert Merchand, a druggist and land-owner residing in Ohio.

John F. Martin was a child of only three years at the time of his father's death. When a lad of ten summers he accompanied his mother on her emigration to America, crossing the Atlantic in a sailing-vessel, which, after a voyage of thirty-six days, dropped anchor in the harbor of New York. They located near Mt. Eaton, in Linn County, Ohio, where Mr. Martin remained until 1838, when he removed to Holmes County, Ohio. In 1840 he became a resident of Coshocton County, of the Buckeye State. He began life for himself at the early age of twelve years, and has since been dependent on his own resources. He first began clerking in a store, and was thus employed for about twelve years in Roscoe, Cleveland, and in Louisville. Attracted by the discovery of gold in

California, in 1849 he started across the plains for the promised El Dorado. The party with which he made the trip went down the river to Cairo and St. Louis, where they purchased outfits, shipping the same to Independence, Mo. They then started across the plains, making the journey by way of old Ft. Kearney. They left home on the 20th of March, and on the 26th of August stopped at what is now Sacramento. There Mr. Martin engaged in prospecting and mining until 1852, and his trip proved a very successful and a very pleasant one, he gaining a considerable portion of gold dust, and also storing away in his mind many pleasant and interesting reminiscences.

In 1852 Mr. Martin by way of the water route returned to his old home. The trip consumed sixty-four days, but the boat was supplied with provisions for only thirty days. However, the vessel at length reached harbor in safety, and the subject of this sketch again made his way to Ohio, where he was once more employed as a salesman. The same year he went to Cleveland, where he secured a position with a wholesale grocery house as solicitor and adjuster, a position which he filled until 1854. Wishing to seek a home in the West he then removed to Iowa, and with the capital he had acquired purchased a tract of land of five hundred acres near Iowa City, but only made his home thereon from June until October. He then sold out, and in the winter of 1854 came to Winona. Locating at Richmond he purchased a tract of land of about three hundred acres, securing the same, or the greater part of it, from the Government. He laid out the village of Richmond in 1855, and immediately established a general store, which he carried on in connection with farming. He was thus engaged in business until 1860, when he removed to the farm on which he now lives, and established a general store at Ridgeway. In July, 1864, he joined the army, becoming sutler of the Seventh Minnesota Infantry, and when the war was over he was discharged at Ft. Snelling, in August, 1865. Immediately after he returned to his home and family.

On the 13th of March, 1853, Mr. Martin was united in marriage with Miss Elizabeth Morrison, daughter of Zachariah and Maria (Butler) Morrison. The lady, who is a native of Holmes County, Ohio, was born on the 4th of July, 1832, and was one of six children, the others being John, William, Isaac, a resident of Effingham, Ill.; Maria, wife of Abraham Barnes, who is living in Winnebago; and Louisa, wife of John Broadwell, a resident of Winona.

After his return home in 1865, Mr. Martin began farming, which he carried on until 1867, when he was elected Sheriff of the county on the Democratic ticket, and for three successive terms he was chosen to that office. He was also appointed Deputy United States Marshal, which position he held for five years. In 1873, after his term of Sheriff had expired, he returned to his old home in Ohio, and visited many different parts of this country, traveling until 1875, when he took up his residence upon the farm which is now his home. Here he owns two hundred and forty acres of land on sections 9 and 16, Pleasant Hill Township, and his time and attention are now given to the cultivation of his land and to stock-raising. He is recognized as one of the leading agriculturists in the community, and has a valuable place, whose many improvements are indicative of his thrifty care and supervision. In 1891 he was appointed by the Governor as Notary Public, to serve for seven years. In politics he is a stanch Democrat, warmly advocating the principles of his party, and in his social relations is a Mason, having attained the Knights Templar degree. In the various public offices he has filled he has discharged his duties with a promptness and fidelity which have won for him high commendation, and made him worthy the trust reposed in him. In business he has won success, owing to enterprise and careful management, and is now the possessor of a comfortable competence.

Volney E. Waffles.

VOLNEY E. WAFFLES, who carries on farming on section 7, Wiscoy Township, was born in Mohawk, Herkimer County, N. Y., on the 3d of July, 1843, and is the eldest in a family of four children, whose parents were John and Sarah A. (Maxfield) Waffles. The family is of German origin, and was established in the United States in Colonial days. The father was a native of New York, and became a harness-maker. For a number of years he carried on a harness and saddlery shop, and thus provided a livelihood for himself and family. His death occurred February 20, 1887, at the age of seventy-two years, and his wife died on the 25th of February, 1863, when only forty years of age. The paternal grandfather, Adam Waffles, was a soldier in the Mexican War. In the family to which Volney E. belongs were the following children: Orlando, who died on the 9th of April, 1880; Clinton, who is supposed to have been killed while serving under General Custer, and Minerva, who died in 1851.

Mr. Waffles, our subject, began his education in the district schools, and completed it in Fairfield Seminary, thus acquiring a good practical knowledge, which has well fitted him for his business career and for contact with the world. He was still under the parental roof when he responded to the country's call for troops to aid in crushing out the rebellion. When it was found that the war was to be no holiday affair, and President Lincoln had issued his call for volunteers to serve three years, Mr. ... joined Battery A of the First New York Light Artillery. He was mustered in at Utica, and going to the South was first under fire at Williamsburg. He afterward participated in the siege of Yorktown, the battle of Fair Oaks, the seven-days Battle of the Wilderness, Savage Station, the first assault on Petersburg, and then went on the Katz Cavalry raid through the Virginias and afterward through the borders of North Carolina. At the battle of Fair Oaks his battery was captured. Mr. Waffles and others escaped, and were transferred to the Eighth New York Independent Battery. He took part in many skirmishes, and was with McClellan on his campaign. He was also present at the time of the surrender of Suffolk, and received his final discharge in the city of New York on the expiration of his term of service.

Mr. Waffles then returned to New York and entered upon his business career as a clerk in a general store, where he was employed until 1866. He then sought a home in the West, coming to Winona County, Minn. He engaged in farming in Wilson Township for about four years, after which, in 1870, he began teaching school. In the spring of 1871 he removed to Milwaukee, where he was employed as shipping clerk in a wholesale grocery house, which position he held for two years. In the year 1871 he began work on the Chicago, Milwaukee & St. Paul Railroad, and then went into the office as yard clerk, where he continued until 1875. That year witnessed his return to Winona ... as salesman in a store, and devoted his energies to that line of work until 1881, when he removed to St Paul, where he served as Chief Clerk for the Chicago, Milwaukee & St Paul Railroad Company, a position which he resigned in January, 1889. He then returned to the farm where he now lives, comprising eighty-seven acres of good land on section 7, Wiscoy Township.

On the 14th of February, 1866, was celebrated the marriage which united the destinies of Miss Lana E Miller, daughter of Nicholas and Magdalene (Abert) Miller, and a native of Burlington, Wis. They have had a family of five children, as follows: Clinton, a resident of Wilson Township; Edwin L., a railroad man living in Colorado; Volney A and Mabel S., who are at home, and Charles M., who died July 17, 1884, at the age of seventeen months.

In his political views Mr. Wallles is independent, holding himself free to support the men whom he thinks best qualified for the office, regardless of party ties or affiliations. He has served as Justice of the Peace. Socially he is connected with the Odd Fellows' society, and is also a member of the Grand Army of the Republic. All who know him hold him in high regard, and his sterling worth and many excellences of character make him well deserving of the esteem and confidence of his friends and neighbors.

Joseph Leicht.

JOSEPH LEICHT, editor and proprietor of the Winona *Westlicher Herold*, is a native of Germany. In that country he received a university education and in 1867 emigrated to America, locating in St. Louis, where he worked on the *Abendzeitung* and *Neue Welt* until 1869. In that year he accepted a position with the *Buffalo County Republikaner*, published at Fountain City, Wis., where he continued as an employe until 1871, when he bought out the paper and began publishing it as a Democratic sheet. This venture was successful and he secured a large circulation.

In January, 1881, Mr. Leicht established the *Westlicher Herold* in Winona, and after carrying on the same for six years enlarged its size to 35x48 inches. It [illegible]
tablished a [illegible] the *Winona*, the subscription price of both papers being $2 per year. This was the first undertaking of the kind among the German publishers in the United States. The *Westlicher Herold* and the *Winona* both have a large circulation in Minnesota, Wisconsin and North and South Dakota, and the new undertaking of publishing twice a week for $2 per year, which was pronounced by some of the fraternity a failure, has since been imitated by other publishers East and West. The circulation of the two papers has increased to such an extent that Mr. Leicht found it necessary in 1892 to place a big Cox-Webb perfecting press in the pressroom to run off his editions. The papers are neatly printed and enjoy a large advertising [illegible] [illegible]mber in a number

of social and secret societies, and at the last session of the Supreme Grove of the United Ancient Order of Druids, held in Columbus Ohio, from August 11 to August 20 1891, he was elected Supreme Arch, the highest office of that order in the United States In politics Mr Leicht is a Democrat, and in 1892 he was the unanimous choice of his party for State Treasurer He never accepted a nomination for a city office, but in 1893 he had to submit to the wishes of the taxpayers of his ward, and he was elected School Director, which position he still holds He is working hard for the elevation of our public schools, and in this work he has the unanimous support of all friends of education

---

William Edward Smith.

WILLIAM EDWARD SMITH, business manager of the D Sinclair Publishing Company of Winona, is an enterprising and prominent business man, devoted to the best interests of this community and its upbuilding He was born in Bridgeport Conn on the 20th of June, 1853, and is the eldest of three sons, whose parents were Haskell G and Lucretia (Collins) Smith The paternal grandfather, Ashbel Smith, was born in Vermont and was of English lineage He reared a large family and lived to a good old age The maternal grandfather, Cicero Collins, was a native of Connecticut, and was of English lineage He also reared a large family and lived to an advanced age One of his ancestors was the first resident minister of Litchfield Conn Haskell G Smith, who was born in the Green Mountain State, was a railroad man, and for some time was general manager for a road on Long Island He afterwards retired to a farm near Goshen, Conn, where he spent his last days, his death occurring August 19, 1883, at the age of sixty-seven His

still survives him. Their three children are William E Edward C and Charles C

The eldest son was reared in Goshen, Conn, and began his education in its public schools, after which he attended boarding-schools in Norwalk and New Haven, Conn, preparing himself to take up a scientific course in Yale College which he entered in 1869 He then continued his studies for three years, fitting himself for a civil engineer, which profession he followed from 1872 until 1874. In that year he returned to the old homestead where he remained until 1877, when he came to the West and entered the employ of the North-western Road, in the supply department at Clinton, Iowa He left that place on the 29th of January, 1878, and came at once to Winona, Minn, to fill the position in that company's shops of chief clerk, in which capacity he served for ten months, when he was made traveling auditor To that position he devoted his time and energies until 1881, when he returned to the shops at Winona

Smith was

united in marriage with Miss Clara M. Sinclair, daughter of Daniel and Melissa I. (Briggs) Sinclair. Three children were born to them: Donald, who died at the age of eight years; and Gordon and Stanley, who are still with their parents.

Mr. Smith is a member of Prairie Lodge No. 7, I. O. O. F., and of Oak Grove Lodge No. 15, Order of Druids. His wife belongs to the Congregational Church. On the 1st of January, 1883, he purchased an interest in the Winona *Republican*, a daily and weekly newspaper, in connection with which there is also carried on a job-printing department and bindery. The publishers also own their building, a fine three-story brick structure at the corner of Third and Center Streets.

Almus H. Smith.

ALMUS H. SMITH, a wide-awake and enterprising citizen of Winona County, and the owner of Hillsdale Park Farm, claims New York as the state of his nativity, his birth having occurred near Elmira, in Chemung County, in September, 1844. He is the eldest of three children, whose parents were Lorenzo D. and Cynthia C. (Chatfield) Smith. His sister Alphia is the wife of Michael Doran, a resident of Winona; and Amelia is the widow of John Kenny, and makes her home in South Dakota.

The father of this family was a cabinet-maker by trade. He resided in the Empire State until 1851, when he determined to seek a home in the West, and emigrated to Oswego, Ill., where he worked at his trade for about a year. In 1852 he came to Minnesota, settling in St. Paul, where he carried on cabinet-making until 1851. In the spring of that year he came to Winona, having been appointed receiver in the land-office at that place, a Government position, which he held for about two years. He was one of the company who organized the [illegible] Chicago & N[illegible] stock in the enterprise, and became one of the Directors of the company, but the road was not completed at that time. It now forms a part of what is known as the Winona & St. Peter Railroad. Subsequently, Mr. Smith turned his attention to the real-estate business, which he carried on in Winona until his death. He passed away on the 3d of September, 1863, and was laid to rest in Winona Cemetery. He held membership with the Masonic lodge, and was recognized as one of the leading business men of the city. He possessed excellent executive ability, was sagacious and far-sighted, and labored not only for his own interest, but was also deeply interested in the welfare of his adopted county.

Almus H. Smith accompanied his parents on their various removals, and at the age of ten years came with them to Winona County. In the public schools he acquired a practical English education, and when seventeen years of age he began life for himself. For a few months he engaged in grading railroads, and then turned his attention [illegible] followed until [illegible] wenty years of age At that time he enlisted in the Union service, becoming a private of Company O, Second Minnesota Cavalry He was mustered in at Ft Snelling, and was sent to Ft Ridgley, on the frontier, where he was engaged in guarding Indians The war having ended, he was honorably discharged in December, 1865 and at once returned to Winona County

Here Mr. Smith resumed farming, and lived upon the old homestead for ten years, from 1866 until 1876, when he rented a farm which was his home for about seven years On the expiration of that period he purchased the Hillsdale Park Farm which is now his home. It is a valuable and desirable place, and yields to the owner a good income

On the 28th of November, 1872, was celebrated the marriage of Mr Smith and Miss Jennie C. Floyd who was born in Lawrence County, Ohio on the 25th of April, 1850, and is a daughter of James M and Elizabeth (Wilgus) Floyd To them were born three children, but Clarence C, born February 27 1877 is the only one now living Harry and Herby, twins, both died in infancy Mr and Mrs Smith are widely and favorably known in this community, having many warm friends and in social circles they hold an enviable position Mr Smith is independent in politics, voting for the man whom he thinks best qualified for office regardless of party affiliations He has served as Township Clerk and Chairman of the Board of Supervisors His life has been quietly passed, yet has been one of usefulness, and he is regarded as one of the leading farmers of Hillsdale Township

William Lewis.

WILLIAM LEWIS is the owner of a valuable farm of forty-two acres on section 19, Warren Township, and in connection with the cultivation of his land carries on stock-raising He is recognized as one of the leading agriculturists of the community, and as such deserves mention in this volume. He is a Western man, his birth having occurred near Bennington, in Decatur County, Ind, on the 3d of April, 1815 His parents, Jonathan S and Mary (Ramer) Lewis, had a family of sixteen children, nine sons and seven daughters When William was a lad of ten summers they left the Hoosier State and emigrated to Minnesota, settling in Utica Township, Winona County

Upon his father's farm the subject of this notice was reared to man of the neighborhood his education was acquired. He was still under the parental roof at the time of his enlistment in his country's service On the 25th of February, 1864, he joined the boys in blue of Company B, Seventh Minnesota Infantry and was mustered in at Rochester then Ft Snelling The troops were ordered to St Louis, and thence to Tupelo, where occurred his first engagement He afterward participated in the battles of Nashville and Mobile, and the siege and capture of Spanish Fort, and was in many smaller engagements He was very fortunate in that he was never wounded or taken prisoner, and when the war was over and the South had laid down its arms he was honorably discharged, being mustered out at St Paul on the 16th of August 1865

ne in Winona County, and purchased a farm of eighty acres on section 23, Utica Township where he lived for seven years. On the expiration of that period he removed to Lewiston and carried the mail from that place to Enterprise. The two succeeding years of his life were passed in Winona, after which he came to the farm which has since been his home.

Mr. Lewis was married on the 29th of September 1867, to Miss Rose Nichols, and six children graced their union. Edward the eldest, died in 1869, Isabel is now the wife of William Mason, a resident of Winona, Ella and Herbert are at home, Lawrence died in 1889; and Harry completes the family. Mr. Lewis is a member of the Dunkard Church. He takes no very prominent part in public affairs, has never been a politician, but is content to devote his time and energies to his home and business interests. He is energetic, and by good management and well directed efforts has acquired a comfortable competence and become the owner of a valuable farm.

Clarke A. Fuller.

CLARKE A. FULLER, one of the highly respected citizens of Wiscoy Township, living on section 11, has been a resident of Winona County for thirty-four years, and well deserves mention in her history. He was born in Addison County, Vt., on the 20th of June, 1836, and is a son of Thomas and Marinda (Gilmore) Fuller. The father, who was also a native of the Green Mountain State, was of English descent. He was married in the state of his nativity, and by this union were born three children: Harriet, who became Mrs. Spencer, and died in 1858, Clarke A., of this sketch, and Angie, who married John Moon and died in January, 1890. By occupation the father was a farmer, and followed that business throughout his entire life. His death occurred at his son's house in Winona County, in his seventy-fourth year, and his wife passed away before the close of the Civil War.

In the us [illegible] Fuller spent th[illegible] f[illegible] H[illegible] education was acquired in the district and select schools which he attended until about nineteen years of age, and in Rochester Academy of Rochester, Vt. He thus became well informed on all the common, and many of the higher, branches of learning, and by reading in later years he has kept well posted on the affairs of the day. On attaining his majority, he entered upon his business career, and chose the West as the scene of his labors. Leaving the Green Mountain State, he traveled by rail, water and team until he had reached Minnesota, when he made a location in Freeborn County, near the city of Freeborn. He took up a claim of one hundred and sixty acres, but never made his home upon the land, for he had secured a position as engineer and sawyer in a steam-mill, where he remained for two years. On the expiration of that period he engaged in teaching school for one year. Mr. Fuller then came to Winona County [illegible]ip, where he pur[illegible]tion 12. This he still owns, it being a part of his present farm, which now comprises two hundred acres of valuable land. His fields are well tilled, his farm is under a high state of cultivation and good improvements are there seen. He raises both grain and stock, and his labors bring him a comfortable competence.

Mr. Fuller has been twice married. On the 3d of May, 1860, he was married to Miss Betsy E. Montgomery and to them was born a daughter, Adelia, now the wife of William Dick, a farmer near Marshland, Wis. Mrs. Fuller died on the 17th of November, 1866, and the subject of this sketch was again married, October 8, 1867, his second union being with Mrs. Julia Jenkinson. They have seven children, namely: Frances, wife of Alonzo Kendrick, a farmer residing in Wiscoy Township; George and Walter, who aid in the operation of the home farm; Herbert, who is engaged in school teaching; Chauncey, Louis and Johnnie, who are still with their parents. The family circle yet remains unbroken by the hand of death.

In his political affiliations Mr. Fuller is a Republican, having supported that party since he attained his majority. He has been three times nominated for the Legislature, but owing to the large Democratic majority in the county has never been elected. His nomination, however, shows his high standing in his own party and the confidence reposed in him by his constituents. He is now serving as Township Clerk, and has held that office altogether for twenty years. With the exception of six years, he has during his entire residence in Winona County served as a member of the Township Board of Supervisors. He was one of the County Commissioners for five years, being first elected to fill a vacancy, at which time he served for two years, after which he was re-elected for a term of three years. He has also been Justice of the Peace for some time. His long continuance in office indicates not only his personal popularity, but also tells of faithful and efficient service and of duties promptly performed. Mr. Fuller is a valued citizen, in that he takes an active interest in everything pertaining to the welfare of the community and its upbuilding. He belongs to the Masonic fraternity, and is an active worker and leading member in the Congregational Church.

Silas Braley.

SILAS BRALEY, ex-Sheriff of Winona County, and a member of the Winona Construction Company, which is engaged in paving, sewer work and general contracting, is recognized as one of the most enterprising business men of the city. He was born near Montpelier, Vt., May 1, 1844, and is one of a family of three children, whose paren[illegible] Braley. His sister, Betsy, is now the wife of Alvin Pierce, of Westboro, Wis., and his brother, Alvin, resides in Winona. The father of this family was born on the old Braley homestead in the Green Mountain State in the year 1819, and was a farmer by occupation. He resided in Vermont until 1849, when, accompanied by his family, he started [illegible] in Oshkosh,

Wis., where he continued to reside until 1864. In that year he removed to Fond du Lac, where he remained until 1868, and then went to Cherokee County, Iowa. His remaining days were there passed. His death occurred in 1894, at the age of seventy-five, many years after his wife was called to the home beyond. She, too, was born in Vermont, and died at the early age of thirty-two years. The Bialey family is of English origin and was founded in America by ancestors who crossed the briny deep on the "Mayflower." The grandfather, Silas Bialey, spent his entire life in Vermont.

The gentleman whose name heads this record was a child of only four years when he was taken by his parents to Wisconsin. He continued at home until eighteen years of age, and then started out in life for himself. During the three years which followed before he had attained his majority, he paid his father $20 per month for his freedom. Going to Oshkosh he engaged in lumbering, following that business about four years, when he entered the shipyards and began learning the ship-carpenter's trade, serving a three-years apprenticeship. On the expiration of that period he resumed lumbering, to which he devoted his time and energies until 1870, when he came to Minnesota, in company with A. J. Haywood, and engaged in logging for two years. He then entered the employ of Laird, Norton & Co., to superintend their rafting and logging business, and continued with them about twelve years, or until 1884, when he purchased an outfit and began logging in his own interest. For six years he carried on business along that line. In 1892, in connection with Otis Abell and C. G. Corey, he organized what is known as the Winona Construction Company.

This company is extensively engaged in paving, in laying sewers and in doing general contract work. The first contract taken was for the paving of some seventy-three thousand yards of the streets of Winona, and putting in about twenty-six thousand feet of curbing. This contract amounted to $120,000, and was completed some two weeks before the time specified in the agreement. The company also took a similar contract for work in Quincy, Ill., for $70,000, and the work was completed six weeks before the specified time, a fact which plainly indicates the thoroughness and rapidity with which the work was carried on. The firm has a high reputation for the excellence of their work and their faithfulness to contracts, and the liberal patronage which they now receive is well deserved.

On the 15th of December, 1863, Mr. Bialey was united in marriage with Miss Marion W. Powell, of Oshkosh, Wis., daughter of Willoughby and Zilpha Powell, both of whom were natives of Nova Scotia, and died in old age. Mr. and Mrs. Bialey have three children: William Wallace and John W., who are engaged in railroading on the North-western Road, and Marion Alice, at home.

In 1888 Mr. Bialey was nominated and elected as Sheriff of Winona County for a term of two years, and on the expiration of that period was re-elected. He had previously served as Deputy United States Marshal for four years, and in the discharge of his duties has ever been found fearless and true. In politics he is a stanch Republican, having supported that party since attaining his majority. Socially he is connected with the Masonic fraternity, belonging to Winona Lodge No. 18, A. F. & A. M., Chapter No. 5, R. A. M., and Cœur de Leon Commandery No. 3, of Winona. He is also a charter member of Winona Lodge No. 21, K. of P. Mr. Bialey is a broad-gauged, liberal-minded and public-spirited man, justly popular in Winona and his adopted county, where he has many friends, who hold him in the highest regard.

Austin Abell.

AUSTIN ABELL, who was numbered among the boys in blue of the late war, now devotes his time and energies to general farming on section 3, Wiscoy Township. He is a native of the Empire State, his birth having occurred in Oswego County, on the 16th of August, 1833. The Abell family is of English origin and was probably founded in America in early Colonial days. Lemuel Abell, the father of Austin, was also born in New York. Having attained to mature years, he was united in marriage with Miss Sallie W. Watson, a lady of Scotch lineage, and to them were born the following children: Austin, of this sketch; Minerva L., widow of Alvin Ford, a resident of Wiscoy Township; Otis, who lives in Winona and is a contractor for laying pavements; Alfred, who resides in Winona; and two who died in infancy.

In the usual manner of farmer lads the subject of this record spent the days of his boyhood and youth. He early became familiar with farm work in all its departments, for as soon as old enough to handle the plow he began work in the fields, and the occupation to which he was reared he has made his life work. For fifteen years he resided in New York, and then left the home of his early childhood for the West, the family removing to Dodge County, Wis., where he remained until after he had attained his majority. The year 1855 witnessed his removal from the Badger State to Minnesota and saw him located in Winona County. He first settled ... remained for a year, when he removed to Waseca County, and in 1856 entered one hundred and sixty acres of land from the Government. It was a wild and unimproved tract, upon which not a furrow had been turned or an improvement made, but with characteristic energy he began its development and made his home thereon until 1861.

In the mean time Mr. Abell had married, Miss Mary A. Small having become his wife on the 16th of September, 1858. Their union has been blessed with four children, three sons and a daughter, namely: George A., Janette, Lemuel A. and Urban S. The family is now widely known in this community, and is noted for its hospitality, its members having a wide circle of friends and acquaintances.

Returning with his family to Winona County, Mr. Abell rented a farm and continued its cultivation until 1864, when, prompted by patriotic impulses, he responded to his country's call for troops, and enlisted as a private of Company K, Eleventh Minnesota Infantry. He was mustered into service at Ft. Snelling and at once sent to Nashville, Tenn., where he was engaged in guarding railroads and property until the close of the war. He took part in no large battles, yet his service was often quite arduous. When the war was over he was mustered out, in July, 1865, and at once returned to his home and family.

Mr. Abell resumed farming and traded his property for a farm of one hundred and twenty acres ... still resides. It has been his home continuously since, and is a well developed tract of land, whose rich fields and good improvements indicate the thrift and enterprise of the owner, and tell of his careful supervision. His life has been a busy and useful one, devoted to his farming interests. He takes no very active part in public affairs, yet is always interested in what pertains to the welfare of the community and its further advancement and upbuilding. He has held the office of Supervisor, yet has never been an office-seeker. He formerly voted with the Republican party, but is now a Prohibitionist, espousing the principles of that organization, for it embodies his views on the temperance question.

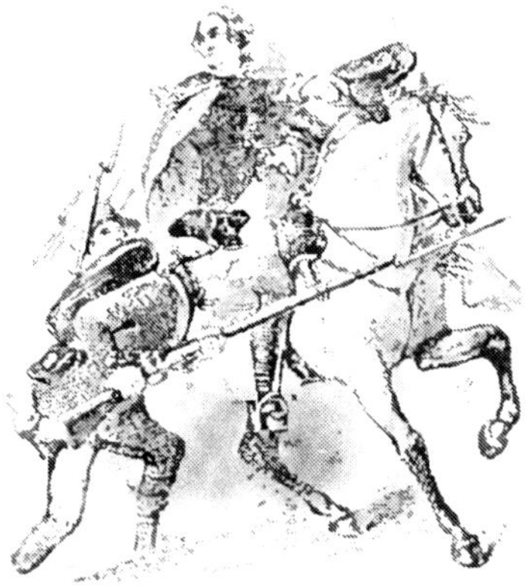

HON. O. B. GOULD.

Hon. Ozro B. Gould.

HON. OZRO B. GOULD, lawyer, came to Winona in the autumn of 1867, and began practice in January following. His legal studies had been pursued in the office of Lee & Brewer, of Tiffin, Ohio, and at the University of Michigan, where he graduated with the law class of '67. He was of New England parentage, his father, Ozro A. Gould, being a native of Rutland County, Vt., from where in early life he emigrated with the family to Genesee County, N. Y. In that state the greater part of his life was passed, and there in 1832 he married Mary A. Barnes, daughter of Elisha Barnes, of Middletown, Conn. In 1837, having purchased a considerable amount of notes and commercial paper which had been given to people in Canada, he removed there to look after his investments. Owing to the disturbed condition of affairs incident to the panic of that year and the Canadian rebellion, returns came in slowly or not at all, and Mr. Gould engaged in other lines of business to help out, remaining in Her Majesty's dominions until his death, which occurred at Toronto, December 15, 1845.

The subject of this sketch, the only child of his parents, was born [illegible]

on his father's death his mother returned with him to the States, where she died three years later, at Attica, N. Y. In 1849 Ozro was taken by an uncle, Isaac N. Howe, to live upon a farm in Sandusky County, Ohio. The uncle dying soon after, the boy at the age of fifteen struck out for himself. Having no fortune but good health and a strong constitution, he labored at such employment as he could find, attending school at odd times when opportunity offered. In 1861 he enlisted as a private soldier in Company G, Fifty-fifth Ohio Infantry, and served during the war, being discharged as Captain of the company in July, 1865. He was wounded and taken prisoner at the battle of Chancellorsville, Va., May 2, 1863. Released on parole, he commanded a division of the Parole Camp near Washington during the summer of 1863. Joining his regiment in northern Alabama in the fall of that year, he participated in the battles of Lookout Mountain and Missionary Ridge under Grant, and the following year was in Sherman's campaign against Atlanta and on the march to the sea.

Mr. Gould was largely instrumental in securing [illegible] are of soldiers' orphans, which was located at Winona. He served as a member of the State Board by appointment of the Governor and acted as the local Director. In 1880 he was elected to the lower house of the State Legislature, serving for the regular and special sessions of 1881. At the special session impeachment proceedings were begun against one of the District Judges, and Mr Gould was selected as one of the managers on the part of the House The trial before the Senate lasted until March, 1882, and resulted in the removal of the accused officer

Mr Gould takes an active interest in public and business affairs, having been a promoter and director in several manufacturing and other corporations In politics he has always been an earnest Republican, and in religious matters claims for himself and allows to others the utmost latitude of opinion

In July, 1865, he was married at Chicago, Ill, to Miss Mary E Couse, a graduate of Butler University, Ind, and of the Cook County Normal School, and teacher in the State Normal School at Winona She was a daughter of Andrew Couse, of Woodstock, Ill Mrs. Gould died at Winona, April 9, 1892, leaving three children: Ozro C., Mary and Ralph Fulton

The following extracts from a recent number of the St Paul *Pioneer Press* in reference to the latest honor conferred upon Mr. Gould will doubtless be of interest to his many friends

"Governor Nelson yesterday appointed O. B. Gould, of Winona, to succeed Chief Justice Start as Judge of the District Court of the Third Judicial District Mr. Gould's appointment is said to be highly satisfactory to the Bar of the district. He is about fifty years of age, and has been a resident of Winona over twenty years He has been a member of the State Legislature, and served in an Ohio regiment during the Civil War."

'O. B Gould, of Winona, who was appointed District Judge yesterday to take Judge Start's place, will now be glad that he was not nominated for Clerk of the Supreme Court. Judge Gould is a loyal Republican worker, who has never received much from the party, and the honor is doubly merited and doubly acceptable on this account"

Peter R. Dickson.

PETER R DICKSON, who is foreman of a brickyard in Diesbach, a position he has filled for a quarter of a century, was born in Lachute, Canada East, May 22, 1845. His parents were William and Christie (Moore) Dickson, and both were natives of Scotland The father during his boyhood crossed the Atlantic to Canada, where he still resides, at about the age of seventy years. During the greater part of his life he has engaged in the manufacture of brick, but now carries on farming. His wife died some years since, passing away at the age of thirty-three

Peter R Dickson was a lad of only ten summers at the time of his mother's death He remained upon the old home farm until twenty years of age, and during that time learned the trade of brick-making, becoming familiar with it in all its details In 1865 he removed to Illinois, where he worked as a farm hand by the month for a year. His residence in Dresbach dates from 1866 Coming to this place, he sought a position in a brickyard and was made its foreman, in which capacity he served for nine years He subsequently went to Sioux City Iowa, and was foreman of a brickyard at that place for one year, but on the expiration of that period he returned to Diesbach and resumed his former position

On the 2d of May, 1869, Mr. Dickson was united in marriage with Miss Minnie Burke, of Diesbach and to them were born ten children, four of whom are deceased. William G., at home, Mabel, who is successfully engaged in teaching school; Roland, Hollis, Erwin and Arthur, who are still under the parental roof. The family circle yet remains unbroken, and the household is noted for its hospitality, its members ranking high in the social circles in which they move

Mr. Dickson now owns a pleasant home in Diesbach He votes with the Democratic party and warmly advocates its principles. For two terms he served as Chairman of the Township Board, and proved a competent official. He belongs to the Episcopal Church, and has lived an honorable, upright life, which has gained for him the confidence and esteem of the entire community His faithfulness to his employer's interests is well indicated by his long service

---

N. V. A. Crow.

N. V. A. CROW, one of the extensive landowners of St Charles, who is now living a retired life, is a native of Indiana, his birth having occurred in Orange County, on the 8th of October, 1822 His father, John Crow, was born in North Carolina, and when a young man emigrated to the Hoosier State, becoming one of its pioneers He there married Polly Millis, who was also born in North Carolina, and with her parents removed to Indiana They soon afterward went to Illinois, and located a mile and a-half from Geneva, on the Fox River, thirty miles from Chicago Indians still visited the neighborhood and caused the settlers considerable trouble Mrs Crow there died, after which Mr Crow removed to Linn County, Iowa, settling in what is known as the "Big Woods"

The subject of this sketch accompanied his parents on their various removals, and was reared to manhood in Iowa Having attained to mature years, he was united in marriage with Miss Eliza Lane, of Linn County, after which he secured land and began the cultivation and development of a new farm By their union were born four children Sylvester, George, John Wesley and Nelson Manley. Mr. Crow was married the second time, in Wisconsin, the lady of his choice being Amanda Lane, who died May 20, 1886 The children born of that marriage were Sophia, who died at the age of six years; Millis Walter, who for three years has engaged in merchandising in St Charles, where he is doing a successful business, Garrison Albert, who died of consumption at St Charles, at the age of twenty-six years; and Eddie, who died in Santa Monica, Cal., of typhoid fever when eighteen years of age

After his first marriage, Mr Crow carried on farming for a few years, and then began working in the lead mines near Hazel Green, Wis, where he continued for five years He engaged in prospecting and mining on his own account, but did not meet with the success he anticipated. In 1850, attracted by the discovery of gold in California, he crossed the plains to the Pacific Slope, leaving home on the 20th of March, and reaching Hangtown on the 10th of August He engaged in prospecting for gold for a month and a-half at that place, and then went to Nevada, where he remained until his return to Wisconsin in April, 1852 He had at first carried on mining beside a stream, but high water caused him to leave that place, and he went to Shelby Flats, where he worked in sluice diggings. This trip proved fairly successful, and he returned home with some capital, making the journey by way of the Isthmus route to New York City

Mr. Crow rejoined his family in Grant County, Wis, and there remained for about three years. In 1855 he came to Winona County, and located a claim in Elba Township, five miles north of St Charles He also purchased other claims, and secured from the Government about four hundred acres of land Upon this he settled continuing its cultivation and improvement until after the breaking out of the war, when he bought a farm in Olmsted County, upon which he resided until his removal to St Charles, which has now been his home for eleven years. He still owns the old home farm of two hundred and forty acres, besides another tract of the same size, together with his first farm of four hundred acres, a three hundred and twenty acre farm in St Charles Township, and a small tract of land within the city limits. He was principally engaged in the raising of wheat, and in his undertakings he met with prosperity He has also engaged in loaning money, and to a limited extent has been interested in mercantile pursuits

Mr Crow is a Royal Arch Mason, and in social and business circles stands high. He has the confidence and regard of the entire community, and has many warm friends His home is an elegant residence, built of brick, and in it he expects to spend his declining days, resting in the enjoyment of the fruits of his former toil His life has been both a busy and useful one

James F. Hennessy.

JAMES F. HENNESSY, the efficient Superintendent of the Winona Wagon Works, was born in Elgin, Ill, on the 6th of June, 1849, and was there reared until twelve years of age His father, William Hennessy, was a contractor and builder At a very early age the subject of this sketch went to Chicago, starting out in life on his own responsibility. He was employed as an errand boy until thirteen years of age, when he became a helper in a carriage shop, his time being thus passed up to the age of fourteen, when he took a [illegible] to Califor[illegible] turned and resumed work at his trade in Chicago, where he remained for a year In his sixteenth year he removed to Dubuque, Iowa, where he worked in a wagon shop, and later took up his residence in Decorah, Iowa, where he made his home until his eighteenth year At that time he located in Rochester, Minn, and worked as a journeyman until 1871. He had become familiar with the trade in all its departments and was recognized as a thorough and efficient workman

In 1871 Mr Hennessy entered the employ of [illegible], Minn., who were the found[illegible] Winona Wagon Company, of which he soon became foreman. This company was soon consolidated with the firm of Albertson & Oleson and the style of the Rushford Wagon Company was assumed. Mr. Hennessy became foreman of the new shops, and in February, 1880, came to Winona as foreman of the Winona Wagon Works. In 1883 he was made Superintendent, which position he holds at the present time.

On the 19th of October, 1876, in the city of North East, Pa., Mr. Hennessy was united in marriage with Miss Elsie A. Palmer, and to them have been born seven children, six of whom are daughters: Jessie, who is now a student in the high school, Mabel, Ada, Helen, Kate, Florence and James. Mr. Hennessy holds membership in the Masonic fraternity, the Independent Order of Odd Fellows and the Modern Woodmen of America. He is also identified with the Baptist Church, and in political views is a Republican.

Much of the success attained by the Winona Wagon Works Company is due to the active and untiring efforts of Mr. Hennessy. He gives his entire attention and skilled training to the details of every department of the business and has a just pride in the exact division of labor, the lack of friction and the general growth of this concern. He has a happy faculty of knowing how to handle men, has a wide acquaintance with the wants of skilled artisans and ever has in mind their welfare and advancement. A pleasant and agreeable gentleman, it does him good to show to the stranger the various departments of the works, and no more pleasant or instructive hour can be passed than one spent in his company, as each particular piece of machinery passes in review.

Martin Schulz.

MARTIN SCHULZ devotes his time and energies to agricultural pursuits on section 19, Fremont Township, where he now owns and operates eighty-four acres of good land, that is under a high state of cultivation and well improved with all the accessories and conveniences of a model farm. He claims Germany as the land of his birth, which occurred in the kingdom of Baden in 1834. His parents, John and Mary (Dear) Schulz, were also natives of that country, and the father followed farming in pursuit of fortune. I children, of whom the subject of this sketch is the youngest.

Martin Schulz remained upon the home farm until nineteen years of age, when he determined to try his fortune beyond the Atlantic, for he had heard much of the privileges and advantages afforded young men in the New World. He sailed on the good ship "Henry Hudson," and after a long voyage of forty days, during which they encountered some very severe weather, the vessel dropped anchor in the harbor of New York. The ed took up his residence in Elizabethtown, N. J., and began work at the carpenter's trade, which he followed in that place for about six months. He then removed to Delaware County, N. Y., where he worked at carpentering for about three years, and in 1856 he sought a home in the West. This was his introduction to Winona County and he located in Fremont Township, where he worked at his trade for a year. On the expiration of that period he was obliged to return to New York to act as witness in a large lawsuit, and he continued carpentering in the Empire State until 1862, when he again came West. He then changed his occupation, removing to a farm of forty acres which he had purchased during his previous stay here.

In February, 1864, Mr. Schulz responded to the call of his adopted country for troops, and enlisted in the Union army, as a member of Company D, Seventh Minnesota Infantry, with which he served until the close of the war when he was honorably discharged. He participated in the battles of Nashville, Spanish Fort, and several minor engagements, but was fortunate enough to escape being wounded or captured. When the war was over and peace restored, he returned to his farm, which he has since operated.

On the 11th of February, 1861, Mr. Schulz was united in marriage with Miss Miranda Smith, of New York, who died in this county in 1887. He is a Republican in his political views, and served as Postmaster of the Clyde postoffice for about thirteen years. He belongs to John C. Fremont Post No. 181, G. A. R., of Fremont, and holds membership with the Presbyterian Church. He devotes his energies to general farming and dairying, and his possessions have come to him as the reward of earnest effort, perseverance and good managment. His life has been well and worthily passed, winning him the respect and confidence of all with whom he has been brought in contact, and as a valued citizen and honored pioneer he well deserves representation in this volume.

Daniel Sinclair.

DANIEL SINCLAIR, Postmaster, and publisher of the *Daily* and *Weekly Republican* of Winona, Minn., claims Scotland as the land of his birth, which occurred in Thurso, on the 12th of January, 1833. His parents, George C. and Margaret (Johnston) Sinclair, were also natives of Scotland. The paternal grandfather, Donald Sinclair, was a Scotch merchant, and died at the advanc[illegible] H[illegible] numbered [illegible] Th[illegible] ther, George Johnston, was born in Scotland, was a sea-captain, and was a great traveler. He sailed numerous vessels to the East Indies, and several times circumnavigated the globe. He belonged to the Presbyterian Church, and died in Scotland at the age of seventy-five.

The father of the subject of this sketch also followed merchandising and, possessed of good busi[illegible]ce of success in his [illegible] H[illegible]wever, occurred [illegible]

1838, at the early age of thirty-five. His wife long survived him and in 1849 came with her family to America, locating first in Meadville, Crawford County, Pa., where they resided for seven years. Her last days were spent in Rochester, Minn., where her death occurred in 1888, at the age of eighty-four. Both Mr. and Mrs. Sinclair were members of the Presbyterian Church. In their family were four children, all of whom are yet living, namely: George, of Ritzville, Wash.; William, who is living in Winona; Anna, wife of Hiram W. Stebbins, a resident of Rochester, Minn.; and Daniel, of this sketch.

Mr. Sinclair, whose name heads this record, was a youth of sixteen when with his mother and her family he crossed the briny deep to the New World. In his seventeenth year he began learning the printer's trade, which he has made his life work. In the spring of 1856 he came to Winona, where he has since made his home. After working in the *Republican* office for about two weeks, he purchased a half-interest in the paper, becoming a partner of W. G. Dye. A stock company was established when this paper was first published, and business was carried on under the name of King, Forest, Dye & Co. until Mr. Sinclair became a member of the firm, and the name was changed to D. Sinclair & Co. Under this style the business was conducted for many years, but in 1886 a stock company was again formed, known as the D. Sinclair Publishing Company. Mr. Sinclair is editor-in-chief, and is well able to fill that position. He is an able and ready writer, who labors for the best interests of the community, and the success which has come to him is well deserved.

In 1855 Mr. Sinclair was united in marriage with Miss Melissa J. Briggs, daughter of Isaac and Lucretia (Field) Briggs. Six children were born of their union, a son and five daughters, but Ida, George and Winnefred are now deceased. Clara, Jessie and Fannie still survive, the first-named being the wife of William E. Smith, who is business manager of the *Republican*. Mrs. Sinclair is a member of the Congregational Church, and is a most estimable lady.

The name of his paper indicates the political affiliations of Mr. Sinclair, who has always been a stanch advocate of Republican principles. He was made Postmaster under President Grant, on the 16th of May, 1869, and filled that office continuously until the 1st of July, 1885, when a change of administration led to his vacating the office. On the 1st of July, 1890, however, he was re-appointed, and still (August, 1894) fills the position. His long-continued service well indicates his fidelity to duty and the confidence and trust reposed in him by his fellow-townsmen. The postoffice building was completed in November, 1891, and with furnishings and heating apparatus cost $182,000. Mr. Sinclair has witnessed the entire development of Winona and the surrounding country. He came here before the first railroad was built, and in the work of progress and advancement has ever borne a prominent part.

Although Mr. Sinclair has never been much addicted to personal activity in politics, he was in 1880 a delegate-at-large from Minnesota to the Republican National Convention at Chicago, and, as chairman of that delegation, is credited (by reason of his persistence in keeping the name of William Windom before the convention) with having largely contributed to the conditions which resulted in the defeat of Mr. Blaine and the nomination of James A. Garfield.

Theodore K. Page.

THEODORE K. PAGE, one of the County Commissioners of Winona County, now living in Wiscoy Township, claims Vermont as the state of his nativity, his birth having occurred in Orange County, on the 15th of June, 1833. His paternal grandfather, Joseph Page, was a native of Massachusetts. His parents, William and Permelia (Chapin) Page, were both born in the Green Mountain State, and when Theodore was eleven months old removed to Lorain County, Ohio, from where they emigrated to Wisconsin in 1840, settling in Janesville, Rock County. The father was a farmer by occupation, and in the West gave his attention to agricultural pursuits. In 1847 he removed to Dodge County, where, with the exception of a few years passed in Nebraska, he resided until called to the home beyond. His death occurred at the age of ninety-one. In politics he was a strong Democrat of the Jacksonian type.

Theodore Page continued at home with his father until he had attained his majority and was early inured to the arduous task of clearing the timber from a new farm. When he had reached man's estate he began to work as a farm hand by the day and month in Dodge County, being thus employed during the summer season, while in the winter months he worked in the pineries. The year 1855 witnessed his arrival in Minnesota and during the succeeding winter he lived in Winona, working on the river. Afterwards he settled in Freeborn County, twelve miles northwest of the present site of Albert Lea, and was the first settler of the township.

In the summer of 1856, in Steele County, he was united in marriage with Miss Jane Montgomery, who came of one of the old families of Wisconsin. Her father, James Montgomery, had become a resident of Wiscoy Township, Winona County, in 1855, and there spent his remaining days, dying in 1865. Mr. Page made a claim in Freeborn County and lived in true pioneer style. A soda-box was the only sawed lumber in his home. He opened up a good farm, transforming the raw land into rich and fertile fields, which he continued to cultivate until 1864, when he sold out and returned to Winona County. He purchased a farm in Wiscoy Township, near the home of his father-in-law, and during the Indian scare in 1862 there was but one other family remained in this vicinity. In 1865 Mr. Page bought the farm on which his son now resides, comprising two hundred acres of good land, a rich and fertile tract, now highly cultivated.

To Mr. and Mrs. Page have been born the following children: James, an engineer and farmer, now residing near Watertown, S. Dak.; Ida, wife of Julius Norton, of Pleasant Hill Township; Charles, who was engineer in the Electric Light Works of Omaha, Neb., where he died of diphtheria, March 2, 1894, Jennie, wife of Levi Vail, a railroad man of Wabasha, Orville, a farmer of Iowa, and Wallace, at home.

Mr. Page has always been a Democrat in politics In 1886 he was appointed a member of the Board of County Commissioners to fill a vacancy caused by the resignation of John Young. This term lasted one year. In 1892 he was elected a member of the Board on the Democratic ticket, representing District No. 5, which is composed of the townships of Richmond, Dresbach, New Hartford, Pleasant Hill, Wiscoy and Wilson He received a majority of seventy-four, being elected over James Finch, of Pleasant Hill, who had served for six years previous He is now acting on the Finance Committee and is proving a capable and trustworthy officer Socially he is a Mason, belonging to Orient Lodge of Money Creek, Houston County.

Thomas Roberton.

THOMAS ROBERTON is one of the honored pioneer settlers of Winona County, now living on section 20, Fremont Township, where he owns a good farm The record of his life is as follows· He was born in Glasgow, Scotland, October 15, 1836, and is the third in a family of seven children, whose parents were Thomas and Janet (Reid) Roberton Two of the number died in infancy. The others are· Thomas; Elizabeth, widow of Duncan Ferguson and a resident of Fremont Township, John, a prosperous farmer of the same township; Joseph, deceased, William, who carried on agricultural pursuits in Fremont Township; Janet, wife of Thomas Nesbit; and James, who died at the age of eighteen years

The parents of this family were both natives of Scotland, and the father was a farmer by occupation. In 1841, accompanied by his family, he crossed the briny deep and located in Canada, where he made his home until 1857 That year witnessed his arrival in Winona County. Here he purchased land in Fremont Township, and upon the farm which thus came into his possession he spent his remaining days. His death occurred at the very advanced age of eighty-three years, and his wife passed away at the age of fifty-six. He served as Supervisor of his township in an early day, and though he lived a quiet and unassuming life, his sterling worth was recognized and he was highly respected.

Thomas Roberton was reared under the parental roof, remaining at home until the age of eighteen years, when, in the fall of 1855, he came to Winona County, Minn, pre-empting land in Fremont Township. He accompanied his parents and their family in the spring of 1857, and the Robertons have since been important factors in the upbuilding and development of this community

The subject of this sketch was married, January 26, 1866, to Miss Agnes Gilmore, who was born June 5, 1843, in Canada, and is a daughter of James and Jessie (Crawford) Gilmore Her parents were natives of Scotland, born near Glasgow, and are still living in Canada, the father having reached the age of seventy-six years In the family of Mr and Mrs Roberton were seven children, but Thomas, their first-born, was killed at the age of twenty-seven years by a street car in Chicago, while attending the World's Fair in the summer of 1893; Nettie is the wife of George Randall, a resident farmer of Fremont Township, Alvin is employed as a bookkeeper in Winona, Isabel, Frederick J., Frank and Willie are still at home

In his political affiliations Mr. Roberton is a Republican, and has served as School Director of his district for twenty years, but is in no wise a politician in the sense of office-seeking His wife and children are members of the Presbyterian Church, and he contributes liberally to its support, and to other worthy interests calculated to benefit the community In his business dealings he has been successful, and is now the owner of four hundred and eighty acres of valuable land, comprising one of the finest farms in Winona County. His prosperity is certainly well deserved, being the reward of honest labor He was one of the first settlers of the county, and has ever taken a commendable interest in all that pertains to its welfare and upbuilding, aiding in its advancement and promoting its progress

---

Reuben E. Maynard, Jr.

REUBEN E MAYNARD, JR, has spent much of his life in Winona County, and is now one of her leading farmers and stock-raisers, carrying on business along that line on section 6, Saratoga Township. He is a native of the neighboring state of Wisconsin, his birth having occurred in Walworth County, near Lake Geneva, on the 11th of January, 1846. His father, Reuben Maynard, was born in Washington County, N Y, July 9, 1815, and was of English descent Upon a farm he was reared to manhood, and in the common schools acquired his education. When he had attained his majority he started out in life for himself, and began work as a farm hand by the month [illegible] who was born [illegible] 21 18[illegible], and they became the parents of a family of eight children, a son and seven daughters, namely Marcia, who died September 27, 1885, Lestina, who died April 12, 1887, Selina, who resides on the old homestead, Reuben E, of this sketch, Celista, who died April 27, 1879; Ella, wife of William Boyd, Hattie, wife of H. A Coe, a resident of St Charles, and one who died in infancy

Mr Maynard, the father of this family, continued a resident of New York until 1843, when he resolved to try his fortune in the West. He made the journey by way of the canal and Lakes to Walworth County, Wis., and then located near Lake Geneva, where he secured from the Govern[illegible] situated about two mi[illegible] from [illegible] lake [illegible] cultivated and improved, and transformed it into a valuable property. It was his home until 1861, when he sold out, and with ox-teams came to Minnesota, settling on the farm where his son now resides. He purchased a partially improved farm of one hundred and sixty acres on section 6, Saratoga Township, but only ten acres had been broken, while a log cabin constituted the only improvement. This is still standing, one of the landmarks of pioneer days, which indicates the progress and advancement which the years have brought to Winona County. Here he continued to spend his remaining days, an honored and highly respected citizen, who by his sterling qualities made many friends. From a financial standpoint his life was also one of success, and he left to his family a good property. He died on the 18th of March, 1893, and his remains were interred in Saratoga Cemetery.

Reuben Maynard, Jr., spent the first fifteen years of his life in the state of his nativity, and then accompanied his parents on their removal to Winona County. His school privileges were limited, and he is largely a self-educated man, but by reading, experience and observation he has become well informed. Being the only son of the family, he always remained on the old homestead with his parents, and from early life aided in the cultivation of the farm. At the age of twenty-five he assumed its management. He and his mother together own three hundred and sixty acres, which are under a high state of cultivation, and improved with all modern accessories and conveniences.

On the 1st of February, 1888, Mr. Maynard was united in marriage with Miss Amanda L. Sheldon, who died May 6, 1889. In his political views Mr. Maynard is a Republican, and has served as Supervisor, but has never been an office-seeker. As before stated, much of his life has here been passed, and an honorable, upright career has won for him the high regard of those with whom he has been brought in contact. The family is one of prominence in the community, and in the history of their adopted county the Maynards well deserve mention.

Henry G. Cox.

HENRY G. COX, one of the enterprising and public-spirited citizens of Saratoga Township, now residing on section 8, was born in Windsor County, Vt., near Barnard, on the 27th of September, 1829, and is a son of Orrin Cox, who was also a native of the same locality. The Cox family is of English origin, and its establishment in America dates back to 1710, when four brothers of that name crossed the broad Atlantic to the New World . . . by trade, and followed that business in early life, but in later years carried on farming. He died in the Green Mountain State in November, 1857, and his wife passed away in 1883. In their family were seven children: Esther, now the wife of Lyman Cox, a farmer of Saratoga Township, whose sketch appears elsewhere in this volume; Edna, widow of Samuel Archer, a resident of Vermont; Orrin E., who makes his home in Seattle, Wash.; . . . engaged in the real-estate business; Mary J., wife of George Wheelock, a retired farmer residing in St. Charles, Minn.; Julia, wife of John Royce, who also lives in St. Charles; and Emma, wife of Harry Rowe, who is located in Brattleboro, Vt. The parents of this family are both deceased, but all the children are yet living.

Upon the farm Henry G. Cox spent the days of his boyhood and youth. His educational privileges were limited to those afforded by the district schools of the neighborhood. He remained under the parental roof until after he had attained his majority, when, at the age of twenty-two, he left home and removed to New York. There he was employed in factories for about four years, or until the spring of 1854, when, attracted by the advantages he had heard were afforded by the West, he sought a home in Illinois, locating in Rock Island. Not exactly suited with that locality, after two months he removed to Indianapolis. Ind., and secured work in the machine and wagon shops. Thus his time was passed until 1855, when he came to Minnesota.

On Christmas Day of 1854 Mr. Cox was united in marriage with Miss Chastina L. Stevens, and to them was born one child, Henry S., who is now proprietor of the Nicollet Hotel of St. Charles. The wife and mother was called to her final rest in 1880, and her remains were interred in the Saratoga Cemetery. On the 13th of April, 1883, Mr. Cox was again married, his second union being with Mrs. Ellen Reed, who bore the maiden name of Ellen Alderneau. They have two children, twins, Harryrowe and Harterowe, who were born July 28, 1884.

In the spring of 1856 Mr. Cox removed to the farm on which he now resides, entering from the Government one hundred and twenty acres of land on section 7, Saratoga Township, which he secured through a land-warrant which he had purchased. The following year he built thereon the first frame house in Saratoga Township, and it is now his place of residence. For several years after his arrival here he carried on both farming and carpentering. In 1857, in connection with Vincent Hicks, he built the first sawmill in this part of the county, locating at what is now Hampton, and for two or three years carried on business along that line. For some time past, however, he has devoted his entire time and attention to general farming and stock-raising. All of the buildings upon the place were erected by him, and stand as monuments to his thrift and enterprise. He has a well improved and valuable farm, under a high state of cultivation, and the well tilled fields yield to him a golden tribute in return for the care and cultivation bestowed upon them.

Mr. Cox has always been a supporter of the Republican party, and warmly advocates its principles, yet has never sought political preferment for himself. He is warmly interested in all matters pertaining to the public welfare, and is recognized as a valued citizen. He started in life a poor boy, and is a self-made man, who by his own well directed efforts has risen from an humble position to one of affluence.

Samuel J. Tomlinson.

SAMUEL J TOMLINSON, one of the well known publishers of southeastern Minnesota and now editor of the Winona *Daily* and *Weekly Herald* and the *Weekly News*, is a native of Lapeer, Mich, born on the 18th of September, 1842 His father, Samuel C Tomlinson, was a carriage-maker by trade, and emigrated to Michigan more than sixty years ago, locating at Detroit, from where he afterwards removed to Lapeer He became one of its pioneer settlers, and engaged in the saw and grist mill business for a time, but afterwards embarked in carriage and wagon making, which he carried on for many years He continued to make his home in Lapeer until his death, which occurred in 1881, on his eighty-fifth birthday. His wife bore the maiden name of Martha Walton, and both were natives of Pennsylvania She survived her husband one year, and passed away at the age of eighty-four. They were members of the Methodist Church, and Mr Tomlinson was a very prominent man in the community in which he lived In the family were seven children, four sons and three daughters, of whom five are yet living, namely William, of Luzerne, Mich Mary, wife of L E. Waterbury, of Highland Mich, Elizabeth, wife of William Graham, of Detroit; Henry R, who is living in Kansas City, Mo, and Samuel J, of this sketch

The last-named was reared and educated in his native town, and also attended the university at Ann Arbor. At th... printing-office and served a five-years apprenticeship to the printing and publishing business, which he has made his life work At the age of nineteen he became the editor of the *Clarion* of Lapeer, and continued its publication for about a quarter of a century with good success, during which time he became quite widely known in journalistic circles in Michigan He then purchased a controlling interest in the Detroit *Evening Journal*, and a year later sold out and purchased a half-interest in the *Daily News* of Elgin, Ill, and the *Weekly Advocate* of that place. There he continued for a year and a-half, when he purchased the *Morning Tribune* and *Evening Press* of Bay City, Mich, publishing the two papers at the same time Subsequently he purchased the *Republican* of Charlotte, Mich, but a year later sold out and bought a half-interest in the Winona *Daily Herald* and the *Weekly News*, his partner being J H Johnson

In 1861 was celebrated the marriage of Mr Tomlinson and Miss Abigail A Gage, daughter of Alvah and Rachel B (Hungerford) Gage, natives of New York, from where they removed to Lapeer County, Mich Six children were born to Mr. and Mrs. Tomlinson, four sons and two daughters, but two died in infancy. Evangeline C. is now the wife of J S McPherson, a resident of Chicago, by whom she has one daughter, Abigail Jean; George Ashley, a vessel-broker of Duluth, married Miss Laura Davidson, of Bay City Mich, Ada ... Samuel Arthur is a lawyer, now in the State Law Library of Lansing, Mich.

Mr. Tomlinson is a Royal Arch Mason, and his wife belongs to the Presbyterian Church. They have a beautiful home property in Lapeer, but since 1893 have been residents of Winona. In the publication of his papers Mr. Tomlinson is meeting with good success. His long experience in newspaper work has made him familiar with the wants of the public along that line, and the *Herald* and *News* are bright, entertaining sheets, well deserving of a liberal patronage.

E. W. Rebstock.

E. W. REBSTOCK, who is officially connected with the history of this county, and is now serving as City Assessor of Winona, claims Germany as the land of his birth, which occurred in Wurtemberg, on the 22d of October, 1832. He came to this country when seventeen years of age, crossing the Atlantic in a sailing-vessel in October, 1849, and settled first at Wilbraham, Hampden County, Mass., where he lived for one year. In 1850 he removed to New Britain, Conn., where he made his home until 1858, working in a brass foundry. He was an expert along that line, and he was thus enabled to command good positions.

On leaving New Britain, Mr. Rebstock sought a home in the West, and became one of the pioneer settlers of Winona County, Minn., locating near Lewiston, on the 19th of April, 1858. Thirty-six years have passed since his arrival, and he has therefore witnessed much of the growth and development of this region, for it was still quite a frontier settlement when he cast in his lot with its citizens. Here he turned his attention to farming, which he [illegible] years. His land [illegible] vation, and the well tilled fields yielded to the owner a golden tribute, while the many improvements upon his farm indicated to the passer-by the thrift and enterprise of the owner. His life has been a busy and useful one, and his industry has brought him a well merited success.

Mr. Rebstock was married in March, 1856, in New Britain, Conn., to Francisca Bickel, a native of Germany, but on the 27th of December, 1873, he was called upon to mourn the loss of his wife, who died, leaving five children, namely: Charles, who is now a resident of Tyler, N. Dak.; Emma, wife of A. J. Schmidt, of Winona; E. W., a druggist and Postmaster of Sanborn, Minn.; John, who is employed by the Bridge Company of Winona; and Carrie, at home.

Mr. Rebstock is a public-spirited man, always earnestly interested in the development of his adopted county. During his long residence in Utica Township, for several years he held the office of Town Clerk, was also Supervisor for two years, Township Assessor for three years, and served as Justice of the Peace. In all of these [illegible] the duties in a [illegible] ed to his frequent re-election and won him the confidence of all. In 1876 he was elected County Recorder of Deeds, and in consequence left the farm, removing to Winona, where he has since made his home. In January he entered upon the duties of the office, and for four years served in that capacity with credit to himself and satisfaction to his constituents. In 1882, after an interval of two years, he was re-elected, and served until the spring of 1885, when he was elected Assessor of the city for one year. In 1889 he was again elected to that office, and has since served in that capacity.

In 1877 Mr. Rebstock bought a set of abstract books of H. W. Jackson, and in 1878 was joined in business by Mr. Fellows. His office is located in the court house, and he has a very complete set of abstracts and is doing a good business. He enjoys the respect and good-will of the entire public, this universal confidence having been gained by his straightforward and honorable methods of conducting business. For thirty-six years he has been a resident of Winona County, and therefore deserves mention among the early settlers. In the work of progress and development he has ever borne his part, and his aid has never been solicited in vain in behalf of any enterprise calculated to promote the general welfare.

Mrs. Ann Cecelia Simpson.

MRS. ANN CECELIA SIMPSON, who resides at No. 226 West Wabasha Street, Winona, was born in Lowell, Mass., on the 17th of March, 1838, and is a daughter of Arthur and Catherine (Mellon) Menehan. Her mother died when she was a mere child, and her father afterward married again. At eleven years of age she entered the family of a maiden aunt in Lowell, where she remained until her marriage, at the age of sixteen years, to Verrazeno Simpson. Soon after the young couple started for Iowa, locating in Dubuque, where Mr. Simpson engaged in the dry-goods business until the fall of 1856, when they came to Winona, bringing with them a daughter, who was then nine months old. After twenty years of wedded

longer live together, a separation ensued, and on the advice of Judge Mitchell, her attorney, Mrs. Simpson secured a divorce. She built for herself a pleasant family residence on West Wabasha Street, where she yet makes her home.

In the family were six children. Elizabeth is now the wife of E. G. Nevins, of Winona. Ben, who graduated at Troy, N. Y., became a civil engineer, and was serving as City Engineer of Winona at the time of his death, which occurred at the age of thirty-one. He had married Mattie Kerdolff, of Lexington, Mo., and now resides in La Crosse, Wis. Their only living child, Verrazano Kerdolff, nine years old, has lived with Mrs. Simpson since the death of his father, when he was three years of

etcalf, of

Tacoma, Wash. Minnie died in her seventh year. Frances died at the age of nineteen months. Harry died at the age of twenty-one months.

Mrs. Simpson has traveled quite extensively during the last fifteen years, visiting many places of interest in this country. She deserves much credit for having reared her family of children. She lives a quiet, retired life in the pleasant home which she erected some years since, and is surrounded by the best wishes of many warm friends, who esteem her very highly. She possesses many excellences of character, and those who know her have for her a very high regard.

Louis Sikorski.

LOUIS SIKORSKI, one of the representative citizens of Winona, well deserving of representation in the history of his adopted county, was born in the province of Pommern, Germany, on the 8th of August, 1845, and was the third in a family of four children, whose parents were John and Elizabeth (Klopotek) Sikorski. The father was a hotel-keeper and grocer in his native land.

After attending the common schools, the subject of this sketch entered college in Konitz, Prussia, where he pursued his studies for seven years, being then graduated from that institution. He was educated for the priesthood, but instead of entering the Catholic ministry, he embarked in business in the city where he attended college, there making his home until 1868. That year witnessed his emigration to America, and saw him located in Winona County, Minn. Later he opened a general merchandise store in Trempealeau, Wis., which he carried on for eighteen months, when he returned to Winona, and established here a grocery, which he conducted for two years alone. On the expiration of that period he admitted a partner into the business, and their connection continued for about two years, after which he was alone again for three years. He then sold out and began clerking in a dry-goods store, spe four years; but preferring to engage in business for himself, he formed a partnership and opened a clothing establishment. After four years he bought out his partner and was sole proprietor for several years.

Mr. Sikorski was married, in 1872, to Josephine Ranswick, of Trempealeau County, Wis., and they are now the parents of four children, two sons and two daughters: Rosie, who is clerking in a music store; and Tracy, Joseph and Harry, at home.

Mr. Sikorski is a stanch Democrat in his political views, and in 1878 was elected City Treasurer of Winona, in which capacity he served for two years. In 1881 he was elected to represent his district in the State Legislature, and so ably did he fill the office that he was chosen his own successor. During his first term of service he was a member of the Standing Committee of the House, and served on the Committees on Insurance, Temperance, Schools for Deaf Mutes, Public Parks, Universities and University Lands. In 1893 he was a member of the Committees on Public Accounts and Expenditures, Military Affairs, State Prison and Reformatory, State Reform Schools, Soldiers' Home and Geological and Natural History. While thus serving, the three public buildings above mentioned were all enlarged. Mr. Sikorski has done good [illegible] estly for the best interests of the community which he represents. At both elections he received the largest majority of any man on his ticket, as he can control the Polish vote which is very strong in the city of Winona, his fellow-countrymen having great confidence in him and his fidelity to their interests

In connection with his other business cares, Mr Sikorski is a clerk for the Minneapolis Brewing Company of Minneapolis He is a member of the Catholic Church, belongs to St. Joseph's Catholic Society of Winona, to the Polish Legion, and is widely recognized as one of the most prominent and influential citizens of Winona County

Hermon Curtis.

HERMON CURTIS, who is now living a retired life in Winona, claims Connecticut as the state of his nativity The place of his birth was New Hartford, and the date January 4, 1810. His father, Elizar Curtis, was born in the Nutmeg State, September 11, 1782, and the grandfather, Job Curtis, was a Connecticut carpenter, who belonged to one of the early families of that state Elizar Curtis was very prominent in church circles, and served as Deacon in Torringford, Conn He married Amanda Steele who was born in Connecticut, April 17, 1783, and both are now deceased They became the parents of eight children, who grew to mature years but only one resides at the old home in the East

The boyhood days of Hermon Curtis were passed upon his father's farm, where he continued until twenty-four years of age, when he left the parental roof. He was then united in marriage with Miss Sophia Stillman, and started out in life for himself with a capital stock of about $100 He received a small amount of land from his father, and to this he [illegible] two hund[illegible] and [illegible] and valuable farm, which he cultivated and improved until 1871

After many years of wedded life, his first wife passed away, in 1851 Two of their children died in infancy, and one daughter, Eugenia, died at the age of twenty-two. A son, Hermon, who came to Winona in 1869, and engaged in the banking business with L C. Porter, died in Florida, March 22, 1878 His wife and two children now reside in California. Edward F. also emigrated to Winona, and, opening a grocery, carried on business along that line until his death, which occurred March 13 1883 His wife, who bore the maiden name of Mary Wheeler, had previously passed away, leaving three children Julius E and Benjamin W., who now comprise the firm of Curtis Bros, of Winona, and Helen B, a young lady of fifteen, now living with her grandfather

After the death of his first wife, Edward F Curtis married Miss Alice C Townsend, of Berkshire County, Mass, who survives him They had one child, Mary Eugenie, now a maiden of twelve sum[illegible] engaged in busi[illegible] or a boot and shoe house of New York, and in the West carried on merchandising. He was also a Director of the Board of Trade, and in his political views was a Republican

Harmon Curtis was married a second time, in 1852, the lady of his choice being Miss Charlotte C Stillman, a cousin of his first wife She died March 21, 1887. After his removal to the West Mr. Curtis engaged in farming for some time, but made his home in the city. He now lives retired, having acquired a competency that permits him to lay aside business cares He still owns some farm land, in connection with his home and property in Winona. In his early life he was a Whig in politics, but since the organization of the Republican party has been one of its supporters For many years he has been a member of the Congregational Church, and in his earlier years he long served as Chorister His life has been well and worthily passed, and his career has been an honorable and upright one, which may well serve as an example to those with whom he is brought in contact. Winona claims him among her best citizens, and he well deserves representation in this volume

Rev. Philip Von Rohr.

REV PHILIP VON ROHR, pastor of St Martin's German Lutheran Church of Winona, and President of the Wisconsin Synod, is recognized as one of the most prominent and influential citizens of his adopted county, and was born on the 13th of February, 1813, in Buffalo N Y His father, Rev Henry Von Rohr, was formerly Captain in a regiment which served as body-guard to the Prussian king The ancestry can be traced back to 1111, and the family has furnished many representatives to the military profession who have become prominent in army life. There are still many of the name connected with the German army

In 1839 the father of Rev Mr Von Rohr became the leader of about one thousand families who emigrated to America in three vessels, and on reaching New . lages near Buffalo and Niagara Falls. Mr. Von Rohr later went to Wisconsin, locating fourteen miles from Milwaukee with the intention of following farming, but soon after returned to New York and became a minister in Bergholtz, Niagara County, where he continued his labors until his death, which occurred in 1875, at the age of seventy-seven years. He was a leader in the ranks of the Lutheran ministry and was President of the Synod of Buffalo for many years.

Philip Von Rohr, the eldest in the family of four children, was reared in western New York, and at the age of eleven years he entered the Martin Luther Seminary of Buffalo, his parents having decided that he should become a minister He carried out their wishes, and in his twenty-first year was ordained in Buffalo His first work was . m October,

1863, until May, 1866. In June of the latter year he came to Winona in response to a call from the church at this place. The congregation consisted of nine families, with a membership of twenty, and had been organized for four years, but had had no minister.

Here Rev. Mr. Von Rohr has remained continuously since. The first house of worship in which he held services was a small frame structure 18x30 feet in dimensions. In the second year after his arrival this was enlarged, and in 1870 a church 36x80 feet in dimensions was erected. This served as a place of meeting for fifteen years, when, in 1885, the present substantial edifice was built. It is 57x133 feet in dimensions, has a seating capacity of eleven hundred, and is valued at $20,000. It stands on the site of the first church. In 1878, through the instrumentality of Rev. Mr. Von Rohr, was erected St. Martin's School, which is 50x60 feet in dimensions and two stories in height. It is divided into two large schoolrooms, a large assembly hall and society and recitation rooms. The two hundred and fifty pupils are in charge of three teachers, who instruct the students in all the common and many of the higher branches and teach in both the English and German languages. They are also instructed in the tenets of the church. The membership of St. Martin's Church has increased from nine to four hundred families, numbering thirteen hundred and sixty communicants.

Rev. Mr. Von Rohr was also the organizer of St. John's Church, of Wilson Township. He established it soon after his arrival in Minnesota and was its pastor for six years. His church is in a thriving condition, and the various societies connected therewith are in good working order. There is a ladies' society for general church and missionary work, a young ladies' society, and a young men's society for fostering a love of music and providing a high class of entertainments. There is also a mutual benefit association organized for aid in case of sickness or death, and a life-insurance society, which was organized under the state laws and has a membership of seven hundred. All these associations have been formed through the earnest efforts of Mr. Von Rohr, who is a most untiring worker in the interests of anything connected with the church. Some time since he became connected with the Wisconsin Synod and for six years has been its President. By virtue of this position he has charge of the seminaries and colleges of that state, including the Northwestern University at Watertown, Wis., which employs eight professors; a theological school, and the Lutheran Theological Seminary at Milwaukee, which was erected at a cost of $60,000. The work of the church in the synod has been carried on in an extremely successful manner.

On the 1st of February, 1866, Rev. Mr. Von Rohr was united in marriage with Miss Emma Schaal, of Buffalo, N. Y. To them were born thirteen children, eight of whom are now living, Hugo, Adella, Freda, Edmond, Ada, Emma, Adolph and Hedwig. Henry died in June, 1886, in his eighteenth year, while a student at Watertown, Wis.; and Philip died from accidental scalding, May 7, 1894, when three and a-half years of age.

Mr. Von Rohr is a man of fine physique, tall and well proportioned. In manner he is very genial and pleasant, and in his composition has a strong vein of humor. He is broad minded, well read, and has made friends wherever he has gone among all classes of people.

Moses Stickney.

MOSES STICKNEY is one of the worthy citizens that Vermont has furnished Winona County. He resides on section 29, Warren Township, where he has made his home since 1855, covering a period of almost forty consecutive years He is therefore numbered among the early settlers of the county, and has been an eye-witness of the greater part of its growth and development Its history is familiar to him from the early days, and he well deserves mention among its honored pioneer settlers.

The Stickney family is of Norman-French extraction, and was founded in America in the year 1637, at which time some of the ancestors of Moses Stickney landed at Rowley, Mass His father, Moses Stickney, Sr, was a native of New Hampshire, and his mother, who bore the maiden name of Mercy Peffer, was born in the old Bay State. By trade the father was a carpenter and joiner, but in the latter part of his life he also gave some attention to farming His father served as a member of the Colonial army during the War for Independence In the Stickney family were three children, two sons and a daughter

The subject of this sketch, who is the only survivor, was born and reared on the old home farm, the place of his birth being in Windham County, Vt, and the date March 27, 1815 He became familiar with all the duties of farm life, for as soon as old enough to handle the plow he began work in the fields He attended the district schools to which he had to . . . a-half, but in this way he obtained a fair business education When he reached man's estate he took charge of the old homestead farm, and cultivated the fields and improved the place for about fifteen years

On the expiration of that period Mr Stickney sold out and purchased another farm, upon which he lived until 1855, when he again sold, preparatory to removing to the West In the mean time he had married On the 2d of February, 1816, he was joined in wedlock with Miss Cynthia Brown, and to them were born nine children Moses A, born November 10, 1816, Cynthia E, who was born October 20, 1818, and died November 16, 1858, Henry, who was born July 6, 1850, and died in 1871, Marshall E, born January 9, 1852, Charles D June 28, 1854, Samuel E, December 14, 1858, Ida A, April 6, 1860; Clinton A, who was born November 22, 1861, and died April 12, 1865; and Raleigh G, born October 4, 1866.

Leaving his Vermont home, Mr Stickney journeyed by way of rail and river toward the setting sun until he had reached Minnesota. Being pleased with the country and its prospects, he stopped in Winona County, and soon afterward made a settlement in Warren Township, pre-empting one hundred and sixty acres of land on section 29 It was mostly oak openings His first home, a board house 16x18 feet in dimensions, still stands, one of the few landmarks of pioneer days that yet remain He began breaking prairie with

as was in

use in that day. Winona contained only a few cabins, and this locality was a frontier settlement, just opening up to civilization. With its development and progress Mr. Stickney has ever been identified, and has borne his part in the work of advancement and upbuilding. His labors have brought to him a comfortable competence, and he is well situated in life. His farm he sold August 22, 1894, to his son, Samuel E.

On attaining his majority Mr. Stickney joined the ranks of the Whig party and voted for William Henry Harrison. When the Republican party sprang into existence he went to its support, and has since voted that ticket. Mr. Stickney has not gained a national reputation, but in the community where he lives he is honored and respected and has the high regard of many friends.

Robert Crooks.

ROBERT CROOKS, a retired farmer of St. Charles, who, having acquired a competency, is now resting in the enjoyment of the fruits of his former toil, was born in Cookstown, County Tyrone, Ireland, on the 16th of November, 1816. His parents were Robert and Jane Crooks. The former was a weaver by trade, and in 1840 he left the Emerald Isle, crossing the Atlantic to America. For two years he engaged in mining in Pottsville, Pa., and afterward engaged in coal-mining in Pittsburg. Subsequently he resumed his westward journey, continuing his travels until reaching Dubuque, where he engaged in mining lead for three years, being paid for each ton that he turned out. In the spring of 1853 he left the mines and sought a home in Minnesota, where he secured a claim on section 32, Elba Township, five miles north of St. Charles. This town then consisted of only two houses, a blacksmith shop and a hotel. Mr. Crooks purchased his land of the Government, securing a quarter-section at $1.25 per acre. H[illegible] began to plo[illegible] crowned with success in the shape of abundant harvests, and for twenty-one years he carried on the farm, making it one of the rich and highly developed places of the county. To his first purchase he added until his farm now comprises two hundred and forty acres. He also had another of two hundred, and one of one hundred acres. These and other tracts of land he has disposed of, but still retains possession of the old homestead.

On the 5th of November, 1855, in St. Charles Township, Mr. Crooks was united in marriage with Miss Agnes M. Barr, a native of Paisley, Scotland, born January 25, 1825. She came to the United States in 1853, and the following year removed to Winona County in company with her brother, Thomas Barr, for whom she kept house until her marriage. She had been previously married, having at the age of fifteen become the wife of John King, who died, leaving her with two children: Margaret, who is now the wife of Samuel Stebbins, of Winona, and Alexander, who carried on farm-[illegible] nd Mrs. Crooks [illegible] e now deceased

Agnes, born May 22, 1858, died the same year, Mary Jane, born in 1860 died at the age of ten years; Elmer E., born in 1862, is now a shoe-dealer in St Charles, and the present Mayor of the city He is a good business man and is a worthy representative of the official and commercial interests of the town

Both Mr and Mrs Crooks are members of the Congregational Church, and take quite an active part in the work of the same. Mrs Crooks has been a member for fifteen years of the Society for the Advancement of Home and Foreign Missions In politics Mr Crooks is a Republican, and ardently advocates the principles of his party. During the years in which he carried on his farm he managed his business with such excellent ability that as a result of his enterprise and industry he became a well-to-do man. His life has been worthily passed, and is deserving of emulation in many respects.

Robert J. Duncan.

ROBERT J. DUNCAN Among the leading and influential farmers of Rolling Stone Township is numbered the gentleman whose name heads this sketch. He resides on section 12, where he has eighty acres of land, constituting one of the good farms of the county. There he carries on general farming and the dairy business, and his place in its neat and thrifty appearance well indicates the enterprise and careful supervision of the owner.

Mr Duncan was born on the 16th of October, 1840, and is a son of Noyes and Mary (Billings) Duncan His father, who was a native of Oneida County, N. Y., there spent his early life and during his youth learned the wagon-maker's trade When a young man he removed to Chautauqua, N. Y., where he carried on wagon-making until 1856, in which year he emigrated to Minnesota Arriving at his destination, he purchased a farm in Fremont Township, Winona County, and was one of its representative citizens up to the time of his death, which occurred at the age of seventy five years His parents were natives of New England but the family is of Scotch Duncan was also born in Oneida County, N. Y., and died in 1842, when Robert was only two years of age, leaving three children Mary, now deceased; Harry, who served in the One Hundred and Twelfth Infantry during the Civil War, and died in Suffolk, Va., while in the service, and Robert J., of this sketch Mrs Duncan's parents were natives of New England, and her father was a soldier in the War of 1812 After the death of his first wife, Noyes Duncan was again married, his second union being with Amanda Howard, by whom he had two children, Mary and Mark, the latter a farmer of this county

In the history of his adopted county Robert J Duncan well deserves representation, for he is regarded as a leading and influential citizen, and the record of his life will prove of interest to his many friends He only remained at home until about twelve years of age, when he began to earn his own livelihood by working as a farm hand Thus he was employed during the summer months, while in the winter season he attended the district schools. After the breaking out of the late war he responded hat every

patriotic citizen should stand by the Union in her hour of peril and aid in crushing out the rebellion. Donning the blue, he was assigned to Company G of the Third New York Infantry. He was the first one to enlist in the town of Stockton, N. Y., and with the company he continued until the 19th of April, 1862, when he was discharged on a surgeon's certificate of disability. He afterward re-enlisted, but his services were not accepted. While in the army he had suffered from an attack of typhoid fever, and was confined in the Union Hotel Hospital at Georgetown, D. C., for some time.

After being mustered out, Mr. Duncan returned to his home in Stockton, N. Y., and learned the profession of dentistry, which he followed for two years, but on the expiration of that period he resumed farming, as he did not like office work. In the spring of 1869 he left his home in the East for Missouri, and in that state purchased a farm, upon which he resided for a few months. He then sold and came to Minnesota, where for about five years he served as Superintendent of the County Poor Farm, discharging the duties of that position in a prompt and acceptable manner. His next place of residence was in Winona City, where he remained for a year. He then rented a farm for two years, after which he purchased the farm on which he now resides.

On Independence Day of 1862, shortly after his return from the scene of war, Mr. Duncan was joined in wedlock with Miss Mary Kelly, of Stockton, N. Y., who died in March, 1875. He later married Miss Helen C. Kelly, a sister of his first wife, and to them have been born two sons, Harry and Herman. Mr. Duncan is a stanch Republican in his political views, and cast his first vote for Abraham Lincoln. He may truly be called a self-made man, for since the age of twelve he has been dependent on his own resources, and his success is the reward of earnest effort.

Samuel Augustus Johnson.

SAMUEL AUGUSTUS JOHNSON, the senior member of the firm of S. A. Johnson & Co., hardware dealers of St. Charles, was born in Stoughton, Mass., on the 7th of June, 1826, and is of English descent. His grandfather, Robert Johnson, was a native of England, and was a sea-faring man, being mate of a ship which sailed across the Atlantic. He was on one of his trips at the time of his death, and was buried in the ocean.

Royal Johnson, father of Samuel A., was a native of Boston, Mass., and engaged in the manufacture of shoes. Having arrived at years of maturity, he married Sarah Winchester, daughter of Samuel Winchester, who was one of the heroes of the Revolution, and fought at the battle of Bunker Hill. He, too, was born in the Bay State, and came of one of the early families of the Massachusetts Colony. Royal Johnson spent his last years in Minnesota with his son. He was born in 1800, and was called to the home beyond at the age of seventy-four. His wife passed away in Connecticut when in middle life.

Mr. Johnson, the subject of this sketch, was a child of seven years when he accompanied his parents on their removal to Connecticut. Under his father's direction he learned the shoe-maker's trade, serving a regular apprenticeship. He was employed at Eastford, Conn., and worked as a journeyman four years, then becoming a partner in the old firm with which he had served his apprenticeship. A branch factory was established at Northampton, Mass., and Mr. Johnson took charge of the Eastford House, having many men under his control. In 1855 he severed his business connections in the East and emigrated westward, bringing with him a capital of about $3,000. His destination was Minnesota, and he landed at Winona, but soon after located a mile and a-half north of St. Charles, where, under the pre-emption law, he secured a claim. He located on the land and at once began to improve the farm. At the time of his arrival there also came to the county his brother, George H. Johnson, now of Blooming Prairie, Wis.; a sister, Mrs. Isaac M. Childs; and his wife's parents, Mr. and Mrs. Carpenter, and their two sons, Loren N. and Uriah L. The latter resides in Dover Township, and the former died from the effects of army service. He enlisted in the Union cause during the War of the Rebellion, was taken sick with fever, lost his eye-sight, and being unfit for further duty was discharged. A sister of Mrs. Johnson is now the wife of Isaac M. Higley, and resides in Chatfield.

On the 1st of September, 1852, was celebrated the marriage of Samuel A. Johnson and Miss Mary C. Carpenter, of Eastford, Conn. To them were born six children: Everett C., who is now engaged in business with his father; Richard H., who is cashier of a bank in Dickinson, N. Dak.; Ella A., wife of J. C. Hendee, of St. Charles; Robert A., who is a member of his father's firm; Alfred P., who is engaged in the hardware business in Garfield, Wash.; and Winnie, who died in childhood.

Mr. Johnson was also found among the boys in blue during the late war. He enlisted in February, 1864, in Brackett's Minnesota Battalion, and did service under General Sully in the Northwest, taking part in the Sioux campaign in Dakota, and going up the headwaters of the Missouri and on to Devil's Lake. He participated in the battle of Killdeer, Mont., about thirty-five miles northwest of the present town of Dickinson, where about three thousand were engaged on each side. He spent one winter at Ft. Ridgely, and one at Ft. Randall, on the Missouri, and was discharged in May, 1866, after a service of two and a-half years.

Mr. Johnson successfully followed farming from the time of his marriage until May, 1877, when he embarked in the hardware business in St. Charles, with a stock valued at about $2,000. This has been largely increased to meet the growing demand, and since his sons have become members of the firm they have also added a line of agricultural implements. They are men of good business ability, and careful management and close attention to all details have brought them a well merited success. Mr. Johnson sold his original farm and purchased two hundred and forty acres of land nearer St. Charles, to the further improvement and cultivation of which he devotes his energies in connection with his commercial interests. He votes the Republican ticket, and is in close touch with his party. He is highly esteemed as a straightforward, honorable business man, and in the history of his adopted county well deserves representation.

John R. Gile.

JOHN R GILE, who is now living a retired life at No. 653 East Third Street, Winona, was born in Addison, Steuben County, N. Y, on the 16th of April, 1829, and is a son of John F and Fanetta (Butler) Gile The father was born in Hartford, Conn, and at an early day removed to Addison His wife was a native of Philadelphia, Pa John R spent the days of his childhood and youth in the East, and when twenty years of age accompanied his parents on their removal to Waukegan, Ill., the journey being made by way of the Lakes They remained in Waukegan only a short time, when, on account of the ague, they removed to the present site of Baraboo, Wis, although the town had not then sprung into existence. The parents settled permanently on a timber claim on Cedar Creek, seven miles from Baraboo, in 1849, and there continued until 1853, when they came to Winona County The father secured a claim seven miles southwest of Winona, and three miles west of Witoka, at Gile's Corners, at the head of Burns Valley, and in 1851 began to build a home. He was one of the first settlers in that locality He assisted in blazing the road to La Crosse, and was connected with many events concerning the early history and development of the county There he improved a good farm, upon which he made his home until his death, which occurred in 1873, at the age of sixty-nine years He was in a runaway and thereby sustained an injury, a log badly hurting his side A week afterward he was caught in a storm, and died a few hours later, on the 24th of December. He had improved a good farm of one hundred and sixty acres, and on the old stage road he kept a hotel, his hostelry being a very popular place with the traveling public For many years he held the office of Postmaster at Wayland, and was recognized as one of the leading citizens of the community His wife survived him about one year

After the family came to Minnesota, John R Gile was engaged in running a mill in Wisconsin, but during the high water of June, 1855, he lost nearly all his property there, it being washed away. This caused him to seek a home in Winona County, and secured for this locality one of its best citizens He obtained a farm near his father's, and for ten years successfully carried on agricultural pursuits, placing his land under a high state of cultivation. He then sold out and came to Winona.

Ere leaving Wisconsin, Mr Gile married in Baraboo, on the 12th of June, 1855, Miss Sarah Jane Howard, a lady of French ancestry, who lost her parents during her early childhood, and was reared by her grandfather. Ten children have been born of this union, eight of whom are yet living, namely Charles A., the efficient City Treasurer of Winona, Mary A, wife of W E Smith, railway agent for the North-western Railroad in Volga, S Dak, Joseph Llewellyn, a farmer of Hart Township, John D., also an agriculturist, Minnie, wife of M M Ostrom, of Winona, James B, who is living in Winona; Andrew J., who is in the employ of the Winona Lumber Company, and George W, at home Eldula and Emma both died in childhood.

On coming to Winona, Mr. Gile came into the

possession of the Winona *Democrat*, which was then owned by A. J. Reed, to whom he had loaned money for the establishment of the paper. He afterward admitted to partnership J. J. Green, and later other changes were made in the ownership of the paper. The business steadily increased, and a joint-stock company was organized. The paper was invoiced for $9,000, but this move proved an unprofitable one, and Mr. Gile lost all he had invested in the venture. The paper was sold at a receiver's sale in 1868, Mr. Gile being the purchaser, but later he disposed of it. For some time he was engaged in the commission business as a member of the firm of R. A. Foster & Co., and to this work his energies were devoted until 1872, when he returned to the farm. From time to time he sold off portions of his farm, and in 1892 disposed of the remainder. He also carried on merchandising at Wilson, and was Postmaster of that place for four years. Since 1860 he has been a member of the Masonic fraternity. He has taken an active interest in political affairs, being a stanch supporter of the Democracy, and has labored earnestly in its interests. He has been an active member of the central committees, and has served as Chairman of the Board of Supervisors, and as Justice of the Peace. He is devoted to his adopted county, doing all in his power for its advancement and welfare, and as a loyal and valued citizen deserves mention in this volume.

Thomas Adams Peirce, M. D.

THOMAS ADAMS PEIRCE, M. D., a homeopathic physician, successfully engaged in practice in Winona, was born in Bath, Me., December 20, 1829, and is a son of Thomas A. and Arabella (Sloane) Peirce, also natives of the Pine Tree State, the former born in 1800, and the latter in 1804. The paternal grandfather, Daniel Peirce, was also a native of Maine, and of English descent. He made farming his life occupation, had a family of four children, and died at the age of seventy years. The maternal grandfather, Samuel Sloane, was born in Massachusetts and was a ship-builder. He belonged to the Congregational Church, and died in Maine at the age of eighty-two. The Doctor's father was a sea captain, and died in Darien, Ga., in 1830. His wife survived him until 1891, passing away at the age of eighty-seven. He was a member of the Methodist Church, while she belonged to the Presbyterian Church. In their family were three children, but Samuel and Arabella are now deceased.

The Doctor was reared in his native city, and acquired his literary education in Litchfield Academy, of Litchfield, Me. In his seventeenth year he took up the study of medicine and surgery, and afterwards entered the Pennsylvania Medical College of Philadelphia, there pursuing his studies from 1846 until 1850. He was graduated from the Homeopathic Medical College in 1850, and the same year began practicing in Norristown, Pa., where he remained until the fall of 1854, when he removed to Wilkes Barre, Pa., where he continued the prosecution of his profession until 1858. In that year he emigrated westward, and after a short who is living in Whitewater, Wis., Edward F., of Hampton, Franklin County, Iowa, and Peter H., of this sketch.

The last-named spent the days of his boyhood under the parental roof, and in his early life carried on both merchandising and farming in New York. He there continued to make his home until after he had attained his majority. He was a child of six years when the family removed to Cayuga County, settling near Oswego, N. Y. The year 1852 witnessed his arrival in Wisconsin, he being the first of the family to become a resident of that state. He afterwards returned to New York, where he remained until the fall of 1855, when, with his father and mother, he again went to Wisconsin, his parents making a permanent location there.

P. H. Williams carried on various lines of business until 1863, when he came to Minnesota, locating in Saratoga Township, Winona County, seven miles south of St. Charles, there becoming owner of the farm which he yet owns. For two years he carried on a hotel at Troy, on the old stage road, but when the railroad was built his business was destroyed. He then turned his attention to agricultural pursuits, operating his farm with excellent success from 1866 until September, 1885, when he came to St. Charles. His farm comprised one hundred and sixty acres, but he added to this from time to time, and at length his landed possessions comprised ten hundred and sixty acres, which were divided into three farms of three hundred and twenty, three hundred and sixty and three hundred and eighty acres, respectively. All are devoted to the raising of grain and are well watered. Mr. Williams engaged in the cultivation of wheat crops and thereby accumulated a handsome competency. He is now engaged in the real-estate business, handling town property.

At Ft. Atkinson, on the 14th of September, 1858, Mr. Williams married Miss Maggie Byron, who was born August 25, 1837, in Cazenovia, Chenango County, N. Y., and is a daughter of Thomas and Mary (Clark) Byron. Her father died when she was quite young, and when she was ten years of age her mother removed with the family to Twin Rivers, Wis. From the age of fifteen until her marriage she resided in West Troy and in Jefferson, Wis. Her mother, who reared a family of eight children, died in Scott County, Minn., September 1, 1868. To Mr. and Mrs. Williams have been born the following children: Flora, who was formerly a successful teacher of Winona County, and is now the wife of P. F. Haynes, a real-estate dealer of Chicago; Annie, the wife of George D. French, of St. Charles; Mary, the wife of Henry Cox, of the Nicollet Hotel, of St. Charles; Nettie, at home; Charlie A., who was graduated from the Wisconsin University at Madison, and is now an attorney-at-law of Chicago; John R., who was graduated from the Illinois University of Chicago, and is now Clerk of the Court under Judge Brentano, of Chicago; Bertie, who died in his sixth year; Elmer, who died at the age of two years, and Johnnie, who died in infancy.

Mr. Williams votes with the Democratic party. He served as Alderman for four years, and on three different occasions has served as Mayor of St. Charles, in which offices he was found true to his duties. His wife belongs to the Episcopal Church. Mr. Williams has lead a busy and useful life and his success has come to him as the reward of earnest labor and good management. He is recognized as one of the most progressive and prominent citizens of St. Charles, and in the history of his adopted county well deserves representation.

Nathaniel Cavis Gault.

NATHANIEL CAVIS GAULT is the senior member of the firm of Gault & Co., manufacturers of the Schonnmaker Lightning Cable, and is a prominent business man, who labors earnestly for the best interests of Winona. He was born near Concord, N. H., June 30, 1822, and is a son of Obed and Mary (Cavis) Gault, the former of Scotch descent and the latter of Welsh lineage. The paternal grandfather emigrated from Scotland to New Hampshire in early Colonial days.

N. C. Gault was reared on the home farm, and at the age of twenty-eight married Miss Martha E. Blood, of Lowell, Mass. He devoted his attention to agricultural pursuits until April, 1856, when he emigrated to the West, becoming a resident of Winona. Here, in connection with Moses Gordon, he opened a hardware store, which they carried on until the failing health of Mr. Gordon compelled them to close out their business, in 1863. He had a commission from Governor Miller to enroll recruits for the army for Companies K and I, of the Eleventh Minnesota Infantry, and he himself joined the former company. On reaching Ft. Snelling he received word to call upon Governor Miller, who said to him, "You are too old to carry a musket or act on guard duty, so I will appoint you Quartermaster of the Eleventh Regiment," handing him a commission. In later life he learned that William Windham and Judge Thomas Wilson had been instrumental in securing for him this appointment. Mr. [illegible] his regiment, and served as Quartermaster until after the close of the war.

When the country no longer needed his services, Mr. Gault was mustered out, and after spending one year in Alabama he returned to Winona, where he engaged in the manufacture of brick. He was appointed to the Internal Revenue service, with which he was connected for some years, and was Oil Inspector for the county for four years. From 1875 until 1881 he was connected with no business enterprise, but on the 28th of June of the latter year he established the manufactory of which he is now the head. They manufacture the Schonnmaker Lightning Cable, which is formed of a galvanized steel wire, overlaid with copper tubes, made from sheet copper and twisted into a continuous flexible cable; they also manufacture copper wire cables. The business has constantly increased, until it has assumed extensive proportions and become one of the leading industries of Winona. The factory is 20x70 feet, and has a capacity of about five thousand feet of cable per day. They manufacture cables in two sizes, of from two hundred and fifty to five hundred feet in length, and also manufacture gold and silver plated points, arrows and vanes, as well as the necessary standards. The manufacture is exclusively for wholesale trade, and they sell direct to the salesmen.

When seventeen years of age, Mr. Gault united with the Baptist Church in his native town. In [illegible] na the first

Baptist Church was organized in this place, and he assisted in raising the funds for the building of the house of worship. He has served as Deacon during his entire existence, and has been one of its most prominent members. He aided in organizing the first Sunday-school, and has been a leader in Sunday-school circles. His wife also shares with him in the good work, and is likewise prominent in the Woman's Christian Temperance Union. Mr. Gault was active in organizing the Old Settlers' Society, and feels a commendable interest in everything that tends to perpetuate the early history of his adopted county. He possesses the confidence of his fellow-townsmen in an unusual degree, for he has lived an honorable, upright life, well deserving the respect of all.

BUEL T. DAVIS

Buel Turner Davis.

BUEL TURNER DAVIS is the efficient Superintendent of the public schools of Winona, and is recognized as one of the able educators of the state, having a reputation for skill and ability in the line of his profession which might well be envied by a teacher of many more years' experience. Professor Davis was born in Decatur, Macon County, Ill., July 31, 1852, and is a son of Hon. John Davis, who comes of an old family of Macon County, Ill., and is a Member of Congress from the Fifth District of Kansas, elected on the Populist ticket. He was also a member of the Fifty-second Congress, and received the unanimous nomination for the Fifty-fourth Congress. His wife bore the maiden name of Martha Powell. She was born in Wolverhampton, England, and is a sister of Maj. J. W. Powell, who is in charge of the Ethnological Bureau at Washington, D. C., and Prof. W. B. Powell, Superintendent of the public schools of t [illegible] tire District of Co [illegible] from Kentucky, and the grandfather of Professor Davis was a warm personal friend of Lincoln.

Buel Turner Davis was named for two friends of his father, Jesse Buel, a noted author, and Professor Turner, of Illinois College, where John Davis was educated. The gentleman whose name heads this record was reared upon a farm near Decatur, and began his education in the district schools. He spent three years in the Decatur High School, and during the summer months pursued some special studies at home. At the age of eighteen he went to Kansas to improve a section of land which had been purchased by his father, and spent two years in developing and cultivating the farm. During this time he taught two short terms of country school, and also attended the State Agricultural College of Manhattan during the greater part of two years. His father having arrived to take charge of the farm, Buel T. entered [illegible] ol in Em- [illegible] o Illinois and made his home with his uncle, W. B. Powell in Aurora. He was graduated from the high school in that place, and was in the normal department of the public schools, receiving the didactical degree in 1876. He next returned to Kansas and completed the course in the State Normal, receiving therefrom a life diploma, which gives him the privilege of teaching at any time in that state without further examination.

After spending the summer of 1876 at the Centennial in Philadelphia, Mr. Davis was elected Principal of the graded public schools in Chetopa, Kan., and with three assistant teachers had charge of two hundred pupils, giving great satisfaction, as was shown by the complimentary notices in the papers of that place. The *Advance* said of him: "He is a man of very superior qualifications, and was an efficient and popular Principal. He is one of the best and most thorough educators in the state of Kansas, and his experience and ability as a Principal and Superintendent eminently fit and qualify him for any position pertaining to educational matters."

Mr. Davis for four and a-half years was Superintendent of the public schools of Emporia and had twenty teachers under his direction. During this time public sentiment greatly changed owing largely to his influence, and the small school buildings in the city were replaced by structures of which the town may well be proud, and great progress was made in the schools. While at Emporia Mr. Davis was chosen by the Board of Regents to organize the training department in the State Normal, and for some months held the double position of Superintendent of the public schools and Principal of the training department, drawing double salary. The training department was raised to a high standard under the management of Mr. Davis. On closing his labors in the public schools, he devoted the following four years to the normal. He at once organized a preparatory and model school, embracing classes from the primary through the grammar grades, and in April, 1882, employed an instructor in kindergarten methods. This feature of the school soon became very popular.

After eig

Davis becai

Winfield, Kan. He had been a member of the firm of John Davis & Sons, proprietors of the Junction City *Tribune*, although engaged in teaching at the time. He had also established the *Little Hatchet*, a school paper, which afterward became *The Educationalist*, and later *The Western School Journal*, and which is now an important factor in education, published at Topeka, Kan. He established the Winfield *Tribune* in 1881, and continued its publication until the fall of 1886, when he resumed school work. That year he went to Chetopa, and in 1887 to Anthony, where he served as Principal two years. In 1889 he was made Superintendent of the schools in Atchison, where he continued two years, and in 1891 entered upon the work at Winona. He had visited the National Association at St. Paul, became interested in Minnesota and soon after was elected Superintendent of the schools of this city. Eighty teachers are employed under his supervision, of which eighty per cent. are normal graduates and rank as able instructors. There are eight good brick school buildings in this city, which are supplied with all modern improvements, and in which there are three thousand pupils enrolled. Mr. Davis found the schools in good condition, and has steadily raised their standard of excellence. One important feature is that he has so arranged the grading that a pupil may advance if qualified and not be held back by delinquent students. He has also introduced changes which enable the principals to give more time to grading and advancing pupils, a kindergarten system has been introduced, and the school age has been placed at five instead of six years. Great attention is paid to the selection of primary teachers, as Mr. Davis believes that a right start greatly determines the future success of a pupil. An assistant teacher serves one year with the primary teacher, and is then placed in an intermediate grade.

Mr. Davis was married in 1882 to Miss Emma Waite, of Oregon, Ill., a lady highly esteemed for her womanly traits of character. She had formerly been a teacher in Kansas. To them have been born five children: Buel, John Jay, Mildred,

...asonic fraternity.

and of the Congregational Church, in which he has been an active worker. He is a member of the Teachers' Association, and during the summer of 1894 he headed a party of twenty-two teachers who went on a pleasure trip to Asbury Park. He is connected with the state summer schools, and has conducted one nearly every year since 1876. He has done much satisfactory work in this line. The course of study in Winona he has thoroughly revised upon the idea of unity of thought and expression. The highest regard of those with whom he is brought in contact is ever given him, and on his arrival in Minnesota the schools of the state received an important acquisition.

George Washington Clark.

GEORGE WASHINGTON CLARK, who is now living retired in Winona, is one of the honored pioneers of the county, and was the first settler on Wabasha Prairie, on the present site of the city. With the growth and development of this region he has since been prominently identified, and with its history his name is inseparably connected. He was born on the 10th of June, 1827, in Copenhagen, Lewis County, N. Y. His father, Orrin Clark, was a soldier in the War of 1812, and took part in the battle of Sacket's Harbor. After his death, which occurred in New York in 1818, he was granted a land-warrant in recognition of his services. This was located in 1855 by his son, George W., in whose possession it yet remains.

The Clark family is of Scotch-Irish origin. Some of the ancestors removed from Argyleshire, Scotland, at the time of the great confiscation and took up their residence in Ireland. John Clark was born on the Emerald Isle in 1655, and in 1699 was married. In 1717 he came to America and took up his resid[illegible] 1738 removed to [illegible] Hampshire County. His children were Matthew, Thomas, John, William, Samuel, James, George, Sarah and Elizabeth, all born in Ireland. Matthew married Janet Bothel, and became a resident of Massachusetts at the same time as his father. His children were Jane, John, Alexander, Agnes, William, Hannah and Elizabeth, all born in Rutland, and James, Margaret, Sarah and Matthew, natives of Colerain. James Clark, of this family, was a child of seven years at the time of his father's death. He became a Captain in the French and Indian War, serving from 1751 until 1763, and commanded a garrison at Ft. Stenwix, near Rome, N. Y. He retained his rank in the Revolution, and was stationed at New London, Conn., guarding the spoils of war captured from Burgoyne at Saratoga. His death occurred in Chester, Mass., in 1800. His children were John Scott, Royal, Silas, David, James, Orrin and Betsy.

John Scott Clark, the grandfather of Winona's pioneer, was the first white male child born in Chester, Mass., the date being 1762. He entered [illegible] Revolution [illegible] is father at

New London, Conn. In 1790 he married Selah Anderson, and they became the parents of the following children: Orrin, Asenath, Electa, John and Lucinda. In 1804 they removed to Copenhagen, N. Y., where the grandfather died, March 1, 1850, in his eighty-eighth year. In religious belief he was a Baptist and a leading member of the church. His wife passed away June 23, 1888. Orrin Clark, father of George W., married Rebecca White Templeton, of Worcester County, Mass., and their children were, Electa, Betsy, Sarah, Rebecca, Orrin, Nathan, Wayne, George W. and John Scott. The father of this family died in Copenhagen, January 13, 1840, in the forty-ninth year of his age, and his wife was called to the home beyond September 23, 1855, at the age of sixty-eight. Their son Wayne came to Winona in 1852, and lived with the subject of this sketch for one season, after which he returned to Copenhagen, where he still makes his home. He is a prominent man, especially in educational matters, and for fourteen years served as County Superintendent. Another brother, Orrin, came to Winona County in 1854, and purchased a farm of Allen Gilmore, one of the original "six bachelors." This farm adjoined the claim of our subject, and thereon Orrin made his home until his death, which occurred February 10, 1894. He married Miss Cornelia Cottrell, and their only surviving child is Julia A. Clark. John Scott Clark came to Winona in 1852, and died in the summer of 1854, when twenty-four years of age. He was buried in what is now Woodlawn Cemetery, but this was six years before the cemetery was established, and his was the only interment up to 1860.

Upon the old home farm, George W. Clark was reared, and the common schools afforded him his early educational privileges, which were supplemented by two terms' attendance at Lowville Academy. In the spring of 1851 he bade adieu to home and friends, having resolved to try his fortune on the broad prairies of the West. He went from Sacket's Harbor to Lewiston, N. Y., thence by rail to Buffalo, by steamer to Detroit, and finally reached Milwaukee. By team he continued his jo[illegible]
he visited re[illegible]

in company with three young men, he started across the country, reaching La Crosse at the time when its second frame building was in process of construction.

Four weeks later, with Silas Stevens and Edwin Hamilton, Mr. Clark started up the river for Wabasha Prairie, the present site of Winona. On the 13th of November, at half-past one in the morning, they landed on the western bank of the Mississippi, near the present site of the big flouring-mill. Mr. Johnson, who ten days before had reached this place, was asleep in his cabin a mile down the river, and they spent the remainder of the night with him. When day broke, they went to the extreme east end of the prairie, drove a stake as a starting point, and began locating claims. The following spring John Evans reached Winona County. There were now six bachelors at this place, and each agreed to hold one claim for himself and an extra one for six months. The members of the party were, Edwin Hamilton, Allen Gilmore, George Wallace, Ervin Johnson, Caleb Nash and George Clark. The last-named secured a claim for himself and one for his brother. John Evans settled on one of those claims, and when persuaded to abandon that one immediately removed to the other. During the winter of 1851-52 Mr. Clark lived on the Stevens claim, but in the spring built a log shanty on his own claim, and has since thereon resided. After about four years he erected a two-story frame dwelling, 22x25 feet, and has since made it his home, although he has greatly enlarged it and improved it in the mean time. To the original farm of one hundred and sixty acres he has added from time to time until he now has nearly half a section. The first tract is embraced in the Evans Addition to Winona. Some trouble was experienced by land-jumpers. Mr. Bummell tried to jump a claim held by Mr. Johnson, and in company with Harry Herrick destroyed the cabin. The first woman to locate permanently in Winona County was Mrs. Augusta Pentler, who located here in March, 1852. The same spring a drove of cattle from Missouri was taken to Winona County for the Indians further [illegible]
he is bought two [illegible]
se, for they were

from New York, where cheese-making was and is one of the chief industries. The question of coagulation was an important one and one of the brothers being somewhat of a chemist, shot a meadow lark and used its stomach to make rennet. With this the curd was made and in course of time the Clark brothers had the first cheese manufactured in Winona County. They also made butter, which was much in demand at gatherings where ladies were expected to be present.

On the 11th of February, 1857, G. W. Clark was united in marriage with Miss Jennie A. Lockwood of Waupun, Wis., whose birth occurred December 1, 1837. By their marriage were born seven children: Frank W., born January 1, 1858; Adah L., January 27, 1860; Jay Scott, November 1, 1862; Florence E., July 28, 1868; Alfred H., March 26, 1870; Jennie A., January 25, 1871; and May, September 13, 1878.

When Winona was incorporated, Mr. Clark's property was included within the city limits, but the following year was set off by act of Legislature. He is the only resident of the township who owns the land on which he originally located, and yet makes his home thereon. He went through all the experiences of pioneer life and for many years devoted his time and attention first to opening up and then to developing and cultivating his farm. He has labored for the best interests of the community, and is an honored pioneer, who is held in high esteem by both young and old, rich and poor.

Benjamin J. Loucks.

BENJAMIN J. LOUCKS is one of the more recent arrivals in Winona County, but is recognized as one of the leading citizens of Wiscoy Township. His home is on section 11, where he follows farming. A native of New York, he was born in Herkimer County on the 15th of April, 1838, and is a son of Peter and Dolly (Petrie) Loucks. Their family numbered four children, three sons and a daughter: Elias, Margaret, Benjamin and Reuben.

The third-mentioned spent the days of his boyhood and youth in the usual manner of farmer lads, and was early inured to the arduous task of developing the

very limited, he

ed through experience, observation and reading. These, however, have proved to him practical teachers. At the early age of eleven years he began to earn his own livelihood, and has since been dependent upon his own resources. He may therefore truly be called a self-made man, for he is deserving all the credit which that term implies.

In 1861 Mr. Loucks was found among the defenders of the Union. In April of that year he joined the boys in blue and was assigned to Company K, Thirty-fourth New York Infantry. The first engagement in which he participated was the long and hotly-contested Battle of the Wilderness

ge of York-

nteen days.

From there he was sent to the hospital, where he remained for two months, unfit for service. Later he participated in the battles of Antietam and Fredericksburg, being for the time assigned to Sedgwick's corps and on the 30th of June, 1863, was mustered out.

Mr. Loucks then returned to New York, where he remained until 1888, when he came to Winona County, Minn., and here has since made his home. Soon after his return from the war he was married to Miss Mary E. Simmons, the ceremony being celebrated on the 23d of August, 1863. Their union has been blessed with one child, Norman H., a resident farmer of Wiscoy Township.

Mr. Loucks is comfortably situated in life, having by well directed efforts in business and by thrift and enterprise acquired a competence. In politics he is a supporter of the Republican party, and socially he is connected with the Grand Army of the Republic.

Fred H. Pickles.

FRED H. PICKLES, City Engineer of Winona, although young in years and comparatively a new addition to the population of this city, has nevertheless left, in the permanent city improvements made under his administration, an indestructible monument to his energy and executive ability. He was born in Nova Scotia, November 5, 1864, and is the son of Rev. F. H. W. Pickles, a Methodist minister of St. John, New Brunswick, and Harriett (Ricketson) Pickles. His paternal grandfather, Michael Pickles, a native of Keithley, Yorkshire, England, arrived in America in 1826 and settled in New Brunswick, where he was united in marriage with Fanny Wilson, who came of an old Baltimore (Md.) family. The maternal grandmother of our subject was a resident of New York during Revolutionary days, and witnessed many of the stirring scenes of that early period in United States history.

Fred H. Pickles graduated at the University of Mt. Allison N[illegible] coming to t[illegible] of Assistant Engineer of the New Brunswick Shore Line Railroad, Assistant City Engineer of St. John for two years, and was also in the employ of James D. Leary, of New York City, in the construction of deep-water docks, grain elevators, and other engineering works at St. John. After arriving in the United States, he accepted the position of resident engineer of the bridge crossing the Mississippi River at Lyons, Iowa, where he remained until the completion of the bridge. Under the employ of C. F. Loweth, of St. Paul, a member of the American Society of Civil Engineers, he was employed in various water-works, sewerage and other engineering constructions. Mr. Pickles came to Winona in May, 1892, whither his reputation for close application and careful work had already preceded him, and one week after his arrival was elected to the office of City Engineer. His first important work here was assisting in the completion of the high bridge across the Mississippi R[illegible] plant. Since Mr. P[illegible] of City Engineer, there have been some $70,000 expended by the city for sewers. He has designed and superintended the laying of the brick pavements of the city, and the brick engine house in the First Ward was also constructed after designs made by him.

Mr. Pickles has produced (mainly from notes taken in the field), and now has on file in the City Engineer's Office, the first and only accurate records ever possessed by the city of matters belonging to his department of the public service. He has found time amidst his multitudinous official duties to design for neighboring towns, the electric-light plant at Rochester, Minn., and the water works at Rolling Stone, Minn., and at Galesville, Wis., being some of his work.

January 13, 1891, Mr. Pickles was united in marriage with Miss Mary Elliott, daughter of Edward and Elizabeth Elliott, of St. John, New Brunswick. They attend the Congregational Church, of which Mrs. Pickles is a member. Mr. Pickles is not a politician and would be considered an independent.

Francis McCormick Cockrell.

FRANCIS McCORMICK COCKRELL, who for many years was engaged in the hotel business in Winona, and was one of the most popular landlords of southern Minnesota, is now living retired, enjoying a well earned rest. A native of Kentucky, he was born in Bourbon County, on the 28th of February, 1811. His grandfather, Peter B. Cockrell, was one of the heroes of the Revolution. Removing to Missouri, he settled in Cooper County, where he spent his remaining days, dying at an advanced age. The family was early founded in Jefferson County, Va. His son, John Cockrell, became the father of our subject. He married a lady who came from a prominent Virginia family, and his last days were passed in his Kentucky home at Maysville. Five children were born to them, but only two are now living.

F. M. Cock[illegible] his own resou[illegible] achieved in life is due entirely to his own efforts. He therefore deserves great credit, for he has worked his way upward from an humble position to one of affluence. He entered upon his business career as a clerk in a store in Maysville, Ky. He afterward engaged in the same business in Cincinnati, whence he came to Winona in 1856. Here he became proprietor of the Huff House, which was built by H. D. Huff in 1855, and on the 5th of June was opened to the public by Willis & Hawthorne. Not long after Mr. Willis sold out his interest to Messrs. Cockrell and Williams, and business was conducted under the firm name of Cockrell & Co. until 1861, when Mr. Hawthorne sold out and the name of Cockrell & Williams was assumed. For thirty-five years the Huff House was the leading hotel of Winona, and one of the most [illegible] of southeastern Minnesota. E. D. [illegible] is a native of

Maine, and an enterprising and progressive citizen. He continued his connection with the hotel until 1872, when he was instantly killed by the explosion of gas in an old gas generator. He was at the head of the first gas works built in Winona, and was largely interested in many of the leading enterprises of the city.

On the death of his partner, Mr. Cockrell became sole owner and proprietor of the Huff House, and there carried on business until 1888, when it was replaced by the Winona Hotel. Since that time he has lived retired. He is a pioneer landlord of the Northwest, and for years did a most successful business. His constantly increasing patronage led him to enlarge his hotel, and brought to him a handsome competence, which now enables him to live retired.

In 1842 Mr. Cockrell was married, but in 1845 lost his wife. In his political views in early life he was a Whig, and on the dissolution of that party joined the Democracy, which he yet supports. He has been actively interested in the welfare of Winona, and has done much for the advancement of those enterprises which are calculated to promote the general welfare. He has for some time been a member of the Board of Trade, a stockholder in the Winona Gas Light Company, and for more than half a century has been a Master Mason. He is a very popular gentleman, and his familiar figure is seen upon the streets every day. The distance is indeed short that he can go without being accosted by an acquaintance. He has many warm friends who hold him in the highest regard, and their confidence and esteem are well merited by this worthy gentleman, who is numbered among Winona's pioneers.

Charles A. Gile.

CHARLES A. GILE, the efficient and popular City Treasurer of Winona and a member of the insurance and real-estate firm of Smith, Posz & Gile, has the honor of being a native of Minnesota. He was born at Money Creek, in Houston County, November 27, 1857, and is the eldest in a family of eight children, six sons and two daughters, who graced the union of John R. and Jane (Howard) Gile. A sketch of the father appears elsewhere in this work. He was born in Addison, [illegible] and is a s[illegible] dence, R. I., born in 1805. In early life the grandfather removed to Hoboken, N. J., and for many years was engaged in logging and rafting on the Susquehanna River. For a long time he made his home in Addison, Steuben County, N. Y., and there all his children were born. Later in life he removed to Wisconsin, and about 1853 came to Minnesota, locating in Wilson, Winona County. For years his was the only house between La Crosse and Chatfield, and the old log cabin was used as a [illegible] recognized as a [illegible] settlers of Winona County, where his death occurred in 1872, at the age of sixty-eight years

John R Gile, the father of our subject, was a youth of about twenty when, with the family, he became a resident of Baraboo, Wis There he lived for several years He first came to Winona in 1850, and a year later made a settlement in Wilson Township. His education was acquired in his native state, and in early life he taught school for several years After coming to Minnesota he was editor and publisher of the Winona *Daily* and *Weekly Democrat* for some time—the largest newspaper enterprise at that period in the southern part of the state Subsequently he engaged in the grain and fruit commission business in the city, but afterward was overtaken by reverses, and then removed to his farm in Wilson Township, where he remained some twenty years He lived the quiet life of an agriculturist. About 1891 he came to the city where he is now living retired For some time he was recognized as one of the leaders of the Democratic party in Winona, and has ever been a stanch supporter of its principles His wife, who has been to him a faithful companion and helpmate on life's journey, is also living. She is a daughter of James Howard, who was born in Canada, and was of French descent

In the Gile family were eight children: Charles A, of this sketch; Joseph L., who is living on a farm in Wiscoy Township; Mary A, wife of T E. Smith, of Volga, S Dak, John D, a member of the Fire Department of Winona, James B, who is yet in school, Andrew J, who is employed in the Empire Mill, George W at home, and Minnie, wife of M. Ostrom, of Winona

The history of Charles A Gile, the well known City Treasurer of Winona, will undoubtedly prove of interest to many readers of this volume, for he has a wide acquaintance throughout the county At the age of twelve he began working on the farm, and during the winter season, when crops were harvested and the labor of the farm was practically over, he attended the district schools His studious habits and aptitude for learning soon made him master of all the common branches, and at the age of sixteen he began teaching, a profession which he followed for seventeen terms in Winona County During the summer months he would engage in farm labor, and during the autumn return to the schoolroom, being thus employed until twenty-one years of age

On attaining his majority, Mr Gile was united in marriage with Miss Ida E. Evans, of Winona, daughter of Royal B and Mary (Parks) Evans, who were natives of Ohio, and came to this state at an early day, being numbered among the pioneer settlers of the county. Four children graced the union of Mr and Mrs Gile Florence Irene, Ray J, Bessie May and Mary Jane

About the time of his marriage, Mr. Gile entered the employ of Youmans Bros & Hodgins to scale lumber, and continued with that firm for two summers, after which he engaged with the Winona Lumber Company as Superintendent of the manufacturing and scaling department There he remained seven summer seasons, teaching school winters, when he bought out the local fire-insurance business of H. P. Hubbell, who is now State Agent of the Springfield Fire and Marine Insurance Company. This was in 1888, and he carried on business for a year On the 1st of November, 1889, he formed a partnership with H. G. Smith and Henry Posz, and has since been engaged in the insurance and real-estate business, under the firm name of Smith, Posz & Gile. This is the leading firm in the city in their line of business.

In politics Mr. Gile has always been an earnest and consistent Democrat. For two terms of two years each he served as School Director In 1893 he was elected City Treasurer for a term of two years, and is now filling that position with credit to himself and satisfaction to his constituents He is an active member of several of the secret and benevolent societies of the city, and is one of the wide-awake and representative young business men of Winona

C. C. Beck.

C. C. BECK is one of the leading wholesale and retail merchants in Winona, and is a prominent business man, who has risen to his present position from humble circumstances. His success in life is the reward of earnest effort, and his example should serve to encourage others who, like himself, have to start out to make their own way in the world empty handed.

A native of Germany, Mr. Beck was born in Goeppingen, Wurtemberg, on the 11th of January, 1831, and is the fifth in order of birth in a family of seven children. His grandfather, a native of the same country, carried on the business of dyeing cloth. His father was born in Goeppingen, and was extensively engaged in dyeing wool and linen goods for many years. He won success in his business, becoming quite well-to-do. He came of a family noted for longevity, and his death occurred at the advanced age of ninety-two. His wife, who was born in the same locality as her husband, died when the subject of this sketch was about five years of age.

C. C. Beck remained at home until the age of fifteen, when he began to learn the brewing trade, which he followed for about two years. He then went to Augsburg, Bavaria, where he was employed in a brewery for six months, after which he went on foot to Mainz, Baden, a distance of four hundred miles. On reaching his destination he sought and obtained employment in a brewery, where he continued

dence was

trade for two years, when on account of failing health, he was obliged to return home. During the two succeeding years of his life he superintended his father's fruit farm, and in August, 1857, he started for America, taking passage on a sailing-vessel, which, after a voyage of seven weeks, dropped anchor in the harbor of New York City in September.

For two months Mr. Beck visited with friends, and then came to the West, locating first in Dubuque, Iowa, where he had a brother living, engaged in the brewing business. For six months he worked with his brother, and then sought a home in Prairie du Chien, Wis., where he was employed in a brewery until the 11th of November, 1858. On that date he arrived in Winona, Minn., and soon after purchased a half-interest in the Gilmore Valley Brewery, which he carried on in partnership with others for three years, when he became sole proprietor. He then successfully carried on the business alone until 1878, when his plant was destroyed by fire, and he thereby suffered a loss of about $20,000. When this misfortune overtook him he turned his attention to farming, and began operating the land which he had purchased in 1862. For some years he then carried on agricultural pursuits, but at length turned his attention to merchandising, and in 1887 embarked in the wholesale and retail hardware business. For four years he had a partner, whose interest he

that period, since

He built a three-story brick store, 40x130 feet in dimensions, at a cost of $12,000, and has it well stocked with a fine line of shelf and heavy hardware, which he sells to the wholesale and retail trade. He has built up a good business and is now at the head of one of the leading commercial concerns of Winona.

On questions of national importance Mr. Beck votes with the Democracy, but at local elections is not strictly partisan. For many years he served as Chairman of the Board of Supervisors of Winona Township, and proved a capable and efficient officer. Socially he is a member of Humboldt Lodge, I. O. O. F. He now owns a farm of one hundred and eighty-seven acres adjoining the city, and in addition to this valuable and desirable property has a beautiful residence, one of the finest in the county, which was erected at a cost of $10,000.

Esbon Skinkle.

ESBON SKINKLE, deceased, was a well known and honored member of the farming community of Wiscoy Township, with whose interests he was closely identified from pioneer times until death removed a valued citizen, and one who had done much to promote its upbuilding. He was born in Wayne County, N. Y., May 20, 1831, and was the son of Henry Skinkle.

For many years Esbon lived in his native place, and then accompanied his father to McHenry County, Ill., where he lived until attaining man's estate. He had received a fairly good education in the inferior schools of that period and locality, and when eighteen years old began to make his own way in the world. His labors were as a farm hand, for which he received a very insignificant sum of money. In 1855 he thought to better his condition financially, and coming to this county began to work for Loren Thomas, remaining in his employ the greater portion of the time until his enlistment as a private in the ranks of the Union army. He [illegible] Company K, Eleventh Minnesota Infantry, August 27, 1864, and until the day of his discharge, June 20 of the following year, did guard duty at Nashville, in the state of Tennessee.

On the establishment of peace, Mr. Skinkle returned to Winona County and moved upon a tract of Government land, which included eighty acres on section 11, Wiscoy Township, for which he paid $1.25 per acre. He had purchased this claim in 1857, but did not live upon it or begin the work of its cultivation until his return from the war. It was thickly covered with timber in some portions, and in clearing this away he spent many weeks of arduous toil. The soil richly repaid him for his hard labors, and until the day of his death our subject reaped handsome returns. His attention was given to general farming and in this industry he was classed among the most progressive and wide-awake men in his community.

Esbon Skinkle was married, September 17, 1865, to Miss Elizabeth Cisler, a native of the Empire [illegible] y 23, 1845.

Her parents were Richard and Dorothy Casler, worthy residents of Herkimer County. To our subject and his wife there were born two children: Frank, who died at the age of eight years, and Myrtle, now the wife of Norman Loucks, a well-to-do farmer of this township. Mrs. Louck's children are Benjamin, Avis Elizabeth and Harry Raymond.

Mr. Skinkle always took an active interest in the success of the Republican party, with which he voted for many years. He was Chairman of the Board of Supervisors in his township, and in various ways aided in promoting the welfare of his community. He was active in the discharge of his duties as School Director, and whether filling office or not did what he could to further the cause of education. He was prominent in Masonic circles, and as a Grand Army man was very influential in Witoka Post. In his death, which occurred April 16, 1891, Wiscoy Township lost one of its best citizens. The fine property which he left stands as a monument to the energy which he put forth in the labors of life and the good judgment which characterized his efforts, while his high standing among his fellow-men was an equally satisfactory proof of his worth as a neighbor and a citizen.

Charles Knopp.

CHARLES KNOPP is a well known farmer and fruit-grower of this county. He resides on section 30, Winona Township, where he owns an interest in three hundred acres of fine land. This is now a rich and valuable tract, owing to the high state of cultivation under which it has been placed and to the many improvements made thereon. In appearance it is neat and thrifty, everything is kept in first-class order and indicates the careful supervision of the owners.

Mr. Knopp is a native of the neighboring state of Wisconsin. His birth occurred on the 8th of April, 1850, he being the eldest in a family born to Michael Knopp, whose biography appears elsewhere in this work. The Knopps are of German extraction [illegible] many, and [illegible] years of age. He made no settlement in the East, but came at once to the Mississippi Valley, and settled on a farm in Wisconsin. There he ran a flouring-mill near Green Bay for about two years, after which he came to Minnesota, in 1861, and purchased land. He makes his home in the city of Winona, but is engaged in farming and fruit-growing. Although seventy-eight years of age, he is an active old man, and personally superintends his business interests. All who know him esteem him highly, for he is a man of sterling worth, possessed of many excellences of character. His wife, who was also born in Nassau, Germany, is yet living, at the age of sixty-seven.

Charles Knopp has resided in Winona County during [illegible] for he was a lad [illegible] family came to

Minnesota. He had previously resided in the Badger State, and in its common schools began his education, which was completed in the schools of this community. Upon the old home farm he became familiar with agricultural pursuits and fruit-growing, which business was to become his life work, and he labored with his father until about thirty-three years of age. He then joined his brother Joseph and engaged in farming three hundred acres of land, the farm which is described above. To its further cultivation and development he has since devoted his energies, and his labors have brought him a comfortable competence.

On the 2d of February, 1882, Mr. Knopp was united in marriage with Miss Amelia Roehning, a native of Germany. Their family now numbers five children, Samuel, Paul, Walter, Martha Mary and Elsie Elizabeth, and the circle is yet unbroken by the hand of death.

In his social relations Mr. Knopp is connected with Friendship Lodge No. 98, A. O. U. W., and Oak Grove Lodge No. 15, Order of Druids, both of Winona. He exercises his right of franchise in support of the Democracy, and is a stalwart advocate of the principles of that party. His fellow-townsmen have attested their confidence in his ability by calling him to public office, and their trust has never been betrayed. He has served as Chairman of the Board of Supervisors for two terms, has filled the office of Town Clerk, and is now serving as Constable of Winona Township. The duties of these offices he has discharged with promptness and fidelity, thereby winning the commendation of all concerned. Mr. Knopp has long resided in this county, and those who have known him from boyhood are numbered among his warmest friends, for they have witnessed his honorable, upright life.

Rev. Nicholas Schmitz.

REV. NICHOLAS SCHMITZ, of Rolling Stone, was born on the 12th of January, 1856, in the village of Neidenbach, Germany, and with his parents came to the United States in November, 1868, when a lad of twelve years. He crossed the Atlantic to New York, and thence came direct to Minnesota, settling in Hampton Township, Dakota County. He remained with his parents upon the farm until 1872, when he began his studies for the ministry. After continuing his studies for some years he was ordained, on the 20th of July, 1882, by Rt.-Rev. R. Seidenbusch, in St. John's Univ [illegible] M

Rev. Mr. Schmi[illegible]

30th of July, 1882, at New Trier, Dakota County. His first field of labor included all the territory west of Glencoe, McLeod County, and extended to Milbank, taking in all the stations on the Hastings & Dakota branch of the Chicago & Milwaukee Railroad. After nearly two years of service in this field he was called by his Ordinary to Adams, Mower County, Minn. At that place he was greatly beloved by his people and his work proved very successful. In the village of Adams, through his instrumentality, was erected the first Catholic church and pastoral dwelling at that place, [illegible] there was [illegible] Creek, a railroad station on the Iowa & Minnesota Railroad, he also built the first church, a structure 40x80 feet. In 1890 he was called by Bishop Cotter to his present mission at Rolling Stone, where he has worked with great success, enlarging his field of usefulness here and greatly adding to the church in numbers. There is now a fine church and good school under the direction of the Franciscan Sisters of Milwaukee. In connection with his work at Rolling Stone, Rev. Mr. Schmitz also has charge of the Oak Ridge Mission, and the one at Elba.

Isaac W. Timmons, M. D.

ISAAC W. TIMMONS, M. D., one of the leading homeopathic physicians of Winona, and a worthy representative of the medical profession in this county, claims Ohio as the state of his nativity, for his birth occurred in Ross County, on the 11th of October, 1835. He is the youngest in a family of five children born to Thomas and Elizabeth (Draper) Timmons. The former was a native of Maryland, and upon a farm in that state remained until he had attained his majority, when he married Miss Draper. The lady, who was born in Delaware, was of English extraction, and died at the early age of thirty-eight. In 1817 Mr. Timmons removed to Ross County, Ohio, where he engaged in farming and stock-raising. He was one of the pioneers of that county, was recognized as one of its leading citizens, and from 1826 until 1850 he dealt extensively in horses and mules. At the time of the War of 1812 he was only a boy, but he hauled supplies to the soldiers. In his business he was very successful, and, overcoming the difficulties in his path, he worked his way steadily upward to prosperity. After the death of his first wife he married her sister, Hester Draper, and a daughter was born of that union. Mr. Timmons was called to his final rest at the age of sixty-eight. He was a faithful and consistent member of the Methodist [illegible] in the Epis[illegible] born in the United States, where his ancestors had lived for several generations, the family having been founded in America at the time of the landing of Lord Baltimore.

Dr. Timmons early became familiar with farm work, for as soon as he could handle the plow he began laboring in the fields. Up to the time he was eighteen years of age he attended the common schools, and then took a course in the graded schools. Not wishing to follow the pursuit to which his childhood labors were devoted, he turned his attention to the medical profession, and for two years read medicine under his brother's instruction. He then embarked in merchandising at Cairo, Ill., in 1856, and carried on business along that line until 1862, when, the war having broken out, he closed his store at that place and removed to Centralia, Ill. There he served as Deputy Revenue Collector until 1869, after which he spent the two succeeding years in attendance at the Homeopathic Medical College of Missouri, located in St. Louis, from which institution he was graduated in March, 1870.

Dr. Timmons first opened an office in Money Creek, Minn., where for five years he engaged in practice, and then came to Winona, where he has devoted his time to the prosecution of his profes[illegible]s always been a [illegible] of medicine, and his abilities, both natural and acquired, have fitted him for a successful career in his chosen work. His knowledge of medicine and his cheery manner in a sick room make him an excellent physician, and he now has a good practice.

On the 25th of June, 1857, Dr. Timmons was united in marriage with Miss C. E. Robinson, of Ross County, Ohio, and to them have been born six children, namely: Kate E.; Virginia E., who is one of the leading teachers in the public schools of Kansas and Missouri; Jessie M., wife of G. A. Collins, foreman of one of the leading lumber companies of Winona; Lydia, a highly educated lady, now the wife of C. F. Spencer, editor and proprietor of the Atwater *Press*, of Atwater, Minn.; S. Luetta, wife of Charles A. Pfeiffer, who is now connected with the O'Neill Elevator Company of Chicago; and John W., who for several years has held a responsible position in the Winona Deposit Bank.

The Doctor and his family hold membership with the Methodist Episcopal Church, and are among the leading citizens of Winona, occupying a high position in social circles. He has been a stanch and inflexible adherent of the Republican party since its organization, and was one of nine Republicans in his county who voted for Fremont in 1856. He was also one of the thirty-seven known Republicans in Cairo who supported Lincoln. Devotion to principle has always been one of his leading characteristics.

John G. Hayes.

JOHN G. HAYES, who is now engaged in farming on section 11, Rolling Stone Township, is one of the worthy citizens that England has furnished to Winona County. He was born on the 5th of March, 1835, in Pannard, England, and was the only child born to Jesse and Harriet (Carpe) Hayes. The father was a farmer and miller, and followed those occupations throughout his entire life. He never left his native land, but died in England at the age of seventy-five. His wife passed away when sixty-five years of age.

Mr. Hayes of this sketch continued under the parental roof until he had attained his majority. He early began work in the fields and soon became familiar with all the duties of an agriculturist. When he had reac[illegible] to home and frien[illegible] vessel bound for America. The hope of bettering his financial condition led to his emigration to the New World, and his hope has been realized. He first made a location in Claremont County, Ohio, where for ten years he worked at the miller's trade, having learned the same with his father while in his native land. On the expiration of that decade he returned to England and embarked in the dairy business, which he carried on for ten years, when, in 1876, he again came to the United States and purchased the farm upon which he has since made his home.

In 1856 Mr. Hayes was united in marriage with Miss Martha Maidmant, who died while in England, leaving four children: Hettie, the eldest, is now [illegible] of Paris; [illegible] England

Mr. Hayes inherited quite a large estate in England, but as he did not care to remain in that country he placed it in possession of his children. In 1874 he was again married, his second union being with Miss Jennie Randall, of England.

Mr. Hayes is a stanch supporter of the principles of the Democracy, but is not strongly partisan. His fellow-citizens have given evidence of their appreciation of his worth and ability by electing him to several township offices, and he is now serving his second term as Township Treasurer. True to every trust reposed in him, he has won the confidence and esteem of all. Mr. Hayes now owns one hundred and twenty acres of rich and valuable land, pleasantly situated five miles from Winona, and carries on general farming. He has also engaged to some extent in the breeding of trotting horses. He is a broad minded-man, who keeps well informed on the questions and issues of the day, and in the community where he lives is regarded as a valued citizen.

W. L. ROBILLARD

Wilford L. Robillard.

WILFORD L ROBILLARD, a well known business man of Dakota, is the senior member of the firm of Robillard & Helsaple, proprietors of a sawmill The gentleman whose name heads this record has the honor of being a native of Winona County, for he was born in the town of Dresbach, August 15, 1851 His parents, Wilford and Mary (Maynard) Robillard, were both natives of Canada, and came to New York State in 1815 From there in 1816 they went to Freeport, Ill Later, in 1850, they moved from there to Wisconsin, locating in the village of Dresbach, Winona County, where the father carried on a tavern To that business he devoted his energies for about twelve years, after which he moved to Dubuque, Iowa where his last days were spent His wife passed away a few years later Mr Robillard and his father-in-law were the first settlers in Dresbach The latter was a pilot on the river Both entered land from the Government, and Mr Robillard operated his farm for some years, after which he sold it to Mr Dresbach, who laid out the village and divided the farm into town lots

To Wilford and Mary Robillard were born seven children Joseph, now a resident of Dresbach, Josephine and Johnnie both of whom are now deceased, Jennie who

a resident of Dakota, Wilford L, of this sketch, Josephine deceased, and Mary R, wife of John Brown, a railroad man, living in Wabasha. After the father's death the mother became the wife of Alfred Purdy, and by their union were born three children Mrs Hattie Caston who is now living in Dakota, Scott F who is at home with his parents; and George who is also yet under the parental roof

No event of special importance occurred during the boyhood and youth of the subject of this sketch He remained with his parents and acquired his education in the public schools, though from the early age of ten years he earned his own livelihood While still a youth he engaged in service on the river steamers being employed as watchman and receiving a man's wages He continued on the river until eighteen years of age, saving some money during that time He then went to Jordan, Minn., and for one summer worked on a farm On the expiration of that period he returned to Dakota, where he engaged in chopping wood during the succeeding winter In the spring he went to the pineries, where for three years he was employed as a cook and in lumbering, after which he removed to the state of Dakota and there gave his attention to selling farm machinery,

...ears His

next journey was across the plains to the West, to California, but after a short time he returned home and purchased a farm on section 12, New Hartford Township, in this county, comprising two hundred and thirty acres of land. To this he at once turned his attention, and for three years engaged in its cultivation.

In September, 1885, Mr. Robillard was united in marriage with Miss Dora Foreman, whose birth occurred May 18, 1863, and who was the daughter of John Foreman. The latter was a native of Pike County, Mo., born November 15, 1829. When a little over two years old he accompanied his father to Pike County, Ill., and in 1848 he went with his brother to Stillwater, Minn. Soon after he went to St. Paul, in or near which place he lived up to the time of entering the army. He served as cook on a Mississippi steamer for several years, but when the war broke out in 1861 he gave up his position, offered his services to the Government, and donning the blue marched to the front. His death occurred in 1866, and his wife passed away shortly after, leaving four children: Silas, who is now Assistant State Oil-tester and resides in St. Paul; Josephine, now the wife of Osgood Fulington, a resident of St. Paul; Edward, who is engaged in editing a newspaper in California; and Dora, now Mrs. Robillard. Our subject and his wife also have four children, and the family circle yet remains unbroken. They are Ella M., Mary R., Wilford L., Jr., and Josie Belle.

After his marriage Mr. Robillard removed to Duluth, Minn., where he engaged in the real-estate business with good success for three years. He then returned to his old home in Dakota, and after a short interval of rest embarked in the sawmill business, which he has since followed. He is regarded as one of the enterprising citizens of the town, and one of its prosperous business men. His success is the result of close application, earnest effort and untiring industry. In addition to his sawmill he owns one hundred and sixty acres of pine timber-land in the South and one hundred and sixty acres in North Dakota. Mr. Robillard is a member of the Methodist Episcopal Church, and takes an active interest in everything pertaining to the welfare of the community and its upbuilding.

Col. John Ball.

COL. JOHN BALL, deceased, was born on the 5th of December, 1835, in Rutland, Jefferson County, N. Y., and was a son of William and Arodyne (Hill) Ball, who belonged to old families of the Empire State. In the usual manner of farmer lads the Colonel spent the days of his boyhood and youth, remaining at home with his parents until twenty-two years old. The year 1853 witnessed his arrival in Minnesota, whither he came [illegible] entered th[illegible] nona, who was then engaged in surveying the Menomonee Indian Reservation in Wisconsin. Later, in the fall of 1855, he went to Dubuque, Iowa, and the following year again came to Winona. He passed one year in Steele County, and until 1861 engaged in surveying and dealing in land, being in the employ of the Government during a portion of that time. Having determined to enter the legal profession, he took up the study of law with [illegible] d was admitted to [illegible] gage in practice

Mr Ball had watched with interest the progress of events which had preceded and brought on the Civil War, and true to the cause of his country he resolved to strike a blow in defense of the Union when the South began hostilities Hardly had the smoke from Ft. Sumter's guns cleared away when, as a private, he joined Company K First Minnesota Infantry This company was formed of seventy-six men, who enlisted for three months' service, but over sixty of them continued in the three-years service When the regiment was organized Mr Ball was made Captain, and in 1864 he was promoted to the rank of Lieutenant-Colonel of the Eleventh Minnesota Infantry He was with his regiment in Kentucky and Tennessee and as his superior officer, Col J B Gilfillan now Chief Justice of the Supreme Court, was often called away, he practically had command of the regiment When a private he shared with his comrades their high reputation for bravery and steadiness, and when he became an officer he was noted for his valiant service and for his unflinching discharge of duty He took part in many of the hard-fought battles of the war, including the battle of Bull Run, Ball's Bluff, Yorktown, Fair Oaks, Peach Orchard, Glendale, Malvern Hill, Charleston, Fredericksburg, that most important battle of Gettysburg, and others.

On his return from the war, Colonel Ball purchased from Col. H. C Lester his abstract books, completed the set, and in connection with John B. Fellows carried on the abstract business He was honored with a number of public offices, to which his worth and ability justly entitled him He served as School Director and as Alderman and in the year 1866 was elected on the Republican ticket to represent his district in the State Legislature After his retirement from that office he was elected County Treasurer a position which he filled with credit to himself and satisfaction to his constituents until his death John Ball Post G. A R. was named in his honor and indicated the high regard in which he was held by his army comrades With the Masonic fraternity he held membership

On the 27th of December, 1865, Colonel Ball was united in marriage with Miss Emma Lewton, of Lewiston, daughter of James J and Cynthia (Parker) Lewton, who came to Winona in 1858 Her father was a contractor and builder, and both he and his wife died in Winona. Mrs Ball was a native of Jefferson County, Ky , and the family removed from Louisville, Ky , to this place She is a lady of high education and is refined and cultured which fact is shown throughout her beautiful home To Colonel and Mrs Ball were born three children Mary Agnes, now the wife of M. P Hanson, who is in the North-Western Railroad office, William Parker, who resides in Goldendale, Wash , and Charles G , who is in the employ of the Edison Electric Company, of Brooklyn N. Y

Colonel Ball was wounded at the battle of Bristol Station, while leading a charge, and never fully recovered from his injuries. This undoubtedly hastened his death, and he died at the home of his parents in Rutland, N Y , September 26, 1875 He was laid to rest in Woodlawn Cemetery and many friends mourned his loss. His life was indeed exemplary He was honest and straightforward in all business dealings, scrupulously self-sacrificing, and was a true gentleman in the highest sense of the term The Bar passed strong resolutions of respect at his death, and throughout the county friends mourned him like a brother

James Hardwick.

JAMES HARDWICK, a farmer and dairyman residing on section 30, Winona Township, was born on the 10th of June, 1830, in Tickenham, Somersetshire, England, his family being an old one of that county. His father, James Hardwick, was born in an old king's palace, on the same estate where occurred the birth of his son James. Having arrived at years of maturity, he led to the marriage altar Miss Mary Ann Baker, who was born in the same neighborhood, and they became the parents of eight children, seven sons and a daughter, all of whom reside in England with the exception of the subject of this sketch. Throughout his entire life the father followed the occupation of farming. His death occurred at the age of seventy-six, and his wife passed away many years previous.

Upon the death of the mother the family was broken up, and James Hardwick went to live with a farmer in the neighborhood, with whom he continued for a number of years. He then entered the employ of a merchant, in whose service he remained for seven years, when, in the autumn of 1856, he came to America, accompanied by his wife and two children. The voyage across the Atlantic was made in a sailing-vessel and six weeks were consumed in making the trip. On reaching the shores of the New World, Mr. Hardwick came at once to Winona, where he worked for one year, and then removed to the Gilmore Valley, where he purchased eighty acres of land. The tract was covered with timber, but the forest has since been replaced by waving fields of grain, which delight the eye of the passer-by and indicate to him the enterprising and progressive spirit of the owner, who has made his home upon his present farm for thirty-seven years.

Ere leaving his native land, Mr. Hardwick was united in marriage with Miss Harriet Hawkins, who was born in Long Ashton, England. Their union was celebrated on the 4th of July, 1852, and was blessed with a family of four children. James W., the eldest, born June 21, 1853, is the largest dairyman of Winona County. He was only three and a-half years of age when he came here, and therefore almost his entire life has been passed in this locality. On the 1st of May, 1877, he married Miss Lillie Cleveland, of Trempealeau, Wis., and to them were born six children: Rosa M. and Nina L., who died in childhood, and Pearl Clara, Winnie Ida, Mabel Olive and Gilbert, who are still with their parents. Mary Ann is the wife of J. J. Keeley, an engineer in the employ of the Great Northern Railroad, and they have four sons, Harry J., William, Bertie C. and Earl J. Harriet is the wife of J. C. Cornelian, a resident of Grand Forks County, N. Dak. William T., who is engaged in gardening in Winona Township, wedded Miss Mary Gallien, and they have two sons, Ray B. and Allen.

Mr. Hardwick and his son are both supporters of the men and measures of the Republican party. He has served [illegible] as supervisor of his township, and is very prompt and faithful in the discharge of his duties In an early day he took quite an active interest in school work, but now leaves that to younger men of the community. His son has served as Assessor of the township for seven terms, and as Town Clerk for two terms. Mr Hardwick is a member of the Episcopal Church He came to this country with the hope of benefiting his financial condition, and by close attention to the details of his business, by good management and untiring labor he has won a comfortable competence.

John Bain.

JOHN BAIN, one of the representative farmers of Winona County, who owns and operates a valuable tract of land on section 17, Fremont Township, is a native of Ontario Canada, born May 15, 1843 His parents, Robert and Barbara (Ferguson) Bain, had a family of twelve children, five of whom died in infancy The eldest is our subject, and the others still living are Barbara, widow of Charles McDonald, a resident of Polk County, Minn., Duncan, who is engaged in farming in that county, Robert, a carpenter of Polk County, James, who carries on agricultural pursuits in Polk County, Isabella, wife of Thomas V Nesbit, of Winona County; and Donald, who is a farmer of Polk County The father of this family was born in Glasgow, Scotland, in 1818, and when nine years of age accompanied his parents on their emigration to Canada The grandfather of our subject was a carpenter and builder Robert Bain became a farmer and followed agricultural pursuits for many years In 1868 he came with his family to Winona County, making it his home until 1878, when he removed to Polk County, where he still resides upon a farm His wife is also a native of the Highlands of Scotland, and both are members

people who are greatly respected on account of the many excellent qualities which they possess

John Bain, whose name introduces this review, remained upon the home farm until he had attained his majority, and in early life became familiar with all the duties that fall to the lot of the agriculturist The common schools afforded him his early educational privileges, and experience, reading and observation have made him a well informed man As a companion and helpmate on life's journey he chose Miss E A Nisbit The wedding was celebrated March 26, 1873, and their union has been blessed with three children, two sons and a daughter, Robert J Maggie and Neil G, all yet at home

Mr Bain and his family are members of the Presbyterian Church, and he exercises his right of franchise in support of the Republican party, the principles of which he warmly advocates. On that ticket he was elected to the State Legislature in 1889, and was re-nominated for a second term, but the increased Democratic vote which was manifest all over the country caused his defeat. He has been Supervisor of his township for the long period of fifteen ... years has ... fact which shows his popularity in the community where he is best known, and the confidence and trust reposed in him by his fellow-citizens

When Mr Bain came into possession of his present fine farm of one hundred and sixty acres, he could not pay for it entirely, but has now cleared it of all indebtedness and has a very valuable property In connection with general farming he is successfully engaged in stock-dealing, making a specialty of the breeding of Shorthorn cattle and English Shire horses He is enterprising and progressive in all business transactions, and his public and private life are alike above reproach, for whether upon the farm, in local office or legislative halls, he is the same honorable and straightforward gentleman.

Frank E. Gartside.

FRANK E. GARTSIDE, who for the past ten years has been extensively engaged in the laundry business in Winona, and is now at the head of one of the leading industries of the city, claims Pennsylvania as the state of his nativity. The place of his birth is in Pike Township, Bradford County, and the date is February 18, 1862. He is one of a family of six children, four of whom are yet living Their parents were Thomas and Permelia L (Brink) Gartside, the former a native of England, and the latter of the Keystone State. The father was born in Oldham, near Manchester, England, in the year 1828, and lived in his native country until he had attained his majority, when, with the desire to try his fortune in America, he took passage on a sailing-vessel bound for New York, in 1849 After arriving in this country he located first near Philadelphia, but afterwards engaged in railroading in Connecticut, and in the early part of the '50s became conne[illegible] which he continued for the long period of twenty-seven years, one of its most faithful and trusted employes During this time his family lived in Hornellsville, N Y In 1877 Mr Gartside retired from active business, and has since lived in Bradford County, Pa, where he now makes his home, a highly respected citizen His wife, who was born in that county, died in 1894, at the age of sixty-four years

Frank E Gartside was in early life taken to Hornellsville, where he grew to manhood and made his home until 1881. In 1881, when nineteen years of age he embarked in business for himself, establishing a laundry, which he carried on for three years He then came to Winona, and established the laundry which he now owns in this city Since 1885 he has been located on East Fourth Street, in a building erected expressly to meet the requirements of his business The rapid increase of trade necessitated in 1891 the purchase [illegible] the east. The plant is fitted with the newest and most complete machinery, and employment is furnished to twenty-five hands. From the beginning the trade has constantly increased, until it has now assumed extensive proportions and the business has become a very profitable one. In addition to the laundry trade, Mr. Gartside has just put in a carpet-cleaning plant, embodying the latest improvements in that direction, and is prepared to do first-class work along that line.

On the 25th of October, 1892, Mr. Gartside was united in marriage with D. C. Edwards, a native of Elmira, N. Y. They are both highly respected in the community and have many warm friends. Mr. Gartside is one of the enterprising, wide-awake young men of the city and is deservedly popular with all classes. He is connected with several civic societies, holding membership with Winona Lodge No. 18, A. F. & A. M., with the Knights of Pythias fraternity and with the Order of Druids. His political views are those of the Republican party, and on that ticket he was elected Alderman of the city in 1888, serving for one term as a member of the council.

Bernard Maceman.

BERNARD MACEMAN, one of the honored pioneers of Winona County, now engaged in gardening in the city of Winona, was born in Westenflander, Belgium, on the 31st of August, 1822, and is a son of James and Cecil Maceman. In the family were ten children, and Bernard was the seventh in order of birth. The father was a farmer by occupation, carrying on agricultural pursuits throughout his whole life. Physically, he was a large, strong man. His death occurred when about sixty years of age, in Belgium, where his entire life was passed.

Mr. Maceman of this sketch remained at home until his father's death, he being then eighteen years of age. After that he began to support the family, and his earnings were thus used until 1851, when he sailed for America. That was before the day of modern steamers, and he took passage at Antwerp on a sailing-vessel carrying eight hundred and eighty passengers, which after a voyage of twenty-eight days dropped anchor in the harbor of New York. It was in May that he landed on the shores of the New World, and found himself among a strange people, whose language he could not speak. He had no capital and had to depend entirely on his own resources. Immediately making his way to Cleveland, Ohio, in the vicinity of that city he sought and obtained a position as a farm hand, working by the month for half a year for $6 per month.

Mr. Maceman continued to make his home in the Buckeye State until May, 1856, when he bade adieu to Ohio and came to Minnesota, locating in Winona. Here he began work in a stone-quarry, being thus employed for three years, when, with the capital he had acquired as the result of his untiring labor and perseverance, he purchased forty acres of land, on which the cemetery now stands. He afterward purchased sixteen acres of land, on which his home is now located, and to gardening he devotes his time and energies. In this business he has prospered, for he thoroughly understands the culture of fruit and vegetables, and the products which he places upon the market are always of a fine variety, and therefore bring a good price.

In Cleveland, Ohio, Mr. Maceman was united in marriage, in March, 1856, with Miss Amelia Spellman, a native of northern Holland, born February 21, 1834. The lady came to America with her parents when a maiden of ten summers. By their union were born five children, two of whom died in infancy. Those still living are James, the eldest, who now rents his father's farm, William, who is engaged in gardening in Winona Township, and Bernard, who is employed in Winona. Mr. Maceman is a member of the Catholic Church, and his wife holds membership with the Episcopal Church. Both are highly respected people and have many warm friends in this community. For thirty-eight years Mr. Maceman has been a resident of Winona County, and has therefore witnessed the greater part of its growth and development. He has always manifested a commendable interest in everything pertaining to its welfare and upbuilding, and deserves mention among its honored early settlers.

John Waltham.

JOHN WALTHAM is a man of strong individuality, possessed of many striking characteristics, among which are those sterling qualities which have gained for him high regard. Those who know him best recognize his honesty of purpose, his straightforwardness and the true nobility of manhood, and his friends in the community are many. He was born in Molton, Lincolnshire, England, May 27, 1817, and in 1836 crossed the Atlantic to New Orleans on the new sailing-vessel, "John Dunlap," which reached its destination after a voyage of eight weeks. He was accompanied by a man and his three children whose wife had refused to leave England. This gentleman had a brother in Alton, Ill., a miller, who had re[illegible] with him and in compliance with this request he brought Mr. Waltham to his brother's home.

On reaching Alton, Mr. Waltham hired out to the miller, and for him took some horses to northern Illinois, riding them two hundred and ten miles across the trackless prairie and through the wilderness. For this he was paid $12, of which he spent $6, wishing to save the remainder to return with, if necessary. He settled at Pecatonica, Ill., where he worked at various labors until 1837, when he went to Dubuque. In the same year he returned to Alton, and hired to his old employer to work in the coal mines, where he was employed for some years. Finally he purchased eighty acres of land near Shipman Station, and opened up a farm. In [illegible] of New Orleans in company with a party of five. They crossed the Isthmus and had some interesting experiences in getting around the rapids, having to change boats several times. They left home in March, and on the 24th of July reached San Francisco. Mr. Waltham suffered from ill health and for a time could only work half a day. He afterward secured a claim, on which he spent the summer, and then returned to Marysville and staged one hundred and fifty miles to Shasta. Beyond that all travel was on muleback. In the fall Mr. Waltham engaged in prospecting, and in the winter took a claim. He worked for $40 per month above expenses and the next summer received $100 per month above expenses. Finding the mountains were covered with snow, he concluded to go fifty miles across to Trinity River. When half the distance was accomplished he and his companion came to the home of four miners, with whom they remained over night. The next day they traveled over the mountains without either food or drink. Mr. Waltham went through many hardships and experiences during his life in California, but also gained much valuable information.

After his return to Illinois, the subject of this sketch purchased eighty acres of land at Shipman. In 1861 he again went to the Pacific Slope, by way of the Isthmus route, taking with him his wife and daughter. He expected to locate in the Umpqua Valley, but the ship could not enter the river on account of fogs and went on to Portland. Mr. Waltham did not like that region, and after visiting several points on Puget Sound returned to San Francisco, and in the spring again went to Illinois.

On the 27th of April, 1856, in Alton, Ill., Mr. Waltham married Lucinda B. Carpenter, who was born December 18, 1827, in Landgrove, Bennington County, Vt., and came to Illinois with her father at the age of thirteen. They resided on the old farm near Shipman until 1861, when they came to Minnesota, and Mr. Waltham entered a farm six miles north of St. Charles. The following year he sold out his household effects and returned to Illinois. He took passage on the "Denmark," which was sunk on a sandbar, one hundred miles above Alton, but took another boat and proceeded on his way. Mr. Waltham settled on the old farm near Shipman, and in 1863, after planting his crop, decided to go to Colorado. He left St. Joseph, Mo., for Denver with a train of freight teams and drove four mule teams across the country. After his return he fitted up the mule-train for trip to Montana, in 1863, but returned to Illinois in 1864, just before the election of Lincoln.

The year 1865 witnessed the arrival of Mr. Waltham in Minnesota. He settled two and a-half miles southeast of St. Charles, and in the fall purchased land a mile and a-half northwest of the town, on which he built a large brick house, now owned by N. V. A. Crow. For twelve years he improved that place. In the mean time he went to England to see his family and old home. He also visited Florida to look up the country, but did not make investments there. In 1877 he went to California with a view to buying land, but was not pleased with the country and returned to Ashland, Neb., where he rented a farm. After raising one crop he returned to Minnesota. In the mean time he had sold his farm in Winona County. The next season he again went West, this time to Hot Springs, Ark., where he engaged in hotel-keeping until 1873. He then returned to Winona County, where he still had business interests, owning a farm near Utica. In 1878 he returned to St. Charles, and in 1881 he began the brewing business, which he carried on for two years. He then sold out, as the business proved unprofitable. He has since twice visited Hot Springs, taking friends both times, visited California in company with Mr. and Mrs. Crow, and attended the New Orleans Exposition, thence going across the country to Los Angeles, Cal. He has five times visited Mississippi. He now owns a farm of one hundred and sixty acres near Utica, another tract of sixty acres, and some residences in St. Charles which he rents.

Mr. Waltham has seen many sides of life, suffered privations, met business reverses as well as successes, has been brought in contact with all kinds of people, and has had varied experiences. A love of travel and change seems inherent in him, and although he has sometimes wished that he might settle down quietly, it has seemed impossible, and he has continued his journeyings. His prosperity is due to his own well directed efforts and also to those of his estimable wife, whose excellent business and executive ability has stood him in good stead, a fact which he recognizes, giving to her due credit. She has indeed been to him a helpmate. Although not possessing the extreme polish of the society man, Mr. Waltham is possessed of true manliness and has a keen appreciation of the beauties of nature and of the high and lofty along other lines. Although his school privileges were limited, travel and experience have brought him a wide knowledge, and he frequently jots his thoughts down in rhyme, which often possesses much beauty, both of thought and diction. His ability as an entertaining conversationalist is widely known and recognized, and he always has a fund of rich anecdotes and interesting personal reminiscences to relate. Some one has said of him that he is a man through whose life runs a strain of humor, earnestness, satire, levity, honesty and cheerfulness. His life has been somewhat as the rolling stone, yet contrary to it in one particular, for he has not only gathered moss, but polish as well. The record of Winona County would be incomplete without this sketch of one of its leading characters.

Otis Crandell Tucker.

OTIS CRANDELL TUCKER has long been one of Winona's prominent business men, and this history would be incomplete without the record of his life, which shows what can be accomplished by diligence, perseverance and well directed efforts. He early learned to make the most of his opportunities, and in this way he has steadily risen from an humble position to one of affluence. He was born near Hoosick, Rensselaer County, N. Y., March 12, 1822, and is a son of Silas H. and Betsy (Crandell) Tucker. On his father's side he is a relative of ex-Secretary B. F. Tracy, a member of President Garfield's cabinet. The father served as an officer in the War of 1812-13, and after his return from the army was extensively engaged in farming, and at the same time carried on a lumber business in Vestal, Broome Co[illegible]

Mr. Tucker was two years of age at the time of his parents' removal to that place. He early became familiar with the work of the farm and of the mill. In his boyhood he attended the common schools, and for two years pursued his studies under Professor Wheeler, of Union, N. Y. When he had attained his majority he started out for himself and began the lumber business on his own account in Broome County, N. Y. He soon after bought a mill, and later carried on business in Pennsylvania. He worked earnestly, trying hard to make a start in life, and at length his labors were rewarded by increasing capital. In 1858 he first came to Minnesota and loaned some money on real estate, but soon after returned to his home.

In the fall of 1860 Mr. Tucker again came West, with a view to seeking a location, and after trav- [illegible] he took up his residence in Winona, in 1861. It was his intention to eventually build a lumber-mill, but instead he opened a lumber-yard. There were only two small mills in this place at that time cutting from twelve to fifteen thousand feet of lumber per day. They were the beginning of what is now the most important industry of the place. In connection with his lumber-yard Mr. Tucker engaged in buying grain for a short time, but soon abandoned this and for fifteen years carried on a lumber business extending over a radius of one hundred miles. Previous to locating in the West he had made investments in pine lands in Michigan, which lands he subsequently sold at a handsome advance. He had also made some loans on land in this locality, and out of these grew a real-estate business.

With various other enterprises was Mr. Tucker also connected. He began loaning money, and became a stockholder in the First and Second National Banks, and subsequently was made a Director of the Second National Bank. His time and attention are now largely given to his real-estate interests, and whatever of success he has attained has not been the result of chance, nor has come to him as an inheritance, but has been achieved through earnest and persistent efforts and is the reward of untiring labor. He votes with the Democratic party, but has never sought political prominence. He is a man of high character and strict integrity, whose standing in business and social circles has made him one of the valued citizens of his adopted county. He is noted for his promptness in meeting his obligations. No one in his long business career ever had to come to him a second time with a bill or other obligation. In a period of more than thirty years he has had but one law suit, and in that particular case he was the defendant, and obtained judgment against the plaintiff for about $2,800.

On the 2d of July, 1860, was celebrated the marriage of Mr. Tucker and Lucinda C., daughter of Benjamin Rounds, of Broome County, N. Y. Their only child, a daughter, Ella, was born April 8, 1861. Her early girlhood was passed in Winona, and after graduating from the Normal School in 1887 she entered the Northwestern University at Evanston, Ill., where she remained two years. Her taste and natural artistic genius, which were of a high order, received guidance and direction through a course of special instruction in art in Chicago, at the Cooper Institute in New York, and through six months of European travel, spent in viewing the work of the old masters. She was amiable and unassuming in character, prominent in society and charitable movements and a favorite with all. She passed to her reward October 17, 1891, regretted by the entire community, and mourned by all who knew her, and is buried in Woodlawn Cemetery.

Samuel A. Alling.

SAMUEL A. ALLING is the owner of Cherry Grove Fruit Farm, one of the finest fruit farms in this part of Winona County. He makes his home in the village of Homer, and is a highly respected citizen, having many warm friends throughout the community. He was born July 27, 1821, in New Haven, Conn., and comes from an old New England family. His father, Samuel Alling, was also a native of New Haven and for thirty-three years was a sailor. At length he abandoned the sea and turned his attention to farming. Having purchased a tract of land in the East, he cultivated and improved the same until about 1856, when he came to Minnesota, and for two years made his home with his son Samuel. He then returned to Connecticut, where he spent his remaining days, his death occurring about 1861. His wife survived him three years, and died in

1864 They had a family of ten children, eight of whom are yet living David, now of Rockford, Ill, Mrs Sarah Baldwin and Mrs Rebecca Baley, both deceased, Mrs Mary Harrison, of Winona County, Jane Scratton, who is living in Florida, Samuel A, Mrs Emily Russell, of East Haven Conn, Mrs Martha Potter, of New Haven, Conn, Mrs Maria Kay, also of New Haven, and Mrs Janet Smith, of Hartford, Conn

Under the parental roof Samuel A Alling remained until twenty years of age. For a short time he then engaged in blacksmithing at $12 per month, after which he began work in the armory, where he received $2 per day After being thus employed for a year he spent two years in an auger and ditch shop, and then embarked in the manufacture of matches, which he carried on for a short time The next event of importance which occurred in his life was his removal to the West in 1847

In the mean time, however, Mr Alling was married, on the 19th of May, 1845, Miss Rhoda Jones becoming his wife She was a daughter of Samuel and Catherine Jones, natives of Connecticut Her father was a farmer After thirteen months of wedded life, Mrs Alling died, leaving an infant daughter, Emma, who is now the wife of Samuel Croffman, of Winona For three years Mr Alling lived alone, and then married Elizabeth Hill, who died of consumption three years later, while living in Michigan For his third wife Mr Alling chose Maria Greenman, daughter of Orange and Sarah (Bouton) Greenman natives of New York. Her father died when she was quite young Her mother afterward came to the West and resided with Mrs Alling for a short time, when she again returned to her old home. She now resides in Battle Creek, Mich, with her son Daniel, who now follows farming at that place In the Greenman family were ten children, five of whom are yet living Jane is deceased; Mortimer is a resident of Michigan, Edward is living in the same state, Ann is the wife of Spencer Pickle, of Michigan, Mrs Maria Alling was born November 1 1835, Daniel lives in Battle Creek, Mich; Pauline is now deceased, Mrs Eunice Cook is a resident of Nebraska Minn, and Jean and Sarah are both deceased.

On coming West in 1847, Mr Alling located in Rockford, Ill where he made his home for six years He then removed to Minnesota locating on a farm in Winona County A few years later he came to Cherry Grove Fruit Farm which has since been his home He has here between six and seven hundred cherry trees, comprising one of the finest cherry orchards in this section His fruit is of a fine variety, and meets with a ready sale. In connection with this property he also owns many town lots

To Mr and Mrs Alling were born three children but only one is now living. Sarah, the eldest, was born in May, 1848, and died in June, 1849, Ida, born May 4, 1853 is now the wife of George O Booth, a contractor and builder of Prescott, Iowa, by whom she has four children, and Homer, born February 28, 1851, died in December, 1855

The educational privileges of Mr Alling were limited to six weeks' attendance at the district schools, but though his advantages were few, he has improved his opportunities, and is a self-made man, who deserves great credit for his success in life He has served as Assessor, Justice of the Peace, Constable, Treasurer and Town Clerk and in fact, has filled all the town offices except that of Supervisor By his ballot he supports the men and measures of the Republican party

Abraham Hesselgrave.

ABRAHAM HESSELGRAVE, who carries on general farming on section 15, Saratoga Township, where he owns and operates a good farm of one hundred and fourteen acres, is a native of New York. He was born in Lisbon Township, St. Lawrence County, on the 2d of July, 1828, and is of English descent. His parents, James and Margaret (Oldness) Hesselgrave, were both natives of England. Their family numbered ten children, nine sons and a daughter. Having emigrated to America, they lived for many years in the Empire State, and there, on a farm, Abraham was born and reared. The school privileges which he received were those afforded by the neighborhood, and he could then attend school only until fifteen years of age.

Mr. Hesselgrave began life for himself at the early age of thirteen by working as a farm hand for $6 per month. He was then employed in that capacity until after his removal to the West. The year 1865 witnessed his arrival in Minnesota. Here he determined that his labors should more directly benefit himself, and instead of entering the employ of others he rented land and began farming in his own interest. The venture proved successful, and he thereby acquired a small capital, with which at the end of the year he purchased forty acres of land on section 16, Saratoga Township. The tract was but partially improved, but his labors soon made the fields very productive and good crops were harvested. The little far[m] of forty acres continued his place of residence until 1873, when he sold out. In 1879 he purchased the farm which has been his home continuously since, and in its improvement and cultivation his time was passed.

On the 16th of August, 1851, Mr. Hesselgrave was married, the lady of his choice being Miss Margaret Champine, and the day on which the historian writes is the forty-third anniversary of their marriage. The lady, a native of Canada, was born March 9, 1832, and is a daughter of John and Rosanna Champine, both of whom were of French extraction. To Mr. and Mrs. Hesselgrave were born eleven children, namely: Jane, Margaret, Henry, John, Emma, James, Minnie (deceased), Fred, Ella, Albert, and Willie, who is also deceased.

In his political views Mr. Hesselgrave is a Republican. He was an opponent of slavery in the days prior to the war, and when a party was formed to prevent its further extension he joined its ranks. When the South attempted secession he was true to the Union, and on the 23d of August, 1862, he manifested his loyalty by offering his services to the Government. He was assigned to Company E, One Hundred and Sixth New York Infantry, and the first engagement in which he participated was at Rolling Stone. This was followed by the battles of Martinsburg, Winchester and Fisher['s] [illegible] Creek, Manassas, the Battle of the Wilderness, Culpeper, Stony Creek, and during many engagements of lesser importance At Petersburg, his last engagement, he was wounded by a minie-ball, which passed through his right wrist, and for a short time was in the field hospital, after which he was sent to the Finley Hospital, in Washington, D C He there received an honorable discharge on the 23d of June, 1865 He was always true to the cause, ever found at his post valiantly defending the Stars and Stripes which now triumphantly wave over a united nation.

After being mustered out Mr Hesselgrave returned to his native state, and thence came to Winona County, with the interests of which he has since been identified He is an honored comrade in the Grand Army of the Republic, and all who know him respect him

---

John Denno.

JOHN DENNO, a retired farmer, now residing in Dakota, was born on the 20th of June, 1820, in Canada and is a son of Joseph and Sampah (Meade) Denno, who were also natives of Canada They came to the United States about 1835, locating in Sheldon Vt, where they made their home for about five years In 1855 they came to Minnesota, and located in the city of Winona. The father was a farmer by occupation, and became well-to-do In his family were eight children, five of whom are yet living

In the usual manner of farmer lads, John Denno was reared, spending his boyhood days midst play and work As soon as old enough to handle the plow, his labors in the field began, and from that time forward he was for many years connected with agricultural interests In fact, he made farming his life work. With his parents he removed from Canada to Vermont when a youth of fifteen, and in 1857 came to Minnesota Here he secured land which he at once began to clear and develop, and in course o ... under a high state of cultivation, while many improvements found upon a model farm were made

As a companion and helpmate on life's journey, Mr Denno chose Miss Mary Bileman, daughter of Enos Bileman, a native of Canada Their wedding was celebrated on the 10th of July, 1840, and for the long period of fifty-two years they traveled life's journey together sharing with each other its joys and sorrows, its adversity and prosperity At length they were separated by death, the loving wife passing away on the 28th of April, 1892 She was a most estimable lady, and her many excellences of character gained her a large circle of warm friends

To Mr. and Mrs. Denno were born eleven children, six of whom are yet living Mrs Jennie Norton, the eldest now living, resides in Homer The next, a son, died in infancy. June, the wife of Levi Brown, is a resident of Winona. Lucinda, the wife of James Donehower, also resides in Wi- ... of Edward Leach, whose home is in the village of Dakota Adeline is the wife of Joseph Tetroe whose home is in Kansas Henry C is the leading merchant and one of the most prominent citizens of Homer He is a very enterprising man, and his success in business is due to his own efforts He wedded Miss Mary Leach, daughter of Charles Leach, one of the pioneer settlers of Winona County.

John Denno was reared in the faith of the Catholic Church, but now holds membership with no religious organization In his political views he is a Democrat His life has been well and worthily passed, and he has gained a competence that now enables him to live retired His honorable and straightforward career has won him universal confidence, and without doubt his many friends will be glad to see this record of his life in the history of his adopted county.

Alvano Benjamin Dyar.

ALVANO BENJAMIN DYAR is a farmer of Saratoga Township, residing on section 9 The record of his life is as follows He was born in Freeman Township, in Franklin County, Me December 17, 1839, and comes of a family of English origin During Colonial days ancestors by the name of Dyar sailed from England to America and became residents of the Pine Tree State. Azor Dyar, the father of Alvano, was there born October 12 1812, and his entire life was spent upon the farm which had been owned by his father His death occurred on the old home place, on the 31st of March, 1892 He was a member of the Methodist Church and a most highly respected citizen, who was widely and favorably known in his native county His wife bore the maiden name of Mary Davis, and was a distant relative of Jefferson Davis. She is now living in Maine, in her eighty-sixth year In the family were three children Alvano B, Emerson D, who is Vice-President of the H J O'Neil Company, leading grain dealers of Winona and Roscoe who is living on the old homestead in Maine which was settled by his grandfather.

The public schools afforded Mr. Dyar, of this sketch, a fair business education, and upon the farm his boyhood days were spent midst play and work No event of special importance occurred during his youth He became familiar with all the duties of farm life, and to his father he gave the benefit of his services until he had attained his majority He then rented a part of the old homestead and began farming in his own interest

It was in the spring of 1865 that Mr Dyar came to Minnesota, settling in Saratoga Township, Winona County. For a year he rented land, and then purchased the farm on which his residence now stands It comprises one hundred and sixty acres of land on section 9, and to this he has added from time to time until he here has three hundred and fifty-six acres, while altogether his landed possessions aggregate about seven hundred acres. The wild prairie land has been transformed into rich and fertile fields and the golden grain pays tribute to his care and labor. His time and attention are given to general farming and stock-raising, and his land is all well improved.

On the 18th of November, 1868, was celebrated the marriage of Mr. Dyar and Miss Adah Gerrish. Five children have been born to them, and the family circle yet remains unbroken. In order of birth they are as follows: Charles A., who is now living in Montana; M. Davis, who is connected with the O'Neil Grain Company, of Winona; John G., Bert A. and Mary O., all of whom are still with their parents.

Mr. Dyar exercises his right of franchise in support of the men and measures of the Republican party. He has served as Township Supervisor, but has never been a politician in the sense of office-seeking. His business career has been one of success. He had no capital with which to begin life, save a young man's bright hope of the future and a strong determination to succeed, and this determination he has carried out. He is now in comfortable circumstances, and is recognized, not only as one of the substantial, but also as one of valued, citizens of the community.

CHARLES GERRISH.

Charles Gerrish.

CHARLES GERRISH, a retired farmer of St. Charles, is numbered among the honored pioneers of Winona County, having here made his home since 1855. He has witnessed the entire growth and development of this region, and has ever borne his part in the work of progress and development, so that his name is inseparably connected with the history of this section.

A native of New Hampshire, Mr. Gerrish was born in Canterbury, Merrimac County, on the 1st of March, 1822. His father, Joseph Gerrish, was also born in that locality, and was the sixth in direct descent from Capt. William Gerrish, founder of the family in America. The Captain was born in Bristol, England, in 1617, braved the dangers of an ocean voyage in 1639, became a resident of Newbury, Mass., and died in 1687. His son, Col. Moses Gerrish, was the father of Col. Joseph Gerrish, and the grandfather of Capt. Stephen Gerrish, who was the great-grandfather of the gentleman whose name heads this record. The grandfather bore the name of Samuel Gerrish.

Charles Gerrish has in his possession many interesting heirlooms, including a worsted comb. This was borrowed from his mother sixty years ago by a lady whose son returned it to Charles Gerrish only three years since. He also has two old silhouettes, the common style of picture at that day, one of his mother at twenty years of age, and the other of Ezekiel Webster, brother of Daniel Webster. He has a block of wood cut from a tree famous in history, the one on which Daniel Webster hung his scythe when, after complaining to his father of the way it hung, he was told to hang it to suit himself. An old pewter plate in his home belonged to his grandmother's mother, and is about two hundred years old. He also has a pewter teapot given to his grandmother, Mrs. Samuel Gerrish.

Joseph Gerrish only lived eight miles from the home of Daniel Webster. He married Sarah Chandler, and after the death of his first wife wedded Sarah Church, daughter of John Church. Her father was a native of Ireland, and a son of Colonel Church, of the English army. When a child of seven years, he came to the United States with a friend. Both the Gerrish and Church families have had many representatives in military life.

Charles Gerrish was reared on a farm in New Hampshire, on the Merrimac River, in the old neighborhood where many representatives of the family resided. At a Gerrish meeting held in 1841 at his home, there were one hundred and seventy-five near relatives present, and with one exception all of these were Whigs These family meetings were a feature in New England society for over half a century Charles remained on the old homestead and operated the farm until 1853 The following year he came West and took up his residence in New Buffalo, Mich The following spring he came to Minnesota, reaching Saratoga on the 19th of June, 1855. A few weeks previous he had secured a claim on sections 3, 4, 9 and 10, Saratoga Township, and at once began to improve that farm, which he made his home for twenty years It comprised four hundred acres of rich land, and was a valuable property His first home was a log cabin, 16x22 feet, with a "lean-to," and in that house the first school in Saratoga Township was taught by Miss Helen Hewitt, daughter of Jason Hewitt She had about twenty-six pupils She was afterward married, and her husband was killed in the Quantrell raid at Lawrence, Kan, where she now lives Her father still resides in Saratoga Township The first election in that township was held in the Gerrish home, and out of the thirty-two votes cast thirty were for Republican candidates

Mr. Gerrish was married on the 18th of March, 1815, in West Hartford, Vt to Miss Olive W. Dimick, a native of the Green Mountain State To them have been born three children Allen, of St Charles a market gardener and breeder of Duroc Jersey red hogs, Adah wife of A B Dyar, of Saratoga, and Etta Veva, wife of Louis H. Dyer, of Quincy Township, Olmsted County

The parents aided in the organization of the Congregational Church in Saratoga, about 1856 and are now connected with the church in St Charles Mr Gerrish, who has always been a stanch Republican in politics, was a delegate to the Constitutional Convention in 1857 After selling his first farm he bought and sold several other tracts of land, and now owns considerable farm property On coming here in 1855, he had a capital stock of about $2 000, but he has made the most of his opportunities, and is now numbered among the substantial citizens of the community, a position to which he is justly entitled He is a large man, of fine physique, with a long gray beard and kindly gray eye, the latter being an index of his character.

Otis Abell.

OTIS ABELL, of the Winona Construction Company, is a man of wide business experience, enterprising and progressive and among the valued citizens of his adopted county he is numbered He was born in Otsego Oswego County, N Y, on the 11th of May, 1844, and is a son of Lemuel and Sallie W (Watson) Abell The father was [illegible] State in the year 1810, and [illegible] moved to the West, locating in Dodge County Wis There he remained for seven years engaged in farming In 1855 he came to Minnesota, and took up his residence in Wiscoy Township, Winona County, where he entered one hundred and twenty acres of land, having obtained it from the Government It was in a wild and unimproved state, but with characteristic energy he began its development and [illegible] it into rich and fertile fields, which yielded to him a good income For many years he was one of the representative citizens of his township, serving for a long period as Chairman of the Town Committee, and in all public affairs was recognized as a leader In early days he was an Abolitionist, and supported that party when devotion to its principles caused much sacrifice When the Republican party was formed to prevent the extension of slavery, he at once joined its ranks and was one of its earnest advocates throughout his remaining days He took a deep interest in religious affairs, and was a member of the regular Baptist Church His wife, a daughter of Pelatiah Watson, was born in Vermont in 1808, and is still living in Wiscoy Township on the farm where they located on coming to the state. The Abell family numbered six children, namely Austin, on the old homestead; Minerva L., widow of Alvin Ford, George, deceased, Otis, of this notice, and two who died in infancy

Pelatiah Watson was a native of Vermont and a farmer by occupation After his marriage he located in New York State, and in 1818 came West, settling in Dodge County, Wis His death occurred at Trenton, that state, when in his eighty-second year. He had a family of three sons and three daughters, namely: Sallie W who is still living, at the age of eighty-six, James, Candice, John, Louisa A and Henry

Otis Abell was a child of four summers when by his parents he was taken to Wisconsin, and was a lad of eleven years when he came to Minnesota The educational privileges afforded him were those of the common schools His services were much in demand upon the farm, and he early became familiar with the arduous task of developing the wild prairie, but to his father he gave the benefit of his services until twenty-five years of age, when he was united in marriage with Miss Mary A Hand, the ceremony being performed on the 25th of July, 1865

Mrs Abell was born in Wayne County, N Y and is a daughter of Alphonso and Mary Ann Hand The family came to the West in 1866, and settled in Minnesota, but the parents are both now deceased, the father having passed away at the age of sixty-three while the mother was called to the home beyond at the age of thirty-three Mr and Mrs Abell now have three children. May, wife of Walter Birdlebaugh, Annie M. and Ida E

After his marriage, Mr Abell built a home and began life in earnest He later engaged in railroading and contracting to which work he devoted his energies for several years, and also sold agricultural implements He then built a store at Centreville, where he engaged in merchandising for eight years, after which he sold out, and in 1885 came to Winona where he has since made his home. For a year and a-half he engaged in merchandising, and then sold out his interest in his store He later embarked alone in the business of laying asphalt sidewalks, which proved a profitable venture, but he is now associated with other parties In 1893 he became one of the partners in the Winona Construction Company, which is to-day recognized as one of the successful business firms of the city. They enjoy a liberal patronage, which is constantly increasing, and the contracts which they have made have yielded them a good income

During the late war, Mr Abell manifested his loyalty to the Union cause by responding to the President's call for troops In 1862 he donned the blue, enrolling his name among the comrades of Company K, Eleventh Minnesota Infantry in which he faithfully served until discharged in 1864 He is now a member of John Ball Post, G A R. holds membership with the Equitable Aid Society, and also belongs to the Modern Woodmen of America In politics he has always been a Republican, and the principles of the party receive his earnest support He is recognized as one of the wide-awake and progressive men to whom the prosperity of a place is due, and Winona recognizes him as one of her most valuable citizens

Hon. William Hall Yale.

HON. WILLIAM HALL YALE occupies a foremost position at the Bar of Winona County, having a high reputation as a lawyer, not only in the county seat, where he makes his home, but throughout the state. He comes of a family prominent in history as among the founders of Yale College, which was named in honor of one of his ancestors, a wealthy gentleman who made liberal donations to the school in the days of its infancy and helped to place it on a firm financial basis. The following on his tombstone attests his worthy character:

"EPITAPH OF ELIHU YALE, WHO DIED JULY 22, 1721.

"INTERRED AT WREXHAM IN DENBIGHSHIRE, WALES.

—o—

"Born in America, in Europe bred,
In Africa travell'd, and in Asia wed,
Where long he lived and thriv'd, at London dead.
Much good, some ill, he did, we hope that all's even,
And that his soul thro' mercy's gone to Heaven.

"You that survive and read, take care
For this most certain exit to prepare,
For only the actions of the just
Smell sweet and blossom in the dust."

The first generation in America of the Yale family were children of David and Ann Yale, natives of Wales, who settled in New Haven, Conn., in 1637 ... Conn., in 1670. He was the father of Capt. Thomas Yale, and those who followed in direct descent were Theophilus, Elihu, Elihu, Stephen and Benajah Yale, the last-named being the grandfather of William Hall Yale. He was a native of Wallingford, and a shoemaker by trade. He died at the age of fifty-five years. Among his five children was Wooster Yale, a native of the Nutmeg State, who became a very extensive shoe manufacturer of Wallingford, where he carried on business for a number of years. On his retirement from that enterprise he removed to New Haven and opened a lottery exchange office. He was made Deputy Sheriff of the county, and, on account of the illness of his superior, virtually served as Sheriff. Subsequently he returned to Wallingford and settled upon the old farm on which his ancestor, Thomas Yale, had located in 1670. He there died in 1842, at the age of forty-five. His wife, who bore the maiden name of Lucy Hall, passed away in New Haven in 1891. Had she lived three months longer she would have celebrated her ninetieth birthday. With the Congregational Church she held membership. To Mr. and Mrs. Yale were born ten children, five sons and five daughters, of whom six are yet living: Esther C., born in 1823, George W., in 1826; William H., in 1831, Edwin A., in 1831, Mary C., who was born in 1836 and is the widow of George Nott, of New Haven, and Susan L., wife of Henry Platt, born in 1811.

W. H. Yale was born in New Haven, November ... ie until six years of age, when with his parents he went to Wallingford. Three years later he went to live in the town of North Branford, Conn., with a farmer by the name of Baldwin, with whom he remained until thirteen years of age. While there he took advantage of the opportunities offered by a good library, and obtained a fair knowledge of books. When a lad of thirteen he returned to his home in New Haven and worked in a paint shop for a time, after which he again attended school, entering the Connecticut Literary Institution at Suffield, Conn., where he studied three years, earning his own living in the mean time. At about the age of eighteen he went to Norwalk and taught school there for about five years, studying law a part of the time. The Sharp Rifle Manufactory of Hartford, Conn., was just then being established and was in need of a bookkeeper. Out of one hundred and fifty applicants he received the preference and was given a salary of $700 per year, but subsequently his salary was increased to $1,200, which was regarded as very large wages in those days.

In March, 1857, Mr. Yale came to Winona, where he has since made his home, and during the entire time has been engaged in the practice of law, winning a large and liberal patronage and gaining the confidence and respect of his clients and all with whom he has been brought in contact. He has been honored with a number of offices. In the spring of 1858 he ran for City Justice on the Republican ticket and was the only Republican on the ticket elected. In 1859, while still serving in that position, he was elected Judge of the Probate Court, serving for a short time. In 1860 he was nominated for County Attorney, and winning in the contest for the office, served for two years, and in 1861 he was re-elected for a second term of two years. In 1866 he was nominated for the State Senate and carried the election by a vote of two to one. In 1869 he was nominated for the position of Lieutenant-Governor, and received a larger majority than any one on the ticket. After serving for two years, he was re-elected by the largest majority given to any candidate at that election, and filled the position until 1871. In 1876 he was again elected to the State Senate from the Eighth District, serving for two years. He was a delegate to the Republican National Convention in 1876, and in 1892 to the National Republican Convention held in the city of Minneapolis. Mr. Yale was re-elected State Senator November 6, 1894, by a handsome majority, in a county largely Democratic.

Turning from the public to the private life of Mr. Yale, the records show that in 1852 he was united in marriage with Miss Sarah E. Banks, daughter of Bradly O. Banks, of Norwalk, Conn. They had one son, Charles B., a lawyer, and General Claim Agent at St. Paul for the Great Northern Railroad, which now reaches to the Pacific Ocean. He married Miss Minnie Huntington, of Milwaukee. Mrs. Sarah E. Yale died in October, 1871, and her loss was deeply mourned by many friends. She was a member of the Episcopal Church, with which Mr. Yale has been identified for forty-five years. In October, 1872, he was again married, his second union being with Mary L. Hoyt, daughter of Charles and Mary (Hoyt) Hoyt. They have one son, William Hoyt Yale.

Mr. Yale has been a resident of Winona for thirty-seven years. He has a state reputation as a lawyer, and has a national reputation as a champion of Republican principles in the Northwest. In the offices which he has been called upon to fill he has ever been found true and faithful to his party's interests and to the people who honored him by their votes. While in the Senate he was often complimented on his fluent and eloquent speeches, and was recognized as a power on whatever side of the question he was found. His oratory has also won him success at the Bar, for it is the robe of logical argument and clear thought

Lyman B. Cox.

LYMAN B COX, a farmer and stock-raiser, owns and operates a good farm on sections 5 and 8, Saratoga Township It is a valuable tract of land comprising four hundred and fifteen acres, and the greater part of it is under a high state of cultivation The place is neat and thrifty in appearance, the fields are well tilled, and there are found all the accessories and conveniences of a model farm

The owner of this desirable property was born in Pierrepont St. Lawrence County, N Y, April 2, 1828 His father, Benjamin Cox, was a native of Vermont, and was of English lineage His mother bore the maiden name of Mary Bowman In their family were the following children Cordelia, now deceased, Caroline, wife of C Wheelock, a resident of Green Bay, Wis, Orvilla, who died in 1850; Jane, who died December 25, 1893, Lyman B, Isabella, who died in September, 1876; Lucy, who died in 1872, and one who died in infancy The mother of this family having been called to the home beyond, Benjamin Cox was again married, his second union being with Clarissa Walker by whom he had two children Daniel, who makes his home in Fond du Lac, Wis., and Edna, wife of Levi Crandall, who is living in Humboldt, Iowa.

No event of special importance occurred during the childhood and youth of Mr Cox, of this sketch. He attended the public schools of the neighborhood until he had attained his majority, thus acquiring a fair business education. He then started out in life the present day has relied entirely upon his own efforts, so that his success is the reward of worthy labor He first earned his livelihood by working as a farm hand, being thus employed until the fall of 1847, when he emigrated to Wisconsin, making the journey by the Lakes and stage to Green Bay There he remained for nine months, after which he returned to New York, where he engaged in farming until 1851

In the year 1853 Mr Cox sought a home in Indianapolis Ind but after about a nine-months stay in that city he again changed his place of residence and Winona County thereby secured a valued citizen He located in Saratoga Township, on the farm where he now lives, pre-empting first a tract of one hundred and sixty acres on section 8 Only about ten acres of this land had been broken, but with characteristic energy he began its further development, and with ox-teams he placed the land under the plow and transformed the once wild tract into rich and fertile fields. He erected a log cabin 16x20 feet in dimensions, in which he lived in true pioneer style for a number of years At length the pioneer home was replaced by a more modern structure and his further labors added to the place all the improvements of a model farm of the nineteenth century

Mr Cox was married on the 3d of June, 1852, to Miss Esther H Cox, and by their union were born four children Francis M, Benjamin C, Mary E. and Julia E., all of whom are still living and

In his political affiliations Mr. Cox has been a Republican since 1860. His first Presidential vote, however, was cast for James Buchanan. He has served in several local offices, having been Supervisor, Township Treasurer and Assessor, and in all of these positions he has discharged his duties with a promptness and fidelity which have won him high commendation. Socially he is connected with the Masonic order. All who know him esteem him highly for his sterling worth and strict integrity, and in the history of his adopted county he well deserves representation.

Sylvester Gardner.

SYLVESTER GARDNER, who is engaged in general farming and horticulture on section 32, Homer Township, his residence being in the village of Homer, was born on a farm at Bennington, Vt., April 28, 1830, and is a son of Abel and Amy Gardner. They, too, were natives of the Green Mountain State, and for many years the father carried on farming near Bennington. His death occurred about 1870. The mother died when Sylvester was about fifteen years of age, and was buried in New York. This worthy couple had a family of eight children, but Harriet Lillie and Electa are deceased. Those still living are: Sylvester, of this sketch; Abel, who now makes his home in Montana; Julia Card, a resident of New York; Alpha, who is located in Winona; Samantha Lillie, of New York, and Anna Hakes, also of the Empire State.

The subject of this sketch spent the first eighteen years of his life in the state of his nativity, his time being devoted to farm work and to study in the district schools of the neighborhood. On leaving home he started westward, and made a location in Green County, Wis., where he remained for three years. On the expiration of that period he returned to Broome County, N. Y., where he spent the succeeding four years, and then came to Minnesota, locating on the farm where he now makes his home. Here he began carpenter work, which he followed until 1861, when he went to Chippewa Falls, Wis., and was a filer in the sawmills at that place until the 4th of July of that year, when he lost his right arm, and was forced to give up his position. In 1865 he returned to Winona County, and worked on the county roads for a number of years, making new and repairing old roads until about 1882, when he turned his attention to agricultural pursuits. He owns a good tract of land of seventy-one acres, and is engaged in general farming, and in raising berries of all kinds, which he sells to the home market.

On the 20th of May, 1851, Mr. Gardner married Charity Decker, daughter of Aaron Decker. The lady was a native of New York, and her father, with his family, came to Winona County in 1855, locating in the town of Homer. He became a well-to-do farmer, and owned a valuable tract of land. Mr. Decker was born September 10, 1802, and his wife, Elizabeth Wells, was born June 20, 1807. They were united in marriage July 6, 1823. The former died September 17, 1867, and the latter September 17, 1861. Mr. and Mrs. Decker became the parents of twelve children: Aaron, Jr., who was born February 10, 1825, and died March 15, 1882; Sarah E., born January 11, 1827, and died October 19, 1839; Hanna L., born April 2, 1829, and died December 21, 1861; Moses, born May 19, 1831, and died December 19, 1877; Peter, born August 21, 1833, and died May 31, 1889; Charity A., the wife of our subject, born January 3, 1836; Clarissa, March 8, 1838; Mary, born July 11, 1840, and died July 11, 1841; Elizabeth, born May 5, 1842, and died July 14, 1842; Elias C., born November 20, 1843, and died March 26, 1871; Harriett E., born September 11, 1847, and Albert James, born June 5, 1851, and died October 1, 1864.

To Mr. and Mrs. Gardner were born five children, but only two are now living. Mrs. Eliza Rogers, born April 20, 1855, is now a resident of Winona. Mrs. Samantha Nash, born June 6, 1858, makes her home in the same city. Nellie, born July 20, 1865, died May 7, 1891. Sylvester, born June 16, 1870, died in September, 1873. One died in infancy.

In his political affiliations Mr. Gardner is a Republican. He has served both as Supervisor and Constable, and is now filling the office of School Director, in which capacity he has served for twelve years. The cause of education finds in him a warm friend, and his public duties are ever discharged with promptness and fidelity. He had but limited advantages in his youth, educational or otherwise, but he has made the most of his opportunities, and being possessed of energy and a strong determination to succeed, he has worked his way steadily upward to prosperity, being now a well-to-do farmer.

Samuel E. Cotton.

SAMUEL E. COTTON, one of the honored pioneer settlers of Winona County, now living on a farm on section 11, Rolling Stone Township, dates his residence here from 1852. The county was then only a frontier settlement, in which the work of progress and civilization was hardly begun, and in its development and advancement he has ever borne his part. He therefore well deserves mention among its founders, and this volume would be incomplete without his sketch.

Mr. Cotton was born in Ellsworth, N. H., September 19, 1821, and is the only survivor in a family of th[illegible] ond in order of birth. The parents were Samuel and Mary (Folsome) Cotton. The father was born and reared upon a farm in Gilford, N. H., and devoted his life to agricultural and mercantile pursuits. His death occurred at the ripe old age of eighty-eight years. For several generations his ancestors have lived in the United States, and their ancestry could be traced back to Rev. John Cotton, of Boston, whose father was an English lawyer, and who came to the United States in the early days of the Colonies. Mrs. Cotton, mother of our subject, was also a native of Gilford, and her death occurred in Dover, N. H., at about the age of [illegible] traction.

Samuel Cotton attended the common and high schools until about eighteen years of age, when he shipped before the mast and for three years sailed on the high seas. He was on a sailing-vessel which at one voyage captured fifty whales. He then spent four years in sailing to Europe, after which he turned his attention to land pursuits, learning the molder's trade in Great Falls, N. H., in which trade he was later employed in Boston and Lowell, Mass., and Dover and Laconia, N. H., until the spring of 1852. In that year he came to the West. He had heard of the advantages and privileges afforded in Minnesota and the opportunities for securing a home, so in April he left New York City, and on the 4th of May reached Minnesota City, coming as one of the members of the Western Farm and Village Association of New York, which numbered about two hundred people. There was only one house in Minnesota City at the time, and two little shanties where Winona now stands. The land had not been surveyed by the Government, and the treaty with the Indians had been passed but not ratified. The little New York colony laid out the village of Minnesota City, and Mr. Cotton built him a house on a lot therein. After the farm lands were surveyed he secured one hundred and sixty acres on the prairie near Utica, about sixteen miles west of his present home. There he did his first plowing, but never planted any crops at that place. Returning to Minnesota City, he secured eighty acres adjoining the village limits, part of which he sold in 1858. He then purchased the farm upon which he has resided continuously since.

On the 28th of October, 1847, Mr. Cotton was united in marriage with Miss Sarah A. Roberts, who was born in Berwick, Me., September 10, 1828. With her husband she came West, and here resided until her death, which occurred October 29, 1893. Her parents were of English and Irish extraction. To Mr. and Mrs. Cotton were born nine children, of whom two died in infancy. Nell is now the wife of Thomas Thorpe, of West Superior, Wis.; John E. is engaged in the operation of the old homestead; Charles Henry occupies the responsible position of foreman in Bemis Bros.' bag factory of Minneapolis; George Walter is a foreman in the Winona Wagon Works of Winona; Fred R. is a telegraph operator in Minnesota; Herbert F. holds a responsible position with the Winona Wagon Works, and Frank L. is on the home farm.

Mr. Cotton is a Republican in politics. When Winona County was organized, however, he was elected Probate Judge, Justice of the Peace and Assessor on the Democratic ticket. He served as Assessor of the county when there were only three people in his district to assess. He was appointed Postmaster of Minnesota City under Buchanan, the second to fill that office, and thus served until 1857, when he resigned, but for many years past he has served as Assistant Postmaster. In 1860 he voted for Abraham Lincoln, and has since been a stalwart Republican. In 1853 he was elected Justice of the Peace, and has held that office almost continuously since. He has also served in other local official positions, and in the discharge of his public duties has ever been found faithful and true.

Mr. Cotton has succeeded in his business dealings and now owns a valuable farm of two hundred acres, which is pleasantly situated a mile from Minnesota City. It is, however, operated by his sons, while he gives his attention to his duties as Assistant Postmaster and Justice of the Peace. He is one of the oldest settlers in the county, there probably being not more than three who located here ere his arrival. He has seen the wild lands transformed into beautiful homes and farms, has seen towns and villages spring into existence, has watched their transformation into cities, has known the hardships and trials of pioneer life, and has ever been found a valuable citizen, ready to aid in all worthy public enterprises.

Lucius Brainard.

LUCIUS BRAINARD, who has served in various official positions and been prominent in the public affairs of the community in which he lives, now resides in Warren Township, where he owns and operates a good farm of one hundred and sixty acres on sections 28 and 33. The place is well improved with good buildings and other accessories of a model farm, the fields are well tilled, and there is a four-acre grove of maple, walnut and butternut trees, which were planted by his hand and stand as a monument to his progressive spirit.

Mr. Brainard was born in Caledonia County, Vt., on the 1st of May, 1824, and is a son of Ira and Verona (Taylor) Brainard. He is the elder of two children, and his brother George yet resides in Vermont. The father was a native of the Green Mountain State, and was of English descent. For some years he carried on merchandising in Danville, doing a successful business, and was also President of the Caledonia Bank at that place.

Lucius Brainard was reared in his native town of Danville, attended the public schools and completed his education at Phillip's Academy. He began to earn his own livelihood when eighteen years of age, entering a woolen factory with the intention of learning the trade. For six years he worked in woolen-mills, after which he was employed on the Vermont & Massachusetts Railroad, and followed that work until 1855, in which year he started for the West. The journey was made by rail and t W

ren Township, Winona County, where he made a location, pre-empting one hundred and sixty acres of land, which constitutes his present fine farm. It was oak openings, and there he built a small log cabin 10x12 feet in dimensions, in which he lived for one year. He then erected a frame house, 16x18 feet, and at once turned his attention to the development of the land. He began breaking prairie with ox-teams, planted crops, and in course of time the rich soil yielded a good return. He was one of the early settlers of the neighborhood, and the county was largely unimproved. Winona contained only one store, and many of the now thriving villages had not then sprung into existence.

Mr. Brainard was married on the 1st of May, 1845, to Miss Emily B. Wright, and to them have been born six children, viz.: George, who now aids in the operation of the home farm; Ira L., who died on the 11th of September, 1848; Frank J., who follows farming at home; Emily J., formerly the wife of John W. Geeslin, an agriculturist of Warren Township; Ira C., who was killed February 8, 1891, by a freight train in the North-Western yards at Winona; and William H., who died on the 17th of July, 1877. Emily J. Geeslin died July 17, 1891.

Both Mr. and Mrs. Brainard, who are members of the Methodist Church, take an active part in its work and are deeply interested in its welfare. For

been Superintendent of the Sunday-school. Everything calculated to elevate humanity receives his approval and support, and he is recognized as a man whose life is worthy of emulation. Socially he is connected with the Masonic fraternity, and in politics he is a Republican. Prior to the organization of that party he supported the Whig party. He has held the office of Chairman of the Board of Supervisors, and has also been Assessor and Constable.

C. C. Chapman.

C. C. CHAPMAN, who is now serving as Postmaster of Minnesota City, was born in London, England, on the 11th of September, 1832, and is a son of Egbert Chapman, who was born in Glastonbury, England, and became an attorney-at-law. Having attained to years of maturity, he married Miss Rebecca Payne, a native of Essex, England. In 1850 he bade adieu to friends and native land and with his family sailed for the New World, locating first on Long Island, where for two years he made his home. In June, 1852, he came to Winona County, as a member of the New York Farm and Village Association, entered land, and resided thereon for a year. He then made a claim in Minnesota City, which he continued to cultivate and improve for a number of years, transforming it into a rich and valuable farm. He now makes his home with his son, the efficient Postmaster of Minnesota City. Although he has reached the very advanced age of ninety years, his faculties are but slightly impaired, and he is a well preserved man. For a number of years he served as Justice of the Peace, and is well known throughout the county as one of its honored pioneers and valued citizens. His wife, who was a member of the Baptist Church for some time and a most estimable lady, was called to her final rest when eighty-five years of age.

C. C. Chapman is the eldest in a family of ten children. His early boyhood years were largely passed in the schoolroom, and at the age of sixteen he entered a shoe factory in London, where he served an apprenticeship until twenty-one years of age, when, in a sailing-vessel, he crossed the briny deep to the New World, whither his parents had preceded him. In October, 1853, he came West, and was engaged in farming near Minnesota City until the winter of 1856, when he went to the western part of the state with a surveying party engaged in laying the division lines between counties. At the time of the Indian outbreak he was at Spirit Lake, and was commissioned Second Lieutenant of what was known as the Watonwan Rifles. Mr. Chapman continued in the service for about eighteen months, and then returned to his home at Minnesota City, after which he engaged in farming until his enlistment for the late war.

On the 18th of August, 1862, Mr. Chapman responded to the President's call for three-years troops, and joined the boys in blue of Company B, Seventh Minnesota Infantry, of which he was made Sergeant. He was present at the battle of

Birch Coolie. He remained in the service until the close of the war, and at the battle of Wood Lake was wounded by a gunshot in the right wrist, which prevented him from taking part in active service for a time. He was afterward on detached service until the close of the war, for his injury prevented the use of the right arm. After the surrender of Lee and the cessation of hostilities, he returned to Minnesota, where he once more resumed agricultural pursuits.

In 1869 Mr. Chapman went to Arkansas, where he was appointed County Assessor by Governor Baxter, thus serving for two years and a-half. He was then postal clerk on the Memphis & Little Rock Railroad for four years, carrying the mail at the time of the siege of yellow fever in the former city. He next gave his attention to the management of a plantation which he purchased near Forest City, Ark., and which was his home until 1880, when he sold out and returned to Minnesota City. The following year he was appointed Postmaster, in which position he has served continuously since with credit to himself and satisfaction to his constituents.

On the 30th of May, 1860, Mr. Chapman was united in marriage with Miss Emma Horner, a native of England. In politics he is a Republican, unswerving in his allegiance to the party and its principles. He has always taken an active interest in political affairs, and keeps well informed on the issues of the day. For several years he has served as district school clerk, and the cause of education finds in him a warm friend. Socially he is connected with John Ball Post No. 20, G. A. R., of Winona. A worthy representative of one of the honored pioneer families of the county, a veteran of the late war, a valued citizen and a man of sterling worth, he well deserves representation in this volume.

Joseph P. Schmitz.

JOSEPH P. SCHMITZ, a leader in business circles in Winona, is at the head of the well known firm of Schmitz & Co., wholesale and retail dealers in saddlery and saddlery hardware. The record of his life is as follows: He was born in Chicago, Ill., on the 11th of August, 1848, and is a son of Ludwig and Susan (Wirtz) Schmitz. The father was a native of Prussia, born in 1805, and in that country lived until about middle life, when he emigrated to the United States and took up his residence in Chicago, where his remaining days were passed. He was a harness-maker by trade, and all ... are yet engaged in some department of the work. Mr. Schmitz died in 1850, at the age of forty-five years. His wife, who long survived him, passed away January 3, 1891, at the age of eighty-three years. She was born in Prussia in the year 1808, and with her husband came to the United States. This worthy couple were the parents of nine children, eight of whom are yet living, namely: John, who now resides in Clinton, Iowa; Anna, wife of M. Mertes, of Winona; Peter J., of Montana; Henry, a resident of Janesville, Wis.; Joseph P., of this sketch; Margaret, wife of Frank Curtis, of Ne... t who is lo cated in Clinton, Iowa, and Mary, wife of Cyrus Bond, a resident of Iowa Falls, Iowa

Our subject spent the first seven years of his life in his native city, and then accompanied the family on their removal to Newport, Wis. where he lived until eleven years of age, when he became a resident of Kilbourn City, Wis. There the succeeding five years of his life were passed, and at the age of sixteen he returned to Chicago, where he worked at the carpenter's trade for about a year. His next place of residence was in St Louis, where he was engaged in making cartridge boxes and saddle bags for army use for six months. On the expiration of that period he again went to Chicago, but after a short time returned to Kilbourn City

The spring of 1865 witnessed the arrival of Mr Schmitz in Winona Here he began making collars in the collar factory of his brother, Peter J Schmitz, with whom he remained for about three years when his health failed him and he went on a hunting and trapping expedition down the river, going as far as Burlington, Iowa A year was thus passed, and the out-door exercise proved very beneficial, he entirely recovering his health After his return to Winona, he joined his brother, P J Schmitz in the manufacture of horse collars, which they sold at wholesale The partnership continued for a year, when Joseph bought out his brother's interest and was alone in business for two years. The old partnership was then resumed for a short time, but afterward he was again sole proprietor, until he admitted to the business H W. Cooper, under the firm name of Schmitz & Cooper, which partnership continued for five years. He then bought out Mr Cooper, and during the succeeding year was again alone in business In 1882 he added a stock of saddlery hardware, and continued to sell to the wholesale trade under his own name having no partner until 1890, when his nephew, Henry H Schmitz was admitted to the business, under the firm name of Joseph P. Schmitz & Co. To the experience, judgment and sagacity of the older man are added the enterprise and progressive ideas of the younger, and the firm is therefore a strong one, which has the confidence of the community and is enjoying a liberal patronage

In November, 1872, Mr Schmitz was united in marriage with Miss Annie Wood, a native of England, and a daughter of James and Betsy Wood Her father was superintendent in a cotton-cloth factory in his native land until about middle life, when he bade adieu to home and friends, and with his family sailed for America For five years he engaged in farming in eastern Wisconsin, and then removed to Kilbourn City, Wis, where he made his home during the succeeding eight years His last days were passed near Mauston, Wis, where he died at an advanced age To Mr and Mrs Schmitz have been born two daughters Mabel V and Lillie Maud

In his political views Mr. Schmitz has been a Republican since attaining his majority He belongs to Winona Lodge No 18, M W. A but takes no very prominent part in civic societies In 1893 he completed on East Wabasha Street one of the most handsome residences in the city, and in that beautiful home now lives with his wife and daughters. He is one of the successful manufacturers of the city, and through good management and diligence has gained prosperity.

John Valentine.

JOHN VALENTINE, one of the representative farmers and pioneers, now living on section 3, Rolling Stone Township, comes from the Emerald Isle. His parents were John and Charlotte (Jones) Valentine The father was born in Dublin, Ireland, and was a tanner by trade. In 1819, accompanied by his wife and five children, he crossed the Atlantic to the New World, and made settlement in New Orleans Subsequently he went up the river to Burlington, Iowa, where he engaged in the tanning business until the spring of 1855, when he came to Minnesota and made a claim, securing as his land the site of the present village of Rolling Stone After a year, however, he sold out and purchased a farm in Mt Vernon Township, where his remaining days were passed Previous to this time he had never carried on agricultural pursuits but he was industrious and enterprising, profited by the experience of others, gained a knowledge of the occupation as he could, and in course of time found himself the owner of a very valuable farm, comprising three hundred acres of rich land His death occurred on the old homestead at the age of seventy-two His wife, who is also a native of Dublin, yet resides at the old home, at the age of seventy-six years

This worthy couple were the parents of six children Margaret, the eldest, is the wife of P Preston, a farmer residing in Winona County; Charlotta is the wife of Peter Giddinger, who is located in Worth County Iowa, William is the next younger, and is now an attorney-at-law of Winona, one sister has passed away and another child died in infan

John Valentine also claims Dublin as the place of his birth, and the date of that important event is October 20, 1844 He was a child of only five summers when his parents bade adieu to the Emerald Isle and sailed for America At the age of eleven he became a resident of Winona County, where he has since made his home He was reared amid the wild scenes of the frontier, for this was then a pioneer settlement, and soon became familiar with the arduous task of developing a farm To his father he gave the benefit of his services until about thirty years of age He received a good common-school education and has kept himself well informed on the issues and subjects of the day by extensive reading

On the 13th of November, 1875, Mr. Valentine was joined in wedlock with Miss Catherine O'Conner, who was born in Ireland, and when a young girl came to the United States. Four children graced this union but only two are now living John Edward, at home; and Eugene, who was born July 21, 1884 Walter died at the age of two years, and Herbert died in infancy

Mr and Mrs Valentine began their domestic life upon the farm which is yet their home He has long been numbered among the most progressive agriculturists of the community, and is now the owner of more than one thousand acres of land in Winona County The home place comprises three hundred acres, and is a most valuable and desirable property The fields are well tilled, excellent improvements have been made, and the place is supplied with all the accessories and conveniences

century. Mr.

Valentine carries on general farming and stock-raising, and also deals in grain in Rolling Stone

With Oak Grove Lodge No 15, Order of Druids, of Winona, Mr Valentine holds membership In politics he is a Democrat, and the principles of the party receive his stalwart support For many years he has served as Chairman of the Board of Supervisors of his township, a position which he yet fills, and at this writing he is also serving as School Treasurer He is a diligent man, possessed of good business and executive ability, and his well directed efforts have brought him a success which is richly deserved. His life demonstrates what can be accomplished by perseverance and good management, and furnishes an example well worthy of emulation

Philip Biesanz.

PHILIP BIESANZ, one of the representative citizens of Winona Township, living on section 30, is the owner of a brickyard and quarry. He was born in Buffalo N. Y, on the 8th of July, 1842, and is one of a family of eight children, and is of French descent His parents, John and Mary (Leberel) Biesanz, were both natives of France When a young man of twenty-two, the father bade adieu to the friends and home of his childhood and crossed the ocean to the New World He settled first in Buffalo N Y, where he embarked in the manufacture of brick which he successfully carried on for the long period of thirty years He then moved to the West, going to Dubuque, Iowa, in the vicinity of that city purchasing a farm, on which he spent his remaining days He died at the advanced age of eighty-two years and many friends mourned his loss, for he was a highly respected citizen His wife passed away at the age of fifty-two

Quietly were the boyhood days of Mr. Biesanz passed His time was taken up by play and work, and by study in the common schools, where he acquired a fair English education In his father's brickyard he als [illegible] now devotes much of his time and attention He remained at home until twenty-two years of age, when, in September, 1864, he enlisted in his country's service, and was assigned to Company C of the Fifth Iowa Cavalry, in which he served until the close of the war He participated in the battle of Nashville, and went across the country with his command When hostilities had ceased, the South having laid down its arms, he received an honorable discharge from the service, and returned to his home

Soon after, Mr. Biesanz came to Winona, and for seven years worked by the month in different brick-yards He had become familiar with the business while at home, and as he was an expert workman, his services were always in demand At length he bought out his employer and has since engaged in business in his own interest He has a large kiln, and turns out about two million brick per year, which, being of a superior quality, finds a ready sale in the market He also has a large stone-quarry, one of the best in the county, and carries on a stoneyard in the city of Winona

In December, 1869 Mr Biesanz married Miss [illegible] ght children graced their union, but Samuel, the second, died at the age of twelve years. The others, who are Lizzie, Charles, Frank, Frederick, Leona, William and Flossie, are all yet at home. The family is widely and favorably known in this community, and the household is noted for its hospitality.

Mr. Biesanz exercises his right of franchise in support of the Republican party, and firmly believes that its principles will produce the best results for the nation. He has been honored by his fellow-townsmen with several local offices, having served as Supervisor of his township for two terms, and as Town Treasurer for two terms. Socially he is connected with the Ancient Order of United Workmen, and with the Order of Druids of Winona, and in religious belief is a Catholic. He now owns two hundred and six acres of land, and is doing a good business, which has made him one of the substantial citizens of the community. He started out in life for himself, working by the month, and thus labored until by industry, economy and perseverance he had acquired a sufficient capital to begin an enterprise of his own. He has trusted not to good fortune, but has made the most of his opportunities, and by determined effort has overcome the difficulties and obstacles in his path. Thus has he become one of the representative business men of the community.

HON. JOHN LUDWIG.

Hon. John Ludwig.

HON. JOHN LUDWIG, who is prominently connected with the business interests of Winona, is now President of the German American Bank. He has been connected with other enterprises in the city, and has thereby aided in the growth and development of Winona and in promoting its material prosperity. The record of his life is as follows: He was born in Canach, Luxemburg, Germany, on the 25th of September, 1839, and is a son of Martin and Mary (Holbach) Ludwig, both of whom spent their entire lives in that country. The father, who was an architect and contractor, did a good business and was recognized as one of the leading citizens in the community in which he made his home. He visited America four times, but never made a permanent settlement in the New World, and died in his native land at the age of sixty-seven.

John Ludwig first came to this country in 1856, being then a young man of sixteen years. He had acquired a good education in his native land, and after starting out in life [illegible] try his fortune in America, having heard much of the advantages and privileges here afforded. He made a location in Fond du Lac, Wis., where he was engaged in merchandising until the breaking out of the war. He had studied with interest the question which brought on the struggle, the attitude of both the North and South, and believed the President's policy was the only safe one for the preservation of the Union. Prompted by patriotic impulses he responded to the call for troops and enlisted in Company C, of the Ninth Wisconsin Infantry. While in Milwaukee he was appointed Corporal, and after serving for three years he re-enlisted as Orderly-Sergeant. His meritorious conduct won him further promotion, and in May, 1865, he was commissioned Second Lieutenant. He was always faithful to his duty, and for more than four years followed the Old Flag, which now floats triumphantly over the united nation. He was mustered out at Little Rock, Ark., on the 30th of January, 1866, having made an army record of

On his return to the North Mr Ludwig settled in Chicago, where he engaged in the hotel business for nearly two years In 1867 he came to Winona and embarked in the hotel business as proprietor of the old Winona House. Later he built the fine building on Third Street, known as Ludwig's Hotel, and for many years there carried on operations, doing a large business, which netted him a good income. Earnestly desiring to please his customers, he supplied his hotel with all possible conveniences, and the hostelry was therefore popular

Ere coming to Winona Mr Ludwig was married, having in 1865 wedded Miss Anna Siegfried, of Chicago They have a family of seven children Elizabeth, who is a fine musician and a member of the Chicago Lady Quintette, Charles M, now a student in Rush Medical College; Ida, who was graduated from the high school in the Class of '94; Mamie, a graduate of St. Mary's College, Winona, who was graduated from a business college, Emma and Otto.

In his political views Mr Ludwig is a Democrat of the most pronounced type In 1877 he was elected City Treasurer, and held the office for three terms For four terms he served as Mayor of the city, and during his administration many excellent and needed improvements were made The city water works were built, the roads were greatly improved, the electric-light plant established, also the street railway, all being in the possession of the city No administration has proved of more substantial benefit than that of Mr Ludwig, and he has received many mementos and testimonials from the people of Winona, showing their appreciation of his earnest efforts in behalf of public improvement and general advancement In 1888 he was a delegate-at-large to the Democratic Convention in St Louis, and was a member of the committee appointed to notify Grover Cleveland of his nomination for the Presidency In 1886 Mr Ludwig was a candidate for State Treasurer, and reduced the Republican majority of forty-five thousand fully one-half In 1894 he was a candidate for Lieutenant-Governor.

In 1892 Mr. Ludwig established the German-American Bank, which at that time was the only German bank in southern Minnesota He was elected its President and still serves in that capacity It is to-day one of the leading financial institutions of Winona, and is a monument to the ability and enterprise of Mr. Ludwig, who is well known as one of the able and enterprising business men of this state. At the Luxemburger Congress held in Chicago in the fall of 1893, he was elected President of the association, which numbers its members by the thousands, all over the United States and Canada, and in 1894 was re-elected to the same office The sagacity and foresight which have characterized Mr. Ludwig's business career and been important factors in his success led him to come to America, and the wisdom of his choice of a home has been made manifest by the prosperity that has crowned his efforts

John Wunder.

JOHN WUNDER is proprietor of a fine greenhouse, situated at the corner of Kansas and Fifth Streets in Winona There he has three and a-half lots, and has eight thousand feet of ground under glass He raises all kinds of flowers, but ... potted plants The place is tastefully and conveniently arranged, and with an eye to the beautiful, the colors being harmoniously blended, while the entire appearance of the place tells of an owner who thoroughly understands his business The ... e year 1866, in small quarters, 12x18 feet, but the facilities have been constantly increased to meet the growing demand, and the quarters are now extensive

Mr Wunder is a native of Holstein, Germany, born on the 1st of November 1832 His childhood and youth were passed in the Fatherland, where he acquired a common-school education, and also learned the florist's trade He has always been fond of flowers, and is an adept in naming different varieties and species, his own conservatories being filled with many different kinds In the year 1851, when nineteen years of age, he bade adieu to the home and friends of his childhood and sailed for the New World His father located in Davenport, Iowa, and he there made his home until 1855, when he came to Winona Here he turned his attention to gardening for some time, growing vegetables near Sugar Loaf, and shipping them to neighboring markets until 1866 He still owns the land on which he carried on this work When he abandoned gardening, he opened his greenhouse, and has since carried on operations along that line

In 1879 Mr Wunder was united in marriage with Miss Elizabeth Veith a native of Hesse, Germany, who came to this country a short time before her marriage In 1891 he was called upon to mourn her loss She had been in delicate health for some months before her death, but her last illness was of only eight days' duration Since the demise of Mrs Wunder, Miss Hettie Rohweder has acted as house-keeper for her uncle, the subject of this sketch

Mr. Wunder votes with the Republican party, which he has supported since his arrival in this country. He belongs to only one civic society, holding membership with Oak Grove Lodge No 15, A O D Mr Wunder has made the study of plants a science and is an expert florist He has not only a large trade in Winona, but also receives many orders from surrounding towns He has a greenhouse complete in all appointments, heated by hot water, and is prepared to meet all demands

Mrs. Mary E. Waterman.

MRS MARY E WATERMAN an estimable lady, who resides in Rolling Stone Township, claims New York as the state of her nativity, her birth having occurred in Otsego County, of the Empire State, on the 28th of October, 1828 She was the ninth child in the family of Barnabus S and Polly (Chase) Fuller, and is the only surviving one Her father was born in New York, and spent his entire life as a farmer near Albany, where his death occurred in his forty-seventh year. He had inherited quite a large estate from his father and was a well-to-do man His ancestors were descendants of Sir Samuel Fuller who came to this country in the "Mayflower" Mrs Fuller was born in Massachusetts, and was a daughter of Josiah and Sarah Chase The Chase family also dates its origin in America back to the landing of the "Mayflower," when William Chase, one of the Puritan fathers, crossed the briny deep to seek a home in the New World His descendants are without doubt the rightful heirs to the Chase and Townley estate The Chase family belonged to the nobility of England

The lady of whom we write acquired her education in her native state, and was reared in her New York home, remaining with her parents until her marriage On the 1st of November 1851, she became the wife of Harrison B Waterman, and in the spring of 1852 they removed to the West, locating upon a claim in Winona County, Minn, where she has since resided To them were born nine children George B was born January 5, 1851 and died August 26, 1881 Clara E, who was born September 11, 1855, died November 17 1886 She was a highly educated lady, and for a number of years was a successful teacher in the Winona High School Clarence Chase, born March 28, 1859, now manages the home farm Amy E born October 2, 1862 died August 17, 1861 Bon, born August 6, 1861, is still living on the home farm Lillie and Rose twins, were born April 3, 1867 Rose died September 10, 1877, and Lillie October 15, 1889 M Edward born March 8, 1869, was married, March 28, 1893, to Clara Milton, and they have one child, George B Harry born October 12, 1871, died March 22, 1873 The children were all born on the homestead farm

In 1882 Mr. and Mrs. Waterman were legally separated and the former is now living a retired life in this county When a young man he was admitted to the Bar, and in an early day was quite prominent After coming to the West he was the first Postmaster of Minnesota City Mrs Waterman, with her three sons, is now living on her good farm, eight miles from the city of Winona, and in the community where she has so long made her home she has a wide acquaintance and many friends who hold her in high regard

---

Rt.-Rev. Joseph B. Cotter, D. D.

RT.-REV JOSEPH B COTTER, D D., is one of the prominent members of the Catholic hierarchy, being now at the head of the Diocese of Winona He was born in England, on the 19th of November 1841, to Laurence P and Ann M. (Perrin) Cotter

Bishop Cotter was about four years of age when he came to the United States, and a youth of nearly eleven years when the family removed to St. Paul. He attended the cathedral parochial school of that city, and later became a student of St Francis' Seminary of Milwaukee Subsequently he entered St Vincent's College of Westmoreland, Pa, where he pursued his studies three years, and then took a three-years course in St John's University of M

Our subject was ordained in St Paul, on the 21st of May, 1871 On the 9th of June following he assumed the pastorate of St Thomas' Catholic Church in Winona, and its mission churches in Winona County His zeal in the work of the ministry, and his marked public spirit, urged his advancement in the year 1877 to the deanship of the Winona district of the Diocese of St Paul, and on the erection of the new diocese comprising the counties of Winona, Wabasha, Houston, Olmsted, Fillmore Dodge Mower Steele, Waseca, Freeborn, Blue Earth, Faribault, Watonwan, Martin, Cottonwood Jackson Murray, Nobles, Pipestone and Rock, he was elected bishop of the diocese His consecration, with that of Rt.- ... of Duluth and

John Shanley, D. D., of Jamestown, N. Dak., was received in the cathedral church of St. Paul, Minn., December 27, 1889, at the hands of the distinguished patriot prelate, Archbishop John Ireland.

Bishop Cotter has under his charge fifty-one priests, ninety-one churches (forty-eight churches with resident pastors and forty-three mission churches), three academies, one hospital, one orphan asylum, one industrial school, a school for Indian girls, and eighteen parochial schools. Since the establishment of the diocese twelve new churches have been erected in his territory, two destroyed by fire have been rebuilt, and several are in process of erection. The founding of the Winona Seminary for young ladies, under the direction of the Franciscan Sisters, marks an auspicious era in the educational work of his administration.

Bishop Cotter is broad minded, devoted to America and her institutions, and ever works for the best interests of the community in which he resides. It is said that no one has done more for the cause of temperance in Winona, and in other interests calculated to elevate humanity he has labored in the same faithful and untiring way. The high esteem and regard in which he is held by all classes of the community have been well earned.

Michael Morgan.

MICHAEL MORGAN, who for many years was extensively engaged in contracting in Winona, is now living a retired life at his pleasant home at No. 126 Winona Street, enjoying the rest which he has truly earned and richly deserves. His birth occurred in County Mayo, Ireland, on the 25th of September, 1823, and in his native land spent the days of his boyhood and youth, there remaining until twenty-three years of age, when he removed to England. Settling in Wolverhampton, he worked at the mason's trade, which he had learned on the Emerald Isle, and while there he was united in marriage, at the age of twenty-seven, with Miss Mary Welch, also a native of County Mayo, Ireland.

Hearing of the advantages afforded in the New World, and hoping to benefit his financial condition, Mr. Morgan emigrated to the United States in 1852. He worked at the mason's trade in New York, where he lived for four years, and in 1856 came to Winona at the solicitation of an old friend, Stephen Mead, who had emigrated hither in 1855. He was the father of Egbert Mead, and here spent the remainder of his days. Mr. Morgan had worked for Mr. Mead in the Empire State. On his arrival in Minnesota Mr. Morgan sought employment as a mason, and as he was an efficient workman his labors were always in demand. He was employed by various contractors in brick and stone work, including the firm of Jones & Butler, the leading contractors of Winona. Mr. Butler is still living in this city.

Mr. Morgan has been engaged in the construction of nearly all of the leading buildings of this place, evidences of his handiwork being seen on all sides. About twenty years since he began contracting in connection with Thomas Hunt, under the firm name of Morgan & Hunt. They made a specialty of constructing stone basements for barns, and had a very extensive trade, their patronage steadily increasing from the beginning. Mr. Morgan continued business until about 1889, since which time he has lived retired.

To the subject of this sketch and his worthy wife were born ten children: John, who is now living in St. Charles; Sylvester, a resident of Winona; Delia, wife of John E. Thibeau, who is living in Winona; William, who makes his home in this city; Mary, wife of John Pheeney, of Des Moines, Iowa; Sarah, wife of Morris O'Heirin, of Winona; Thomas, who died September 3, 1886, at the age of nineteen years; Maggie, wife of T. J. Cleary; and James, who completes the family, and is still under the parental roof.

Mr. Morgan affiliates with the Democratic party, having supported its principles since becoming an American citizen. He has, however, never sought office, preferring to give his entire time and attention to his business interests. He has prospered in his undertakings, and although he began life here as a laborer he has not only built wisely and well in a literal sense, but also in a figurative sense, gaining for himself a comfortable competence, which now enables him to live retired. He has been industrious and enterprising, and his success is well merited.

George B. Mallery.

GEORGE B. MALLERY has the honor of being a native of Winona. He was born in this city on the 9th of May, 1860, and is the elder of two children, his brother being Fred A., who was born in 1862, and is now a railroad man in the employ of the Winona & St. Peter Railroad Company. The parents were Joel and Matilda (Brisco) Mallery. The father was born in Delhi, Delaware County, N. Y., March 2, 1830, and was one of the five children of Peter L. and Anna (Baldwin) Mallery, both of whom were natives of the Empire State. When Joel was a child of three years they removed to Chemung County, settling in Savannah, where Mr. Mallery engaged in the lumber business, and also carried on farming for about seven years. He then embarked in boat-building, and was engaged in the construction of canal-boats for some fifteen years, after which he emigrated westward. Attracted by the advanta

Winona in 1856, and embarked in the teaming business between La Crosse and Winona before the extension of the railroad, and later in the manufacture of lumber. His death occurred in 1880, at the age of seventy-two years.

Joel Mallery came to Winona ere his father's arrival, reaching this city on the 30th of June, 1855. Here he has made his home continuously since, and among its early settlers he well deserves mention. He is an engineer, and for many years followed railroading. For several years he had charge of a locomotive on the North-Western Road, but since 1890 has lived retired. He is now well advanced in years, and deserves the rest which he is enjoying. In early days he was a supporter of the old Whig party. His wife was born in Chemung County, N. Y., and is a daughter of Nathan Brisco.

In his father's home George B. Mallery was

tarted out in life

for himself He first engaged in the grocery business in connection with O H Griswold, and for nine years successfully carried on operations along that line From the beginning his trade constantly increased, and the venture proved a very profitable one, but in February, 1892 Mr Mallery sold out his interest in the grocery and embarked in the livery business, buying out F E Clark He now has a stable of twenty-two horses, including several very fine animals His barn is equipped with the latest styles of turnouts and he does a large general livery business He also has a funeral line Earnestly desiring to please his patrons, he has built up a good trade, and his well directed efforts have brought him the prosperity which he so richly deserves

Mr Mallery takes considerable interest in civic societies He belongs to the Odd Fellows' society, holding membership with Prairie Lodge No 7, and Fidelity Encampment No 26, in which he has filled all the offices, and is also a member of the Grand Lodge and Grand Encampment He is a worthy member of Winona Lodge No. 21, K. of P., in which he has served as Vice-Chancellor, and in his political views he is a Republican having been unswerving in his allegiance to that party since attaining his majority.

William Noonan.

WILLIAM NOONAN, a contractor and builder of Winona, is a native of Canada, born April 11, 1839. His parents, James and Jane (Rudsel) Noonan, had a family of eleven children The father was a farmer by occupation, and followed that business throughout his entire life He was born in 1792, and died in 1871, at the age of seventy-nine years His wife passed away the following year, at the age of sixty-seven

No event of special importance occurred during the childhood and youth of our subject, who spent his early life in his native province, there remaining until twenty-four years of age, during which time he learned the carpenter's trade. He then came to the United States, with the intention of making a home in the Mississippi Valley, however, he went first to Buffalo and thence to Detroit, Mich, spending some time in those cities In 1861 he removed to Chicago, where he remained for two years, working at the carpenter's trade. In 1866 he came to Minnesota, locating in Winona, where he has made his home continuously since, with the exception of two years passed in Wisconsin For the first eight years after his arrival he worked at his trade in the employ of others, and then began contracting and building on his own account, receiving patronage within a radius of five hundred miles He has been connected with the construction of many of the leading buildings of the city, including fine business blocks, residences, elevators, mills and churches, and has done much work both in Minnesota and Wisconsin In 1888 and in 1890 he went to West Superior, where he erected buildings, the aggregate cost of which was about $1,000,000 By close study, earnest effort to please his customers, and an uncommon insight into the underlying principles, Mr. Noonan has deservedly gained an enviable reputation as a contractor and builder

In 1862 was celebrated the marriage of the gentleman whose name heads this sketch and Miss Eliza Fortune, also a native of Canada, and a daughter of James Fortune They have a family of five children, four sons and a daughter, David J, William, Mary Agnes, Albert and George H, all of whom reside in this city.

Mr Noonan keeps well informed on the issues of the day, votes with the Democratic party, and has taken quite an active interest in local politics In 1877 he was appointed to fill an unexpired term as Alderman of the First Ward, in 1878 was elected to that office, and in 1880 was re-elected, serving in all for five years in a most creditable manner His popularity as a broad-gauged man and the confidence reposed in him are indicated by the fact that in a Republican ward he was elected by a majority of one hundred and seventy. He has ever been actively interested in the growth and development of the city, and is a public-spirited and progressive man In his business dealings he is ever straightforward, taking no undue advantages, and the faithfulness with which he lives up to his part of a contract has won him an enviable reputation and gained him a large trade

---

William A. Chamberlin, M. D.

WILLIAM A CHAMBERLIN, M D, who is engaged in the practice of medicine in St. Charles is a native of the Green Mountain State, his birth having occurred in Putney, Windham County, on the 30th of November, 1852. His parents, William M and Nancy Sophia (Kelley) Chamberlin, were also natives of Vermont The grandfather was Cyrus Chamberlin, and the great-grandfather was one of the heroes who aided the Colonies in their struggle for independence They came from an old Colonial family, which in pioneer days was founded in the Green Mountain State The father was a civil engineer and machinist, and his entire life was passed in the East

The Doctor spent his boyhood days upon his father's farm, there remaining until seventeen years of age, when he became a student in Powers' Institute, of B Vt. years course he was prepared to enter college It was his intention to enter Dartmouth College, but his health failed him and he had to abandon that hope. He completed the academical course in 1875, when twenty-two years of age. By teaching and in other ways he had earned the money necessary to pay his tuition, and therefore may truly be called a self-educated as well as self-made man In the summer of 1875 he visited California on a pleasure trip, and the following winter again taught school, in West Brattleboro Vt, where he had lived from the age of five years

In 1876 Dr Chamberlin visited near Corry, Pa, where he engaged in teaching for a year. In the mean time he read medicine with Dr Wright, of Columbus, Pa, and Dr Whitney, of Lottsville, Pa Returning to the Empire State in 1877, he spent the summer season upon the farm, and in the artment of the

University of Michigan at Ann Arbor, which he also attended in 1878-79 taking a complete regular course, although he did not graduate. In July, 1879, he came to St. Charles but he had no particular point in view for a location. He wished, however, to live in Minnesota on account of the climate. He visited Dr. Guthrie, asking for the privilege of reading with that physician, who, however, on seeing his credentials, advised him to engage in practice, as there was no state law to prevent it. He had assisted other physicians and in December, 1879, became Dr. Guthrie's partner. This partnership was continued until the fall of 1881, when Dr. Guthrie removed to California and Dr. Chamberlin entered Rush Medical College of Chicago, from which he was graduated in February, 1882, with the degree of M. D. Returning to St. Charles, he soon won a liberal patronage, and has remained here almost continuously since. In the year 1883 he purchased a drug store, which he carried on until 1891, when he sold out with the intention of going to the South to locate permanently, but after a time he returned to St. Charles, and is now numbered among its leading physicians. He has attended special lectures at Ann Arbor and Rush Colleges on the subject of surgery and clinical work, is a member of the American Medical Association, and in 1893 attended its annual meeting which convened in Milwaukee. He belongs to the Minnesota State Medical Society, before which he read an article on obstetrics, and also holds membership with the Southern Minnesota Medical Society, and the societies of both Winona and Olmsted Counties.

In March, 1882, Dr. Chamberlin married Miss Etta Warner, daughter of J. R. Warner, formerly of St. Charles, but now of Hamline, Minn. The lady was born in Winona County, and was a teacher of music before her marriage. They had one son, William, who died at the age of twenty-two months. Dr. Chamberlin is a member of the Methodist Episcopal Church, takes an active interest in its work, and is a leader in the musical department of the church.

In his political views the Doctor is a Republican. He was elected Mayor of St. Charles in 1890, and was filling that office at the time of the construction of the Winona & South-Western Railroad, in which the city assisted by giving $12,500 in bonds, and also by giving the right of way. The Doctor also served as a member of the School Board.

David Whetstone.

DAVID WHETSTONE, a farmer of Rolling Stone Township, residing on section 12, is numbered among the early settlers of Winona County, dating his residence here from 1855. On his arrival here he found the county but sparsely settled. Its leading cities were then small villages, or had not yet sprung into existence and the greater part of the land was wild and unimproved. He has watched with interest its progress and advancement, and in the work of development has ever borne his part. To the early settlers is due much of the credit of making the county what it is to-day, for they laid the foundation upon which its present prosperity has been built. Among those deserving of prominent mention is Mr. Whetstone.

This gentleman was born near Cincinnati, Ohio, July 7, 1821, and was the fifth in order of birth in a family of eight children, whose parents were John and Susan (Ramer) Whetstone The father was a native of North Carolina, and spent the days of his boyhood and youth upon a farm in that state. When a young man he left his childhood's home and removed to Ohio, where he remained for several years He then became a resident of Ripley County, Ind., where he remained until his death, which occurred at the age of sixty-five His father was one of the heroes of the Revolutionary War and was of German extraction The mother of David Whetstone was also born in North Carolina, and her death occurred at the advanced age of ninety years Her parents were natives of the same state, and her father aided the Colonists in the struggle which made this an independent nation Her father lived to the advanced age of one hundred and seven years, and obtained the prize given the oldest man in Indiana.

Mr Whetstone, whose name appears at the beginning of this record, acquired his education in the common schools, which he attended through the winter season During the summer he worked upon a farm, aiding in the planting and harvesting of crops, and in such other duties as fall to the lot of the agriculturist When he was twenty-three years of age, his father gave him forty acres of land, and he began farming on his own account. He cultivated that tract until 1855, when he sold out and came to Minnesota locating on a farm in Winona County, near Lewiston The land which he purchased was a tract of raw prairie, on which not a furrow had been turned or an improvement made, but he at once began its development, and in course of time, waving fields of grain were seen in the place of the barren prairie. That farm continued to be his home until 1882, when he purchased one hundred and sixty acres of land where he now resides To this he has added ninety-two acres, having in all two hundred and sixty acres

On the 4th of October, 1844, Mr Whetstone married Nancy Parker, who was born in Dearborn County, Ind, on the 3d of March, 1825 She is a daughter of Henry and Katie (Ramer) Parker, the former of whom is of German and Irish extraction To Mr and Mrs David Whetstone were born thirteen children, but four of the number died in early life George, the eldest is now a farmer in Rolling Stone Township, Jane is the wife of Jonathan Lewis, a resident of Lewiston, Minn, Mary is the wife of George Ingram of Winona County, Daniel is an agriculturist of Rolling Stone Township, Susanna is the wife of James Sweazey, of Winona, David follows farming in this county; Silas devotes his energies to the same occupation; Lydia is the wife of Frank Kennedy, of Winona, and John is engaged in gardening in this county.

Mr Whetstone is an Elder in and has charge of the congregation of the German Baptist Church that is built on his farm near Lewiston For forty-five years he has been one of its members, and during nearly this entire period has been engaged in preaching, giving his services to the cause without charge or compensation of any kind. His life has been in harmony with his professions, and his career has ever been a straightforward and honorable one

To George Whetstone, son of the subject of this sketch, and his wife have been born seven children, all of whom are now living Nancy, David and Charles (twins), May, Lawrence, John and Esther, all residing at home Mr. Whetstone has recently sold the place on section 12, and will remove in the spring of 1895 to a new home four miles south of Utica in this county

Nathan Medberry Cross.

NATHAN MEDBERRY CROSS is a farmer and stock-raiser of Saratoga Township, residing on section 27, and is a citizen who has been true to public duty and to private trust. He was born in Chautauqua County, N. Y., near the town of Nashville, November 9, 1835, and is a son of Joel Cross. The father was born in Milford, N. Y., July 21, 1800, and was a son of Jerris Cross, who came of an old English family. The mother of our subject bore the maiden name of Julia A. Medberry, and was born in the Empire State, on the 4th of May, 1812. Her parents were Joseph and Mehitable (Jackson) Medberry. In the Cross family were four children, namely: Jonas J., Agnes, who died in 1876, Nathan M., of this sketch, and Julia, wife of Stephen Irons, a native of Pennsylvania. The father of this family having passed away, the mother afterward married James Ball, and to them were born five children, two of whom are yet living, Joseph D. and Jeptha.

The subject of this sketch was born and reared upon a farm. The first thirteen years of his life were spent in his native state, and he then went to McKean County, Pa., where he remained until he had attained his majority. When he had reached man's estate he started for the West, with the intention of trying his fortune upon its broad prairies, for he believed that superior advantages were afforded to those of the older states of the East. He went first

spent the winter and then crossed the Mississippi, going to Ottawa, Minn., where he pre-empted one hundred and sixty acres of Government land. He lived upon it long enough to establish his claim to the place, and made some improvements upon it during the next two years. He then returned to Pierce County, Wis., and in the spring of 1861 came to Winona County, where he worked out by the month, engaged in breaking prairie and in other farm labor. He was thus employed until 1864, when he removed to the farm on which he now resides, securing one hundred and sixty acres of land on section 27, Saratoga Township. Of this sixty acres had been broken, and with characteristic energy he at once began its further development.

On the 10th of April 1865, Mr. Cross enlisted as a private of Company I, First Minnesota Infantry, and was mustered into service at Ft. Snelling, from where he was sent to Washington, and thence to Virginia, where he was engaged in doing guard duty until after the close of the war. On the 28th of July, 1865, he received an honorable discharge and returned to his home.

On the 7th of April, 1866, Mr. Cross was united in marriage with Miss Annie Lane, and to them were born the following children: Newton, who died in 1881, Willie, who is engaged in clerking

ome; Burton,

who died at the age of two and a-half years and Merton. The mother of this family was called to the home beyond on the 8th of September, 1888. Mr. Cross was married, December 27, 1891, to Mrs. Dent, widow of John B. Dent. She bore the maiden name of Nellie Hyatt, and by her first marriage she had four children, namely: Frank B., who carries on farming in Wisconsin; William H., who is also living in the Badger State; and Ethel and Archie J., who are still with their mother.

Mr. Cross advocated the principles of the Republican party for several years, but now supports the men and measures of the Populist party. He has long served as Township Treasurer, and for twenty-four years has held one or another local office, a fact which indicates faithful service and the confidence and trust reposed in him by his fellow-townsmen. His attention is now largely given to his farming interests, and he owns a valuable and desirable place, comprising three hundred and sixty acres of rich land, which yield to him a good income.

Jerod Brown.

JEROD BROWN, a farmer residing on section 7, Diesbach Township, claims New York as the state of his nativity. He was born in Clinton County on the 4th of March, 1830, and under the parental roof was reared to manhood, the days of his boyhood and youth being quietly passed. When he had arrived at man's estate he started out in life, and has since been dependent on his own resources, so that whatever success he has achieved is due entirely to his own efforts. His first work was in a sawmill, where he received $16 per month in compensation for his services. This mill was located on the Hudson River, and he was there employed for about three years, after which he started westward, having determined to try his fortune on the broad prairies of the Mississippi Valley. He started in April, 1852, and on the 8th of May reached Bunnell's Landing. Soon after he came to Dakota, where he engaged in chopping wood and working on the railroad. He [illegible] he might earn an honest living until his marriage, when he turned his attention to farming.

On the 4th of November, 1855, Mr. Brown was united in marriage with Miss Harriet C. Mott, daughter of Annis Mott. They began their domestic life on section 4, New Hartford Township, where Mr. Brown had a farm of one hundred and sixty acres. There he made his home for thirty-five years, giving his time and attention to agricultural pursuits. He prospered in his undertakings, and his enterprise and industry were rewarded by a comfortable competence. He afterward removed to his present home, where he owns ten acres of land, which is devoted to the raising of berries. This is his only business, and it yields him an income sufficient for his present wants, and he has a snug sum laid by for a rainy day.

To Mr. and Mrs. Brown were born five children, three of whom are yet living: Ann Eliza, born January 10, 1857, died December 30, 1861; Olive [illegible] wife of Edward

F. Shippey, who resides on the old homestead farm in New Hartford Township; Leonard J., born October 21, 1862, lives on the farm with his sister; Vincent C., born March 21, 1866, makes his home in Appleton, Minn.; and Charles L., born March 26, 1873, died November 3, 1882.

Mr. Brown is numbered among the pioneer settlers of Winona County. On leaving his old home in the East he went by stage from Glens Falls to Fort Edward, and thence by rail to Buffalo, N. Y., where he took passage on a boat bound for Detroit, Mich. From that place he proceeded by rail to New Buffalo, Mich., and thence took a boat to Milwaukee, whence he proceeded to the end of the railroad, a distance of twenty-nine miles. Here he again took a stage and went across the country to Galena, Ill., and thence by boat continued on his way to Homer, Minn. Here he went through all the experiences and hardships of frontier life. His first home was a log cabin, which was later replaced by a good frame residence. He also built a good frame barn, cleared his land of the timber, and has transformed one hundred and sixty acres of raw prairie into one of the finest farms of the county.

Mark Willson.

MARK WILLSON is President of the Merchants' Bank of Winona, and one of the leading financiers of Winona County. His connection with the banking interests of this community has continued since 1868, and the institution of which he is now the head has become one of the solid financial concerns of the city. Mr. Willson is a native of Newmarket, Ontario, Canada, born February 27, 1820, and is the only son of John L. and Mary Willson. His parents removed to western Pennsylvania in 1821, locating at Sugar Grove, Warren County, where they spent their remaining days. The family there lived until 1863.

Mark Willson was reared in his father's home, and on entering upon a business career embarked in merchandising, which he followed in the Keystone State until 1863. He has also been prominently connected with political affairs, and has ever discharged his duties with a promptness and fidelity which have won for him the commendation of all concerned. On attaining his majority he was elected Justice of the Peace, which position he filled for the long period of twenty-five years. He also served as Postmaster and in other offices, and was ever true and faithful to the trust reposed in him. His loyalty to friends and to public trust is one of his chief characteristics.

In 1853 Mr. Willson was united in marriage with Miss Elizabeth Hallock, of New York City. Ten years later he severed his business connections in the East, and sought a home in Minnesota, going first to Hastings, where he had friends living. There he opened a mercantile establishment and carried on business for three years. During that time he served as Mayor of Hastings for one year.

In 1866 he brought his family to Winona, where they have since resided, being numbered among the prominent citizens of the community. Here Mr. Willson carried on a dry-goods store for two years, when, in 1868, he disposed of his business and became connected with banking interests. He took an active part in the organization of the Second National Bank, which began business April 29, 1871, with a capital stock of $100,000. He was elected a Director, and in October was made Assistant Cashier, which office he filled until January, 1873, when he was elected Vice-President. In January, 1875, he resigned that position and aided in the organization, on the 18th of May, of the Merchants' National Bank of Winona, of which he became President and also member of the Board of Directors. On the 1st of July, 1879, it was voted to change the organization from a national to a state bank, under the laws of Minnesota, and to transfer its entire business to the new organization. The Merchants' Bank of Winona sprang into existence in August, 1879, and Mr. Willson has since been its President. The success of the institution is largely due to his untiring efforts.

In his political views Mr. Willson is a stanch Republican, having supported the principles of his party since its organization. He is an exemplary and public-spirited man, in whom the best interests of the community find a friend. His success in business is owing to careful attention to all details, diligence and enterprise, and his prosperity is well deserved.

Edson Gates.

EDSON GATES, deceased, was born in Elizabethtown, Essex County, N. Y., March 28, 1831. His parents were Willis and Almira (Hulett) Gates, the former a native of New Hampshire, born October 11, 1793, and the latter a native of Hampton, N. Y., born December 10, 1806. They were married January 12, 1823, in Hampton, N. Y., at the home of her father, Mason Hulett. The latter married Hannah Kidder, a descendant of Oliver Kidder, who lived and died at Wethersfield Corners, Rutland County, Vt. Mason Hulett was born in Rhode Island and died in Hampton, N. Y.

Edson Gates was a descendant on his father's side of Am... settled in Stowe, Mass. His son, Isaac, Edson's grandfather, was born October 22, 1747, and was eighty-three years old when he died. His wife was Mary Wheeler. They had nine children, Willis Gates, Edson's father, being the youngest. He lived to the age of eighty years. Edson's parents immediately after their marriage removed to Elizabethtown, where his father owned quite a tract of timber-land, which necessitated building mills to prepare the lumber for market.

Our subject lived with his parents until he was twenty-six years old, with the exception of one year in Chazy, Clinton County, N. Y., where he took charge of a lady's farm. He came to Minne... ng in Stockton,

Winona County, where he had a sister living. He made this his home, taking trips around the country, finally buying eighty acres of land in Utica Township. In the winter of 1860 he went back to his native state and married Millie A. Braisted. They were married at her father's home, April 2, 1860, and immediately started for their western home. Edson found after arriving at his farm that there were for sale sixty acres across the road, which he immediately purchased, and proceeded to erect a comfortable house on this land. Here he resided until the spring of 1865, when he sold to John Stock. In company with several others he went to Missouri and purchased a farm of three hundred acres, but for various reasons decided not to live there, and finally sold the farm. In the fall of 1865 he moved to Winona and resided on the corner of Washington Street and Broadway for one and a-half years. He then erected a house on East Fifth Street, where he resided two years, after which he sold his home and bought on Johnson Street, where he lived until his death, April 12, 1891.

Mrs. Millie (Braisted) Gates was born in Bridport, Addison County, Vt., June 15, 1835. She was the eighth child in a family of eleven, and removed with her parents in her infancy to Essex County, N. Y., where she spent the most of her life until she was married. Her parents were William and Anna Braisted. Her grandfather, William Braisted, Sr., went to Bridport, Vt., from New Jersey when the country was quite new. His wife's name was Mary Little. The farm on which he resided has always been owned by William Braisted, a brother of Mrs. Gates, now residing there.

William Braisted was born October 11, 1795, and died May 21, 1875. Anna Russell, his wife, was born July 17, 1799, and died April 13, 1885. Her father, William Russell, was a native of Scotland. He was a farmer by occupation and somewhat of a musician. They lived and died in Addison County, Vt.

Edson and Millie Gates were the parents of three children: Minnie, born September 10, 1862, died at the age of fourteen days; Burton N., born November 21, 1863, died at the age of ten months; and William W., born August 22, 1866, died at the age of sixteen months. They adopted a child, the daughter of his youngest brother, who was drowned in Kansas. Jessie Maud Gates came to them at the age of one and a-half years and has ever been considered as one of the family.

Mr. Gates is remembered as a genial, social man, who was fond of doing charitable deeds in a quiet, unostentatious way, was a modest, unobtrusive, whole-souled man, and politically was a stanch advocate of Republican principles.

Franklin Laberee.

FRANKLIN LABERLE, deceased, was born in Whitefield, Me., on the 17th of November, 1828, and died in Winona on the 23d of July, 1893, respected by all who knew him. While in his native state he served an apprenticeship to a ship-carpenter and became an expert workman, gaining great proficiency. For twenty-eight years he was an employe of the North-Western Railway, doing carpenter work. His services were used for the fine interior finishing work on the palace cars until that branch of the business was transferred to Chicago, after which he was employed for the interior finishing of depots, etc.

During the late war Mr. Laberee responded to

the call for troops enlisting in Company F, Thirtieth Wisconsin Infantry, on the 11th of August, 1862 He served for three years and one month, and when the war was over was honorably discharged, on the 20th of September, 1865

Mr Laberee was married on the 4th of March, 1869, in Winona, to Mrs Sarah Jane Eastey, whose maiden name was Alden She is a native of Milo Yates County N Y, but was reared in Steuben County that state To them was born one son, Rolla I who is now in the employ of the Chicago & North-Western Railway Company

Mr Laberee was a trusted employe, and the confidence reposed in him was well deserved, for he was always faithful to the company and its best interests. His time and attention were almost entirely given to the work, which was in no way neglected He voted with the Democratic party, but was not actively interested in politics.

Very Truly

Marshall Bailey Webber.

MARSHALL BAILEY WEBBER is a worthy representative of the Bar of Winona County, and is successfully engaged in practice in the city of Winona. He was born in Raymond, Racine County, Wis., on the 2d of August, 1850, and is the son of Samuel and Sabra A. (Bailey) Webber. Their family numbered four children, three of whom are yet living. He is descended from the Puritan forefathers who founded the colony of Massachusetts. His grandfather, Loring Webber, was a native of the old Bay State, and was a Puritan Baptist of the strictest type. He was born February 16, 1791, and in 1837 emigrated to the territory of Wisconsin, where he secured from the Government a large tract of land, and engaged in farming, locating in Racine County, Raymond Township, at which place he died on the 1st of January, 1885, at the advanced age of ninety-four years. The grandmother on the father's side was Sarah Upham, who was born in Brimfield, Mass., January 18, 1791, and died March 21, 1886. The grandfather and grandmother on his mother's side were of New Hampshire stock, his grandfather being Jonathan Bailey, who was born in Weare, N. H., January 19, 1792, and was engaged in teaching and farming. His grandmother was Sarah Marshall, who was born in Deerfield, N. H., January 28, 1790. Jonathan Bailey and wife emigrated from New Hampshire to the state of Wisconsin in September, 1841, with a family of several children, including the mother of the subject of this sketch, who was then but a small girl. Jonathan Bailey died in Clifton, Pierce County, Wis., June 11, 1866, and his wife died in the same place, January 17, 1865. Sabra Amelia Bailey, mother of Marshall B., was born in Unity, Sullivan County, N. H., July 13, 1826, and was united in marriage with Samuel Webber October 2, 1842. Samuel Webber, the father of Marshall B., was born July 11, 1822, in Holland, Hampton County, in the state of Massachusetts, and for three years previous to his father's emigration to Wisconsin worked in the cotton factory at Sturbridge, Mass. On coming to the then territory of Wisconsin, he engaged in farming with his father, Loring Webber, upon a section of land upon which he now resides in Raymond, Racine County, Wis. He is now the oldest resident in that county, and has always been one of the public-spirited, leading and influential citizens of his county, throughout the community being held in the highest esteem by old and young, rich and poor alike.

Marshall B. Webber was reared amid the wild scenes of the frontier, and lived with his parents upon the home farm until eighteen years of age, assisting in the work of his father's farm. His early education was acquired in the common schools, which he attended during boyhood, subsequently entering the Racine High School. After leaving the latter, he continued his studies for a couple of years in the Rochester Academy, preparatory to his entering Hinsdale (Mich.) College, from which institution he was graduated with honor, carrying off the prize membership of his class, June 17, 1875. Thus he obtained an excellent literary education, which furnished the solid foundation on which to rest the knowledge he would gain along special lines.

September, 1875, witnessed the arrival of Mr. Webber in Winona, Minn. Here he began reading law in the office of Hon. W. H. Yale, and in the fall of 1877 was admitted to the Bar of Winona County, since which time he has been actively engaged in the practice of his profession. He first formed a partnership with Governor Yale, which continued for about three years, when he was elected Prosecuting State's Attorney, which position he filled for two years. On being elected Prosecuting Attorney, the partnership existing between himself and Governor Yale was dissolved, since which time he has been alone, devoting his energies entirely to his increasing legal business, and is now recognized as one of the leading attorneys of the state. He is attorney for the Chicago, Milwaukee & St. Paul Railroad Company, and also for the Chicago, Burlington & Northern, and has been extremely successful in the trial of cases, his ability, both natural and acquired, being such as to command the admiration of all, and justly winning for him a well earned reputation as a lawyer and citizen. On the 2d of January, 1879, Mr. Webber was united in marriage with Miss Agnes M. Robertson, daughter of John and Matilda (Goheen) Robertson, both of whom were natives of the state of New York. She is a most estimable and cultured lady, and, like her husband, holds an enviable positon in social circles. Where true worth and intelligence are received as passports into good society, Mr. and Mrs. Webber are always found.

In his political views Mr. Webder has always been a Republican and a firm protectionist, but is not what may be termed a politician. He is a member of the order of the Knights of Pythias, being one of the first members of Winona Lodge No. 21, in which lodge he has occupied all the chairs. He is an earnest and enterprising young man, devoted to the interests of the city and state, and his support and co-operation are withheld from nothing that tends to benefit the community.

John Staniels French.

JOHN STANIELS FRENCH, one of the self-made men of Winona County, who now carries on general farming and stock-raising on section 9 Saratoga Township is a native of the old Granite State. He was born and reared on a farm, his birth occurring on the 18th of February, 1826 His father, George French, was a native of New Hampshire and when he had arrived at years of maturity married Effie Baker. They became the parents of a family of seven children Lydia N and George, both deceased; Nathaniel B, who has also passed away, John S, of this sketch, Andrew J, David D, who makes his home in Humboldt, Iowa, where he does business as a mechanic, and Chauncey who is engaged in the painting business in Humboldt By occupation the father of this family was a farmer and carried on business along that line for many years. He served in the War of 1812, and died in New Hampshire, where both he and his wife spent their last days.

John S French acquired his education in the district schools, which he attended at intervals until sixteen years of age He then started out to make his own way through life, and his untiring labors and perseverance have been the factors which have brought him success He first worked as a farm hand by the month, receiving about $1 for his services He continued to make his home in the state of his nativity until about 1850, when he went to Massachusetts, there spending the two succeeding years of his life With the hope of benefiting his financial condition, he emigrated to the West in the fall of 1852, settling first in Illinois, where he was employed on the construction of the Illinois Central Railroad, laying tracks from La Salle to Bloomington When that task was completed he returned to his home

While in the East Mr. French was married to Miss Catherine A McGillis, the wedding being celebrated in May, 1854 They traveled life's journey together for almost forty years, and the lady was to her husband a faithful companion and helpmate, but on the 25th of January, 1893, she was called to the home beyond and her remains were interred in St Charles Cemetery Many friends mourned her loss, for she was widely known in this community Two children were born of this union George D married Miss D Williams, by whom he has a son, George Bayard, and their home is in St Charles Edward B now carries on the old homestead He wedded Mary Bell, and they have three children, Edith Lillian, Revettie May and one unnamed

Soon after his marriage John S. French started with his young wife for Minnesota, and took up his residence in Saratoga Township, Winona County, where on section 9 he entered from the Government one hundred and sixty acres of good land, paying the usual price of $1.25 per acre He built a log house and lived in true pioneer style, experiencing all the hardships and privations of frontier life Winona was the nearest trading-post and the county was but sparsely settled Mr French was industrious and enterprising, and in course of time had placed his once wild land under a high state of cultivation. He had also secured many improvements, which add to the value and attractive appearance of the place and indicate the progressive spirit of the owner. Farming and stock-raising have been to him a profitable business, and although he started out in life a poor boy, dependent entirely upon his own resources, he has steadily worked his way upward by good management, diligence and perseverance, and is now the possessor of a comfortable home and property. Since the organization of the Republican party he has supported its principles. He is a member of no church or society, is an independent thinker, true to his views, and is a citizen who manifests a commendable interest in everything pertaining to the welfare of the community.

Edgar A. Bradley.

EDGAR A. BRADLEY, a leading contractor and builder of Winona, who occupies a prominent position in business circles, claims New York as the state of his nativity, his birth having occurred in Madison County, on the 5th of December, 1848. His father, P. Bradley, came to Winona in the fall of 1866. He was engaged in dealing in cattle, and also took contracts for the construction of the Milwaukee & Green Bay Railroad. He was also interested in the erection of a number of public buildings, and took contracts for laying about five miles of water mains in this city. Here he continued to make his home until 1892, when he removed to Lake Park, Iowa, where he now resides.

Edgar A. Bradley spent the first eight years of his life in his native state, and then accompanied the family on their removal to Lake County, Ill. They settled near Waukegan, and in 1860, when he was twelve years of age, removed to Minnesota, locating on a farm in Fillmore County. At the age of eigh ... W ... and has since been connected with its business interests. He learned the carpenter's trade with John Keenan, and worked most of the time as a journeyman until thirty years of age, when he began business for himself as a contractor. Since 1880 his time has thus been passed, and in his undertaking he has met with success. He has not only erected a number of residences, but in connection with his father he also graded several miles of the Green Bay Railroad, and keeps an outfit for removing houses. This branch of his business yields to him a good income. He employs from seven to twelve men, and is now enjoying a constantly increasing trade.

On the 24th of November, 1875, Mr. Bradley was united in marriage with Mrs. Mary Moak, who bore the maiden name of Mary Grant. She is a native of Chicago, and came to Winona in 1854 with her parents, W. W. and Clarissa (Avery) Grant. Her father was a carpenter and contractor, and continued that line of business until his death. ... ected on Second

Street, between Main and Center Streets, one of the first hotels in the city, known as the Grant House, and was its landlord for several years. He aided in the erection of the old Huff House, and was recognized as one of the best contractors and builders in this locality. Mrs. Grant survived her husband for a number of years. Their son, Frank Grant, is now a carpenter of Winona. Their daughter Mary in early womanhood became the wife of Harry Monk, a conductor on the Winona & St. Peter Railroad. He died in Minneapolis, and his widow became the wife of Mr. Bradley, as before stated. The worthy couple have a beautiful home at No. 1120 West Broadway, which was erected in 1892. They hold an enviable position in social circles, and their household is noted for its hospitality. Mr. Bradley votes with the Republican party and warmly advocates its principles, but has never been a politician in the sense of office-seeking, preferring to give his entire time and attention to his business interests, in which he has met with good success. He has lived in Winona through all the days of his manhood, and those who have longest known him are among his best friends, a fact which indicates an honorable and well spent life.

L. G. Wilberton, M. D.

L. G. WILBERTON, M. D., one of the skillful physicians of southeastern Minnesota, is now successfully engaged in practice in Winona. A native of New York, he was born in Hornellsville, on the 18th of April, 1853, and is the only child of George and Martha (Merrill) Wilberton. His father was born in Albion, N. Y., about the year 1827, and completed his education in Albion University, from which he graduated at an early age. His entire life was spent in Hornellsville, N. Y., and he became a very successful merchant of that place, doing a good business. He was also one of the contractors on the early building of the Erie Railroad. He was an indefatigable worker, an energetic business man, and made a notable record for one so young. His death occurred at the early age of twenty-seven years, in the year 1854. His wife was born in Hornellsville, N. Y., and was a daughter of Andrew Merrill, a leading farmer of that vicinity. The paternal grandfather of the Doctor was a native of New York, born near Poughkeepsie. He was appointed land agent of the Government for that region, was a man of prominence in the community in which he lived, and was numbered among the honored pioneers of central New York. The leading part which he took in public affairs made him well known, and his sterling worth was recognized by many friends.

Dr. Wilberton was reared in the Empire State, and acquired his early education in the public schools of Rochester. After graduating from the high school of that city, he entered Cornell University, where he continued his studies for some time. On leaving school he became a teacher in the Lima Seminary at Lima, N. Y., where he remained for a year. He then determined to enter the medical profession and make its practice his life work. To this end he began reading medicine in the office of Dr. White of Rochester, N. Y., and subsequently entered the Hahnemann College of Philadelphia from which institution he was graduated in the Class of '80

Dr Wilberton at once came to Minnesota, located in Winona, and has since been continuously engaged in active practice at this place, with the exception of twenty months spent abroad August 29, 1891, he sailed for the Old World for the purpose of further perfecting himself in the science of medicine by study in the leading schools of Europe. He spent one year in Vienna studied for three months in Berlin, three months in London, several weeks in Paris, and returning in the spring of 1893 to his native land, at once resumed practice in Winona

On the 11th of September, 1882, Dr Wilberton was joined in wedlock with Miss Sarah Dow, daughter of James C Dow, a native of the state of Maine Mrs Wilberton is a graduate of Kent College in Maine, having taken the degrees of A B and A M Her brother, Prof James I Dow, is Superintendent of the Blind Asylum in Faribault, Minn The Doctor and his wife have two children, Laura and George

Dr Wilberton is a member of the American Institute of Homeopathy, and has been honored with an election to the vice-presidency of the Minnesota State Homeopathic Association, a position which he is now filling He is an earnest worker, well informed on everything connected with the science of medicine, and devoted to his profession He is recognized as one of the representative physicians of Minnesota, and has a reputation for skill and ability which places him among the best in the state

---

Samuel C. Dick.

SAMUEL C DICK, deceased, was for some years a well known and leading citizen of Winona County, and his widow, a most estimable lady, resides in Dakota Mr Dick was born in Steubenville, Ohio, on the 19th of April, 1816, and was a son of William and Jane (McClintock) Dick, the former a native of Ireland, and the latter of Scotland Crossing the Atlantic to America William Dick took up his residence in Ohio, where he followed the tailor's trade, and made his home until his death, which occurred in about the year 1819

Samuel C. Dick remained with his parents until seventeen years of age when he started out in life for himself, [illegible] Morefield, Ohio, where he served a three-years apprenticeship On the expiration of that period he joined a brother, and for some time thereafter was employed in Londonderry, Ohio, at blacksmithing The year 1818 witnessed his emigration westward He made his first location in Le Claire, Iowa, where he remained for three years, working at his trade. His next place of residence was in the section of Port Byron, Ill, where for two years he carried on a brickyard In the mean time he built two churches and several residences, doing business as a contractor

While in this place, Mr Dick renewed the acquaintance of a young lady whom he had formerly [illegible] M[illegible] Young, who was then visiting her sister in the section of Port Byron. Their friendship ripened into love, and on the 9th of May, 1850, they were married. The lady is a daughter of Hercules and Anne (Chandler) Young, both of whom were natives of Pennsylvania. In their family were eleven children: Mrs. Rachel Chandler, born in September, 1806, now deceased; Mrs. Sarah Stockton, who was born March 8, 1808, and is now living in Fulton County, Ill.; James, Dinah and Eli, all now deceased; Mrs. Ann Baker, of Illinois; Morgan, now a resident of Arkansas; John, who is deceased; Mrs. Hannah Craft, now living in Martin County, Minn.; Margaret Carroll, born in September, 1828, now living in Lansing, Iowa; and Mrs. Dick, who was born July 21, 1824.

To Mr. and Mrs. Dick were born ten children, eight of whom are yet living. Thomas C., the eldest, who was born March 10, 1851, is now living in Dakota, Minn., and is a carpenter by trade. Margaret E., born August 4, 1853, died on the 3d of August, 1857. Anne E., born November 13, 1855, is now the wife of William Foote, of Preston, Minn. A daughter born July 12, 1858, died in infancy. Emma L., a graduate of the Winona Normal School, born July 23, 1859, is now the wife of T. T. Geddes, a clothier of Anoka, Minn. Clarence F., born November 18, 1861, also a graduate of the Winona Normal School, is engaged in the commission business in Keokuk, Iowa. William W., born May 21, 1864, follows farming in Winona County. Charles G., born November 5, 1866, a bright and promising young man, who graduated from the Winona Normal College, is now studying medicine. Ulysses S., born October 19, 1868, is employed as a traveling salesman by a wholesale paper-bag firm. Elizabeth M., who completes the family, was born April 15, 1871, and is now employed as a teacher in the high school of Preston. Five of the family have taught school in Winona County.

Mr. and Mrs. Dick began their domestic life without capital. For two years they resided in Iowa, and then removed to Illinois, where they remained until the fall of 1855, at which time they came to Minnesota, locating in Richmond, Winona County. Here Mr. Dick established a grocery and general store, which he carried on until the fall of 1858. At that time he removed to a farm, having purchased a tract of wild land, which he at once began to clear and improve. From that time he successfully followed farming until the spring of 1889, and transformed the once raw prairie into rich and fertile fields, which yielded him a comfortable income. He also erected good buildings and made the place one of the best improved farms of the community. It comprised one hundred and eighty acres, and this valuable property makes his family in good circumstances.

Mr. and Mrs. Dick were ever thoughtful of the welfare of their children and provided them with good educational advantages which would fit them for the practical duties of life. Mr. Dick erected two schoolhouses in his neighborhood, one of which was named in his honor, and for some time he served as clerk of the school district. He also held other offices of trust, having been Justice of the Peace for six years and also Treasurer of his township. In politics he was a Republican, in his social relations was a Mason, and in religious belief he was a Methodist. His wife and nearly all of his children belong to the same church. He was ever a kind and affectionate husband and father, devoted to the interests of his family, and they in turn are an honor to him. His wife is a lady held in high esteem, and to her husband ever proved a faithful helpmate.

Philo B. Palmer.

PHILO B PALMER, one of the pioneer settlers of Winona County, now living a retired life, claims Pennsylvania as the state of his nativity. The date of his birth is April 21 1824, and the place Susquehanna His parents, James S and Hannah (Heath) Palmer, were both natives of New England The paternal grandfather, who was born in Vermont, was of English descent, and was a preacher of the Friends' or Quakers' Church. When ninety years of age he rode three hundred miles on horseback on a missionary tour His death occurred at the age of ninety-three The maternal grandfather, Jacob Heath, was also born in Vermont, and came of an old English family. He spent most of his life on the frontier, engaged in clearing land and in the work of the ministry, as a preacher of the Methodist Episcopal faith He was a soldier during the War of 1812 His last days were passed in northern Pennsylvania where he died at the age of seventy

James S Palmer was a carpenter by trade, and in 1856 left the Empire State, emigrating to Winona, where he aided in the erection of some of its first houses. He made the shingles, which are still in use, on one of the oldest houses on Second Street He, too, defended his country during the War of 1812, and was wounded in the leg at the battle of Plattsburg Both he and his wife were active members of the Methodist Church, in which he served as Steward. This worthy couple were the parents of five children, two sons and three daughters, of whom three are yet living, namely: Abigail w[illegible] wife [illegible] Calvin Hitt, of Dover, Olmsted County, Minn; and Philo B

Mr Palmer, of this sketch, remained in the county of his nativity until twenty-two years of age, his time being passed in attendance at the district schools of the neighborhood, and in clearing and developing the farm. He was thus early inured to arduous labor, but thereby developed a self-reliance and force of character which have proven of incalculable benefit to him in later years In 1855 he sought a home in Minnesota, and entered one hundred and sixty acres of land in Dodge County and eighty acres in Winona County, and purchased some property in Winona. Here he carried on carpentering for some time, and then embarked in business as a dealer in agricultural implements, having a large trade which came from all over the country. He did a very successful business, and thereby acquired a handsome competence About 1879 he retired to his farm some six miles from the city, and made it his home for six years, after which he returned to Winona

January 3, 1858, Mr Palmer was united in marriage with Miss Helen L Perry, daughter of Samuel and Minerva (Mather) Perry Four children were born to them Laura M, who died at the age of four years and four months; Mary L, wife of Forest Stansfield, of Winona, Albert L., who married Miss Millie Cosgrove, and is engaged in the grocery business in Austin, Minn, as a member of the firm of Harrobin & Palmer; and Clara H, who [illegible] ville Minn The mother of this family passed away in October, 1881, and on the 8th of January, 1891, Mr. Palmer wedded Mrs. Angeline (Van Housen) Townsend widow of Squire Townsend.

Mr. and Mrs. Palmer are members of the Methodist Episcopal Church, in which Mr. Palmer has served as Class-Leader and Steward for thirty-five years. In his political views he is a stanch Republican, and has held some minor offices. The cause of temperance finds in him an inflexible adherent. He has been Chairman of the Executive Committee of the Old Settlers' Association of the county, a position he has filled for many years. When Mr. Palmer came to Winona the land was still in possession of the Government, the first sale not occurring until October, 1855. He sold his farm in Illinois in 1854 with the intention of removing to Iowa, but came instead to Winona, and has been instrumental in inducing probably fifty families to locate here. He used to haul grain and lumber a distance of seventy-five miles, and has gone through all the experiences of pioneer life, but now has a fine home and other city property, and is resting in the enjoyment of the fruits of his former toil.

Harry Cassius Farrar.

HARRY CASSIUS FARRAR, who is now serving as County Superintendent of Schools, and makes his home in Stockton, has the honor of being a native of Winona County, his birth having here occurred on the 3d of May, 1861. His parents, John L. and Calista J. (Cheney) Farrar, had a family of seven children. The father, who is represented elsewhere in this work, was a native of New Hampshire, as was his wife, but they met for the first time in the West. His early years were spent in his native state, and at the age of twenty-four he left home. On the tide of emigration which was steadily progressing toward the setting sun, he drifted westward, and for two years spent the winters in hunting deer. He then purchased a farm, in 1855, married Miss Cheney, and began life in earnest. Since that time he has devoted his energies to agricultural pursuits. He has always been a man of progressive spirit, taking an active interest in public affairs which are calculated to promote the general welfare, and at an early day he served as a member of the State Legislature. He also held a number of local offices, serving as Township Clerk, Township Treasurer and Justice of the Peace. The cause of education has found in him a warm friend, and one who labors untiringly in its interest. He has long been officially connected with the schools and his labors along that line have been productive of good results. He votes with the Democratic party, of which he is a local leader, and in politics, as in all other matters, he is true to his convictions and fearless in the expression of his opinions.

The early life of H. C. Farrar was spent upon his father's farm and in gaining a rudimentary education in the district schools. His father's belief in education and in its necessity led him to be supplied with good advantages for obtaining at least a practical knowledge, which would be of much benefit to him in any ordinary business career which he might undertake. After leaving the public schools Mr. Farrar entered the State Normal School at Winona, which he attended for four years, spending three years of that time in the normal department He was also engaged in teaching for a limited time during that period In 1888 he was graduated from the normal school, and from that time was constantly engaged in the profession of teaching until he was elected, in the fall of 1892, to the office of County Superintendent of Schools, which position he occupies at the present time

Mr. Farrar has within his jurisdiction in this county one hundred and fifteen schools, and to the arduous duties of County Superintendent he devotes his entire attention He is deeply interested in educational development which is so marked at the present day, and has done much toward advancing the standard of excellence in the schools of Winona County His is a responsible position but the office is ably filled and he has the confidence of the majority of voters in the county

Mr Farrar was married on the 3d of October, 1889 to Miss Mabel C Nettleton of Minnesota, daughter of Charles Nettleton a native of New York The father died in this state in 1892, at the age of seventy-two years, but his widow is still living. Mr and Mrs Farrar have a family of three children Vera, Harold Cheney and the baby

W. D. Abbott.

W D ABBOTT a member of the law firm of Brown & Abbott, of Winona, was born in Steele County Minn, July 13 1859 His grandfather, William Abbott, was born in the town of Sanbornton, N H, in 1800, in the same house which was the birthplace of his son, A. J, and his entire life was passed on the old homestead farm, where he died at the age of forty-five. His father was a native of Pembroke, N H, and spent his entire life in the old Granite State, dying in Sanbornton at a ripe old age He was a son of Samuel Abbott, who long prior to the Revolution removed from Andover, Mass, to Pembroke, where he spent his remaining days He located among the Indians, who were sometimes troublesome, and ex[illegible] tions incide[illegible] back than Samuel Abbott, the ancestry of the family cannot now be traced.

A J Abbott, the father of W D, was born in Sanbornton N H, in 1829 and after arriving at years of maturity wedded Mary H Piper also a native of that city, and a daughter of Daniel Piper, who spent his entire life in the Granite State Mr and Mrs Abbott there lived until 1856, when, hoping to better their financial condition, they emigrated westward and made a home in Steele County, Minn., where the father followed farming during his active business life He still resides on the old homestead but is now retired. He went to the county in an early day and is numbered among its honored pioneers

W D Abbott spent his early life in the county [illegible] chools afforded him his first educational privileges. There he became familiar with the "three R's," and later took a preparatory course in Pillsbury Academy. Subsequently he continued his studies in Carleton College of Northfield, Minn., from which he was graduated in 1883. Having studied law, he entered upon the practice of his chosen profession in Waseca in 1885, and there continued in active business until the fall of 1892.

At that time Mr. Abbott came to Winona and entered the law office of Lloyd W. Bowers, who was then the attorney for the Winona & St. Peter Railway Company, and with him continued until June, 1893, when Mr. Bowers was appointed General Counsel for the Chicago & North-Western Railway Company, and removed to Chicago. Mr. Abbott then formed a partnership with L. L. Brown, under the firm name of Brown & Abbott, and this connection still continues, the firm occupying the law office of Wilson & Bowers. They received the appointment as attorneys for the Winona & St. Peter Railway Company, and are also successfully engaged in general law practice.

Mr. Abbott was married, in the fall of 1886, to Miss Lorena M. Adams, daughter of Thomas Adams, a farmer, residing near Faribault, Minn. She was one of five children, and comes of a family which for several generations past has resided in Vermont. Both Mr. and Mrs. Abbott are highly respected citizens of this community, and have a large circle of friends in Winona.

Clark Gilbert Corey.

CLARK GILBERT COREY is a member of the Winona Construction Company. He is a leader in business circles and is recognized as a valued citizen of Winona, on account of the active interest which he has ever taken in the development of the city and the promotion of the general welfare. Almost his entire life has been passed within the borders of Winona County, and here he has many friends who will receive with interest this record of his life.

His parents, H. A. and Phoebe Ann (Place) Corey, were both early settlers of this county. The father was born in Vermont January 20, 1821, and lived in New England until about twenty-five years of age, when he came West, settling near Oshkosh, Wis., where he engaged in farming for a short time. He then came to Minnesota, and located in the Money Creek Valley, in Winona County, in 1855. In this locality he has since made his home. He and his brother were the first two settlers in that part of the valley. H. A. Corey made a claim before the land was placed on the market, securing a half-section, which he transformed into a rich and highly cultivated farm. He is recognized as one of the representative agriculturists of the community, and is a highly respected and prominent citizen, who has taken a leading part in public affairs. In politics he has been a stanch advocate of the Republican party since its organization, and for two terms served as a member of the State Legislature. His wife was a native of Fond du Lac, Wis., and died in Winona County in January, 1885. Her parents, Joseph and Henrietta Place, were natives of New England. The paternal grandfather of our subject, Alpheus Corey, was born in Vermont, but spent the later years of his life in the West, his death occurring at the advanced age of eighty-eight years.

To H. A. and Phœbe Ann Corey were born three children: Carrie, wife of Clark Wood, of Amboy, Wash.; Etta, wife of F. B. Holbrook, who is also living in Amboy; and C. G., the subject of this sketch. Mr. Corey had been previously married, his first wife having borne the maiden name of Lydia Page. By that union he had two children: Sylvester A., a resident of Wheeler, Iowa; and Alice B., who became the wife of Alfred Jewell, and died in March, 1894.

Mr. Corey, of this sketch, remained upon the home farm until twenty-two years of age, and in his boyhood attended the district schools. He further continued his education by one year's study in the Winona High School, and later spent about three years in the Hillsdale College, of Hillsdale, Mich. Thus he became familiar with all of the common, and many of the higher, branches of learning, and by reading in later years has kept well informed on all of the issues and questions of the day. At length he left home and turned his attention to mercantile pursuits, for he did not wish to follow the life of an agriculturist. He embarked in the grocery business in company with Otis Abell and W. S. Crandall, a connection which was continued for two years, after which he spent the year 1888 in taking contracts for building sidewalks, in company with Mr. Abell. In 1889 he went to Lansing, Iowa, and accepted a position as bookkeeper in the office of the Lansing Lumber Company, where he remained for two and a-half years.

On the 25th of April, 1888, was celebrated the marriage of Mr. Corey and Miss Winnefred Bialey, daughter of Alvin Bialey, of Winona. She died December 30, 1892, leaving two children, Irene and Hamden. Mr. Corey was again married, March 8, 1894, his second union being with Katharyna McKenzie, of Winona, one of the seven children of Hugh McKenzie, of Oshkosh, Wis. Her father was a native of Scotland, and in New York City married Albina Powell, who was born in Nova Scotia.

Mr. Corey returned to Winona in 1892, and again began taking contracts for laying sidewalks. In the following year the Winona Construction Company was formed, the partners being Silas Bialey, Otis Abell and C. G. Corey. This firm engages in street-paving, sewer work and general contract work, and the business has rapidly developed until it has now assumed extensive proportions. Mr. Corey is a member of Winona Lodge No. 21, K. of P. He is one of the energetic young business men of the city, is held in high regard, and those who have known him from boyhood and witnessed his straightforward career are numbered among his warmest friends.

Chauncey Doud.

CHAUNCEY DOUD, who is connected with a large manufacturing industry of Winona, as a member of the firm of Doud Sons & Co., was born in Turin, Lewis County, N. Y., August 15, 1809, and is a son of Giles Doud, a native of Connecticut. The family was founded in America by Henry Doud, who was probably a resident of Guilford, Surrey County, England, and thence emigrated to the New World in 1639, settling in Guilford, Conn., with the colony then under the direction of Rev. Henry Whitfield. This became the permanent home of the family, and a number of the descendants of the original American progenitor still reside in that locality.

The paternal grandfather of our subject was Capt. Giles Doud, who won his title while serving in the French and Indian War. His son Giles removed from Connecticut to New York in an early day. In his native state he was united in marriage with Rhoda Scoville, of Connecticut, and then went to Vermont, from where he removed to the Empire State. Afterward he emigrated westward, settling in Lexington, Sinclair County, Mich., and about 1815 took up his residence in Oswego, Kendall County, where his death occurred in 1853, at the advanced age of eighty-six years. He was a cooper by trade. Capt. Giles Doud, his father, took part with his company in scaling the Heights of Abraham. He had organized and equipped a company for service in the French and Indian War, and led them to the front. Smallpox breaking out among his men, he was stricken with the disease and died at Crown Point, N. Y., while on his homeward journey. He was a son of David Doud, of Middleton, Conn., whose father, John Doud, was the second son of Henry, the founder of the family in America.

Mrs. Doud, mother of Chauncey, died in 1837. He is now the only survivor in a family of eight children, seven of whom grew to mature years. During his boyhood he learned the cooper's trade with his father and soon mastered the same, becoming an excellent workman. He remained at home until twenty years of age, when he started out in life for himself, working in a dairy for a time, and then opening a cooper shop in Rutland, N. Y., where the family had lived from the time he was seven years of age.

Mr. Doud was married, March 7, 1831, to Miss Sarah Comstock, daughter of William Comstock, and in 1837 removed to Michigan. In St. Clair County he secured a timbered farm and at once began to clear and develop it, continuing its cultivation for a period of five years. He was nine miles from any settlement, and the work was so unprofitable and of so difficult a nature, that he became disgusted with it and removed to Oswego, Kendall County, Ill., in 1842. There he carried on farming during the summer months, while in the winter season he engaged in coopering. Eight years later he removed to Lockport, Ill., where he opened a cooper shop, employing six men. In 1857 he became a resident of Trempealeau, Wis., where he built a sawmill, securing the machinery and the men to operate the same in Chicago This he carried on until 1862 His son, Roscoe F, joined him in business, and they also carried on a cooper shop In the year just mentioned they sold out and came to Winona, where they opened a shop which has been carried on continuously since Mr Doud furnished barrels for the Huff & Stecklen Mills, gave employment to three men, and continued his personal supervision of the business until about ten years since When he began operations here he had only about $5,000, but the capital stock has since been increased to $100,000.

To Mr and Mrs. Doud were born the following children: Roscoe T, a partner in the coopering business, Gertrude A, wife of E. W Heydon, of La Crosse, Wis, Anna D, widow of Abner Harris, of Winona, Marietta C., and George W, both of whom died in infancy, Maria Louise wife of George M Brush, of Minneapolis; Cornelia L, who is the widow of Fred Bonner, and now keeps house for her father, and George S, a member of the firm of Doud Sons & Co. Fred Bonner was a brother of Charles Bonner, of Winona, and was at one time connected with the Harvester Works He died in Mississippi, where he was employed as bookkeeper in the Doud Mill Mrs Doud died May 13, 1888, at the age of seventy-seven, her birth having occurred April 2, 1811 She was a lady of excellent business and executive ability, and her judgment and advice often proved very valuable to her husband.

In early life Chauncey Doud was a Democrat, and cast his first Presidential vote for Andrew Jackson, but on the organization of the Republican party he joined its ranks, and has since been one of its warm advocates He keeps well informed on the issues of the day both political and otherwise, and is a valued citizen of the community His home is one of the finest residences in Winona, and stands as a monument to his enterprise

Since an early day Mr Doud has been one of the leaders in business circles in this section of the state, and his progressive spirit has been an important factor in the upbuilding of Winona He was a stockholder in the Second National Bank, and a Director in [illegible] posed of his interest in the same when it was made a state bank He was one of the organizers and original stockholders in the Winona Flouring-mill Company The capital stock was $80,000, and he owned a fourth interest He continued his connection with the same until the mill was burned, about six years ago He then gave his stock to his children They have two mills at Pittsville, employing forty-seven men, one at Marsh, Wis, employing fifty men and barrel factories in Winona La Crosse (Wis), Mankato, Stillwater and Superior

Some years ago Mr Doud purchased a tract of pine land in Mississippi of four thousand acres A company was organized, of which he was made President, more land was purchased to the amount of nine thousand acres, and a mill was erected at a great cost, but after a year's unsuccessful business it was deemed best to sell out Whatever Mr. Doud has given his personal attention and supervision to has proved profitable, for he possesses most excellent business ability, is sagacious and far-sighted, and his management has brought him wealth. He was also interested in a stock-mining company in Idaho and served as its President

The most important enterprise, however with which Mr Doud has been connected is that now carried on under the name of Doud Sons & Co., manufacturers of barrels This company was incorporated in 1880, with a capital stock of $100,000, and about $140,000 is now used in the business This is the outgrowth of the cooper shop which was established by Mr Doud and his son Roscoe in 1857 in Trempealeau, Wis They built a sawmill doing a general milling business, and soon after a stavemill and cooper shop were added in Winona About 1865 stave machines were established at various points in Wisconsin and Minnesota They now have a stavemill at Pittsville, Wis, employing about fifty men, and a sawmill has been erected. There are a sawmill, stave factory and heading-mill at Marsh, Wis, with shipping facilities on the Wisconsin Central, and about seventy-five men are employed They have about nine thousand acres of timber-land in that part of the state, and also secure timber from elsewhere [illegible] urnishes employment to twenty men, at La Crosse to thirty men, the one in Mankato to fifteen men, in Stillwater to fifteen men, and in Superior employment is given to sixty men. Each is presided over by a foreman, and the main trade is among flouring-mills. These factories together on an average turn out about three thousand barrels daily, and the Superior mill alone has a capacity of two thousand barrels per day if necessary. The annual business amounts to about $315,000, and the pay-roll to about $100 000 per annum. This gigantic enterprise is the outgrowth of a small concern, and has really resulted from the good management, methodical and systematic methods, and the careful attention to details of the gentleman whose name heads this record.

Michael Knopp.

MICHAEL KNOPP, a retired farmer now living in Winona, claims Germany as the land of his birth, which occurred in Westphalia, on the 13th of March, 1819. During his youth he learned the stone-cutter's trade, and became an expert workman along that line. He followed the business in the Fatherland until twenty-three years of age, when he sailed for the New World. He had heard much of the advantages and privileges here afforded young men, and resolved to test the truth of these reports, hoping that he would thereby be benefited financially. The voyage across the Atlantic was made in a sailing-vessel. After his arrival he worked for a time in Missouri, and then secured a position on a steamer on the Mississippi River. Shortly afterward, however, he engaged in chopping wood, and was thus employed for two years, but after all his hard labor he was beaten out of his wages by his employer.

Mr Knopp then went to Missouri, where he joined a party en route for California. In 1846, upon his arrival at the Sacramento River, he enlisted in the U[illegible] months during the war with Mexico. In acknowledgement of the services rendered at that time, he has been put upon the list of pensioners of the Mexican War. He remained upon the Pacific Slope about two years, and built the first schoolhouse in Monterey. He also engaged in mining to some extent. Later he went to the Sandwich Islands, but spent only a short time there, when he took passage on a vessel bound for Germany. After visiting his native land and the home and scenes of his childhood, he once more came to America and this time located in Sheboygan County, Wis., where he purchased a tract of land. It was covered with timber, which he at once began to clear away, and in course of time much of the forest had been replaced by waving fields of grain which yielded to the owner a good income. There he lived for thirteen years, after which he sold a part of his farm and built a mill in Kewaunee, Wis., which he operated until his removal to Winona, Minn., in 1861. At that time he purchased the farm in Winona Township which he yet owns.

As a companion and helpmate on life's journey, [illegible] sch, a native of Germany. The wedding was celebrated on the 6th of May, 1849, and their union has been blessed with a family of ten children, nine of whom are yet living. Charles, the eldest, is a farmer of this county; John is a contractor and builder in Winona; Mary is at home; Gertrude is the wife of Henry Felenger; Joseph carries on agricultural pursuits in Winona County in partnership with his brother Charles; George follows farming on the old homestead; Martha is the wife of Charles Richardson, an agriculturist; William is living in St. Paul, Minn.; Jacob was drowned at the age of three years; and Lena is a teacher.

In his political views Mr. Knopp is a Republican, and has held a number of local offices. He belongs to the Evangelical Church, and has led an honorable, upright life. His business career has ever been a straightforward one, and his success is justly merited. He started out in life empty-handed, with no capital save a pair of willing hands and a strong determination to succeed. He has met obstacles and reverses, yet has overcome these by diligence and perseverance, and is now the possessor of considerable property, including three hundred acres of land. Owing to his prosperity, he is now enabled to live retired, enjoying a rest which he has truly earned and richly deserves.

H. S. WAHL, M. D.

H. S. Wahl, M. D.

H. S. WAHL, M. D. The record of the medical fraternity of Winona County would be incomplete without the sketch of Dr. Wahl, who is recognized as one of the leading practitioners in this locality. He occupies a prominent place among his professional brethren, and possesses the skill and ability which have gained for him a high reputation, and won him an extensive business. He was born in the county of Perth, in the province of Ontario, Canada, on the 19th of August, 1860, and was one of a family of four children, whose parents were Frederick and Catherine (Seip) Wahl. His father, Frederick Wahl, was a native of Buffalo, N. Y., born in 1831. The following year his parents removed to the province of Ontario, Canada, settling on a farm near Waterloo, and under the parental roof he remained until twenty-four years of age, when he was united in marriage with Miss Seip, who was born in Waterloo County, Canada, in 1836. Immediately after he removed with his bride to the county of Perth, where he secured a farm, upon which he has since resided, devoting his time and attention to agricultural pursuits.

As the name indicates, the family is of German origin, and was founded in America by the Doctor's grandfather, Henry Wahl, a native of Germany, who in early [illegible] lantic to America, accompanied by his young wife. He was a butcher by trade, and had followed that business in the Fatherland, and to some extent in Buffalo after his emigration to the New World, but on his removal to Canada he turned his attention to farming, and followed that occupation during his active business career. He is still living, at the advanced age of eighty-eight, but his years rest lightly upon him and he is yet enjoying good health.

Dr. Wahl, of this sketch, spent the days of his childhood in the old home in Canada, where he remained until about twenty-one years of age. In his boyhood he attended the common schools near his home, and later spent two years at Stratford High School, after which he entered the commercial college of Belleville, and was graduated from that institution. He then entered upon his life work, and from that time forward has been dependent on his own resources. He first secured a position as bookkeeper in the office of an agricultural-implement establishment, where he remained for two and a-half years, and on leaving that situation he entered a drug store, where he continued for six months.

Having formed a desire to make the practice of medicine his life work, Mr. Wahl, in order to fit [illegible] entered the medical department of the Northwestern University, of Chicago, where he spent three years in pursuing a thorough and systematic course of study. He was graduated in the Class of '84 with the degree of M. D., and immediately after coming to this state located in Minnesota City, where he opened an office and began practice. There he continued his practice for three years, when in 1887, he came to Winona, which has since been his home. In the seven years which have passed he has built up a large business. He practices both medicine and surgery, and in his chosen work he has met with prosperity.

On the 13th of July, 1885, was celebrated the marriage of Dr. Wahl and Miss Clara E. Waterman, of Minnesota City, who for eight years was a successful teacher in the public schools of this state. She died November 26, 1886, leaving one child, Harry, who was born on the 5th of May of that year. The Doctor was again married, March 27, 1888, his second union being with Miss Annie Kaizer, of Winona. One child graces this union, Herbert, born July 24, 1889. The Doctor is a member of the Winona County Medical Society and the Southern Minnesota Medical Association. He is a pleasant, genial gentleman, and outside of professional circles has many warm friends, who esteem him highly for his sterling worth and strict integrity.

Elisha B. Huffman.

ELISHA B. HUFFMAN, one of the highly respected citizens of Homer, who is now practically living a retired life, was born on a farm in Trafalgar, Canada, October 6, 1825, and is a son of Jacob and Elizabeth (Finch) Huffman, both of whom were natives of New York. The father was born in January, 1786, and died February 2, 1851. He was a farmer by occupation and owned a valuable tract of land. He was only about two years of age when with his parents he went to Canada. He enlisted for the War of 1812, and continued in the service until its close. His wife was called to her final rest in 1871. In their family were eleven children, but only two are now living. John died in Michigan in 1888; Christopher has also passed away; Henry died in Minnesota in Septe[illegible] two years, Mary [illegible] Paul G. has passed away; Nathaniel died April 18, 1874; Lorana is deceased; Phœbe is the wife of William Livingston, a railroad man of Canada; Elisha is the next younger; and Joseph has also passed away.

Mr. Huffman of this sketch remained upon the home farm until twenty-six years of age. Some time previous he had assumed its management and the care of his parents. At length, on leaving home, he began to learn the trade of blacksmithing, wagon-making and repairing, and afterward embarked in business for himself, carrying on operations along that line for five years. On the expiration of that period he emigrated westward and spent one year in Iowa. On the 12th of November, 1857, he arrived in Minnesota, making the [illegible] Homer and located [illegible] Township, where he purchased forty acres of land. To this he added from time to time as his financial resources were increased until he had four hundred acres of valuable land, the greater part of which is under a high state of cultivation. He built a good house and barn, made other improvements, and the well tilled fields and neat appearance of the place indicated the thrift and enterprise of the owner. He carried on general farming, and was the first man who ever raised a thousand bushels of wheat in one season in this locality. He also engaged in blacksmithing, and that work proved to him a profitable source of income.

On the 6th of January, 1848, was celebrated the marriage of Mr. Huffman and Miss Caroline E. Currey, daughter of Ephraim and Nancy Currey, who were natives of Canada. The father died in Canada, September 6, 1864; the mother was called to the home beyond October 10, 1887, and she was laid to rest in Homer Cemetery. In their family were eleven children, of whom five are yet living, namely: Hamilton, Carleton, George, Caroline (who was born October 21, 1830,) and Walter. Mr. and Mrs. Huffman are now parents of eight children: Miles J., who was born January 28, 1849, and is the present County Attorney of Scott's Bluff County, Neb.; Henry H., who was born July 6, 1850, and is now in South Dakota; James N., who was born February 25, 1853, and is living in Homer; Jacob W., who was born May 12, 1855, and is a farmer of Minnesota; Ephraim E., who was born March 30, 1857, and is located in Huntsville, Ala.; Elizabeth B., who was born March 16, 1859, became the wife of William Horton, and died February 28, 1890, leaving two children; Elsie C., who was born May 27, 1864, and died February 19, 1866; and Mary A., who was born January 6, 1870, and is still at home with her parents.

Mr. and Mrs. Huffman have always given their children good educational privileges to fit them for the practical duties of life and have supplied them with other advantages. About four years ago Mrs. Huffman suffered from a paralytic stroke, and has since been a cripple, but she bears her misfortune uncomplainingly. She has been a faithful companion and helpmate to her husband, and together as man and wife they have traveled life's journey for forty-six years.

Mr. Huffman is an enterprising and progressive farmer and carried on agricultural pursuits until September, 1891, when he removed to Homer, and has since made his home in this place. He has led a busy and useful life, and has always been a hard worker. He yet engages in labor to a limited extent, for he cannot bear to sit down in idleness, that quality being utterly foreign to his nature. In politics he has been a Republican since he became a subject of the United States and warmly advocates his party's principles. He has served as Justice of the Peace, as Assessor and in all the other town offices, and has ever been true to the trust reposed in him by those who gave him their support.

Richard Perrin.

RICHARD PERRIN is one of Winona County's well known agriculturists, who in his business career has won success, and in all the relations of life has gained the confidence and esteem of those with whom he has been brought in contact. He carries on general farming and stock-raising on section 15, Saratoga Township, where he owns valuable property, comprising two hundred and forty acres of rich land, which is improved with good buildings and all the accessories of a model farm.

Mr. Perrin was born in Yorkshire, England, on the 13th of August, 1825, and is a son of John and Emma (Wilkes) Perrin, who were also natives of the same country. By occupation the father was a farmer, and followed that business through life. The family numbered eight children, three sons and five daughters, of whom Richard is the eldest. Sarah and Elizabeth are both deceased. Thomas and John follow in order of birth. Mary Ann has also passed away. Priscilla is the youngest living, and one died in infancy.

When a child of five years, Richard Perrin left his native land and was brought by his parents to America, the family crossing the Atlantic in a sailing-vessel, which after a voyage of six weeks dropped anchor in the harbor of New York. The family located in Monroe County, N. Y., near Rochester, and there Richard was reared to manhood. His education was acquired in the district schools, wh[illegible] sixteen year[illegible] servation, however, have made him a well informed man. His father was in limited circumstances, and, as he was the eldest child, he remained at home and gave to his parents the benefit of his services until twenty-five years of age. He then started out in life for himself, and began by renting land. This he did for five years, making his home in New York until the spring of 1855, when he emigrated to the West. The journey was made by way of the rivers and lakes to Beloit, Wis. Near that city he purchased one hundred and sixty acres of land, and for two years carried on farming, but on the expiration of that period he removed to Waupun, Wis., where he rented a farm until 1866. In that year he came to Winona County, and has since been numbered among the agriculturists of Saratoga Township. He bought eighty acres of partially improved land on section 15, where his home now stands, and began the development of a farm that has become one of the most desirable places of the neighborhood. As his financial resources have been increased he has extended its boundaries, until it now comprises two hundred and forty-eight acres of rich land, which yields to him a golden tribute in return for the care and cultivation he bestows upon it.

On the 3d of April, 1849, Mr. Perrin was united in marriage with Miss Jane Drake, a native of New York, who was born in 1829. They have two children. Emma became the wife of Peter Bratt [illegible], and they have [illegible] Ada Jennie is the wife of Clarence Statser. They reside on the old homestead and have a daughter, Ora M

In his political affiliations Mr Perrin is a Democrat, but has never aspired to public office In 1890 he was called to mourn the loss of his wife, who passed away on the 30th of August, and was laid to rest in Saratoga Cemetery She had been to him a faithful companion and helpmate on life's journey, and her loss was mourned by her family and many friends. Mr Perrin's success is well deserved, and he also merits the high regard in which he is held

Watson I. Lamson.

WATSON I. LAMSON, one of the honored veterans of the late war, now living in Winona, was for some years connected with the agricultural interests of this county He has also represented his constituents in several offices, thus becoming well known, and in this volume is deserving of representation Mr. Lamson is a native of Massachusetts, his birth having occurred in Mt Washington, Berkshire County, on the 23d of April, 1844. His father, William Lamson was born in Massachusetts, September 1, 1815, and in early life engaged in the insurance business He married Miss Lucy A Lee, who was born in the old Bay State, January 12, 1820, and with his family started for the West in 1851 He first located in Rockford, Ill and after about three years came to Winona County, Minn., settling first in the village of Homer He purchased eighty acres of land, and continued its cultivation for several years, when he was taken sick Not being able to meet payments upon his farm, he lost his property, but afterward bought one hundred and five acres, which he owned up to the time of his death He passed away on the 8th of September, 1892, having for four years survived his wife, who was called to the home beyond in April, 1888 In their family were four children, but Watson the second in order of birth, is the only one now living. [illegible] died April 24, 1887 Livingston M, born January 9, 1846, is also deceased, Mary W born September 23, 1847, died November 23, 1854 In his political affiliations the father of this family was a Republican, and was honored with a number of offices In connection with his other work he engaged in teaching school to some extent He was an excellent mathematician, and never failed to solve any problem which was given him

No event of special importance occurred during the childhood and youth of Watson I Lamson, who lived upon the home farm until after the breaking out of the late war, when he bade adieu to parents and friends and started for the scene of battle On the 13th of August, 1862, he enrolled his name as a member of Company B, Seventh Minnesota Infantry. The company, commanded by Capt S B Sheardown, was engaged in fighting the Indians for about a year, and then went to St. Louis from where they were ordered to Mississippi There they took part in the battle of Tupelo, which continued at intervals for three days, and were afterward at Nashville. Later Mr Lamson took part in the siege of Mobile, where he was under fire for about six weeks, and there remained until honorably discharged, in August, 1865 He was never wounded by a bullet, but his health was greatly impaired and never has been

When the war was over, Mr Lamson returned to his parents' home, and there remained until his marriage, at the age of twenty-five years On the 5th of August, 1869, was celebrated his union with Mary E Richardson, whose death occurred April 23, 1870 On the 24th of March, 1875, he was again married, his second union being with Lucy O Hammond, daughter of M H Hammond a native of Connecticut, who removed to Michigan in 1836, and came to Minnesota in 1865, locating in Pleasant Ridge, Homer Township There he reared his family, and there his death occurred in 1872 His widow is still living with Mrs. Lamson, at the age of eighty-four years, and is a well preserved old lady, who has many friends in this community Mr. and Mrs Lamson have two children William H, born June 19, 1878; and Herbert H, born January 10, 1880 They are good and intelligent lads and are an honor to their parents

At the time of his first marriage, Mr Lamson purchased eighty acres of land, but his wife died shortly after, and he did not then remove to the farm, but instead went to Kansas, where he spent about two years. After his second marriage he added thirty acres and located thereon, devoting his time and attention to farming until 1887, when he removed to Homer, there he resided until 1894, when he removed to his present home at No 263 East Howard Street, Winona In the mean time he had further extended the boundaries of his farm until it now comprises one hundred and eight acres. He yet retains possession of this, having it now rented, and it yields to him a good income Mr. Lamson has been a hard worker and by a busy life has achieved a success which is well merited. In politics he is a Republican He served for one term as Town Treasurer, and for ten years has been Chairman of the Town Board of Supervisors Socially he is connected with the Grand Army of the Republic

William Kaiser.

WILLIAM KAISER, who is engaged in plastering in Winona, was born on the 4th of November, 1832, in Hottenbach, Russia, where he remained until about nineteen years of age, when he sailed for America In his native land he had learned the mason's trade, having provided for his own maintenance for some time. At length he determined to seek a home beyond the Atlantic, hoping thereby to benefit his financial condition, and in a sailing-vessel crossed the briny deep to New York He did not tarry long, however, in the eastern metropolis, but went at once to Scranton, Pa, where he worked at his trade for a year He then resumed his westward journey, and took up his residence in Cincinnati, Ohio, where the [illegible] years of [illegible] life were passed [illegible] came to Minnesota, locating in New Ulm, where he made his home for a short time The year 1862 witnessed his arrival in Winona, where for nearly a third of a century he has engaged in business as a plasterer, taking large contracts for such work

The lady who now bears the name of Mrs Kaiser was in her maidenhood Amelia Kaiser She was born in Baden, Germany, and their marriage was celebrated in 1858 Ten children graced their union, but three of the number are now deceased Those still living are Minnie, wife of Henry Hess, a resident of Winona, Charles, who makes his home in this city, Albert, who is living in Fosston, Minn., where he is engaged in the banking business, Edward, a printer, who resides with his father, Carrie, William G. and Hattie, who are yet under the [illegible] [illegible] one of prominence in the community, and its members hold an enviable position in social circles where true worth and intelligence are received as passports into good society.

Mr Kaiser votes with the Republican party and is a warm advocate of its principles, but has never sought or desired public office, preferring to give his entire time and attention to his business interests and to the enjoyment of his home. He is now the owner of a pleasant residence on King Street, together with a business block on Center Street. These represent his own labor and are monuments to his thrift and enterprise. He is one of the leading men in his line of business, and has received a fair share of the public patronage, whereby he has secured a good income. He has had no special advantages in life, but has made the most of his opportunities, and his success is due to earnest application, untiring effort and good management.

Edwin D. Wilmot.

EDWIN D. WILMOT, who follows farming on section 12, Saratoga Township, is recognized as one of the prosperous and progressive agriculturists in Winona County, and in its history well deserves mention. The record of his life is as follows: He was born in Oneida County, N. Y., May 23, 1841, and is a son of Allen G. and Sarah (Remore) Wilmot. The father was a native of the Empire State, and was of French descent, while the mother was of German lineage. They became the parents of ten children, seven sons and three daughters, of whom eight are now living, namely: Edwin D., of this sketch; Stewart J., Sarah J., Louisa, Isaac G., Julia, Henry and Solon. Eugene and an infant are deceased.

Edwin D. Wilmot was born and reared on a farm, and the occupation with which he was familiar from earliest youth he has made his life work. He attended the district schools of New York, and completed his education in the public schools of Winona. In 1856 he came with his parents to Minnesota, the family locating in St. Charles, where the father secured land from the Government and began the development of a farm. Edwin was thus inured to the arduous labor of breaking and cultivating new land, and became familiar with farm work in all its departments. He was still at home with his parents at the breaking out of the late war, but in 1862 he bade adieu to home and friends and entered the service.

It was on the 15th of August of that year that Mr. Wilmot enrolled his name among the boys in blue of Company D, Seventh Minnesota Infantry. He was mustered into service at Ft. Snelling, and his first engagement was under Sibley, at Big Mound, N. Dak., during the Indian troubles, June 24, 1863, and on the 28th at Stony Lake, the severest engagement of the expedition. He was then sent South, and participated in the battle at Tupelo, after which he went on the raid through Missouri in pursuit of Price, where a running fight was kept up for many days. Later he went to Nashville, and took part in the battle at that place. With his command he also met the enemy at Spanish Fort, and participated in the siege and capture of that stronghold. He went through as a private, and on the 17th of August, 1865, was honorably discharged, for the South had laid down its arms, the Union was preserved, and the war was over.

Mr. Wilmot immediately returned to his home, and in 1866 he began farming in his own interest, purchasing one hundred and fifty acres of land in Saratoga Township. It was partly improved, and he at once began its cultivation and made it his home for three years On the expiration of that period he removed, in 1869, to the farm on which he now resides, and which has been his home continuously since He first purchased one hundred and sixty acres on section 12, but as his financial resources have increased he has added to this until now two hundred and ninety acres of rich and valuable land pays a golden tribute to the care and cultivation he bestows upon it. He also carries on stock-raising, and is the owner of one of the best farms of the neighborhood

Mr. Wilmot was married, on the 1st of March, 1868, to Miss Idella Watson, and their union has been blessed with four children, all of whom are yet living, namely Minnie, now the wife of Monroe Ball, a resident farmer of Saratoga Township; Alfred, Daisy and Pearl, all at home Daisy is a graduate of the high school, and also of the normal school of Winona, and by her study has fitted herself for the profession of teaching The family is one of culture and refinement, the household is noted for its hospitality, and its members are highly respected people of the community

Mr. Wilmot started out in life a poor boy, with no capital save a young man's bright hope of the future and a determination to succeed He has labored earnestly, and his diligence and perseverance have made his career a prosperous one He is now in comfortable circumstances, and can supply his family with all the comforts of life. In politics he has always been a Republican, and warmly advocates the party principles He belongs both to the Odd Fellows' society and the Grand Army of the Republic

---

John C. Laird.

JOHN C LAIRD, of Winona, was born in Lewisburg, Union County, Pa, October 6, 1825, and is a son of Robert Hoyt and Maria (Nevins) Laird The father was born in Derry, Northumberland County, Pa, June 22 1796, and was of Scotch-Irish descent. In 1820 he married Mrs Maria (Nevins) Fruit, a widow. Her father, Christian Nevins, was born in Holland, November 1, 1759, and married Lucretia Chamberlain, who was born in 1765 The great-grandfather of our subject on the maternal side, John Hayes, was born in Londonderry, Ireland, and came to America in 1730 His son, Robert Hayes, was born in Northumberland County, Pa, in 1742, and wedded Mary Allison.

Matthew Laird, the great-grandfather of our subject, was born about 1765, and became a resident of Cu[illegible] County [illegible] His son Moses Laird, married Jane Hayes, and their son, Robert H., became the father of John C Laird, of this notice The grandfather of Mrs Maria Laird was a Revolutionary soldier. He was born in Hunterdon County, N J, September 27, 1736, and was the eldest of twelve children born to William and Elizabeth Chamberlain, who were natives of England, and came to America in 1680. Col. William Chamberlain served in the Colonial army, and his commission bears the date of September 9, 1777. He was a member of General Armstrong's brigade and General Wayne's division, and took part in the battles of Franklin, Princeton and Brandywine At the last-named his son Louis was killed. He was also present at the surrender of Cornwallis, October 19, 1781. His services were recognized as so valuable to the American forces that the English [illegible] his head His old uniform epaulettes are still in possession of the family

Robert Laird and his wife lived and died in Pennsylvania. He made farming his life work and was quite an influential citizen His death occurred at the age of ninety-one years. John C. Laird was one of a family of eight children. He was reared on the old home farm, and at the age of twenty-five determined to go to California, but his family objected and instead he emigrated to northern Illinois in 1850 In the fall of that year he went up the Mississippi to Winona Prairie, passing St Paul, which then contained a population of five hundred He stopped at La Crosse when there were but five families in the town After two weeks he went to Galena and thence to Freeport, Ill. In the spring of 1851 he entered a claim above La Crosse, but clerked in a store until the following fall, when he was made Deputy Register of Deeds of La Crosse County, under William T Price, since United States Senator His eldest sister, Catherine, now the wife of Abner S. Goddard, taught school in La Crosse in the winter of 1851 In May, 1852, Mr Goddard came to Winona, being one of its first settlers He was appointed the first Postmaster of the place, but died the following August His widow afterward married A B Smith and was long a resident of Winona, being one of the best known and most highly respected ladies of the county She had three children when she came here, but two died soon after her arrival One son Charles Goddard, enlisted before he was seventeen years of age for service in the Civil War, and was wounded at the battle of Gettysburg, after which he returned to Winona He was elected Register of Deeds, but died before the time came for him to enter upon the duties of the office

John C Laird arrived in Winona in August, 1852, and the following year made a claim His time was largely spent in driving settlers over the country until 1855 In the spring of that year he was joined by his brothers, Matthew J. and William H., and the firm of Laird Bros was formed They would go up the Chippewa River and buy lumber, which they would raft down and sell to the settlers who were rapidly flocking to this place. The venture proved a very profitable one, and from this grew the extensive business of the firm of Laird, Norton & Co In 1856 the Norton brothers joined the Laird brothers in business, and the subject of this sketch continued with the firm until 1865, when he withdrew. The first mill was erected in the fall of 1857 In 1860 John C Laird went to Olmsted County to improve a farm which he had entered in 1856, and there remained until 1863 He had six hundred acres of land, which he sometimes operated with help and sometimes rented.

On the 9th of April, 1855, was celebrated the marriage of Mr Laird and Miss Charlotte M Jarvis, of Chautauqua County, N Y, who came to Winona in 1853, with Mr. and Mrs. Charles Eaton. Their children are Will Hayes, who for eighteen years has been employed in the office of Laird, Norton & Co, Allison W, a bookkeeper in the Second National Bank, and Scott, who was graduated from the high school in the Class of '94 Mr Laird was one of the first members of the Congregational Church at this place, and has led an honorable, upright life, which has gained for him the confidence and good-will of all with whom he has been brought in contact. In politics he was first a Whig and then a Republican

Willard Harrison.

WILLARD HARRISON, one of the prosperous farmers and highly respected citizens of Winona County, now living on section 17, Homer Township, is a native of the Nutmeg State, his birth having occurred in the town of Branford, New Haven County, on the 19th of May, 1823. His parents, Sylvester and Nancy (Bradley) Harrison, were also natives of Connecticut. The father, who was a sailor, shipped before the mast at the age of fourteen, followed the sea twenty years, and was lost while on a voyage, at the age of thirty-four. He left a widow and three children: Willard; William, who is now deceased; and Timothy I., who was killed while in the Confederate service at the battle of Murfreesboro. The father was lost January 9, 1837, and the mother afterward married again. Her second husband was Mr. Lindsey, by whom she had one son. For her third husband she married Mr. Bryan.

Willard Harrison remained with his mother until eight years of age, when he went to live with a farmer, with whom he continued for five years. He then returned to his mother's home, and was a member of her household until seventeen years of age, when he began learning the blacksmith's trade, following the same until he had attained his majority. He then turned his attention to the machinist's trade, and was engaged in the construction of engines until 1856, when he came to Minnesota, the month of September witnessing his arrival in the state. He spent some time in seeking a location, and finally settled in Fillmore County, where he rented a twelve-acre tract of land, upon which he made his home for a year. On the expiration of [illegible] Minn., where he entered land and made his home until 1862. Since that time he has been a resident of Winona County. For two years he rented a farm, and then, in 1864, purchased an eighty-acre tract of land, on which he now resides. The boundaries of that place, however, he has since extended, until it now comprises one hundred and sixty acres of rich land. He turned his attention to general farming and was thus employed until April, 1865, when he manifested his loyalty to the Government by enlisting in the service as a member of the First Minnesota Heavy Artillery. He was under Capt. John Hammond and remained at the front until the following October, when, the war having closed, he was honorably discharged and returned to his home. He then began to extensively engage in the cultivation of fruit and his entire farm is now devoted to the raising of apples and berries, which he markets in the neighboring towns and cities.

On the 3d of July, 1842, Mr. Harrison was united in marriage with Miss Mary E. Alling, daughter of Samuel Alling, who was born in Connecticut January 9, 1820, and was a farmer by occupation. Mr. and Mrs. Harrison have one child, Mrs. Frances A. Merritt, who was born October 31, 1843, and has always resided at home. By her marriage she has a son.

When Mr. and Mrs. Harrison began their domestic life they had no capital, but he was possessed of a good knowledge of his trade, and thereby was enabled to provide for himself and family. He was recognized as an expert workman, and in all his life was never discharged from a shop. He [illegible] ods with one em[illegible] ployer, and then left on his own account. He came to the West with the hope of benefiting his health, and has since given his time and attention to agricultural pursuits, which he has successfully followed, winning thereby a competence that now numbers him among the substantial citizens of the community. While living in Martin County, he served for two terms as Sheriff. In politics he is a Democrat, and in his social relations is a Mason. All who know him esteem him highly for his sterling worth, and in the community where he lives he has many friends.

Charles Butler.

CHARLES BUTLER, a prominent contractor and builder, resides at No. 369 West Broadway Street, Winona. There is probably no more popular man, or one who has more friends, in this city than he, and in the history of his adopted county he well deserves mention. Mr. Butler was born in Rugby, Warwickshire, England, on the 28th of July, 1832, and his boyhood days were passed amidst the beautiful scenes of that locality. He now has in his possession many views of English landscape, showing lovely scenery and old mansions and cathedrals near his English home. At the age of fourteen he was apprenticed to learn the trade of a mason, brick-layer and plasterer. In June, 1853, in his twenty-first year, he crossed the broad Atlantic to Oswego, N. Y., making the journey with his old employer, with whom he remained until he attained his majority.

Mr. Butler then worked as a journeyman in Oswego until the fall of 1855, when he removed to Toledo, Ohio, where he was engaged in the building of the roundhouse of the Wabash Valley Railroad at that place until the spring of 1856. He then went to Chicago, and on the 17th of May of the same year reached Winona, which he believed would prove a favorable location. Here he again worked as a journeyman, and was first employed in plastering a house on Broadway Street. He laid the first brick in the town, it being used in the construction of the Orrin Smith & Sons Bank on First Street, where the North-Western freight depot now stands. This was in June, 1856. Mr. Butler formed a partnership with James Beasley, his old employer, with whom he had come to America, and in a short time this firm became the leading one of the town. They erected a brick bank building on Second Street, which was known by the name of Smith & Sons Bank, and was destroyed by the big fire in 1862. In 1860 Mr. Butler's partner was killed while quarrying rock for the normal school, and thus death dissolved the partnership which for several years had continued with mutual pleasure and profit.

In July, 1858, the subject of this sketch returned to Oswego, N. Y., and in the fall of that year made a trip to his native land, where, in 1859, he married Miss Ann Harris, one of the friends of his youth. In the spring of that year he sailed with his bride for the New World, and for a short time lived in Oswego, where he was engaged as foreman on the construction of the court house. He then came to Winona, but shortly after went South, spending some time in Memphis, Tenn., and in Mississippi. Returning to Winona, he then resumed contracting, which he continued until 1866. The big fire which swept over the city in 1862 brought him much work, and he was engaged in the construction of many of the leading buildings of the city, including the Winona County Bank and the Kendall drug store. In 1865 he erected the Presbyterian Church. The following year he formed a partnership with John H. Jones, and the first contract which they took was for the erection of the Central School. In 1867 they built the Buffner Block, and did the brick work on the present normal school. They also did the mason work on the North-Western Railroad bridge, carrying on most of the work in the winter, when the river was a sheet of ice, and furnishing employment to some eighty men. In 1871 the partnership with Mr. Jones was dissolved, and Mr. Butler made a contract with the North-Western Railway Company to construct its car-shops, roundhouses, bridges, engine stalls, depots, water-works and elevators. In 1873, in connection with Monk & Gechler, he built the St. Peter Asylum, and continued in partnership with Mr. Monk until 1877, during which time many large buildings were erected.

Mr. Butler was then alone in business for some years. He served as City Marshal in 1870, but in 1880 resumed contracting, and did much work on the big sawmills then being constructed. In 1881 he formed a partnership with John Lohse, and the firm took a $50,000 contract for the erection of a part of the asylum at St. Peter which had been burned. In 1882 they built the Winona Wagon Works, at a cost of $12,000, and the partnership was then dissolved, after which Mr. Butler was alone in business until 1888. In that year he was chosen superintendent of the building of the new court house, and was thus engaged until the summer of 1889, when, in connection with Fred Kratz, he erected the new Winona House, at a cost of $32,000. In 1890 he took a contract and built the first and only brick arched bridge at Minnesota City. This has an elliptical arch, with a span of sixty feet, and an elevation of twelve and a-half feet. In 1891 Mr. Butler put in some of the sewer work in the city and the shore piers and the approach to the new bridge. In 1893, in connection with John Lohse, he erected the basements to the two new wings of the normal school, at an expense of $6,800. He then acted as foreman for Samuel Van Gorder, who had the contract for building the levee wall along the river front.

In 1870 Mr. Butler was called upon to mourn the loss of his wife. He has also buried five sons. His one daughter, Josephine H., on the 3d of October, 1894, married Albert Chappell, a farmer of Kasota. In politics Mr. Butler has always been a Republican, and for four years he acceptably and creditably served as Alderman of the city. In addition to his other business interests he has conducted a brickyard for some five years, and has traded to some extent in real estate. He is a large man, possessed of superior mental ability, and is a whole-souled, kind-hearted gentleman, who has won hosts of friends.

Gilbert M. Corey.

GILBERT M. COREY wore the blue during the War of the Rebellion, and made a good record as a brave and valiant defender of the Stars and Stripes. Though he was among the first to enlist, and served until the close of the war, he was never wounded nor taken prisoner, though he took part in many important campaigns, and participated in numerous battles and engagements. For the past quarter of a century he has been a resident of Wiscoy Township, and is now the owner of an excellent homestead situated on section 28. His estate comprises four hundred and eighty acres of land, all in one body, and this is well improved with good fences, barns and necessary buildings. In addition to the management of his own affairs, he also supervises the Butler estate, a tract of about nineteen hundred acres.

The nativity of our subject occurred in Fair Haven, Vt., August 9, 1839. His father, Alpheus, was born November 2, 1796, and died in his eighty-eighth year. The mother, whose maiden name was Laura Brewster, was born in June, 1808, and died in 1882. The first years of our subject were passed in the town of his birth, but while he was still a mere child his father removed to New York State, and there engaged in farming for several years. Then returning to the Green Mountain State, he located in Worthington County, and there the boy received the main part of his education up to his eighteenth year.

In 1857 G. M. Corey, in company with his father, came to this township, and here the latter took up eighty acres of Government land on section 26. He put up a board shanty, and for several years after his coming to the county served as a local preacher of the Baptist denomination. Until he was twenty years of age our subject remained with his father, and then he began the active duties of life on his own account by working on a farm for the next three years.

August 15, 1861, Mr. Corey enlisted as a private in Company D, Seventh Minnesota Infantry, and was mustered into the service at Ft. Snelling. From there he was sent to Ft. Abercrombie, N. Dak., near which point he took part in two severe encounters with the Indians. In 1862 he worked on the fortifications and blockade, and in the summer of 1863 left with his company and went on the Sibley Expedition, fitted out for the purpose of going across the plains. Later he was sent to St. Louis, where he did garrison duty and guarded Government property until the spring of 1864. At that time he was ordered to go to Kentucky, where he arrived a few days after the battle of Paducah. On the 19th of June he went to Memphis, and thence proceeded along one of the railroads to Moscow, a point about thirty miles distant. June 25 he was sent to La Grange, and from there to Tupelo, Miss. After taking part in the battles in and about Nashville, he was sent to Eastport, Tenn., then to New Orleans, and from there to Dauphin Island, where he camped for a short time. For thirteen days during the siege of Spanish Fort he was under fire, and after this arduous duty was obliged to march all the way to Montgomery, Ala. His long and severe service was terminated August 16,

1865, when he received his final discharge at Ft Snelling

On his return from the South Mr Corey, of this sketch, was employed at a fixed salary by his father, and had the management of the latter's farms for about three years He was enabled to save the main portion of his earnings, and later invested them in a farm of two hundred and forty acres, lying in this township. The land was entirely unimproved and in a state of nature. The young man set to work with energy to improve the place, which he cleared and brought under good cultivation When an opportunity offered he sold the farm and purchased the one where he still resides. This was in 1870, and the farm which he bought then comprised one hundred and sixty acres To this he has constantly added, until his estate numbers four hundred and eighty acres, all in a body and well improved

January 29, 1866, occurred the marriage of our subject and Miss Esther Todd, youngest daughter of William and Mary (Craton) Todd, of Money Creek Township, Houston County Minn Seven children have been born of their union, as follows: Bertha E, who was born October 5, 1866 and died October 16 of the same year, Levi W, born February 6, 1869, Kiza M., May 12 1873, Guy, October 25, 1875, Roxey, July 29 1879, Mark February 19, 1882; and Harry, January 19, 1886

In politics Mr Corey has been an active supporter of the Republican party since becoming a voter. He has served his township as Supervisor, and by holding other local offices Fraternally he is identified with the Masonic order, and is a member of the Grand Army of the Republic. He is a man who merits the great respect in which he is held by all who have the pleasure of his acquaintance for he is honorable and upright in his dealings with one and all, and ever has the best interests of others deeply at heart

---

Rev. John Horan.

REV. JOHN HORAN, pastor of St Charles Catholic Church of St. Charles, Minn, was born in Limerick, Ireland, on the 24th of June, 1819 His boyhood days were passed in his native city, and at the age of fourteen he entered the Jesuit Classical School, where he pursued his studies for two years, preparatory to entering college He then attended Mt Mellery College, of County Waterford, completed the regular course, and passed the examination necessary for entrance to the Univer[illegible] College, the d[illegible] not decided to enter the priesthood, but during the vacation of 1867 he determined to become a student in the latter institution, his parents strongly urging him to enter upon the work of the church He spent five years in the divinity school, pursuing a thorough course of study, and in 1872 was ordained for work in Melbourne, Australia

Father Horan then sailed for that field of labor, and in Melbourne found a fine church the members of which, he says, were unsurpassed for their gen-[illegible] ship of fifteen [illegible] Pro-Cathedral.

with a congregation consisting mainly of English and Irish people, but also of some French and German. He there continued his work for ten years, when his health failing he was forced to seek a change of climate. He then returned to the Emerald Isle but expected to again go to Australia on recovering his health. He remained two years in Ireland and in 1884 he was transferred to the United States. For two years he was in the East, then spent two years in Cincinnati and in 1890 came to St. Charles, succeeding Father Keenan. He has two other churches under his care, those of St. Rose of Lima, at Lewiston; and St. Peter and Paul's Church at Hart. He gives his entire time and attention to the work of the church, and St. Charles' Church is now in a flourishing condition.

Father Horan is a close student along the lines of science, philosophy and history. He is oftentimes considered rather reserved, but to those who know him best he is a genial, companionable man. He makes great friends of his books, and is a close student along the deeper lines of thought. He is much devoted to the study of resemblances between the great philosophers, touching the problems of human life, and also closely studies their discrepancies. Although he is not a public lecturer, he frequently appears before audiences, and his speeches always bring him friends. He gains approval but antagonizes no one. He is in hearty sympathy with American institutions, and is looked upon by those in authority as a man whose history will be closely interwoven with the affairs of the church in this diocese.

Martin Frederick Gensmer.

MARTIN FREDERICK GENSMER, the efficient and popular Postmaster of Lewiston, Winona County, was born on the 4th of March, 1841, in Alt-Ruednitz, Prussia, and is a son of Martin and Caroline (Kastner) Gensmer, who were also natives of the same locality. On emigrating to America, his parents settled upon a farm in Dodge County, Wis., and after residing there for a time came to Minnesota, locating in Winona County in the spring of 1862. Here they settled upon the farm in Norton Township which is still their home, and the worthy couple are numbered among the honored and respected citizens of the community. The father, who is remarkably strong and well preserved for one of his years, has reached the advanced age of eighty-five, and the mother is eighty-four years of age. Mr. and Mrs. Gensmer had a family of six children, four sons and two daughters, as follows: Mary, now the [illegible] Township; Minnie, the wife of August Hilke, a resident of Mayville, Wis.; Martin F., of this sketch; Louis, a farmer of Norton Township, Winona County; and Henry and P. Ferdinand, who are also agriculturists of Norton Township.

Martin Gensmer was a lad of eleven summers when he was brought by his parents to the New World. He remained upon the home farm and gave his father the benefit of his services until about twenty-eight years of age. At that time, in 1868, he came to Lewiston, Minn. Here he engaged in the hardware business, which he conducted for a time, but on account of ill-health he was afterward obliged to sell out. Since that time he has been engaged in various lines of trade, including grain dealing.

On the 28th of May, 1871, Mr. Gensmer was united in marriage with Miss Mary Callies, of Le Sueur County, Minn., a native of Dodge County, Wis., [illegible] in 1859. Their union has been blessed with a family of ten children: William, the eldest, who is now in partnership with his father in the grocery and general mercantile business in Lewiston; Emil, a tinner by trade, working in Winona; Julia, a saleslady in her father's store; and Mary, Martin, Minnie, Amelia, Ida, Alfred and Grover C., all of whom are still with their parents.

Martin Gensmer votes the Democratic ticket, and is a stanch supporter of the principles of his party, doing all in his power to advance its interests. He is now serving as Postmaster of Lewiston, to which position he was appointed in 1886, serving through both the Republican and Democratic administrations. He has been Treasurer of his township, Village Trustee, and a member of the School Board for several years, and in all these offices has discharged his duties with a promptness and fidelity that have won him high commendation. He and his family are members of the Lutheran Church, and are well known and highly respected people of the community. He is one of the oldest and most trusted business men of Lewiston, and the development and upbuilding of the community are largely due to his earnest efforts in its behalf.

J. R. WATKINS.

J. R. Watkins.

J. R. WATKINS, the subject of this sketch, is the President of the J. R. Watkins Medical Company, of Winona, Minn., proprietors and manufacturers of Dr. Ward's remedies. He is a native of the Buckeye State, his birth having occurred at Cincinnati, on the 21st of August, 1840. He was reared in the state of his nativity, spending his boyhood and youth in his parents' home, and was educated at College Hill, Ohio. In 1862 he accompanied his father's family to Minnesota, and became a resident of Stearns County, where soon after they were subject to great hardships on account of the Indian War.

In 1868 Mr. Watkins secured from Richard Ward, of Cincinnati, the right to manufacture and sell his remedies, and later bought out Mr. Ward's entire business. For a valuable consideration he purchased the world-wide right to use his name as a trademark, and had the same registered in the United States Patent Office at Washington, D. C. By more than twenty-six years of hard labor, by honest and upright dealing with the public at all times, and by the expenditure of many thousands of dollars in advertising, Mr. Watkins has made his trade-mark, "Dr. Ward's," a household word in hundreds of thousands of homes, and has succeeded in building up by far the largest medicine and extract business in the Northwest. In order to protect his own interests, as well as those of his multitudinous customers, at the beginning of the year 1891 Mr. Watkins incorporated his business under the name of the J. R. Watkins Medical Company, placing the capital stock at $500,000, with himself as President and Treasurer, and Paul Watkins, his nephew, as Vice-President and Secretary. The business is constantly increasing, and furnishes employment now to more than two hundred men.

Mr. Watkins has been in the city of Winona since the year 1885. In 1890, in order to meet the demands of his increasing trade, he put up a large, substantial brick building, and in the spring of 1894 completed an addition (larger than the original building), which includes large offices, perfect in all their appointments, forming one of the most complete medical laboratories in the country.

Mr. Watkins was married in 1868 to Miss Mary Ellen Heberling, a native of Harrison County, Ohio, and a daughter of George H. Heberling, who lived many years in the Buckeye State, but was born in Virginia, of German parentage. Mr. and Mrs. Watkins have one daughter, Grace.

The following facts with reference to Mr. Watkins' ancestry are of interest. His parents, Rev. B. F. and Sophronia (Keeler) Watkins, had a family of four, all of whom are yet living. The father was born in Hamilton County, Ohio, in the year 1811, and continued his residence in the state of his birth until 1862, covering a period of more than half a century. He followed the ministry, and was a man of more than average ability and power, his labors therefore proving very successful. In the year 1862 he removed with his family to Minnesota, where nearly twenty years of his life were passed. From Minnesota he removed to Cameron, Mo., where he lived a peaceful life until called to the home beyond, in March, 1891, having reached the advanced age of fourscore years. His was a noble life and he left to his family the priceless heritage of an untarnished name. Mrs. Watkins was born at Crown Point, N. Y., on the shore of Lake Champlain, and came of a family that settled in the northern part of the Empire State during pioneer days.

James Watkins, the grandfather of the subject of this sketch, was born in New Jersey in 1764, eleven years before the breaking out of the Revolution. In 1800 he started across the mountains with an ox-team, and became one of those sturdy pioneers who opened up the great state of Ohio to modern civilization. He was one of the first settlers in the western part of the state, and located on what was known as the Sims' Purchase, between the Miami Rivers, at a point then called Ft. Washington, where the city of Cincinnati now stands. He took an active part in the development and advancement of that region during a long life, and his name is inseparably connected with the history of the community in which he lived. By trade he was a blacksmith and brought from New Jersey the first nail-cutting machine ever taken west of the mountains of Pennsylvania. During those early days nails were sold as high as thirty-five cents a pound. The anvil used by James Watkins, and which he brought over the mountains with him, is still in the family, and is engraved with appropriate inscriptions, with the names and dates of birth of the original owner, his son, grandson and great-grandson, and will be handed down to future generations. The death of James Watkins occurred in 1848, at the ripe old age of eighty-four years.

The great-grandfather, Tobias Watkins, was born in New Jersey, in the early part of the eighteenth century, and his entire life was there passed. During the Revolutionary War he took contracts for furnishing beef to the army. At the end of the war he was in possession of a great roll of continental money, which he is remembered to have described as being "as large as his thigh," and which he burned, being utterly worthless, as there were no funds with which to redeem it. Mr. Watkins came of a family of Welsh descent, which for more than two hundred years has resided in America.

Edwin Hill.

EDWIN HILL, an attorney-at-law of St Charles, Minn, was born on the 6th of February, 1831, in Franklin County, Vt, and is a son of Rufus and Mary (Farwell) Hill His father was a native of Troy, N. Y, and when a lad of nine years went with his parents to Vermont, where he afterward carried on farming In the early part of his life he also engaged in brickmaking. By his marriage he had a family of twelve children, seven of whom grew to mature years, while six are yet living. George, who was born October 18, 1828, is now a retired blacksmith of Eyota, Minn Charles A., born October 9, 1831, is now engaged in farming near Morristown Vt Hiram W is editor of the *Times* of St Charles Willard F., born March 12, 1842, was a soldier in the late war, enlisting in the Thirty-sixth Wisconsin Infantry After serving for about a year he was taken sick and died in the hospital at City Point. Georgiana A, born January 9, 1851, is living with her mother in St Charles Charlena D, born in 1853, is now the wife of L Wheeler, a resident of Dane County, Wis, and a brother of Ella Wheeler Wilcox, the poetess of Wisconsin. The parents of this family were married in May, 1821, in Fairfax, Vt., where the father engaged in brickmaking Having saved some money, he in connection with his brother, purchased land and carried on a sawmill, becoming fairly well-to-do In the year 1856 he bade good-bye to his Vermont home and emigrated westward, locating in New Lisbon, Wis., where his [illegible] passed He was born in 1800, and died on the 18th of August, 1879 He witnessed the last battle of the War of 1812, which took place on Lake Champlain He was a Republican in politics, and was a highly esteemed citizen After her husband's death Mrs Hill came to Winona County where she is yet living at the advanced age of eighty-six, her birth having occurred in 1808 She, too, is a native of the Green Mountain State

During his early boyhood days Edwin Hill remained with his parents and acquired a fair English education, but at the age of sixteen he started out in life for himself and began shoemaking in Massachusetts After he had attained to man's estate he chose as a companion and helpmate on life's journey Miss Mary I Powell of Eau Claire Wis., their wedding being celebrated on the 4th of July, 1861 The lady is a daughter of John Powell, a native of Wales, who became one of the early settlers of the Badger State

At the time of his marriage Mr. Hill was serving as Sheriff of his county, and also owned a farm, being thus quite comfortably situated His possessions were all acquired through his own efforts and were the just reward of his earnest labors. The home of Mr and Mrs Hill was blessed with the presence of ten children seven of whom are yet living Minnie E., born July 12, 1862 died on the 18th of April 1870 Ulysses S. G., born November 17, 1864, was a bright young man and at the time of his death which occurred [illegible] bookkeeper in his uncle's store in Eau Claire, Wis. Jennie, born October 31, 1867, is now the wife of Floyd J. Stebbins, a druggist of Thief River Falls, Minn. Nettie St Charles, born March 11, 1870, was the first child born in the town after St. Charles was made a city. Maud M., born April 30, 1871, was a bright and interesting little girl and loved by all who knew her. She died December 2, 1880. Maggie, born January 13, 1874, is now at home. Ben F., born September 2, 1876, is employed in the drug store of Mr. Stebbins at Thief River Falls, Minn. Goldie, born April 24, 1879, is at home. Bessie, born February 16, 1882, is still under the parental roof. Edwin, born February 23, 1885, completes the family.

Mr. Hill is a member of the Masonic fraternity, and has taken the Knight-Templar degree. He exercises his right of franchise in support of the Republican party, but has never been an aspirant for office, preferring to give his entire time and attention to his business interests. He has made a success of the law, and holds an enviable position among his professional brethren.

Nathan Brown.

NATHAN BROWN, who follows farming on section 1, New Hartford Township, was born on the 24th of April, 1820, in Clinton County, N. Y., and is a son of Charles and Sarah (Newton) Brown. The father was a native of Rhode Island, and a farmer by occupation. In the family were eight children: Renolds, now of Dakota, this county; Mrs. Mary Guynarup, now deceased; Nathan; Mrs. Elizabeth Baker and Mrs. Mercy Boyington, both deceased; Leonard, who is living on the old homestead in Washington, N. Y., which belonged to his grandfather; Fred, now of Dakota, Winona County; and Sarah, wife of James Wilson. The father of this family was a successful man of business. He had no educational privileges in his youth of any importance, but was a great Bible student, and was a member of the "Iron-Jacket" Baptists. He served in the War of 1812, and his father was one of the heroes of the Revolution. [illegible] of ninety-tw[illegible] away in 1870, at the age of seventy-nine. He had a strong constitution and death came very suddenly. He several times visited his children in Winona County, and while at the home of his daughter Mary, he passed away. His wife, who was a native of Vermont, died at the age of about fifty-eight years.

Nathan Brown enjoyed no special advantages in his youth and from early life has been inured to hard labor. His school privileges were indeed limited. After attaining to man's estate, however, he began to realize the need of an education, and through his own efforts has obtained a practical business knowledge. He has also read quite extensively, and is now well informed on the leading questions of the day. He was still a young man when he determined to come West. He had left home on attaining his majority, and began work for himself, scorning no labor which would yield [illegible] [illegible]ustrious and en-[illegible] [illegible]perseverance he had secured a capital of about $8,000 at the time of his removal to the West

It was in 1849 that Mr Brown started for Minnesota and on the 29th of September arrived in Winona County He had obtained a permit to engage in business as an Indian trader Land had been entered by a company for a town site and Mr. Brown was entitled to a homestead He also secured one hundred and sixty acres of land on the same section, and afterward bought another one hundred and sixty acres of a company paying $1,900 for the entire amount He has here since made his home, and is now the owner of four hundred acres of valuable land, situated on sections 1, 7 and 12 of New Hartford Township He was the second white settler in the county, and during all the years which have passed since his arrival he has lived upon the old homestead, where he yet resides In his business he has prospered He made judicious investments in land, which he sold when a favorable opportunity presented itself, and when he was thirty six years of age, had he sold out, he could have realized $20,000 in cash

In 1852 Mr Brown started for Milwaukee He went by boat to Galena, and thence by stage to within thirty miles of Chicago, where he took a train upon the first railroad which ever ran out of Chicago The road was built upon the old flat-bar system and now forms a part of the Illinois Central After going about ten miles the train was ditched, plunging down a bank about fifteen feet Mr Brown thought the railroad very treacherous, but at length safely reached Chicago, where he boarded a boat for Milwaukee. The object of the journey was made known when he returned with a bride On the 3d of October, 1852, he married Eliza A Bartholomew, daughter of Isaac and Firza (Houghton) Bartholomew, the former a native of Vermont, and the latter of New Hampshire In their family were twelve children, six of whom are yet living The father was a farmer, and both he and his wife died in New York

Mr. Brown would not risk his bride upon a railroad train but took a stage across the country from Milwaukee to Galena, and thence proceeded by boat to his home in Dakota On the 21st of July, 1854, Mrs Brow[illegible]

and on the 9th of April, 1856, Mr Brown married Julia E. Bartholomew, a sister of his first wife. They became the parents of ten children, eight of whom are now living Isaac C, born April 16, 1857, died September 23, 1861 Leslie L born November 5 1858, is one of the leading lawyers of Winona Hoyt N, born January 4, 1861, is now engaged in railroading in Arkansas Carlos H, born April 16, 1863, carries on farming at home Giles H, born January 23, 1865, is a farmer Cora born December 15, 1867, is at home Mrs Gracie Cass was born April 19, 1869 Dora, born December 16, 1870, is attending school in Milwaukee. Arthur J, born February 11, 1874, is at home. Evelyn, born February 3, 1876 died January 18, 1889

When Mr Brown was first married he returned with his wife to Dakota, here he had a two-story house and a store, where he sold goods to the few pioneer settlers of the neighborhood, and to the Indians, who were his principal customers When Mr Brown arrived here Winona had not yet sprung into existence It was laid out in the fall of 1850, and the first house was built by a Mr Johnson, and furnished by Capt Orin Smith an old steamboat captain. Mr Brown has therefore witnessed the entire growth and development of the county, and is one of its most honored pioneers The land which was in possession of the Government at the time of his arrival, and which was the home of Indians, has been transformed into highly cultivated farms, towns and villages have sprung up, and the work of progress and civilization has been carried forward, until now Winona County occupies a leading place in the state Mr Brown has ever borne his part in the work of improvement, and none are more familiar with pioneer history in this community than he In his business he has prospered and is now in very comfortable circumstances

In his social relations Mr Brown is a Mason, and in his political affiliations is a Democrat He was one of the first County Commissioners At the first election there were three chosen for the office. The one who received the most number of votes was to serve for five years, the second for [illegible] s, and when the ballots were counted it was found that Mr Brown had the largest number. He served from 1853 until 1859, and in 1874 was again elected County Commissioner. He has never sought office, but his fitness for the position was recognized by his fellow-townsmen, and he therefore received the election

The following is an unsolicited tribute from a gentleman who is fully competent to judge of Mr Brown's many good qualities

"Mr Brown has been from the first a most rugged and conspicuous figure in our history, distinguished for his manly courage, his fidelity to friends as well as to truth and principle. He does not seek contention, yet, when thrust upon him, he does not retire from the ordeal He can be depended upon to stand by the right as he understands it, without counting the cost He has met and unflinchingly faced many dangers incident to frontier life, and if his environment should ever be such as to require the qualities of real greatness, he would not be found wanting in the hour of trial."

William G. Christie.

WILLIAM G CHRISTIE, a farmer residing on section 16, Saratoga Township, has for a quarter of a century resided in Winona County, and is therefore numbered among its early settlers. He has watched its growth and progress, has aided in its development and upbuilding, and much of its history is known to him. He has a wide acquaintance in this community, and many will receive with interest this record of his life, which well deserves a place in this volume

Mr Christie was born in Dundee, Scotland, December 18, 1830, and is a son of James and Elizabeth (Gilchrist) Christie, who were also natives of the same country. Their family numbered eight children, six sons and two daughters William G. was reared in the city of his nativity, his boyhood days being passed amidst play and work and in attendance at the common schools, where he acquired a fair business [illegible] When [illegible] teen he accom[illegible] tion to Ame[illegible] Dodge County, Wis., where the father took up Government land William then became familiar with the arduous task of developing a new farm, breaking the oak openings, and plowing and cultivating it until it was transformed into rich and fertile fields He continued under the parental roof until twenty-three years of age, when he began working in his own interest, being employed as a farm hand by the month In 1856 he came to Minnesota, locating in what is now Dover Township, Olmsted County He settled on school land, purchasing one hundred and twenty acres, and began life in earnest He was one of the pioneers of that locality, and aided in the organization of Dover Township

In 1861, however, Mr Christie laid aside all business cares and responded to the President's call for volunteers, enlisting as a private in the First Minnesota Light Artillery He was mustered into service at Ft Snelling on the [illegible] of November, and [illegible] St. Louis, where he [illegible] until March,

1862. From that time forward he was engaged in active service. The first battle in which he participated was Pittsburg Landing. This was followed by the siege of Corinth and the battle of that place. He was under Grant during the entire siege of Vicksburg, and after the surrender of the city, on the 4th of July, did garrison duty until the following February at that place. He was next stationed at Cairo, where the battery was re-organized. With his company he then went up the Tennessee River to Clifton and across the country, joining Sherman's army at Acworth. He was with General Sherman during the entire Atlanta campaign, participating in its many battles, and after the surrender of Atlanta went on the celebrated and victorious march to the sea. He was taken prisoner at Bentonville, March 21, 1865, but soon after was paroled and returned home. At the battle of Pittsburg Landing he was wounded by a minie-ball, but otherwise was uninjured. At the siege of Atlanta, July 30, 1864, when the battery to which Mr. Christie was attached had just moved into park, a sixty-four-pound rebel shell struck the right caisson, exploded the powder in two limber chests and some of the shells. The exploding powder ignited the tow plugs in the ends of the remaining shells in the chests. Mr. Christie at that moment was resting in his tent after thirty-six hours' continuous service in the trenches. One piece of the damaged caisson was blown through the tent and landed within an inch of his head. In the excitement he ran out bareheaded, seizing a pail of water as he went, and running to the injured caisson found the tow plugs of the shells on fire. This fire he extinguished with his hands and deluged the chest with water from the pail he had with him, and thus, at the risk of his own life, saved an unknown number of his comrades from death by their own ammunition. He returned a paroled prisoner on the day of the Grand Review at Washington, D. C., the most celebrated military pageant ever seen in the western hemisphere, and on the 1st of July, 1865, was honorably discharged at St. Paul. He was a faithful and valiant soldier, always found at his post of duty, and ever wore the blue with honor.

Mr. Christie at once returned to his home, where he remained until the spring of 1866. He then came to Winona County and purchased a farm of eighty acres on section 16, Saratoga Township, forty acres on section 36, St. Charles Township, and twenty acres on section 9, Saratoga Township. He now has one hundred and forty acres. Shortly before his arrival here he was married, the lady of his choice being Miss Mary B. Aimer. The wedding was celebrated on the 31st of December, 1865, and their union has been blessed with a family of eleven children: William A., who resides at home and carries on the farm; David, James and Thomas, all of whom died of diphtheria in 1880; Jessie Elizabeth, Robert J., Bertie, Grant S., Richard and Mary M.

Mr. Christie is a public-spirited and progressive citizen, devoted to the best interests of the community in which he has so long made his home. He has served as Justice of the Peace for some time, and is now filling that office with credit to himself and satisfaction to his constituents. He votes with the Republican party, whose principles he warmly advocates, and with the Grand Army of the Republic he holds membership. His time and attention are largely given to general farming, which has been his life work and which has brought to him prosperity, making him one of the substantial citizens of the community. All who know him respect him, for he is a man of sterling worth.

John Keenan.

JOHN KEENAN is numbered among the early settlers of Winona, and has been prominently identified with its growth and development. As a contractor and builder his handiwork is seen on all sides, but aside from the line of his business he has also aided largely in promoting the best interests of the city. He was born in Wayne County, Pa., September 17, 1840, and is one in a family of eleven children, five of whom are yet living. His parents were James and Elizabeth (O'Farrell) Keenan. The father, who was born in 1807, spent thirty-five years of his life in the Keystone State, and in 1866 came to Minnesota, locating in Winona, where he spent one year. He then removed to Austin, where his remaining days were passed, and in 1879 he was called to the home beyond, being then seventy-two years of age. During the greater part of his life he followed farming. His wife was called to her final rest in 1884, at the age of sixty-five. Their children who are yet living are: John, Mary, widow of M. J. Riley, and a resident of Austin, James and Joseph, who are engaged in dealing in agricultural implements in Austin, and M. J., a dealer in music and sewing machines in the same city.

The days of his boyhood and youth John Keenan passed in his native state, where he remained until 1860, when, at the age of twenty years, he removed to New York City. There he made his home until 1867, and during a part of the time was engaged in business as a carpenter and joiner. In that year he came W[illegible] home almos[illegible] operations as a contractor and builder, and has erected many of the most notable buildings in the city. He has during some very busy seasons employed as many as seventy-five hands, and with his helpers has done a vast amount of work. In partnership with N. C. Munck he built the city water-works and the Winona County court house, one of the finest county buildings in the state. Since dissolving partnership with Mr. Munck, Mr. Keenan has built the A. F. Hodgins residence, the Judge Mitchell residence, the Slade Block, the American Express Building, the H. J. O'Neill residence, and many churches and other private and public buildings.

On the 2d of April, 1865, Mr. Keenan was united in marriage with Miss Honora Martha, daughter of James Martha, and the wedding was celebrated in New York City. Three children have graced their union, Anna, Mamie L. and Leo J., all of whom are yet at home.

In his political views Mr. Keenan is a Democrat. He has long been interested in city affairs and in public matters pertaining to the general welfare, but has never sought notoriety through politics. For years he refused to accept office, but in April, 1891, was elected Alderman-at-large and in 1893 was re-elected. For two years he has served as Chairman of the board, and during his connection with public affairs many important improvements have been made, creditable to the wisdom and energy of the council. Under his administration [illegible] ross the river, a [illegible] y-million-gallon pump has been placed in the water-works, while large distributing pipes have been laid through the city more than three miles in length. Wishing to improve the streets by paving them, Mr. Keenan was obliged to have an act passed by the Legislature, but the undertaking did not prove too formidable for him, and the work was accomplished. At least nine-tenths of the stone sidewalks laid in the city have been put in during the past three years. In 1893 the board determined upon beginning the levee improvement, which is now well under way, and will eventually be one of the finest levees upon the Mississippi River. It will be a marked addition to the attractiveness of the city and creditable to the enterprise of the men who made it a possibility.

Mr. Keenan is also a member of the board of the Hospital Association. Probably no man in the community, especially during the last few years, has taken as important a part in the development and progress of Winona, and the city certainly owes to him a debt of gratitude. He is one of the most wide-awake and enterprising men of the day, respected alike for his business ability, his genial manners and his sterling worth.

Herman Canfield.

HERMAN CANFIELD devotes his time and attention to agriculture on his farm, which lies partly within and partly without the corporation limits of the village of Saratoga. He was born near Elmira, Schuyler County, N. Y., on the 25th of September, 1841, and is the eldest in the family of nine children whose parents were Nelson and Jane (Durham) Canfield. The family is of German origin, but the father was born in the Empire State. The children were Herman, Alvin, Augusta, Nettie, Jennie, Nelson, Charles, Annie and Robert.

During the first seven years of his life, Herman Canfield lived on the old homestead farm in New York and was then taken by his parents to Jackson County, Iowa, where he remained until the spring of 1857. He then came to Minnesota by team, and located in Saratoga Township, Winona County. He is practically self-educated, for he attended school only in the winter season, and then but to a limited extent. His training at farm labor, however, was not meager, and to his father he gave the benefit of his services until the 4th of October, 1861, when, at the age of twenty years, he responded to the country's call for troops to aid in crushing out the rebellion. His services were accepted, he was assigned to Company D, Seventh Minnesota Infantry, and was mustered in at Ft. Snelling, from where he proceeded by rail and boat to St. Louis, and thence was ordered to St. Joseph, Mo. He then went to Sedalia, where he joined his regiment and went on the march after Price. The first active engagement in which he participated was at Nashville, and this was followed by the one at Spanish Fort, and the siege of Mobile. He was at Selma, Ala., when the news of Lee's surrender was received. He went through the service as a private, and was never wounded or taken prisoner. After the war was over he was honorably discharged, on the 16th of August, 1865, and returned to his home with the consciousness of having been faithful to his country in her hour of peril

Soon after being mustered out, Mr Canfield was again in Winona County, and during the succeeding five years lived on the old homestead with his father, operating the same, and placing it under a high state of cultivation He was married on the 16th of November, 1870, to Miss Mary Ames, and to them has been born a son Harry E., born December 10, 1888

Upon his marriage, Mr Canfield rented land for two years, after which he removed to Chatfield and engaged in carrying the mail from that place to St. Charles His time was thus passed for three years, when he again resumed farming, living on rented land for two years On the expiration of that period, with the capital he had acquired, he purchased a farm of one hundred and sixty acres in Saratoga Township, and made it his home for two years, when he bought his present farm, comprising one hundred acres, lying partly within the village limits of Saratoga

Mr Canfield votes with the Republican party and has always been a stanch supporter of its principles Socially he is connected with the Masonic fraternity A self-made and self-educated man he deserves great credit for his success in life, which has been achieved through his own efforts and has come to him as the result of earnest labor, enterprise and industry

Henry Ruehman.

HENRY RUEHMAN, who devotes his energies to agricultural pursuits on section 32, Winona Township, is a native of Germany That country has furnished to the county many leading citizens, prominent among whom is the gentleman whose name heads this record He was born on the 9th of August, 1841, and was reared upon a farm, spending the days of his boyhood and youth in the usual manner of farmer lads. The common schools afforded him his educational privileges

It was in May, 1866, when twenty-five years of age, that Mr Ruehman sailed for America He bade adieu to the home and friends of his childhood and came to the United States to seek his fortune With the years has come no regret over the step then taken, for here he has prospered in his business undertakings, winning a success which would probably not have come to him in the Fatherland He first located near Chicago, digging ditches on a farm for a month, after which he continued his westward journey to Davenport, Iowa Near that place he worked at harvesting until the autumn of 1866, when he came to Winona For two years he was employed as a farm hand by the month, and was then engaged in a brickyard for a similar period Wishing that his services might more directly benefit himself, he began farming in his own name [illegible] eight years On the expiration [illegible] purchased one hundred and twenty acres of land on section 32, Winona Township, and has since made it his home.

On the 5th of April, 1888, Mr. Ruehman and Miss Minnie Suckstorf were united in marriage. The lady is also a native of Germany. Two children were born to them, but one died in infancy. Annie, a bright little maiden, is still with her parents. In the community where they live Mr. and Mrs. Ruehman are widely and favorably known and have many friends who esteem them highly for their sterling worth and many excellences of character.

In his political affiliations Mr. Ruehman is a Republican. He warmly advocates the principles of that party, and by his ballot has supported its men and measures since becoming an American citizen. For eight years he has been a member of the Board of Supervisors, and his long-continued service in that office is a high testimonial to his fidelity. Socially he is connected with the Order of Druids of Winona. The greater part of his time and attention, however, are given to his agricultural interests. When he came to his farm it was covered with timber, but he at once began to clear it, and as the trees fell before his sturdy strokes they were replaced by grain fields, which in course of time yielded golden harvests. Of the farm seventy acres are now under a high state of cultivation, and upon it have been placed many excellent improvements, which stand as monuments to the progressive spirit of Mr. Ruehman.

Hon. Fares B. Martin.

HON. FARES B. MARTIN, the leading merchant of Witoka, and one of the prominent citizens of the county, claims Indiana as the state of his nativity, his birth having occurred in Lebanon, Boone County, on the 25th of February, 1851. His father, Wesley Martin, was born on the shores of Lake Chautauqua, in the Empire State, and at a very early day emigrated to the West, locating in Lebanon, Ind. There he owned and operated a sawmill, and had other property. He was also a merchant, and did a good business in commercial circles. He afterward removed to Jamestown, Boone County, in that town carrying on a woolen-mill and gristmill for about four years. On the expiration of that period he came to Minnesota, and purchased a farm in Homer Township, Winona County, in the year 1863. Here [illegible] he made his home for about twenty years. He was successfully engaged in agricultural pursuits, and was a well known farmer of the community. His wife died about four years ago and since that time he has made his home with his children, who are all well-to-do people. In his undertakings he has prospered, and is now the owner of considerable property in Indiana, the rents from which yield him an income more than amply sufficient to supply all his wants.

The public schools afforded F. B. Martin his educational privileges. He came with his parents to Minnesota and remained with them until about eighteen years of age, when he started out to make his own way in the world. Returning to his birthplace, he was there engaged in selling goods for the Grange store, of which he had charge for about [illegible] Minnesota and aided his father in carrying on a farm. He also became a music teacher, being for a year and a-half engaged as a vocal instructor. As a companion and helpmate on life's journey he chose Miss Jennie Smith, born February 25, 1856, a daughter of C. P. and Jane Smith, who were natives of New York, and now reside in Watertown, S. Dak., where the father carries on agricultural pursuits. The wedding of Mr. and Mrs. Martin was celebrated on the 14th of October, 1877, and their union was blessed with two children, but Pearl, the elder, who was born August 7, 1878, died February 7, 1879. Earl F., born July 11, 1890, is a sturdy little fellow of four summers.

Mr. Martin embarked in general merchandising in Witoka in 1886 with a very small capital, but he has constantly increased his stock to meet the growing trade, and now has about $6,000 invested in the store. He is ever fair and honest in his dealings, and courteous in his treatment, and his pleasant, genial manner and earnest desire to please have won him a large trade, which is constantly increasing. He is a very enterprising and public-spirited man, and has recently erected a fine hall at a cost of $2,500 for the purpose of giving his fellow-townsmen a place of entertainment. He labors earnestly in the interests of the community, and his support and co-operation are withheld from no worthy enterprise calculated to be of public benefit. In fact, he is a prime mover in many such undertakings. Socially he is connected with the Knights of Pythias lodge and the Masonic fraternity. In his political views he is a Republican, and was elected to the Legislature in the fall of 1894, obtaining a plurality of some two hundred votes in a district having an average Democratic majority of over two hundred, thus running about four hundred ahead of his ticket.

Joseph D. Ball.

JOSEPH D. BALL, a farmer of Saratoga Township, residing on section 9, is a native of New York. He was born in Chautauqua County, on the 14th of November, 1813, and was six years of age at the time of his parents' removal to McKean County, Pa. There he grew to manhood and in its public schools acquired his education. He started out in life for himself when sixteen years of age and from that time forward has been dependent on his own resources, so that the success he has achieved in life is due entirely to his own c[illegible]

Mr. Ball [illegible] country during the late war. He watched with interest the progress of events which preceded that struggle, and his sympathies were all with the Union so that when the attempt at secession was made he resolved to stand by the Government, and hardly had the smoke from Ft. Sumter cleared away when, on the 21st of April, 1861, he responded to the call for three-months troops. He was assigned to Company A, McLean's Erie Regiment, and was stationed at Pittsburg during his first term. On the expiration of the three months [illegible] Company G, One [illegible] ania Infantry known as the Pennsylvania "Bucktails," or sharpshooters. This was in August 1862, and he was mustered into service at Harrisburg, Pa. The first engagement of the regiment was at Fredericksburg, which was followed by the battle of Chancellorsville and that most important battle of the war, Gettysburg. There Mr. Ball was wounded by a minie-ball, a shot entering his right arm. He was taken to the field hospital and thence sent to a hospital in Philadelphia, where he was forced to remain from July, 1863, until May, 1864. He was then placed on detached duty and went to Washington, where he served as an Orderly until the close of the war. His services being then no longer needed, he was honorably discharged on the 29th of June, 1865.

Mr. Ball at once returned to his home in the Keystone State, where he remained until March 1866, when he came to Winona County and located in Saratoga Township. For two years he rented land, and then purchased one hundred and sixty acres on section 23, which he subsequently sold, and bought the farm upon which he has since made his home. This was an improved farm, and Mr. Ball applied himself to its cultivation until September, 1894, when he sold out for the purpose of retiring from active farming. Success attended his efforts, and he not only placed his land under a high state of cultivation, but also added to it until he had three hundred and three acres, all in one body.

On Christmas Day of 1867 was celebrated the marriage of Mr. Ball and Miss Augusta F. Smith, daughter of Thomas S. and Julia A. (Scott) Smith, who were natives of Cattaraugus County, N. Y., the former born June 30, 1824, and the latter March 13, 1825. The paternal grandfather, John Smith, was a native of England and came to America when a child of twelve years. Mr. and Mrs. Thomas Smith married November 23, 1845, and became the parents of seven children: James D., who is engaged in the butchering business in Humboldt, Iowa; Augusta F., now Mrs. Ball; Julia A., wife of Edgar Howes, a resident of Ellington, Iowa; John T., who is living with his parents; William W. A., who is engaged in the butchering business in Fertile, Iowa; Wealthy A., wife of Stephen Streeper, who makes his home in Ellington, Iowa, and one who died in infancy. The father of this family was a blacksmith and cooper by trade. He made his home in New York until 1851, when, by way of the Lakes, he went to Milwaukee and thence drove across the country to Freeport, Iowa, where he established a blacksmith and cooper shop. There he carried on business for ten years, after which he purchased a farm in Hancock County, Iowa, where he now makes his home. He owns one hundred and sixty acres of land, but leaves its cultivation to his son, while he lives retired. He is a Republican in politics, has served as a member of the Board of Supervisors, and is a highly respected citizen.

To Mr. and Mrs. Ball have been born three children, and the family circle yet remains unbroken by the hand of death. Monroe, the eldest, is a resident farmer of Saratoga Township; Nellie is the wife of Edwin Smith, who resides in St. Charles, where he is engaged in clerking in a store; Dwight, who completes the family, is still at home. The parents are prominent and highly esteemed citizens of the community, and their friends in this locality are many.

Mr. Ball has always affiliated with the Republican party, and by his ballot supports its men and measures, but has never been an aspirant for office, his time and attention being fully occupied by his business interests, in which he has prospered. Socially, he is connected with the Masonic fraternity and with the Grand Army of the Republic. He manifests a commendable interest in public affairs, especially those calculated to promote the general welfare, and is as true to his duties of citizenship in times of peace as in days of war. His record as a soldier is an honorable one, for he valiantly followed the Old Flag on many a Southern battlefield, and even after disabled for active service stood by his country until the Stars and Stripes were victoriously planted in the capital of the confederacy.

Samuel Brammer.

SAMUEL BRAMMER is numbered among the early settlers of Winona, and for long years has not only witnessed the growth and development of this county, but has also aided in its progress and advancement. He therefore deserves mention among its founders, and his sketch deserves a place in its history. Mr. Brammer was born in Newark, Nottinghamshire, England, August 18, 1823, and was the sixth in a family of eight children whose parents were John and Sarah (Taylor) Brammer. The father was a shepherd, and died at the age of about sixty years. The mother passed away when about seventy-five years of age. Of their children, John and Sarah are still living in England; Thomas and Elias are now deceased; Edward makes his home in Canada; Samuel is the next, and Mary and Elizabeth are still living in England.

Mr. Brammer of this sketch attained his education in the common schools of his native land, and remained at home until seventeen years of age, when he started out in life for himself. He first engaged in railroading in Scotland and Wales, and was thus employed until the spring of 1849, when he bade adieu to the friends and home of his childhood, and in a sailing-vessel crossed the Atlantic to the New World. Here he sought and obtained employment on the construction of the Hudson River Railroad, being thus engaged for six months. On the expiration of that period he visited his brother in Genesee County, N. Y., where he continued [illegible] emigrated [illegible] took up his residence in Chicago, which was then but a small town, and for a short time worked in a livery stable. He was afterwards for a limited period employed on the farm, and then rented land in McHenry County, Ill., where he carried on agricultural pursuits in his own interest for three years. Returning to Chicago at that time, he then secured work with a drainage company, building plank roads for two years.

On the expiration of that period Mr. Brammer sought a home in Wisconsin, removing to Sauk County, where he bought one hundred and sixty acres of land. After a short time, however, he came to Winona, where he has made his home during the greater part of the time since the summer of 1856. He worked at the carpenter's trade until 1859, after which he engaged in railroading in Missouri for a time. He also served in the engineer corps for about six months in North and South Carolina, after which he returned to Winona, being made foreman of pile-driving for the Winona & St. Peter Railroad, a position which he held for eleven years. He then had charge of the wrecking car for five years, and for a time had charge of the construction of bridges. He has since been engineer on the drawbridge at Winona across the Mississippi River, in which capacity he is now serving. He is a faithful and conscientious business man, always true to his duties and to the trust reposed in him.

Mr. Brammer has been twice married. In Feb- [illegible] wedlock with Miss Mary Smith, [illegible] death left a daughter,

Evelyn, who is still residing with her father. In August 1862, Mr. Brammer was again married, his second union being with Miss Elizabeth Smith, of Winona, who died at the age of fifty years. To them were born five children: Jessie, who was graduated from both the high school and state normal school of Winona, has now been the efficient Principal of the Jefferson School of this city for five years; Sallie is also a graduate of the state normal, and is now successfully engaged in teaching in the Madison School of Winona; William S. is station agent of the Winona & St. Peter Railroad at Jaynesville, Minn.; and Mary and John are yet at home.

The Republican party receives the support of Mr. Brammer, who has advocated its men and measures since its organization. Socially he is connected with Winona Lodge No. 7, I. O. O. F., and is a faithful member of the Methodist Episcopal Church. Those who know him esteem him highly for his sterling worth, and he has the respect and confidence of a large circle of friends and acquaintances. The history of the community has been familiar to him from an early day, and in the development of the county he has ever manifested a commendable interest.

Jacob Haesly.

JACOB HAESLY, a manufacturer of cigars in Winona, embarked in business for himself in 1889, and now enjoys a good trade. He is enterprising and progressive, and is ranked among the leading business men of the city. Mr. Haesly is a native of Switzerland, his birth having occurred in the land of the Alps on the 16th of July, 1846. His parents, Jacob and Catherine (Bumgartner) Haesly, had a family of nine children, of whom he is the eldest. The father was a carver by trade, and carried on business along that line in the Old Country until 1848, when he bade adieu to friends and native land and with his family sailed to America. He first located on a farm in Green County, Wis., but now, at the age of sixty-nine years, is living a retired life in Dodge, Wis. He has been successful in his undertakings, and has acquired the capital which enables him to lay aside business cares and yet enjoy the comforts of life. His wife has now reached the age of seventy-two years.

Of the family of this worthy couple two died in childhood. The [illegible] Paulus, a resident farmer of Rochester County, Minn.; Frederick, who carries on a farm and is also proprietor of a hotel in Dodge, Wis.; Katie, now deceased; John, who is engaged in the manufacture of cigars in Winona; Casper, a resident of St. Paul; Marks, who is living in Winona; and Christina, who died in early girlhood.

The gentleman whose name heads this record was a child of only two years when by his parents he was brought to America. In the usual manner of farmer lads he was reared, and in the district schools of the neighborhood he acquired his education. To his father he gave the benefit of his services until 1862, when, at the early age of sixteen years, he responded to the President's call for troops to aid in crushing out the rebellion. His services were accepted and he was assigned to Company K of the Second Wisconsin Infantry, in which he served until the close of the war. He was present at Appomattox Court House at the time of General Lee's surrender. In the hotly contested Battle of the Wilderness he was wounded in [illegible] taken to the

Columbian Hospital in Washington, where he remained for about three months. As soon as he had sufficiently recovered he hastened to rejoin his regiment, with which he continued until the cessation of hostilities. He participated in twenty-two hard-fought engagements and many of lesser importance, and took part in the siege of Richmond. Although so young when he entered the service he was true to his oath of allegiance, and men whose years were double his own showed no more bravery when before the cannon's mouth than the farmer boy.

After being mustered out of the service, Mr. Haesly returned to Madison, Wis., and engaged in the cigar business, which he had followed for two years before the war. In October, 1867, he came to Winona, and remained in the employ of others until 1889, when he embarked in business for himself. He had acquired the necessary capital through industry, perseverance and economy, and his business career is that of a self-made man. He employs three workmen and enjoys a good trade, which yields to him a fair income.

On the 9th of March, 1877, Mr. Haesly was joined in wedlock with Miss Emma A. Surdan, of this county, and to them have been born two children, a son and daughter: Clayton J., born March 11, 1879, and Goldie Emma, born on the 20th of August, 1884.

Mr. Haesly holds membership with Winona Lodge No. 18, A. F. & A. M.; Winona Chapter No. 5, R. A. M., Cœur de Leon Commandery No. 3, K. T., all of Winona, and the Order of the Mystic Shrine of Minneapolis. He was quite prominent in Masonic circles. He also holds membership with the Odd Fellows' society of Winona. In local politics he takes quite an active interest and votes with the Republican party. He is a loyal citizen, and is as true to every duty as when on Southern battlefields he followed the Old Flag.

H. A. COREY.

Hamden A. Corey.

HAMDEN A. COREY is one of the old settlers of Wiscoy Township, Winona County, for he has made his home within its boundaries, upon his present homestead, for upwards of forty years. When he came here in 1855 he took up three hundred and twenty acres from the Government in company with his brother Sylvester. It was necessary for him to begin farming in an humble way, and his first home was in a log cabin, 15x18 feet in dimensions. Under its roof he lived until 1869, when he removed to the house which is still his residence, and which was the first one built of brick in this township.

The birth of our subject occurred in Northampton, Mass., January 20, 1822, his parents being Rev. Alpheus P. and Lilly (Pratt) Corey, natives of Massachusetts. They were married in the Bay State, and to them were born six children, namely: Almira, Mrs. Johnson, of La Crosse, Wis.; Julia, wife of Rev. D. Wilson, also of Wisconsin; Sylvester, whose home is in Money Creek Township, Houston County, Minn.; Augusta, wife of Harmon Waldron, of Winona; Minerva, deceased; and our subject. The mother of these children died in 1833, when Hamden was only eleven years old, and his father afterward married a Miss Brewster, by whom he had three children. He followed the shoemaker's trade, and being an industrious and enterprising business man, gained a good competence for himself and family. He had been a Free-Will Baptist preacher for many years.

Our subject passed his early years on a farm, and received his preliminary education in the district school. Later he attended a seminary at Bristol, Racine County, Wis. On attaining his majority, he began working for farmers by the month, and continued so doing until he came to the West. This event occurred in the spring of 1846, the journey being made by the canal and the Lakes as far as Kenosha, Wis. For a time he worked on a farm in Bristol Township, Kenosha County, taking a place on shares, and during this period he went to school through the winter months. In 1848 he returned to New York, and was there until the following year, when he moved upon a piece of Government land in Winnebago County, Wis., which he had entered in 1847. The tract comprised one hundred and twenty acres, and on a cleared piece of ground he erected a shanty with some lumber which he had obtained, and there he resided until 1855, when he sold out, and with three yoke of oxen started for Minnesota. Soon after his arrival here he became a permanent farmer of Wiscoy Township, where he has since been engaged in general agricultural duties and stock-raising.

May 29, 1849, Mr. Corey married Miss Lydia Page, and of their union were born three children: Sylvester A., who lives in Mitchell, Iowa; Wheeler, a merchant of Wheeler Station, Iowa, on the Winona & South-Western Railroad; and Alice, who married Alfred Jewell, and died on the 23d of March, 1891. Mrs. Lydia Corey died July 3, 1854, and on the 29th of the following October our subject married Miss Phœbe A. Place. Their marriage was blessed with the following children: Carrie, who became the wife of Clark P. Wood, a farmer in the state of Washington; Clark G., who is a member of the firm known as the Winona Construction Company; Etta, wife of Frank B. Holbrook, a real-estate dealer in Portland, Oregon; and one who died in infancy. The mother of these children was called to her final rest in January, 1885. The present wife of our subject was formerly Mrs. Betsey Amon, daughter of Joshua and Salley (Hadley) Emery, a native of Vermont.

In 1870 Mr. Corey was elected to represent this district in the State Legislature, his name being placed on the Republican ticket. His fidelity to the interests of his constituents resulted in his being re-elected in 1872, and this time also he made for himself a good record. For some two terms he served as County Commissioner in the early days of his residence in this place, and before the organization of the townships he served as Justice of the Peace. At various times he has held minor local offices, such as Township Assessor, Road Overseer, etc. From the first he has been prominently identified with the upbuilding and development of the community in which he dwells, having assisted in laying out roads and used his voice and influence in favor of everything which would elevate mankind and tend toward the prosperity of this region. He has long been a faithful member of the Free-Will Baptist Church, and takes a great interest in its growth and good works.

Dingman Speelman.

DINGMAN SPEELMAN, of Winona, is one of the honored pioneers of the county, having since an early day resided within its borders. Forty years have passed away since his arrival, and therefore he has seen not only the growth of the towns and cities, but has watched with interest the transformation of wild land into beautiful homes and farms, and has seen the march of progress and civilization, bringing in its wake [illegible] prises and [illegible] manifested an interest in the advancement of the county, and among its early settlers is well deserving of mention.

Mr. Speelman was born October 10, 1811, in Nauwstede, island of Schouwen, Zealand, in the kingdom of the Netherlands, and the days of his childhood and youth were spent in his native land. No event of special importance occurred. He was early inured to hard labor, and his life has ever [illegible] He continued in the [illegible] years of age, when he came to America. The day that witnessed his embarkation was an important one in his career, for he has undoubtedly attained a success in the New World which he would not have achieved in the Old He settled first in New York, where he worked as a farm hand and on the canal for several years Later he removed to Cleveland, Ohio, where he spent three years, and in 1855 he came to Winona Here he has been employed in various ways For a time he engaged in gardening, and subsequently in digging wells He now carries on a boarding-house, and in this business is meeting with success

In the year 1811 Mr Speelman was united in marriage with Miss Minnie Dewder, who for many years traveled life's journey with him, but in 1885 was called to the home beyond Thirteen children were born of this union, but ten of the number are now deceased Minnie, the eldest, is the wife of B Maceman, whose sketch will be found on another page of this work, John is now a resident of Des Moines, Iowa, and Jane is the wife of John Kecker, who is living in Winona

Mr Speelman affiliates with the Democracy, which he has supported since becoming an American citizen He belongs to the Presbyterian Church, and is now the oldest member of the congregation in Winona He owns a pleasant home, and is one of the honored pioneers, throughout the community being held in the highest regard His long residence here has made the people familiar with his honorable, upright life, and has gained him universal confidence and esteem He has never had occasion to regret the fact that he left his native land for the New World, and no native citizen of America is more loyal to this land and its free institutions than Mr Speelman

Lewis B. Ferrin.

LEWIS B. FERRIN, who is now living in St Charles, but for many years carried on farming in Winona County, is a native of the far-off state of New Hampshire his birth having occurred in Hebron, on the 2d of February, 1820 His parents were Aaron and Phœbe (Jackson) Ferrin, the former also born in the Granite State, and the latter in the state of Maine. The father was a farmer and land-owner in New Hampshire. He was born August 25, 1775, and died on the 22d of September, 1851. His wife, who was born September 23, 1778, passed away March 1, 1855 They had a family of twelve children, ten of whom reached maturity but the subject of this sketch is the only one now living Bradden born November 1, 1799, lived to a very advanced age, but never came West Hannah born February 3, 1801, died in 1816. Alice, born March 3 1802, died in infancy. Enos, born June 15, 1803, died January 18, 1837 Jerusha born December 13, 1804, died April 14, 1887 Aaron, born April 24, 1807 died December 8, 1812 Freeman, born April 9 1809, came to the West and spent his last days in St Charles Minn where he passed away October 7, 1871 Cummings, born September 13, 1810 died June 2[illegible], 1837 Walter J. born June

7, 1812, died in California. Lodema, born July 21, 1814, died March 11, 1881, in Lewiston, Winona County.

The parents of this family were married January 3, 1798. Mr. Ferrin was then in very limited circumstances, but he possessed energy and enterprise, and by the assistance of his estimable wife he became fairly well-to-do. He was an honorable, upright man, was a faithful member of the Methodist Episcopal Church, in which he served as Class-leader, and all of his children became respectable men and women. He gave them good educational advantages, and they never brought disgrace upon the untarnished family name which he left them.

Upon the old home farm Lewis Ferrin was reared, and to his father he gave the benefit of his services until nineteen years of age. He then started out in life for himself, paying his father for one year's time, after he had earned that sum. After his marriage his parents came to live with him and found there a pleasant home for about twelve years, when the son decided to remove to the West and they went to live with their eldest son, at whose home their last days were passed.

Lewis Ferrin was married on the 28th of February, 1841, the lady of his choice being Miss Margaret D. Brown, a native of New Hampshire and a daughter of Deliverance and Mary (Emerson) Brown, both of whom were also natives of the old Granite State. The father died when Mrs. Ferrin was quite young. He was twice married, and by his first union had three children, while by the second marriage twelve children were born. The mother lived to the age of about eighty-four years. In 1855 Lewis Ferrin started with his wife for the West, and on the 10th of June they located in Warren, Winona County. Here our subject purchased a claim, paying $1,000 for three hundred and twenty acres, on which he made his home until November, 1867. He then sold out and removed to Mankato, where he purchased a home, but not long after he again bought a farm in the neighborhood, continuing its cultivation until the fall of 1893, when he removed to St. Charles, where he has since lived retired.

Mr. Ferrin has been honored with some public offices of trust, having served as Postmaster while living in New Hampshire, and as County Commissioner and Supervisor in Winona County, while for three terms he filled the office of Alderman. In his political views he is a Democrat and warmly advocates the party principles. He has improved three farms in this county, and now owns one of the neatest homes in St. Charles, where he is living retired, enjoying the rest which he has so truly earned and richly deserves. His life has been an honorable and upright one, and all who know him esteem him highly for his sterling worth and strict integrity.

Joseph Reynolds.

JOSEPH REYNOLDS, deceased, was for many years widely known and highly respected by the citizens of Winona County. His honesty and integrity were proverbial, and won him the confidence and regard of all with whom he was brought in contact. He was born in Sullivan County, N. Y., June 8, 1819, and died February 21, 1891, in the seventy-second year of his age, his loss being widely and deeply mourned. He was reared on a farm in New York. His brother Silas was of late a large stock-grower of Aurora, Ill., and his brother Isaac also lived in Aurora. In early life Joseph and his brother James left home and came to the West, and the latter died in Aurora some six years ago. On leaving the farm they bought a stock of groceries at Buffalo and opened a country store in the state of New York, which they conducted for a year. They afterward carried on a tannery and a gristmill. James having received an injury the brothers drifted apart, James going to Aurora, while Joseph went to Chicago.

It was in 1850 that Mr. Reynolds, of this sketch, took up his residence in Chicago, which was then a small place without railroads, and the traders had no good facilities for transportation. He visited all the country trading points buying furs, riding from one place to another on horseback through Iowa, Minnesota and Wisconsin. He was always quick to take advantage of opportunities afforded him, and this characteristic was one of the important factors in his success. He carried on a prosperous business as a fur-trader for some time, and then engaged in the grain trade, his western headquarters being at McGregor, Iowa, but his main place of business was in Chicago. He bought grain all along the northern part of the river, everything being put in sacks and shipped by boat to Prairie du Chien, where he handled his grain by means of the Chicago, Milwaukee & St. Paul Railroad elevator, from which he loaded cars for Chicago. As the steamboat owners did not handle his grain to suit him, he began to load barges of his own, which he hauled with a small steamer which he had built for that purpose. Mr. Reynolds was familiarly known as "Diamond Jo," which came from his special mark upon the sacks of grain. At that time buyers usually marked each sack of grain in a certain way, and Mr. Reynold's mark was a diamond, inside of which was the name "Jo." This soon became familiar over a wide extent of territory, and he was thereafter called "Diamond Jo," a name which he also gave to his steamer. His business was usually conducted under the names of other men. He was the "company" of the great grain firm of Bassitt, Hunting & Co., of McGregor, Iowa, the predecessor of the present firm of Hunting & Co. This firm had a line of elevators on the Milwaukee Road into Iowa and Dakota. At Winona the business was under the name of L. B. Strong & Co., and the concern operated all of the Chicago & North-Western elevator lines as far west as Sleepy Eye, having the business of what is now the Marfield Elevator Company, the McNeill Grain Company and the Winona Mill Company. At Winona as high as two million bushels of grain were handled in some seasons. This firm also had an extensive river trade, extending from Cassville, near Dubuque, and including all points north to the first town below St. Paul. Mr. Strong had previously been employed in buying grain at Brownsville, near La Crosse. He was afterward called upon to take charge of the business in Winona, and soon became a partner, but when the first year was over he withdrew, although the name of E. B. Strong & Co. was retained and he continued an employe. In 1878 he went to Chicago, and the business was then carried on by Mr. Reynolds until 1881, when it was transferred to Dubuque, and became the business of the E. M. Dickey Company, which handled a large line of elevators on the Illinois Central. Mr. Dickey had been superintendent of the boat line, and had formerly been connected with Mr. Reynolds in the grain business at points below Dubuque.

In other business relations Mr. Reynolds was also found. He was a member of the Chicago Board of Trade, and one of the successful operators on the same. In 1867 he started the "Diamond Jo" line of steamers, in order to secure better transportation for his grain. At first he only hauled grain down the river, but soon started an agent in Chicago to solicit consignments of goods to take up the stream, and the result was very successful. He had five regular passenger and freight boats, valued at about $100,000, besides about thirty barges, costing $1,000 each, with a capacity of from eight to twelve thousand bushels of grain. In later years nearly all of the grain was handled in bulk. About $350,000 was invested in the steamboat business, and employment was furnished to from five hundred to six hundred men. E. M. Dickey served as Superintendent, and is the present manager of the Reynolds estate, which continues the steamboat business, but has recently closed out the line of elevators to the O'Neill Grain Company. Mr. Reynolds always gave his personal attention to both the steamer line and grain business. He made Chicago his headquarters, but was usually on the river or visiting the points where he had elevators or bought grain. He also attended personally to sales in Chi[illegible] under his s[illegible]

About 1876 Mr. Reynolds became interested in mines in Georgetown, Colo., but that venture did not prove a success. Later he became a stockholder in mines at Leadville, and there won back all that he had lost in mining ventures. He afterward met a mine-owner in a hotel in St. Louis and bought a mine in Arizona, for which he paid $50,000, but it proved to be a salted one and he lost it all. He then purchased the Congress Mine, a group of eight mines at Congress, Ariz., and incorporated the Congress Gold Mining Company, with a capital stock of $600,000. He put in about $350,000, but this was all reimbursed to him, and the mines have recently been sold for $1,000,000. The steamboat business having proved successful, he turned his attention to railroads in 1875. He visited Hot Springs, and finding no road at that place, he secured a charter for building what became the Hot Springs Narrow Gauge Railroad, for a distance of twenty-two miles. This required an investment of $300,000, but proved a great success financially. It was afterward made a regular gauge road and the capital stock was increased to $600,000, most of which was owned by Mr. Reynolds. During the time of the construction of the road he made his home in Hot Springs. He would carry in a little grip-sack the money with which to pay off all bills, and the Hot Springs Road was probably the only one whose obligations were promptly met, the road never having any debt of any kind. No man gave more close or careful attention to the details of business.

Some time before his death, Mr. Reynolds sank an artesian well in the beautiful park in McGregor, Iowa, and placed therein a fountain. He always considered McGregor his home. With the Democratic party he voted, but was never prominent in political affairs. He was reared in the faith of the Society of Friends, and always adhered to its principles. He was undemonstrative, retiring in disposition, and never very talkative. When he suffered loss he would merely remark, "It's tough, boys," and with renewed energy begin work again.

At the age of about twenty-six Mr. Reynolds wedded Mary Morton, who still survives him. The[illegible] son Blake, who died of consump[illegible] M[illegible] [illegible]ighth year. Mr.

Reynolds was fond of a good story and possessed a genial, pleasant nature, which won for him friends wherever he went. For some time he was in poor health, and in 1891, accompanied by Jay Morton, his brother-in-law, and Marshall Nez Perce, he started for Arizona, intending to visit his mines at Congress. On the way he was attacked by pneumonia, and was forced to remain in Phœnix, Ariz., for a week. After a two-days drive across the country to Congress he felt quite tired, and the next morning complained of headache, but his illness was serious, and he grew steadily worse until at ten o'clock p. m. on the 21st of February, 1891, he passed away. His remains were taken back to Chicago, and he was laid to rest in Mt. Hope Cemetery.

Hans Hanson.

HANS HANSON, deceased, was for many years a well known citizen of Winona County, and was highly respected by all who knew him. He was born on the 29th of December, 1830, in South Lan, Norway, and in his native land was reared to manhood. No event of special importance occurred during his boyhood and youth. His educational privileges were meager, being those afforded by the common schools, but he always endeavored to keep himself well informed on topics of general interest.

Having arrived at years of maturity, Mr. Hanson was married, in October, 1849, the lady of his choice being Miss Christine Myhre, a native of Norway. Their wedding was celebrated in that land, and there they remained until the following year, when they bade adieu to early friends and sailed for the New World. That was before the days of steamers, and after a long voyage in a sailing-vessel they reached the harbor of Quebec. On reaching this country they at once made their way to Wisconsin, where they spent the succeeding fifteen years of their lives. On the expiration of that period they crossed the Mississippi into Minnesota, and located on section 9, Homer Township, where Mr. Hanson purchased two hundred and eighty acres of land. He afterward bought eighty acres adjoining the first purchase, and thus became the possessor of a valuable tract of three hundred and sixty acres, all in one body. He crossed the Atlantic a poor man, and began life in a strange country without capital, but a pair of strong arms and willing hands stood him instead of money, and he at once began work. The success which comes as the result of industry, perseverance and good management crowned his efforts and made him one of the prosperous farmers of the community.

To Mr. and Mrs. Hanson were born nine children: Hans, now of this county; Ola, at home; Mrs. Mary Larson; Mrs. Annie Thompson, who departed this life on the 23d of June, 1893, leaving five children; Mrs. Tillie Erickson; Mrs. Angie Bergh; Mrs. Christine Bergh; Hannah, wife of Eric Bahrud; and Mrs. Minnie Gilbertson. Mr. and Mrs. Bahrud now occupy the old home farm. They were married on the 9th of December, 1891, and their union has been blessed with two children: Gilbert, born May 6, 1893, and Bertine, May 3, 1891. The parents are well known and highly respected people, and their friends in the community are many.

In his political views Mr. Hanson was a Repubhim, and warmly advocated the principles of the party but never sought political preferment. In his religious belief he was a Lutheran, and was a consistent member of the church with which he held membership. He might truly have been called a self-made man, for his prosperity was the result of his own earnest application and untiring labor. He continued to carry on farming and stock-raising until his death, which occurred on the 12th of April, 1878. Many friends mourned his loss, for they knew him to be a high-minded gentleman, of sterling worth and strict integrity.

Mrs. Hanson, who was born in Norway, on the 11th of March, 1828, still survives her husband, and bids fair to live for many years to come, for she is well preserved, both physically and mentally. She, too, is a member of the Lutheran Church. Her life has been devoted to her family, who know her to be a faithful and loving wife and mother. At the time of this writing she is visiting with her daughter in Wisconsin, but makes her home on the farm in Winona County. The children are doing well in life, and all are members of the Lutheran Church and highly respected people.

William Parkhurst.

WILLIAM PARKHURST, one of the intelligent and highly respected farmers of Winona County, now living on section 31, Winona Township, and one of its oldest citizens and honored pioneers, was born in Framingham, Mass., on the 30th of June, 1803. He was reared upon the old homestead, and at an early age began work in the fields, so that he was soon familiar with all the duties that fall to the lot of an agriculturist. On attaining his majority, with the tide of emigration which was steadily flowing westward, he made his way to Illinois, which was then one of the frontier states. He there engaged in teaching school for a number of years, and also carried on farming until 1853, when he came to Minnesota. His first settlement was made in Fillmore County, where he secured a homestead claim, on which he resided until 1865.

In the spr[illegible] Mr. Parkhurst came [illegible] Winona Co[illegible] home, and purchased one hundred and sixty acres of land in the Gilmore Valley, constituting his present farm. He was married on the 16th of March, 1837, the lady of his choice being Miss Hannah Work, who died, leaving two children, Henry and William. The former now resides in St. Louis County, Mo., but the latter was called to the home beyond during his boyhood days. After the death of his first wife, Mr. Parkhurst was again married, October 2, 1841, his second union being with Miss Laura Smith, a native of Vermont, born in Williamstown. Six children graced this union: Alice, now the wife of A. C. Smith, a resident of Sargent County, N. Dak.; Charles, who is still on the home farm; Harriet, wife of L. O. Maxham, who is located in Winona; Alfred, who is living on the old homestead, which he operates in connection with his brother Charles, the two taking care of their parents in their old age; Emma, wife [illegible] and Lizzie, wife of Henry Robinson, who is also living in Sargent County, N. Dak.

Mr. Parkhurst is descended from a family which traces its ancestry back to George Parkhurst, who was born in England, and in 1613 sailed from his native land to America. His wife comes from a family which has long been established in the New World. The Parkhursts are noted for longevity, and the gentleman whose name heads this record has now reached the advanced age of ninety-one. He has long resided in Winona County, and has become widely known. Throughout the community he is held in the highest regard, and the history of Winona County would be incomplete without this sketch of one of its oldest and most honored citizens. Both he and his estimable wife are members of the Congregational Church.

Frank L. Randall.

FRANK L. RANDALL, the honored and efficient County Attorney of Winona County, is numbered among the native sons of Minnesota, his birth having occurred at Ft. Ridgely, Nicollet County, November 20, 1856. His grandfather, William Randall, was a native of Vermont, and was probably of English descent. He served in the War of 1812, and made farming his life work. His death occurred at the age of seventy. The maternal grandfather, Urban B. Auskau Lange, was a native of Copenhagen, Denmark, and came to America about 1828, locating in Philadelphia. He was a practical watch-maker, surveyor and inventor. Removing to Illinois, he located near Quincy about 1839, and there died in 1858, at the age of seventy. He was a great hunter, taking much delight in that sport.

Benjamin Randall was born in the Green Mountain State, and having arrived at mature years he married Wilhelmina H. Lange, a native of the Keystone State. They became the parents of eight children, seven of whom are yet living, namely: Mary Louisa, wife of George H. Noble, of Winona; Frank L.; wife of Dr. B. M. Randall of Graceville, Minn.; Rev. William E., of St. Louis; Richard A., a well known lawyer of Winona; Dr. Henry R., deceased; A. Josephine, a teacher and elocutionist; and Freth, of Winona. The father was a school teacher in Missouri for many years, afterward ran a canal-boat and subsequently engaged in merchandising in Peoria. Later he moved to Ft. Snelling, Minn., where he was engaged in business as a sutler for four years. For three terms he served as a member of the Territorial Legislature. In 1853 he went to Ft. Ridgely, where he remained until 1867, when the fort was abandoned. He then engaged in manufacturing and merchandising until 1889, when he removed to Winona, where he has since made his home. He served with the citizen soldiers during the Indian War at Ft. Ridgely, where, in connection with J. C. Ramsey, he commanded the defensive forces. He is one of the pioneers of the state, and belongs to the Old Settlers' Association of Minnesota. He belongs to the Masonic fraternity and to the Odd Fellows' society, and at St. Peter he was President of the School Board. He also served as Alderman and Mayor, and in 1883 was a member of the Legislature He is recognized as one of the prominent citizens of this state, and is widely and favorably known.

Frank Randall was reared in St Peter, Minn and after acquiring his early education in its public schools he entered St John's College of Prairie du Chien, Wis He followed farming from the age of eighteen until twenty-three after which he engaged in teaching school for some years. At length he determined to enter the legal profession, and in 1875 began reading law with G. S Ives, of St Peter In 1880 he was admitted to the Bar, and immediately opened an office at Tracy, Minn, where he continued practice for a year. The succeeding five years were passed in New Ulm, where he did a good business, and in 1885 he came to Winona, and formed a partnership with Mr Tawney, the connection continuing for five years In 1893 he was joined by his brother, Richard A, and they now do business under the firm name of Randall & Randall.

On the 3d of May 1886, was celebrated the marriage of Frank Randall and Miss Winona E. Pierce, daughter of Z B and Mary E (Ross) Pierce. Three children have been born to them Hortense, Cotter and Mary. Mr Randall is a member of the Catholic Church, and in politics is a Democrat In November 1892 he was elected to the office of County Attorney, which position he is now filling in a creditable and acceptable manner At the early age of twenty years he was appointed County Superintendent of Schools of Nicollet County, and was elected to that office in 1877 He has taken an active interest in educational affairs, aided in building the large school in Tracy and was a member of the board when the New Ulm school was built The best interests of the community ever find in him a friend, and the county finds in him a valued citizen and worthy official. At the Bar his ability is also recognized

---

Michael Einhorn.

MICHAEL EINHORN, a farmer residing on section 30, Homer Township, is one of the worthy citizens that Germany has furnished to America He was born in Selz, April 8, 1828, and is a son of Peter Einhorn, also a native of Germany Having arrived at years of maturity, the father there married Margaret Wisham He was a contractor and builder, and followed that business in his native land until 1844, when, with the hope of bettering his financial condition, he sailed for America Locating in Cook County, Ill, he there purchased land and turned his attention to farming, which he carried on up to the time of his death He passed away in March, 18[illegible] to mourn his [illegible] dred and sixty acres of land, and upon his farm his wife remained for two years, when she, too passed away, in March, 1853 The parents therefore did not long enjoy their new home Upon the mother's death the heirs sold the property, receiving for it about $8 per acre

Michael Einhorn continued a resident of Cook County until 1862 He was a young man of sixteen years at the time of his emigration to America When he had attained his majority his father gave him $200 in money and he started out in life for himself He first turned his attention to farming, but soon after went to Chicago, where for fourteen years he was employed by the McCormick [illegible] and industrious. [illegible] the expiration of that period a not inconsiderable sum. As before stated, he left Cook County in 1862, and came to Winona County, Minn. In Wilson Township he purchased one hundred and forty acres of land at $10 per acre, and upon that farm made his home for five years. In the mean time it had more than doubled its value, and he sold out for $35 per acre, thus realizing a good profit. He next purchased a quarter-section of land in Wilson Township. This was an unimproved tract, for which he gave $5 per acre. Not a furrow had been turned thereon, but with characteristic energy he began its development, and the raw prairie was soon made to yield to him bounteous harvests in return for the care and labor he bestowed upon them. For fifteen years he continued its cultivation and made it a valuable tract. At length he sold out for $4,000 and removed to Winona, where the two succeeding years of his life were passed. On purchasing another farm he became the owner of a one hundred and sixty acre tract, on which he made his home for four years. He then sold that property and bought the farm on which he now resides.

On the 6th of May, 1851, Mr. Einhorn was united in marriage with Miss Barbara Kraudwick, daughter of Arnold and Annie (Schwartz) Kraudwick. Both parents were natives of Germany, and came from Prussia to America in the year 1843. They located on a farm in Cook County, Ill., where they made their home for some time, and then came to Winona County, settling in the town of Wilson, on the Chatfield road. There Mr. Kraudwick engaged in keeping a tavern, which was largely patronized by the traveling public, and therefore yielded to him a good income. He carried on business along that line until his death, which occurred on the 2d of February, 1867. His wife met her death October 29, 1880, when seventy-nine years of age, being cruelly murdered by robbers, who killed her and then took all her money, which amounted to a considerable sum, as she did a large business and handled considerable cash. The rogues also fired the house, but it did not burn. Mr. and Mrs. Kraudwick had four children, of whom two are now living.

To Mr. and Mrs. Einhorn were born fourteen children, of whom the following are living, the others having died in infancy: Michael, born October 11, 1856; Mary, November 24, 1859; Tracy, November 8, 1860; Annie, August 29, 1863; Henry, September 8, 1865; Elizabeth, April 2, 1867; Sophia, May 18, 1869; Bernard, December 20, 1871; Herman, May 22, 1873; Catherine, March 7, 1875; and George, May 22, 1877. Michael was married April 11, 1882, to Anna Carpenter, after whose death he married Mary Koenig; Tracy became the wife of Nicholas Lombard, April 13, 1885; Annie wedded Conrad Koenig, October 12, 1886; Mary became the wife of Bernard Weiser, November 13, 1888; and Henry was married to Bertie Harvey, November 13, 1891.

Mr. Einhorn is a self-made man and deserves great credit for his success in life. He started out empty-handed, and, depending entirely upon his own resources, he has steadily worked his way upward, overcoming the difficulties and obstacles in his path by diligence and earnest effort, and thus has won prosperity. He is not only recognized as a leading farmer, but is also one of the progressive and public-spirited citizens of the county. In his political views he is a Democrat, and he and his family are members of the Catholic Church.

James Holt.

JAMES HOLT, a prominent farmer and stock-raiser of Winona County, now living retired in the village of Utica, was born on a farm in Somerset County, Me., November 19, 1825, being the second of six children born to the union of Timothy and Betsy (Smitt) Holt, also natives of Maine. The children in order of birth were: Sarah, Mrs. Stephen Judkins, deceased; James, our subject; Mary J., the wife of Taylor Davis, a farmer of Maine; Mehitable, Mrs. George Shafton, also of Maine; Alvira, wife of Otis Emerson, a hatter residing in Methuen, Mass., and one that died in infancy.

The Holt family originally resided in England, but emigrated to America in an early day and settled in Maine. The parents of our subject were very poor, and in 1863 they came to Minnesota, where they made their home with their son James until they died. The father departed this life in 1874, and the mother passed away in 1879, being laid to rest beside her husband in the Utica Cemetery. Both were consistent members of the Reformed Church. In politics he was a Democrat, and a firm believer in the principles of that party.

July 14, 1853, James Holt married Miss Thirza, daughter of John G. and Thirza (Smith) Dugley, natives of Maine, and of English ancestry. The family removed to Wisconsin in 1850, and settled in Green Lake County, where Mr. Dugley bought some land and proceeded to make a home for his family. That county was then in its primeval condition, an[illegible] sitated a larg[illegible]ance. The father was called to the land beyond May 21, 1876. The mother is still living and is quite active for one of her years (eighty-five). Mrs. Holt was born in Franklin County, Me., April 25, 1835, and is an amiable and estimable lady.

The family of Mr. Holt consists of four children. Newton M., who was born May 24, 1854, was a carpenter and bridge-builder, and formerly was with the American Bridge Company, but is now living retired in California. Leroy I. was born September 6, 1855, and now resides on the old homestead in Winona County. Alvira was born January 27, 1858, and is the wife of D. M. Brown, a stenographer of Minneapolis. Willard F., whose birth occurred May 23, 1860, is a carpenter and builder of Sioux Falls, Iowa. Walter E. was born June 24, 1873, and died January 17, 1881.

In 1849 Mr. Holt started westward from Maine, and the following year reached Wisconsin, stopping in Green Lake County. He was young and energetic, willing to work at anything honorable whereby he might get a start in life. For eleven years he remained in Wisconsin, being employed at various occupations during that time, but mainly engaged as a farmer. By industry and economy he was enabled to save a neat sum of money, and when, in 1861, he came to Winona County, he was enabled to purchase one hundred and seventy-five acres on section 12, St. Charles Township. The land was in its primitive state, and all the improvements now on the place were put there by our subject. [illegible] successful, and and [illegible]essions until he became the owner of three hundred and thirty-five acres of as valuable farm land as can be found in the county. One hundred and seventy-five acres of this he still retains, the remainder belonging to his son Leroy.

For a number of years Mr. Holt carried on general farming and stock-raising, making a specialty of sheep and Norman horses. In this line of industry he was one of the most successful men in the county, and also became widely known in the state. In 1882 he retired from active farm life, giving over the management of the farm to his son Leroy. For some time after coming to Utica he employed his leisure time in working as a blacksmith, which trade he had learned in his youth. He is not obliged to work, having accumulated a sufficient amount of this world's goods to keep him and his family in comfort for the remainder of their days, but it is an utter impossibility for him to remain idle. Politically he is a staunch Populist. He is public spirited and ever ready to assist in all the needed improvements of his home locality, and is highly esteemed in the community in which he lives.

Mrs. Ruth M. Cogswell Rowell.

MRS. RUTH M. COGSWELL ROWELL is a direct descendant of the Rt.-Hon. Sir Humphrey Cogswell, otherwise Lord Humphrey Cogswell, of England, to whom, in 1447, was first granted the coat of arms which appertaineth to the name of Cogswell. Paintings of these ensigns armorial are still retained in the family. She is of the seventh generation in descent from John Cogswell, who was born in Westbury, Leigh, County of Wilts, England, in 1592, and who married September 10, 1615, Elizabeth Thompson, daughter of Rev. William and Phillis Thompson. Rev. William Thompson, the father of Elizabeth Thompson (the great maternal ancestor of all the descendants of John Cogswell), was vicar of the Westbury parish church from 1603 to 1623, the time of his death. Westbury parish church was very ancient, dating to the time of William the Conqueror. Westbury, England, was granted its charter of incorporation by Henry IV. The place is of great antiquity. It occupies the site of the old Roman military and trading station, Verlucio. It is ninety-eight miles from London. The name is of Saxon origin, and here, according to tradition, was the palace that belonged to the West Saxon kings. The inhabitants are supplied with water from springs and a small stream that flows into the Avon. On the register of the Westbury parish church are found recorded at this date the marriage of John Cogswell and Elizabeth Thompson, as also accounts of the baptisms and burials of their ancestors.

Edward Cogswell, the father of John Cogswell, was a man of wealth, and bequeathed not only large sums to his wife and children, but also certain sums to his godchildren. His wife, who survived him less than a year, on her decease bequeathed not only moneys to her children and godchildren, but also sums to Westbury Church and to the poor.

John Cogswell with his wife and children embarked on board a ship, May 23, 1635, at Bristol, England, and sailed for New England. He took with him from England farming implements, housekeeping utensils, valuable pieces of carved furniture embroidered curtains, damask table linen, much silver plate and a Turkey carpet. He also brought several farm and household servants, and sums of money. He settled in Ipswich, Mass. where in 1636 we read of a grant of three hundred acres of land being given him, as also deeds of lots for building purposes. Mrs R M C Rowell's great-grandfather Nathaniel Cogswell was a leading merchant and prominent citizen of Haverhill, Mass. He married, January 31, 1740 Judith Badger, the only surviving daughter of Joseph and Hannah (Peaslee) Badger, her father being also a merchant in Haverhill, Mass. Her mother was a woman of culture, having been a member of the first high school taught in Boston, Mass. Nathaniel Cogswell was a man of integrity and business capacity, and deeply religious, as was his long line of ancestry. His wife was a person of commanding figure and cultured manners. After a successful business life he retired in 1776, and settled in Atkinson, N H where he at once became active in establishing religious and educational institutions in the town. Prior to the completion of the meeting house (to which completion he contributed freely), meetings were conducted in his own house. During the Revolutionary War his patriotism was shown by his advancing large sums of money to provide equipments and provisions for the soldiers. These loans of money by reason of a depreciated currency, proved almost a total loss. Besides providing money, Mr Cogswell gave eight sons to the army, who served with distinction, and fulfilled an aggregate term of service of more than thirty-eight years, said to be the longest rendered by any family in the country. They were tall men, their aggregate height measuring fifty feet. They all survived the war and became prominent in professional and civil life.

Mrs Row[illegible]
well was b[illegible]

February 26, 1770, Ruth Badger, daughter of Gen Joseph Badger, of Gilmanton, N H. They at first resided in Haverhill, Mass., but at the close of the war he purchased a farm and built a frame house (said to be at that time the best house in the state) near his father-in-law in Gilmanton, N H. The house is still standing, with furniture in it furnished by him, and all in good repair and occupied by Cogswells.

Hon. Thomas Cogswell was a commissioned officer in the army of the Revolution during the whole war. He was Captain, then Major (January 1, 1777), then Lieutenant-Colonel (November 26, 1799) and afterward Wagon-master General. He led a company in the battle of Bunker Hill, was present at the siege of Boston, and continued in the service until peace was declared. We subjoin an extract from a letter penned by George Washington.

"Major Cogswell has always been represented to me as an intelligent, brave and active officer."

"Given at headquarters, June 7, 1881.

(Signed) "GEORGE WASHINGTON."

At the close of the war his country called him into another sphere of action. When peace was declared, as a citizen he displayed such firmness and benevolence with all that goes to characterize a good statesman, that he was at once called upon to hold offices of trust. He was twice nominated for Representative to Congress from New Hampshire. He filled with dignity and honor the office of Judge of the Court of Common Pleas from 1784 to his death in 1810. His great generosity to the first Congregational Church while living (donating them a sacramental service, as well as other presents), and respect to his memory, induced the church to erect a stone to mark the spot of his burial. (For confirmation, see the book entitled "Cogswells of America.")

Rev Frederic Cogswell, the father of Mrs Rowell, an ordained minister in the Christian Church, was the son of Hon Thomas Cogswell, of Gilmanton, N H. He commenced his work in the Gospel ministry while a young man. He married, May 18, 1817 Hannah Rogers Peavey, daughter of Col Anthony Peavey, of Farmington, N H.
[illegible] [illegible]n of Pike, Alle-
[illegible] 1821 in which

state her parents then resided, her father being engaged in evangelistic work, in company with his cousin Joseph Badger, editor of the *Christian Palladium*, and his brother-in-law, John L. Peavey. When she was two years of age her parents returned with her to New England, where she was reared and educated, her parents and all her people being New Englanders. When she was nine years old she gave her heart to Christ in a meeting led by her father (in the house of Robert Foster, editor of the *Christian Herald*) in the city of Portsmouth, her father being pastor of the Christian Church in that city. In the schools of Portsmouth she received much of her early education, which was afterward continued in the academy at Rochester, N. H. While attending this school she had the privilege of being with her father's only sister, the wife of Hon. Nathaniel Upham. Mrs. Upham was a noble woman, and did much to mould the character of her niece. She was the mother of Prof. T. Upham, of Bowdoin College, and several other illustrious children.

June 9, 1841, the lady whose life is here given married Warren Rowell, son of Hon. Charles Rowell, of Allenstown, N. H. In 1853 they removed with their children to Homer, Winona County, Minn. In 1856 she commenced her work in the ministry, thus following in the footsteps of her ancestors, her parents both being preachers. When her maternal grandmother died it was said in a local paper that she was a mother in Israel, seven of her children having been preachers. Mrs. Rowell was for some time pastor of the Advent Christian Church in Utica, also in Winona. She at length resigned her position as pastor, and went on a number of missions West and South, having preached the Gospel in nine different states. She has written articles for publication which have been printed in nine different papers in different states. In 1891, from a sense of duty, she retired from the Advent Christian Church and State Conference, and by letter united with the Free-Will Baptist Church of Winona; she also became a member of the Yearly Meeting with which she is still connected. She was a member of the Woman's Christian Temperance Union almost from its organization. In 1888 she was appointed President of the Woman's Christian Temperance Union for Winona County. In June, 1889, she was elected President of the First District Woman's Christian Temperance Union, which office she held until April, 1894, when a sad bereavement and also a call to more effectual evangelical work in the ministry, induced her to resign that position. While holding that office she traveled largely over the four counties comprising it, organizing unions and lecturing on temperance and different departments of Woman's Christian Temperance Union work. Though now over seventy-three years old, she is still busy, preaching the Gospel of Christ from time to time, doing evangelical work, Sunday-school work, and also state and local work for the Woman's Christian Temperance Union. She is State Superintendent of Hospitals, and is also earnestly engaged in the local and quarterly mission work of the Free-Will Baptist Church, having been elected President of the Quarterly Mission Board.

We subjoin the following extract from a Winona County History printed in the year 1883: "In connection with the early history and settlement of the town of Homer, there is no name, perhaps, that figures more prominently than that of Mother Rowell. Born of illustrious parents, she was reared and educated in all that appertains to true womanhood, and inherited from her ancestors those great moral and intellectual traits of character which enabled her in after years to wield such an influence in the wilds of the West that unborn generations will yet feel. * * * The education of the people in Christian and moral principles has been the life work of Mrs. Rowell, but few women, indeed, could stand to do the amount of missionary work that she has done, and nothing but a strong will power, supported by the sustaining influence of an all-wise Providence and the convictions of right, could have sustained her in the performance of the amount of physical labor required of her in attending to her itinerant life's work, always ready at a little warning to go to the sick-room, and soothe the dying with words of cheer, preach the funeral sermon and attend the last sad rites of the dead, meanwhile speaking words of hope and consolation to the living, then again on the rostrum or pulpit, explaining the great mysteries of salvation through Christ; and when we reflect that she has done all this at great pecuniary sacrifice to herself, we must conclude she is a sincere worker in the Master's cause. Besides her ministerial duties, she has given birth and reared to honor five children, two of whom are now dead. The eldest, Mary Adeline, graduated in the normal school in Winona, taught three years in the public schools in the city, and also taught in the collegiate institute at Red Wing. She married an estimable gentleman of that place, and now resides there. Her second child, Fred C., is also a graduate of the normal school at Winona. He taught successfully several district schools, married an accomplished young lady in Pleasant Valley, by the name of Anna M. Preston, and now lives upon the farm with his father. Her third child, Anna M., a highly educated young lady, was also a teacher, and for her amiable qualities was very highly respected. She married E. G. Lord, son of the County Superintendent, O. M. Lord, but their earthly lives were soon cut short, she dying in a little over a year, leaving an infant son, and he soon followed, both dying of consumption. The fourth child died at the age of thirteen months. The fifth and last, Warren C., is now attending the city schools at Red Wing, and is a very promising boy, and expects to graduate next year. Who can say that Mrs. Rowell has not done her part in the Christian work and development of Winona County, and in the education of the youth in all those virtues that adorn society and form the palladium of our civil and religious liberties? May her life be spared to continue the good work."

Mrs. Rowell's youngest son, Warren C., has graduated with honor from the State University at Minneapolis, and has his business office at Nos. 408 and 409 Boston Block, Minneapolis, Minn.

S. D. VAN GORDER.

S. D. Van Gorder.

S. D. VAN GORDER, of Winona, is the owner of extensive stone-quarries along the Mississippi, and takes large contracts for furnishing stone for river improvements. He is a man of excellent business ability, and his diligence, enterprise and good management have brought him a success of which he is well deserving.

Mr. Van Gorder was born on the 4th of November, 1837, in Chemung County, N. Y., and is a son of Jonathan and Elizabeth (Westbrook) Van Gorder. The grandfather, Jeremiah Van Gorder, was one of three brothers who emigrated from Amsterdam, Holland, to America long before the Revolution. He settled in New Jersey, and when the Colonies tried to throw off their yoke of British tyranny, he joined the Colonial army and served with distinction as an officer of the Revolution. He died some years after independence had been achieved, from the effect of wounds received in battle.

Jonathan N. Van Gorder was born in Sussex County, N. J., in 1785, and when nineteen years of age removed to New York, with a colony locating in Chemung County, where he spent his remaining days. He was a shoemaker by trade, and followed that occupation in early life, but later bought a sawmill and engaged in the lumber business for many years. After retiring from active business life, he came to Winona and spent his last years with his son, S. D., in whose home he passed away in 1861, at the age of seventy-nine. He was for years one of the leading citizens of Chemung County, public spirited and progressive. Mr. Van Gorder married Miss Elizabeth Westbrook, daughter of Hon. James Westbrook, who served as a member of the Legislature in 1812, at which time the slaves were set free in New York. He was one of the most prominent and influential citizens of the Empire State, and his name was inseparably connected with its early history. His father, Maj. Lowell Westbrook, won his title while serving in the Revolutionary army, under Washington. He was a member of the State Senate of New York while his son was serving in the House, in 1812. Mrs. Van Gorder died in 1859. In her family were ten children.

At a very early age S. D. Van Gorder started out in life for himself, and when a youth of fifteen he was captain and owner of a boat on the Erie Canal. At the age of sixteen he became Postmaster in the village where he then lived, and was recognized throughout the community as a young man of much promise and ability. Industry and enterprise have been numbered among his chief characteristics through life and have been important factors in his success.

In June, 1856, when eighteen years of age, Mr. Van Gorder emigrated westward and cast in his lot with the early settlers of Winona, where he has made his home almost continuously since. He has been connected with many of its leading industries and business interests. He helped to build the stone road to Sugar Loaf and was later one of the promoters of a sash, door and blind factory, establishing the enterprise in company with Messrs. Simpson and Evans. He then embarked in the sawmill business with L. C. Porter, and this partnership continued for four years, after which he engaged in contracting for the construction of railroads. In 1861 he established a lumber-yard, which he conducted three years and then sold out. He then entered the employ of the railroad company as superintendent of the timber and lumber department, receiving for his services $200 per month and expenses. After a year and a-half he was taken ill with typhoid fever and for six months was unable to do any work. He then secured a charter for a ferry-boat across the Mississippi, which he ran until 1880 and then sold to the city. During that time he also owned a steamer.

In later years Mr. Van Gorder has taken many Government contracts to furnish stone for river improvements, and is engaged in the stone-quarry business. He now owns thirteen hundred acres of land along the Wisconsin bank of the river, opposite the city, in which are fine stone-quarries, and to their management he now devotes the greater part of his time and attention. They yield an excellent quality of stone, which finds a ready sale in the market, and the income derived therefrom has made the owner one of the prosperous citizens of the community.

Mr. Van Gorder exercises his right of franchise in support of the Democratic party. In early life he took an active part in politics, but does not do so at present. In 1887 he was elected Chief of Police for a two-years term and in 1880 was re-elected, serving in all for four years. Since 1864 he has been a member of the Masonic fraternity, and now belongs to Winona Lodge No. 18, A. F. & A. M.; Winona Chapter No. 5, R. A. M.; and Cœur de Leon Commandery No. 3, K. T.

Henry S. Cox.

HENRY S. COX, landlord of the Nicollet Hotel, St. Charles, Minn., was born December 25, 1866, in Saratoga Township, Winona County, Minn. He is a son of Henry G. and Chastina (Stevens) Cox, both of whom are natives of Vermont.

Our subj[illegible] until he wa[illegible] gaged as a bridge-builder on the Chicago, Milwaukee & St. Paul Railroad, being thus engaged for about four years, and later was employed by the South-Western Railroad. He was married, June 7, 1894, to Mary Williams, a daughter of P. H. Williams and a native of New York. Mr. Cox is now prop[illegible] and is the owner [illegible] of land in Saratoga Township, Winona County He is recognized as one of the leading citizens of the place, and takes a general interest in all things pertaining to its welfare. The hotel of which he is the proprietor is considered one of the best hotels in southeastern Minnesota

The mother of our subject died when he was about fourteen years of age, and the father subsequently married again, and is now residing on the old homestead and is one of the leading citizens of his township

---

Harmon Waldron.

HARMON WALDRON, one of the highly respected citizens of Winona, now living at No 1207 West Fifth Street, is a native of New York born in Warren County, August 2 1828 His father, William G Waldron, was a native of Rensselaer County, N Y, and was descended from ancestors who came from Holland, and received patents for the Harlem Commons under Governor Duggan Resolvent Waldron, who belonged to one of the leading families of his native land, sailed from Amsterdam, Holland, to New York His descendants in direct line were William, Cornelius, Garrett, William G and Harmon

The father of our subject after his marriage settled in Warren County, N Y, then a new country, which he assisted in opening up to civilization He wedded Judah Bratt, who died at the advanced age of eighty-two They had a family of fourteen children, of whom four are yet living, and with the exception of one who died in infancy all reached mature years The father died at the ripe old age of ninety years. He served for a short time in the War of 1812, but took part in no active battles He had one son, Rev. John B Waldron, who was a popular minister, and preached for a few years in Winona He organized the Money Creek Free-Will Baptist Church in Houston County called meetings at various other places, and was a powerful speaker He died near Syracuse, N Y, some twenty years ago

Harmon Waldron was the youngest of the family, and as the others had left home he remained under the parental roof until twenty-five years of age and gave his father the benefit of his services He assumed entire charge of the farm at the age of eighteen, and continued its management for seven years

On the 14th of February, 1853, Mr Waldron was united in marriage with Miss Augusta Corey, a native of East Rutland, Vt born March 7, 1829, and a daughter of Alpheus and Lillie (Pratt) Corey, both of whom were natives of Massachusetts The grandfather, Isaac Corey, was born in the Bay State, and served his country in the Revolutionary War, being afterwards granted a pension by the Government When Mrs Waldron was a maiden of eleven summers her parents removed to New York, settling in Chestertown, Warren County For one year after his marriage Mr Waldron continued on the old homestead, and then, in 1854,

he at once

began to clear and improve. Subsequently he abandoned agricultural pursuits and entered the employ of an extensive lumberman, Orson Richards, serving in various capacities. To this business he devoted his energies for about ten years, usually buying standing timber and then preparing it for the market. He also did some trading on his own account.

In 1868 Mr. Waldron came to Winona County, and purchased a tract of land of three hundred and twenty acres in Pleasant Hill Township. Upon this farm he located, and made it his home for nearly three years, when failing health induced him to return to New York, in 1871. He sold his farm and spent the succeeding two and a-half years in the Empire State, again connected with lumber interests. It was in 1873 that Winona gained him as a citizen, and here he embarked in the dairy business, which he continued for about six years, his sales amounting to $3,000 annually. When he abandoned that enterprise he turned his attention to stock-dealing, which he yet follows, buying cattle and hogs, which he ships to market in Chicago. For ten years he did the most extensive business in this line in the county. He is a careful buyer and trader, and his business has proved very satisfactory. He has made a study of the business, and finding that stock need close attention while in transit, he usually accompanies each shipment. In connection with his stock-dealing he is also largely interested in farming land in the Great Jim River Valley in South Dakota.

To Mr. and Mrs. Waldron were born three children. Robert, the eldest, is a commercial traveler, residing in Aberdeen, S. Dak. Edward C. is a railroad conductor, residing at Colorado Springs. He married Aleda Cross, of Warren County, N. Y., and lived in Winona County for some years. She died in this city in April, 1885, leaving two children: Mildred, who now makes her home with her grandparents; and Eldredge, who is with his father. Howard H., the youngest of the Waldron family, is now a stenographer of Winona.

Mr. Waldron was formerly a Republican in political sentiment, but on account of his strong temperance principles he has of late years supported the Prohibition party. He was reared in the Methodist faith and both he and his wife are faithful members of the Methodist Episcopal Church of Winona. For thirty years he has been a member of the Masonic fraternity. In all business dealings he is straightforward and honorable, and his life has been a useful one, that has gained for him the confidence and esteem of many friends and acquaintances.

James M. Drew.

JAMES M. DREW, one of the leading farmers of Rolling Stone Township, and a worthy representative of a pioneer family, was born on the old Drew homestead, which is yet his place of residence on the 17th of February, 1862. His parents were Edward B. and Sarah (Meddick) Drew. His father, who was born in Hammondsport, N. Y., was reared upon a farm in that state, and began his education in the common schools. His privileges in that direction, however, were supplemented by a course of study in Franklin College. He was thus fitted for the practical duties of life, and by experience, observation and extensive reading in later years he has always kept himself a well informed man. On emigrating westward he located in Indiana, where he spent about three years, when, in 1852, he joined the Land and Village Association of New York. He met the party in Chicago, but traveled from Indiana to Galena, Ill., with ox-teams and thence came to Winona, where he arrived in the spring. From the Government he secured the land on which James Drew now resides.

At that time the land was not open to settlement, and Edward Drew had to give the Indians a barrel of flour for the right to build a cabin. He then staked out a claim and spent the succeeding winter in chopping wood. The next year he went to Wisconsin, and planted some wheat, raising the first crop of that grain ever harvested in Winona County. His land, which was entirely unimproved in 1852, was transformed into a rich and valuable farm, and the pl... thrift and enterprise of him who secured it from the Government forty-two years ago. In 1891 Mr. Drew left the farm, removed to Chicago, and has since lived retired. He comes of a family which was established in this country at an early day, but is of Scotch and Irish extraction. His wife was born in New York, and her parents were natives of New Jersey. Her death occurred in Winona County about twenty-seven years ago.

Mr. and Mrs. Drew were the parents of three children: John M., who died at the age of fifteen years; James M., of this sketch; and Janet, a stenographer of Chicago. The gentleman whose name heads this record is now the only representative in Winona County of the family so long prominent here. The name of his father is inseparably connected with the history of this community, for he bore a most important part in its development and progress and is numbered among its most honored pioneers.

James M. Drew was reared amid the wild scenes of the frontier, and the work of the farm was familiar to him from an early age. He aided in the labors of the field in the summer months, and in the winter attended the State Normal School of Winona, from which he was graduated in 1883. He then attended school in Danville, Ind., for one year, after which he spent the succeeding winter as a teacher in a district school of this county. He was then made Principal of the village schools of Appleton, Minn., in which capacity he served for one year, when he returned to the farm, making his ... t the beginning of the school term of that year he entered Cornell University, where he took a special course on agriculture, and the following spring was assigned the position of assistant to the director of that institution. A year later he returned home to take charge of the farm, a step made necessary by his father's failing health and to the management of the old homestead he now devotes his time and energies.

On the 25th of September, 1890, Mr. Drew was married to Miss Elsie Salisbury, of Elkhorn, Wis., daughter of one of the first settlers of Walworth County, Wis. Mr. and Mrs. Drew have two daughters, Helen Louise, born November 3, 1892, and Margarette, an infant.

In his political views James Drew is liberal. His father, who was quite prominent in political affairs, votes with the Democracy, and was three times elected on that ticket as a member of the State Legislature from Winona County. An enterprising and progressive citizen, he took an active interest in everything pertaining to the welfare of the community. In his business dealings he was successful and accumulated seven hundred acres of fine land, which is now successfully and ably managed by James M. Drew, the worthy subject of this sketch.

August J. Cooper.

AUGUST J. COOPER, who is an old Union soldier, is the owner and occupant of a fine tract of land on section 15, Pleasant Hill Township, which in its improvement and general appearance will compare favorably with any estate in the county. It consists of one hundred and seventy-two acres, occupying a good location.

Mr. Cooper spent the first twelve years of his life in Germany, where he was born January 1, 1843. Like all the youths of that country, he attended school, and his father being a farmer, he also assisted in performing many of the lighter duties on the farm.

When only twelve years of age, young Cooper, accompanied by his father, embarked on a sailing-vessel bound for American shores, and after a very slow and tiresome voyage was landed several weeks later in New York harbor. Their destination being Wiscon[illegible] thither and located in Watertown, Dodge County. After five years spent there, our subject changed his location and came to Pleasant Hill Township, this county, where he purchased a tract of land in partnership with his father. The property, which could not at that time be called a farm, included one hundred and twenty acres, which they immediately set to work to improve and cultivate in a most thorough manner. It now forms a portion of Mr. Cooper's present estate, and the home-like dwelling and various outbuildings which adorn it indicate to the passer-by that it is occupied by a family of enterprise and good taste.

September 27, 1864, during the progress of the late war, Mr. Cooper joined Company B, First Minnesota Heavy Artillery as a private, and was mustered into service at Ft. Snelling. The regiment was soon ordered to Chattanooga, Tenn., w[illegible] duty until the close of the war. On receiving his honorable discharge, he turned to the peaceful pursuits of farm life, and has ever since been engaged as an agriculturist.

Mr. Cooper was married July 27, 1871, and to himself and wife has been born a family of six children, bearing the respective names of William, Ida, Harrison, Lewis, Albert and Annie, all of whom are living with the exception of the eldest. In politics our subject is a stanch advocate of the Democratic party. He belongs to the German Lutheran Church, and earnestly endeavors to practice in his daily life the principles in which he believes. He is a member of the Grand Army of the Republic, and as such is well liked throughout the community. He has been greatly prospered as an agriculturist, and is one of those citizens who have contributed their quota toward the development of their adopted land.

Michael F. Walz.

MICHAEL F. WALZ is now serving as Water Commissioner of Winona, and is a most efficient and faithful officer. He was born in Columbia, Lancaster County, Pa., December 7, 1855, and is of German descent. His grandfather, Daniel Walz, was a native of Wurtemberg, Germany, and was quite a well-to-do citizen, owning an estate, which was operated by others. His death occurred at the age of seventy-five years.

Daniel Walz, the father of Michael F., was born in Wurtemberg, Germany, in 1816, and his wife, Mary, was also a native of that land. They were there married, and continued to make their home beyond the water until 1857, when they sailed for the New World, and became residents of Lancaster County, Pa. There Mr. Walz secured a position as foreman of the smelting works, discharging the duties of that position for six years, or until 1863, when he removed to Saginaw, Mich. He there embarked in the lumber business, which he carried on until 1884, when he retired from active life. He has since followed no business enterprise and is now resting in the enjoyment of the fruits of his former toil. Both he and his wife are well advanced in years.

Michael F. Walz is one of a family of sixteen children, fourteen of whom are yet living. He was a child of eight years when the family removed to Saginaw, Mich., where he resided until 1879. His early education, acquired in the common schools, was supplemented by study in the Normal School of the Missouri Synod, in Addison, Ill. He entered that institution in 1869, and was graduated therefrom in 1873, after which he entered the lumber business, but after following that enterprise for three years he was forced to abandon it on account of ill-health. During the next three years he gave his time and attention to teaching in Saginaw County, and in 1879 he went to Milwaukee, Wis., where he taught in St. Marcus' Parochial School for one and a-half years. In August, 1880, he received a call to come to Winona as Principal of St. Martin's Parochial School in this city, and that position he creditably filled until May, 1893, when, on account of failing health, he was obliged to give up educational work, in which he has always taken a great and abiding interest He was an able instructor, and the schools over which he had charge made rapid progress

Ere crossing the Mississippi, Mr Walz was married, in Saginaw County, Mich, July 25, 1880, to Henrietta Goppelt, a native of that county, and a daughter of Michael Goppelt This worthy couple have many friends throughout the community and are highly respected citizens. They hold membership with St Martin's Lutheran Church, and for several years Professor Walz has been its organist He gained a good musical education in Addison, Ill, and in Saginaw, Mich, under Professor Guenter, and yet conducts the male choir in the Harmonia Society. He is Secretary of the Winona Mutual Benefit Association, which has a membership of some six hundred It was organized in 1878 and pays death claims only. Mr. Walz became connected with it, and had the society incorporated in 1888, and the membership at once began to increase and has continued steadily to do so, eighty members having been taken into the organization in 1893, while a larger number will be admitted in 1894

In April, 1893, Professor Walz was called to office being elected Water Commissioner of Winona On the 1st of May he entered upon his duties, and so well were they discharged that in April, 1894, he was re-elected for another term The affairs were in a very bad condition, but Mr. Walz has succeeded in bringing order out of chaos, has ascertained wherever city water is used, and has made a complete record of the length of mains, the amount of water rentals, etc. He put up the first complete record of taps or connections in the department In the year 1893 he increased the water receipts over $3,000, and the additional income will be at least that much more in 1894, making the receipts $16,000, against $10,000 in 1892 Meters have also been introduced under his administration, and a great amount of water is saved by that means Mr Walz has labored earnestly to perfect everything connected with the water-works system, and the ability and faithfulness which he has displayed in the discharge of his duties have won him the confidence of all During his residence in Winona he has become widely known and has gained a large circle of friends and acquaintances, who hold him in the highest regard

Henry Mazy.

HENRY MAZY, who resides at No. 301 East Fifth Street, Winona, was born in Chicago, Ill May 15, 1832 His father, Louis Mazy, was a native of Germany, and a shoemaker by trade He went to Chicago in 1831, and located near old Sand Ridge. He subsequently purchased a farm in Cook County, Ill, upon which he made his home There he was one of the pioneers and resided for many years When our subject was seventeen ye[illegible] others, he crossed the plains to California being seven months en route. For about five and a-half years after his arrival in California he worked for C C. Reynerson, in buying and selling cattle He then engaged in the milk business in San Francisco, where he continued to reside until 1862, when he enlisted in the service of his country becoming a member of Company A of the Second Massachusetts Cavalry, joining the regiment in Boston [illegible] nt was sent to

Baltimore, and then was attached to the Army of the Potomac under General Sheridan. He served under that eminent commander and was engaged in all the various raids and battles of that celebrated army, being present at the capture of Lee. Of the original company of one hundred who enlisted in 1862, only seven were discharged at the close of the service, the remainder having been killed in battle or taken prisoner. Mr. Mazy was one of the number who took part in the Grand Review at Washington.

The parents of our subject having removed to Minnesota, on his discharge he joined them in Faribault County, and engaged in farming near the city of Faribault. In the spring of 1875 he came to Winona and, buying a street sprinkler, he has since, under contract, engaged in street sprinkling during the regular season.

On the 24th of December, 1865, in Faribault County, Mr. Mazy was united in marriage with Miss Louisa Fisher, a native of Germany. They have no children, but have reared a son and daughter of one of her brothers, Ervin and Bertha. The former is Deputy Clerk of the Courts, and the latter is preparing for a teacher in the public schools.

Mr. Mazy politically is a Republican and at present is serving as Alderman of the Third Ward. He is a member of the German Lutheran Church, and is held in high esteem by all who know him.

Abraham Nelson.

ABRAHAM NELSON has been for more than thirty years one of the leading agriculturists of Wiscoy Township, and is the owner of a valuable and improved homestead, situated on sections 25 and 32. He is a practical and progressive farmer, which facts may be easily seen by the traveler who passes by his well kept farmyard and dwellings. He is one of the native sons of Norway, his birth having occurred February 2, 1837, and the first ten years of his life were passed on his father's farm, since which time, being left an orphan, he has supported himself and made his own way.

When seven years old, Abraham Nelson set sail for America with his father, who bore the Christian name of Andrew. After eight weeks spent on the Atlantic they arrived on the shores of the New World, and at once continued their westward journey to Wisconsin. In that state the boy attended the district schools during the winter months until he was in his seventeenth year. At the age of eleven he was bound out to a farmer, for whom he worked for four years, receiving only his board and clothing. The summer he was sixteen he was given $10 per month for his services, this being the first money he ever earned. In the fall of 1854 he came to Minnesota with the family of O. R. T. Kingsley. The journey was made in a wagon drawn by two yoke of oxen, and the Mississippi River was crossed at LaCrosse. This country was then but little settled or improved, and between the points of LaCrescent and Gile's Corners there was not a house to be seen.

Abraham Nelson took up a tract of one hundred and sixty acres from the Government, but did not prove up the land. For a few years during the summers he ran a breaking team and in the fall engaged in threshing. In 1856 he purchased one hundred and sixty acres of Government land near where the village of Money Creek, Houston County, is now located. For this land he paid at the rate of $1.25 per acre, and after putting up a log cabin he cleared and broke forty acres of land. In 1862 he sold out his interest and then purchased the farm where he now lives, this place being located on sections 25 and 32 and comprising one hundred and ninety-five acres. This homestead he sold in 1863 and re-purchased in 1879. September 20, 1864 he enlisted in Company A, First Minnesota Heavy Artillery. He was mustered in at Ft. Snelling and from there was sent to Chicago, Louisville and Chattanooga. In the latter place he was put on guard duty, and was so serving at the close of the war, when he received his honorable discharge, dated June 20, 1865. Returning from Tennessee to Minnesota, he bought a farm in this township, which he cultivated until the following year, when he went to Faribault County, this state, and on his arrival there bought one hundred and sixty acres of railroad land. Owing to the failure of crops and the plague of grasshoppers in 1878, he returned to this county, and as he had lost nearly all his possessions by his unfortunate settlement in the western part of the state, he was obliged to begin life almost at the bottom round of the ladder again. Being a man of determined will and energy, he set sturdily to work to repair his fortune. He took up a homestead of eighty acres on section 30, Pleasant Hill Township. The tract he leased for five years, after which he came to his present farm, this being in 1883.

August 26, 1860, Mr. Nelson married Adeline Clarke, and to the worthy couple were born four children. Dora E., the eldest living, is the wife of E. J. Kingsley, who operates a farm near Money Creek; Flora died in 1875; and two children died in infancy. Mrs. Nelson was called from this life March 16, 1892. The present wife of our subject was united in marriage with him September 13, 1892. She is Hannah, a daughter of John and Catherine (McNaughton) Gordon, and widow of George Brenaman. The latter died April 24, 1885.

In his political belief Mr. Nelson has until recently been a stalwart Republican. Of late he has identified himself with the Prohibition party, as he is a strong believer in temperance and thinks that national laws and legislation would tend toward a better condition of affairs in this country. A patriot both in times of peace and war, he is a member of the Grand Army of the Republic and a loyal citizen. Religiously he is a member of the Methodist Episcopal Church, to which his wife also belongs. Self-made and self-educated, he deserves the credit which is freely accorded him by those who know his history, for in spite of many discouragements which would have seemed insurmountable to most men he has come forth triumphant and successful.

William Duncanson.

WILLIAM DUNCANSON, a farmer who resides on section 20, Warren Township, is numbered among the honored pioneers of Winona County. He was one of its first settlers, and is familiar with its history from the time when the city of Winona was a mere frontier hamlet. With interest he has watched its progress and advancement, and has aided in its development, so that his name is inseparably connected with the record of its upbuilding. Such a man is well worthy of representation in this volume. He was born in Nova Scotia, on the 5th of May, 1825, and is a son of William and Eleanora (Benjamin) Duncanson. In their family were six children, five sons and a daughter, but Eunice, Benjamin, Jacob and Thomas are all now deceased. William is the eldest survivor. Jerome, who completes the family, is now living in St. Paul. The father was a native of Nova Scotia, and throughout his life carried on agricultural pursuits.

William Duncanson was reared upon the old home farm, and from early boyhood its work was known to him, so that when he began business for himself he had a fund of practical experience on which to rely, even though he had no cash capital. He attended the subscription schools at intervals until sixteen years of age, but is practically a self-educated as well as a self-made man financially. His life has been a busy and useful one. He started out for himself at the age of nineteen years, and began to earn his livelihood as a farm hand. His home was with his father until 1851, when he came to the United States, going from Nova Scotia to Boston, and thence to Dodge County, Wis., making the journey by way of the canal and Lakes to Milwaukee, and thence across the country by team to his destination. He crossed the Mississippi on a scow, pushed with poles, and after spending the night with Indians, started through the unbroken forest, blazing his way from the river banks at La Crescent to his present home. He made a location near Beaver Dam, and devoted his energies to farm work, being thus employed until the spring of 1851.

That year witnessed his arrival in Minnesota, and thereby Winona County gained one of its valued citizens. He secured a squatter's claim in Warren Township, and in 1855 pre-empted the land, a tract of one hundred and sixty acres on section 20. Here he built a log cabin 12x10 feet and brought to the county the first boards ever sold in Winona. There were less than twelve buildings in the city at that time, including one small store and a tavern. The Indians still lived in the neighborhood, and Mr. Duncanson had lived for six months in Warren Township ere he saw a white settler within its borders. The Chippewa Indians were very numerous in the neighborhood, but were always on friendly terms with their pale-faced brother, occasioning no trouble. All of the events of pioneer life in Winona County are familiar to Mr. Duncanson. He came thither with ox-teams, and then used his oxen in developing his farm. He aided in surveying this section of the county, and with its history has been identified from a very early day.

On the 21st of February, 1844, was celebrated the marriage of the subject of this sketch and Miss Rebecca Dodge, daughter of Stephen and Rebecca Dodge. Their union has been blessed with a family of ten children: Margaret; David; Rebecca, who died February 23, 1869, and Jeremiah, Theodore, Orrin, Julia, John, William, and Charles, who died February 9, 1869. Theodore is supposed to have been the first white child born in this neighborhood, his birth occurring in the fall of 1854. He was killed by lightning on the 31st of May, 1871. In the fall of the first-mentioned year Mrs. Duncanson remained for four weeks alone with her four little children while her husband returned to Wisconsin to move his brother here.

In his political views Mr. Duncanson is independent, voting for the man and not the party, upholding principle and not politicians. He has served as a member of the Board of Supervisors, but has never been an office-seeker. Both he and his wife belong to the Baptist Church, and are worthy people, who take a commendable interest in everything pertaining to the welfare of the community and its advancement. He is both a self-educated and self-made man, and for his success in life deserves great credit. In his business he has met with good success and now owns three hundred acres of valuable land, all in one body, his farm being now operated by his son. He is also a stockholder in the Farmers' Elevator, located in Lewiston. As a self-made man, substantial citizen and honored pioneer, he well deserves representation in the history of his adopted county.

Chris Michel.

CHRIS MICHEL, deceased, was born in Germany in December, 1820, and died at his home in Winona County on the 24th of October, 1888. The days of his boyhood and youth were spent in his native land, where, in January, 1842, he was united in marriage with Miss Gustine Ernson. The lady was there born March 29, 1819, and is still living. By their marriage they became the parents of two children, but both died in infancy.

Mr. and Mrs. Michel began their domestic life in the Fatherland, and there continued for ten years. In 1852 they bade adieu to the home and friends of their youth and took passage on a westward-bound sailing-vessel, which at length dropped anchor in the [illegible] New York. Continuing their journe[illegible] they finally reached Wisconsin, where they made a location. Subsequently they left the Badger State and, removing to Minnesota, settled on a farm. They had no capital at the time of their arrival, and were dependent entirely upon their own resources. The husband and wife labored together, his industrious efforts being ably seconded by her work in the house. They practiced economy in their living and by good management, industry and perseverance at length became the possessors of considerable property, and to-day Mrs. Michel is one of the wealthy ladies of the county.

Mr. Michel made farming his life work, and placed his farm all under a high state of cultivation, until the once wild land was transformed into [illegible] [illegible]lded to him a golden tribute [illegible]re and labor he bestowed upon it He was also an excellent financier Mr. Michel met with a severe accident, a tree falling upon him and striking his head From that time forward his mind was impaired, but his faithful wife kept him at home tenderly caring for him, until he was called to his final rest, on the 24th of October, 1888 In politics he was a Democrat and with the Methodist Church he held membership.

After her husband's misfortune Mrs Michel assumed the management of the farm and property, and soon showed that she was a woman of excellent business ability. To her sagacity, foresight and enterprise is due the well deserved prosperity which has come to her and made her one of the wealthy citizens of the county She now owns sixty-five acres of rich and arable land, has mortgages on a number of farms, and has considerable money loaned She watches her opportunity, and when she thinks a profitable sale or purchase can be made, takes advantage of the same. Her farm is now rented, so that she has little to care for

Like her husband, Mrs Michel holds membership with the Methodist Church She is now in quite poor health, and with her lives her niece, Elvina Barnholtz, who will remain with her during her declining years Mrs. Michel is a most excellent lady, and her sterling worth and many excellences of character have gained her a large circle of friends and acquaintances

Rev. P. J. Gallagher.

REV P J GALLAGHER, pastor of St Thomas' Pro-Cathedral of Winona was born September 8, 1854, in County Mayo, Ireland, and when about ten years of age came to America with his sister and brother He was the youngest in the family of nine children born unto P J and Bridget (Ragen) Gallagher The father was a farmer by occupation, and the mother died when our subject was only about six months old On reaching this country he came direct to Winona, to his brother-in law, with whom he made his home for some time He attended the common school of the neighborhood, and was afterward graduated from the high school of this city, at the age [illegible] tered St John's University at Collegeville, in Stearns County, Minn, where he completed the regular classical course in five years

Mr Gallagher was then sent by Bishop Grace to the Grand Seminary at Montreal Canada, where he completed the theological course of four years, after which he was ordained to the priesthood by Rt-Rev Bishop Fabre, D D He afterward returned to Winona where he celebrated his first mass on the Sunday after Christmas in the year 1877 For a time he continued a guest of Father Cotter, after which he was appointed assistant pastor of St Paul's Cathedral in St Paul, Minn, and had charge of the missions of western St. Paul and [illegible] for about two years He then built a parsonage in western St. Paul, organized a new parish, built a brick house of worship, and founded a parochial school which had an average attendance of seven hundred pupils and was taught by the Sisters of St Joseph He there remained for about ten years, and did a most excellent work in the interest of his church

In 1890, when Rev. Mr. Cotter was made Bishop of the diocese, Rev Mr Gallagher was placed in charge of St Thomas' Pro-Cathedral of this place, with which he has been connected continuously since The church has a membership of about three hundred families and is in a flourishing condition Father Gallagher is an earnest and untiring worker, whose time and attention are given unremittingly to his pastoral duties, and by his own people and those of other denominations he is held in high esteem He acquired an excellent education and is a well informed man

---

John Thill.

JOHN THILL, who is a worthy representative of the agricultural interests of the county, now resides on section 8, Wilson Township where he owns and operates one hundred and sixty acres of good land This is a valuable and desirable farm, pleasantly located, and the rich land yields to the owner a golden tribute in return for the care and labor he bestows upon it. The improvements are in keeping with those of a model farm, and include a two-story residence, a fine barn and other necessary outbuildings The place is neat and thrifty in appearance, and to the passer-by indicates the careful supervision of the owner

Mr Thill is still a young man He was born on a farm in Asch, Germany, on the 15th of May, 1865, and is a son of John and Mary (Morris) Thill, both of whom were natives of that country The father was a farmer by occupation, and was also master of the carpenter's trade, which he followed at various intervals. In the family were seven childr[illegible] Angeline who also live in Germany, John, of this sketch, Mary, who was born in Paris, France, and is now Mrs Rencher, of Winona Township, Matthew, now living with his parents in the Fatherland, and Catherine who is yet under the parental roof.

In the public schools of his native land John Thill acquired a good education He early became familiar with the duties of farm life, and to his father gave the benefit of his services until after he had attained his majority He was twenty-two years of age when, in February, 1887 he bade adieu to home and friends and crossed the broad Atlantic to the New World On reaching the United States he continued his journey across the country to Minnesota and took up his residence in Winona County, where he has since made his home At the time of his arrival he had only $2 but he came here with the hope of bettering his financial condition, and at once set to work to reach the desired end He is industrious and en[illegible]d in prosperity [illegible] who makes [illegible] ed, he has steadily worked his way upward, and is now in comfortable circumstances, being the possessor of a valuable property.

Mr Thill now lives with his sister, Mrs Reucher who keeps house for him, her husband being a partner of Mr Thill. He is a public-spirited and progressive citizen, interested in everything pertaining to the welfare of the community, and in his religious belief he is a Catholic. He exercises his right of franchise in support of the Republican party and warmly advocates its principles. A jovial, genial young man, his pleasant nature has gained him many warm friends and all who know him esteem him highly.

Jacob Frederick Fleischer.

JACOB FREDERICK FLEISCHER, general foreman of the Chicago & North-Western Railway shops at Winona, occupies a responsible position and discharges his duties with a promptness and fidelity that have won him the confidence of his employers and the respect of those who serve under him. He was born in Norway, and when a child of two years was brought by his parents to the United States, the family settling in Madison, Wis. The father, K. J. Fleischer, established at Inmansville, Rock County, Wis., the first Norwegian newspaper published in America. It was called the *Emigranten*, and the first edition was printed in 1851. Subsequently Mr Fleischer removed the paper to Madison, where he continued its publication for several years. He was then for a number of years employed in the *State Times* office of Wisconsin, after which he became Vice-Consul of the United States at Madison. Thus he served for several years, and did much to induce the people of his native land to emigrate to America. He also established a general banking business and European exchange at Madison. He was an intimate friend of Ole Bull, and in Norway the two gentlemen formed a project to establish a colony in Pennsylvania, but the people were not ready for such a abandoned. Whenever Mr Bull came to the United States he was the guest of Mr Fleischer. The latter, after a prominent and well spent life, died in Chicago in 1892.

From his early years J. F. Fleischer passed his boyhood days in Madison, Wis., where he remained until a youth of fourteen. He acquired his education in Wittenberg College, of Springfield, Ohio, after which he enlisted in the one hundred days' service in the Eighty-sixth Ohio Infantry, when the call was made for troops to protect Washington. He served in Virginia and West Virginia, escorting artillery over the mountains and on the expiration of his term was honorably discharged.

In 1863, having returned to the North, Mr Fleischer entered the employ of the Milwaukee & Prairie du Chien Railroad Company, and has since been engaged in railroad work. He learned the machinist's trade in the shops at Milwaukee, and worked in the jobbing shops at La Crosse, Sparta and in other places. His residence in Minnesota dates from 1868, at which time he located in Hokah, being then in the employ of the Southern Minnesota Railway. He continued in the shops at that place, and remained with the same company until 1880, with the exception of a period of three

he Illinois

Central Road at Waterloo, Iowa, with the Northern Pacific at Brainard, Iowa, and was foreman for a year and a-half in the Dean & Smith jobbing shops of La Crosse, Wis., engaged in building Hoyt's automatic millstone dresser. In 1880 he entered the employ of the North-Western Railway Company at Winona, under W. A. Scott, then Master Mechanic. In that year he was sent to Huron, S. Dak., as foreman under W. W. McIntosh, Master Mechanic, and in 1887 he came from Huron to Winona to accept the position of general foreman at the repair shops at this place, where two hundred men are employed.

Mr. Fleischer was married on the 1st of June, 1871, in Hokah, Minn., the lady of his choice being Miss Anna Dibbell, of that city. They have a pleasant home at No. 223 West Broadway Street, and have many friends in this community.

In his political views Mr. Fleischer is liberal, connecting himself with no political party. He was made a Mason in Hokah, Minn., and soon became an active member of the fraternity. He became Worshipful Master in 1875, and was prominent in the Grand Lodge, taking an active part in establising lodges and chapters. He was a charter member of the lodge in Huron, S. Dak., of which he was made Master, and in the chapter he was elected High Priest. He is also a member of the Knights of Pythias. His social and genial manner and his many excellences of character make him popular and he has many warm friends.

JUDGE J. A. TAWNEY.

Hon. James A. Tawney.

HON. JAMES A. TAWNEY, of Winona, is a Member of Congress from the First District of Minnesota, and his connection with many of the leading questions that have been before the Fifty-third Session has brought him into prominence and gained him a reputation throughout the country. The history of his life is one of much interest, for from an humble position he has steadily arisen to a place of honorable notoriety. He was born on the 3d of January, 1855, in Adams County, Pa., near Gettysburg, and is a son of John E. and Sarah (Bobiitz) Tawney. He comes from the same ancestry as the late Chief-Justice Taney, of the Supreme Court. The founder of the family in America was John Tawney, who landed at Baltimore about 1650, and settled in Lancaster County, Pa. The Tawneys are a sturdy race, possessed of physical perfection and great powers of endurance. John E. Tawney and his father were both blacksmiths. He became a prominent citizen of the community in which he lived, and took an active interest in public affairs.

Between the ages of fourteen and seventeen years James A. Tawney worked at the blacksmith's trade for his father. He then went to Du Bois, Clearfield County, Pa., where he had charge of a shop, and did the blacksmith work for the Du Bois Sawmill until 1877. In the mean time he had learned the machinist's trade, and in August of that year he came to Winona, where he worked in a machine-shop and at the forge until January, 1881. Mr. Tawney now resolved upon a change of work. For two years previous, unassisted and undirected, he had read law, and he now entered the law office of Bentley & Vance, where he made rapid progress. He applied himself closely, and in an incredibly short time had mastered much of the knowledge which is essential to successful legal practice. He was admitted to the Bar July 10, 1882, and went to Madison, Wis., to further pursue his legal studies in the State University, but owing to Mr. Bentley's death he returned home, and at once entered upon what has been a most brilliant professional career. To a casual observer his success seems almost phenomenal, and to one more acquainted with his methods it cannot but fail to excite admiration and wonder His reading has covered a wide range, and his general knowledge has been brought into use at the Bar His ability as an advocate was soon recognized, and he has been connected with many of the important cases in the district Steadily his business has increased until, when not occupied with his official cares his time is almost entirely taken up by attention to his many clients

A successful lawyer often makes an able official, and such has been the case with Mr. Tawney. In 1883 he was elected Judge Advocate of the Second Minnesota National Guards, in which position he served until January, 1891, when he was made Judge Advocate-General on the staff of Governor Merriam In the fall of 1890 he was elected State Senator from the Fifteenth District, and served four years In Winona County the Democratic candidate for Governor received a majority of sixteen hundred the same year but Mr. Tawney overcame that majority, and carried the county by a vote of four hundred This was the result of his great personal popularity, and, more than that, of the confidence and trust reposed in him In the expression of his political views he had given forth no uncertain sound, and was recognized as one of the leading Republicans of the state He was Vice-President of the Republican State League from February, 1888, until March, 1891, and since that time has served on the Republican State Central Committee While in the Senate he served on the Judiciary Committee, and was one of the chief opponents of Ignatius Donnelly and other Populist members who attempted impracticable and "wild-cat" legislation

Mr. Tawney was married on the 19th of December, 1883, to Miss Emma Newell, a lady of culture and refinement, who is well fitted to be the companion of her illustrious husband. They have four children Everett Franklin, James Millard, John E and Maud Josephine.

To follow in detail the career of Mr Tawney in the State Senate and in Congress would be to write a volume, but much is deserving of mention on the pages [illegible] He was Chairman of the Senator Davis Committee in 1893, when Davis was candidate for the United States Senate and was largely instrumental in securing his election He was ever an earnest worker for the interest of his constituents, and his careful policy and recognized ability made him the choice of his party as candidate for Congress in Waseca, July 26, 1892 Two other names were proposed—Allen J. Greer, of Wabasha, and G W Rockwell, of Rushford He received the majority on an informal ballot, and on the first ballot was nominated by acclamation During the campaign he made sixty-five speeches His Democratic opponent was Hon W H. Harries, of Caledonia, who two years before had been elected by a majority of twenty-three hundred A Populist and a Prohibition candidate were also in the field. A vigorous campaign followed, and Mr Tawney was elected by a plurality of thirty-one hundred and sixty

Mr. Tawney took his seat in Congress in the extra session of the Fifty-third Congress, August 7, 1893 He was made a member of the Committee on Pensions and of Irrigation of Arid Lands, with which he is still connected Under Act of December 21, 1893 it became unlawful for the department of the Interior to refuse to pay pensions without giving pensioners thirty days' notice of charges, and a chance to refute the same. The department, however, paid no attention to the law but continued disallowing pensions. Mr. Tawney had a number of cases among his constituents who were unjustly affected by the ruling of the department, their claims being clouded by the Van Leuven pension litigation He secured the passage of legislation, reciting the fact that certain constituents, naming eight men, had pensions suspended without notice, and that payment had been withheld in violation of the Act of December 21, 1893, for three months and asked the Department of the Interior why the act had not been complied with. The bill was reported on favorably by the Committee on Invalid Pensions, and passed by the House, and as a result it obtained a ruling from the Department of Justice that enforced the provisions of the act providing that notice should be given of the suspension of pensions This ruling affected [illegible] and resulted in the payment of over $1,000,000. His speech on pensions, delivered March 5, 1894, was a masterly effort, setting forth in a powerful way his views on the question, and won repeated applause.

Mr. Tawney delivered his maiden speech in the extra session on the repeal of the Federal Election Law. He delivered three brilliant speeches on the tariff and one on reciprocity, and their reception by the members of his party was shown by the frequent cheers which greeted him. He made an able argument in behalf of the tariff, when he showed that on account of the duty on Canadian barley, there was an increase in the state of Minnesota from seven million bushels in 1890 to sixteen million bushels in 1892.

Mr. Tawney was associated with such men as Reed, Burroughs, Cannon, Boutelle and other leaders, and in the Congress of the Nation won the recognition of merit and ability. Hon. C. E. Town, of Duluth, said of Mr. Tawney in the Republican State Convention, that one of the leaders of the House, Mr. Boutelle, had remarked that in his experience in the House he never knew of a new member who had made a more favorable impression than had Mr. Tawney.

Asahel B. Quimby.

ASAHEL B. QUIMBY, Master Mechanic in the Winona & South-Western Railway office and shops of Winona, claims New Hampshire as the state of his nativity, his birth having occurred in Dunbarton, near Concord, on the 26th of September, 1851. His father, John Quimby, was a native of Lincolnshire, England. At the age of eighteen A. B. Quimby entered the "Amoskeag" shops at Manchester, and, serving his three-years apprenticeship, he received a diploma as a machinist. He then entered the shops of the Concord Railroad, at Concord, N. H., as a journeyman, and later secured employment in the shops of the China Manufacturing Company, where he continued for three years. In 1879 Mr. Quimby came to the West. He worked in Milwaukee, Wis., and was employed by the Hokah & Minneapolis, and by the Minnesota & Wells Railroad Companies. He then entered the employ of the Chicago & North-Western Railway Company, and was stationed in the shops in Winona, where he continued for eleven years, or until 1891, when the Winona & South-Western Railway was established and the position of Master Mechanic was offered him. This he accepted, and entered upon his duties on the 1st of February. Forty-one men are employed under him, and for their superior officer they entertain a high regard, for he is ever fair and just in his dealings, never manifesting any of the overbearing tendencies of many task-masters. In the shops all of the engines are overhauled and all repair work is done. Mr. Quimby gives his entire attention to the business, and sustains very pleasant relations with the road and its Superintendent, J. T. Mahoney.

Mr. Quimby was married November 20, 1875, in Manchester, N. H., to Miss Emma I. Bingham, a native of the old Granite State. They had an adopted son, Elmer, who came to them in infancy, and died August 12, 1892, in his fourteenth year. Both Mr. and Mrs. Quimby are faithful members and active workers in the Free Baptist Church. The congregation was organized in their home, and at the beginning had only a few members. A new building was erected at the corner of Lincoln and Howard Streets, at a cost of $5,000. It is a neat brick structure, built in modern style, and was dedicated on the 24th of June, 1894. The church has a membership of about one hundred, with fully organized societies and Sunday-school, and Mr. Quimby is now serving as Clerk of the church. He has also been active in Sunday-school work, and does all in his power to promote those interests which are calculated to elevate humanity and advance the general welfare. He is a man of strong temperance principles, and now votes with the Prohibition party, but was formerly an advocate of the men and measures of the Republican party.

Moses Laberee.

MOSES LABEREE, of Winona, residing at No. 218 West Wabasha Street, was born in Whitefield, Me., July 14, 1827, and is a son of Benjamin and Nancy (Jewett) Laberee, who were also natives of the Pine Tree State. The paternal grandfather, Peter Laberee, was born in New Hampshire, whence he went to Maine. His wife was a Longfellow, and came from Massachusetts.

The gentleman whose name heads this record spent the days of his boyhood and youth in the usual manner of farmer lads, his education being acquired in the district schools, which he attended through the winter months, while in the summer season he aided in the labor of the field. On attaining his majority he left the parental roof and in 1849, on the tide of emigration which was steadily drifting westward, he went to Wisconsin, locating in Sauk, with his elder brother. They there assist... were then e... the Yellow River. Moses Laberee remained in Wisconsin until 1856, engaged in milling and lumbering, and then came to Winona, where his brother, Franklin Laberee, now deceased, was then living, having located here in the spring of 1855. For several years Moses engaged in teaming, and then began to work for the Chicago & North-Western Railway Company, on car work. He began operations in 1871, and has since been in the employ of that road. He has worked all of the time in the shops, repairing cars, getting out material and running machinery.

For thirty-eight years Mr. Laberee has resided in his present home, which was erected in 1856. He was married on the 2d of July, 1851, in Sauk County, Wis., to Miss Emeline C. Turner, a native of Alna, Me. For almost forty years they traveled life's journey together, and the lady proved to her husband a faithful companion and help- ... 1893, she was ... them were born the following children: Edwin, who is now engaged in milling in Minneapolis; Ruth Ella, wife of Wallace Galbraith, a resident of Ransom County, N. Dak.; Willett, who follows farming in Deuel County, S. Dak.; and Harriet M., who graduated from the normal school, and for some years has taught in the public schools of Winona City, and also keeps house for her father. Ruth for four years has successfully taught in the public schools, and Harriet is taking an active part in educational work.

Mr. Laberee exercises his right of franchise in support of the Republican party, but has never sought or desired office. In connection with his business interests he has for several years been a Director in the Winona Building and Loan Association. He aided in its organization, July 6, 1882, and believes firmly in the principles which underlie the association. The best interests of the community ever find in him a friend, and his hearty support and co-operation are given to those enterprises which are calculated to benefit the community.

Nathan Harris.

NATHAN HARRIS, one of the honored early settlers of Winona County, who since 1856 has resided within her borders, is now located on a farm on section 12, Wilson Township, where he owns two hundred and twenty-five acres of rich and valuable land. The entire amount is under a high state of cultivation, and is well improved with all the accessories and conveniences of a model farm. Buildings and fences are kept in good repair, the fields are well tilled, and there is an air of neatness and thrift which pervades the place and indicates the careful supervision of the owner.

The life record of Mr. Harris is as follows: He was born on a farm in Nova Scotia, February 22, 1813, and his parents, Alpheus and Rebecca (Eaton) Harris, were natives of the same country. The father, who was a farmer, began life in fair circumstances, and as he made the most of his opportunities he became quite well-to-do, his business and executive ability and good judgment winning him prosperity. Mr. and Mrs. Harris were united in marriage about 1800, and began their domestic life in Nova Scotia. Twelve children were born unto them, and with one exception all grew to mature years. They were Elisha; Mrs. Sarah A. Hall, who now occupies the old homestead; Mrs. Olive Robblee, who is living in the East; Mrs. Nancy Pingree; Stephen E.; Mrs. Elizabeth Chipman; Nathan; James E.; Thomas A.; Lucy, deceased; Daniel K., and Mary J.

Nathan Harris remained at home until he had attained his majority, and then embarked in general merchandising, which he carried on for a period of five years. He afterward carried on various pursuits for a time. In 1815 he came to the United States and made a location in Boston, Mass., where he spent one year, after which he went to New Hampshire. During the succeeding nine years he remained in the old Granite State.

Ere that period had elapsed Mr. Harris was married. On the 20th of September, 1817, he wedded Miss Martha J. Fuller, daughter of Capt. Edward Fuller, who was a native of Massachusetts, and served as a Captain in the War of 1812. On his return to private life he engaged in the manufacture of paper, and conducted a very prosperous business, winning thereby considerable capital He came to Minnesota at the same time as Mr Harris, having lost his wife some years previous In the family were six children, four of whom reached mature years Thomas U died at the home of his sister, Mrs. Harris, in 1886; Ezra and Edward are also both deceased, Martha was born July 5, 1809

In New Hampshire Mr and Mrs. Harris continued to make their home until 1856, when they came to Winona County. They had three children, two of whom are yet living Lucilla, born November 25, 1847, died May 15, 1872, and was laid to rest in Woodlawn Cemetery. Edward F, born March 28, 1850, resides on a farm adjoining that of his parents, and is recognized as one of the successful agriculturists of Winona County; and Orlando U, born May 2, 1854, now carries on the home farm, and is a most highly respected citizen They also have ten grandchildren, all living

Both Mr and Mrs Harris are members of the Congregational Society Mrs Harris is a member of the church, to which their son Orlando also belongs, and in its work and upbuilding they take an active interest. The cause of education finds in Mr Harris a warm friend, and for many years he has served as School Director In politics he is a Democrat, but has never been an aspirant for office, preferring to give his entire time and attention to his business interests It is his close attention to the details of his business, combined with diligence, prudence and careful management, that has brought him the success which has crowned his efforts

The Winona Wagon Company.

THE WINONA WAGON COMPANY was incorporated in October, 1879, as the Winona Rushford Wagon Company by A J Stevens, John Albertson and O B Gould The last-named became President The capital stock was originally $15,000, and the first year about five hundred Rushford wagons were sold. From that time the business has steadily increased until now the annual sale amounts to ten thousand wagons Business is done in a three-story brick shop, 50x100 feet, with a two-story L, in which is stored the raw material which comes in from the yards. There is also a blacksmith shop, 65x190 feet, a seasoning shed, 25x500 feet, full of smaller timber, and a larger building [illegible] about ten thousand sets of hubs All the timber for the more important parts of the wagon is seasoned for three years, either in protected sheds in the yards, or in buildings enclosed from the weather, and for three months before using is kept in the seasoning rooms in a bath of hot air at a temperature of one hundred degrees, day and night, until every particle of greenness or moisture is thoroughly extracted. Many important parts, such as hubs, etc., are then dipped in boiling oil, which prevents checking and imparts an especial toughness to the fibre

At the extreme end of the factory, where the finished property is kept, are side-tracks from all the [illegible] that it is no trouble to load goods A new contrivance has lately been introduced into the factory—a powerful hydraulic tire-shrinking machine, used in shrinking tires on wheels The tires are first heated to two hundred and sixty-five degrees in a steam heater, too hot to handle by hand, but not hot enough to burn wood The tire is then laid on the wheel, which is placed horizontally on the machine, the tire slips down into place, and with a touch the operator causes plungers to move up against it all around it The pressure forces it to contract, and it is set against the wheel so forcibly as to place the proper "dish" in the wheel, and is then held in place still more tightly when it cools and contracts This is a most excellent piece of machinery, and with it one man can do the work which would otherwise require ten men The bands are put on the hubs by a machine working on the same principle.

A spoke-driving machine, which is operated by a boy, drives spokes for forty wagons in a day—the work of four men This consists of a hammer at the end of a handle three and a-half feet long, so swung on an axle moved by friction wheels that its strikes a powerful blow, and yet is as easily controlled as is a small hammer in the hands of a skilled blacksmith. Three blows will drive the most obstinate spoke to its shoulder in the hub, and much more solidly than is possible by hand. New machines of most improved patterns are being added in each department, and many of the special machines are made in one part of the plant by skilled machinists, who are thoroughly conversant with every need of each machine

The Rushford wagon is known from Maine to California, from Manitoba to Texas, and its fine lines of construction, combined with the best material the finest workmanship, and honest effort in each department, has given it a name second to none among wagons The great demand can be partially appreciated when it is known that over one hundred styles of wagons are made in this factory alone, styles differing in details of dimensions rather than in finish and general appearance Every department of this large plant is under the trained eye of its Superintendent, Mr. Hennessy, whose generalship in handling men and meeting emergencies is unquestioned This has proven one of the very few manufacturing plants started in Winona that have had a steady improvement and advancement, there having never been one day of disaster. It has been one of the really important institutions, and has ever afforded sure employment, summer and winter, to hundreds of employes, many of whom are almost fixtures, not a few having been in its employ for ten or more years. It has been the policy of its management to so conduct business that each employe could feel that so long as he attended to duty he could depend upon his position, and situations are not held through favoritism, but through merit

John Dobbs.

JOHN DOBBS, deceased, was born in New York, on the 24th of January, 1827, and died in Winona on the 23d of September, 1890 His early years were passed in Albany, where he learned the book-binder's trade, and there he continued until 1849, when, attracted by the discovery of gold in California, he made his way to the Pacific Slope There he engaged in mining for about a year, meeting with only average success He then returned to his native state and resumed work at his trade in Albany.

Soon after his return Mr Dobbs was united in marriage with Miss Elizabeth Porter, and to them were born five children, of whom two died in childhood Edward T, the eldest living, is a dentist of Brooklyn, N. Y., William J is now station agent on the Elkhorn & Missouri Valley Railroad at O'Neill, Neb, Charles died in infancy; Jennie died in childhood, and Herbert Orr died in O'Neill, Neb., December 11, 1893 He had served as operator and station agent, and had also been in the employ of the Lansing Lumber Company. His first wife having died, Mr Dobbs was again married, his second union being with Miss Mary E Potts, of Albany. Her father, William Henry Potts, died in Columbia County, N Y, at the age of thirty-three Her mother, who bore the maiden name of Lucinda Moore, was born and reared in that county, but for some years had resided in Albany, where, on the 20th of March, 1872, her daughter Mary became the wife of John Dobbs. By this union were born three children Frank Nelson, who is in his nineteenth year and is employed as clerk in the shops of the North-Western Railway Company; Arthur Emil and Percy Moncrief

Mr Dobbs continued to engage in book-binding in Albany until 1857, when he came to Winona, hoping that a change of climate would prove beneficial, for he was then in poor health He secured a farm near Utica, but remained thereon only about a year for the financial panic of 1857 brought ruin upon the country, and like many others he suffered some loss He then returned to New York, much improved in health, and resumed work at his trade in Albany He was a skilled binder, and his services were always in demand, so that he found steady work in the East until he abandoned the old occupation to again seek a home in Minnesota. He established a book-bindery in Winona, but soon consolidated it with the *Republican* newspaper, which was published by the firm of Sinclair & Dye Mr. Dobbs became an equal partner in the concern, and continued in charge of the bindery until within a few months of his death. He devoted his time and attention assiduously to his business interests, and won a success which was well deserved

Mr. Dobbs was an enthusiastic Republican and in deep sympathy with the principles advocated by the paper with which he was connected. Socially he was a Knight-Templar Mason, and took an active interest in that fraternity. He was very influential in organizing the original fire department of Winona, when the business men protected themselves [illegible] He continued his close connection with the fire department until its efficiency had been fully established, and was a member of the advisory or directing board of fire protection. On the 15th of October, 1887, he resigned as a member of the company, and at that time the department presented him with a fine cane, which was highly prized as a token of their esteem and respect for him The best interests of the community ever found in him a friend, and his hearty support and co-operation were ever given to all enterprises which he believed would prove of public benefit He passed away September 23, 1890, and throughout the community the loss of this valued citizen was mourned

Mrs Dobbs is a lady of refinement and culture, and is well known as the proprietress of an excellent boarding-house Her pleasant home is situated in the center of the city, close to the normal school, and the comforts of home life are had by those who share her roof She possesses many sterling qualities and is endeared to all who know her.

Alexander C. Sinclair.

ALEXANDER C. SINCLAIR Though he has passed from the scenes of time, Mr Sinclair is still remembered by a host of warm personal friends, and especially by the citizens of St Charles Township, where for so long he made his home He was a man of great energy and force of character, who through his own industry and perseverance accumulated a valuable property, including his well improved farm on section 32

The birth of our subject occurred in New Hampshire, December 20, 1821, and his parents, Joseph and Ann (Cornell) Sinclair, were also natives of that state His father followed the trade of a carpenter in addition to the occupation of a farmer In 1851 he decided to try his fortune in what was then considered the far West, and with his family he started for Minnesota They went by rail to Peoria, Ill, and from there proceeded by stage to Dixon, Ill, where they took passage on a boat and came direct to Winona They arrived on the 19th of August, and within a few hours after landing the wife and mother died of cholera This was a sad blow to the family. Two days after placing the remains of their loved one in the cemetery at that place they proceeded to St. Charles Township, and located a claim on section 32, where they entered one hundred and sixty acres of Government land

A small log cabin stood on one corner of the property, and in this humble abode the family made their home for about six years At the expiration of that time they erected the commodious building that now occupies the site of the former cabin This is one of the best farm houses in the neighborhood, and the farm is the best improved in the section, having all the necessary farming implements and stock of all kinds that are generally found on a first-class estate

On the 18th of February, 1846, Mr Sinclair was united in marriage with Miss Betsy, daughter of Nathan and Clarissa Merrill, natives of New Hampshire Four children blessed their union, of whom one died in infancy. Clarissa the eldest, married

William Groger, and resides on a farm adjoining the old homestead; Ann died December 12, 1863, and Ella married Angus Ross, a banker of Rock County, Minn.

Mr. Sinclair was what may be termed a self-educated man, not having had the advantages of good schools in his youth, but with the aid of good books and the current literature of the day, combined with his natural intelligence, he became well posted in both local and national affairs. In his business career he was very successful, and was widely and favorably known, having the esteem and confidence of his neighbors. For twenty years before his death he was a great sufferer from asthma and lung trouble, but bore his sufferings patiently until the end came. His death occurred February 4, 1892, and his remains were laid to rest in the private cemetery of the family on his farm. He was greatly missed by his friends and mourned by the entire community. Politically he always affiliated with the Republican party, but was never actively engaged in public affairs, preferring to give his attention to his private interests.

Nicholas Schell, Jr.

NICHOLAS SCHELL, JR., one of the leading merchants of Rolling Stone, is now at the head of a good store, stocked with a full line of general merchandise, and is doing a constantly increasing business. He was born in Fischbach, Marche County, in Luxemburg, Germany, on the 24th of December, 1854, and is a son of John and Katie (Loutsch) Schell. Their family numbered seven children, of whom Nicholas was the fourth in order of birth. The father worked as a common laborer in his native land until 1869, when, with the hope of bettering his financial condition, he sailed for America. Coming to Minnesota, he bought a farm in Rolling Stone Township, Winona County, and during the remainder of his life carried on agricultural pursuits. He was in very limited circumstances at the time of his arrival, but he worked hard, and as the result of his enterprise and perseverance secured a comfortable competence, leaving to his family a good property. He was called to the home beyond at the age of sixty-nine years; his wife passed away at the age of seventy-two. They were laid to rest side by side in Rolling Stone Cemetery. Both were members of the Catholic Church, and throughout the community were held in high regard.

Nicholas Schell spent the first fifteen years of his life in the Fatherland and then came with his parents to the United States. He worked upon the home farm until sixteen years of age, and then began working as a farm hand by the month in the neighborhood. In this way he passed the summer, while in the winter season he attended the public schools. His early educational privileges were afterwards supplemented by a course of study in St. John's University. He paid his own tuition with money which he acquired by labor in the field, and thus is a self-educated, as well as a self-made, man financially.

When twenty-one years of age Mr. Schell began teaching school in Mt. Vernon Township, Winona County, and then took charge of the Oak Ridge school, which he successfully taught for a period of ten years. His long continued service there well indicates the confidence reposed in him by those interested, and plainly demonstrates that the confidence was not misplaced. At length, after this period of successful teaching, he turned his attention to agricultural pursuits and purchased eighty acres of land. He afterwards rented a farm, which he operated through the summer months, while in the winter season he was for three terms employed as a teacher in the Rolling Stone schools. In 1889 he sold his farm and embarked in merchandising, which he yet follows.

Mr Schell was married on the 6th of October, 1880, the lady of his choice being Miss Mary Kimmel, daughter of Nicholas Kimmel, one of the early settlers of this county. He votes with the Democratic party and is a stanch advocate of its principles. For two years he served as Assessor of Mt. Vernon Township, for about eight years was Town Clerk, and was also clerk of the Farmers' Fire Insurance Company of Rolling Stone. He is a man of pleasant, genial manner, and his gentlemanly deportment, his earnest desire to please his customers and his fair and honest dealing have won for him a liberal patronage, which is well merited.

John Evans.

JOHN EVANS, deceased, was one of the honored pioneers of Winona of 1856. He was born in England in 1800, and during the days of his early manhood emigrated to the New World, locating first in Canada. He afterward removed to Michigan, and in 1833 left that state to become a resident of Ohio. He later removed to Wisconsin, and in April, 1852, he came to Minnesota. It was his intention to locate at Lake City, on Lake Pepin, but instead he decided to settle on Winona Prairie. He made a journey up the river on a steamer to Menomonee, and then started out to seek a location. The claim which he entered comprised what is now the finest residence part of Winona. He became the owner of one hundred and fifty-two acres, and during the first winter after his arrival he spent his time in getting out rails, splitting enough that year to fence forty acres of land. He then began the cultivation and development of a farm. Mr. Evans took a very active part in securing Winona as the county seat, went to the State Legislature for that purpose, and bought the two lots on which to build the court house. He was a valued and prominent citizen, and had the high respect of all who knew him. His death occurred in 1856, and his wife passed away fifteen years later. In their family were two children, a son and daughter.

The former, R. B. Evans, was born in Detroit, Mich., August 3, 1833, and at the age of eighteen years came to Winona. He now resides on the Evans Subdivision, which was laid out by his father and is a part of the original claim which was entered from the Government in 1852. When he began business for himself R. B. Evans settled on a farm in the Gilmore Valley, three miles from the river. He also had a farm seven miles away, on the ridge, where he lived for thirteen years. In 1882 he returned to the city, and now is living on a part of the old homestead. In 1885 he built the first stable in Winona, and embarked in the livery business. This was the first in the place

In 1857 Mr Evans was united in marriage with Miss Mary Parks, a native of Ohio, who came here with her cousin, Ervin Johnson, who married Abigail Evans, a sister of our subject In 1857 he returned to Pennsylvania, where he engaged in the oil business, but after a time again came to Minnesota, where he died in 1869. His wife passed away in 1862. Their daughter, Winona Johnson, married Dr Flowers, of Ohio, and died a few years later For his second wife Mr Johnson married a sister of Mrs Evans, who still lives in North Bloomfield, Ohio She has one daughter Myra who is married and lives in the Buckeye State To R B Evans and his wife were born four children George, who married Frankie Bozburg, was a successful insurance solicitor He died in New Mexico after a year's illness, May 2, 1893, at the age of thirty-six years. Edwin died at the age of four years Anna died at the age of thirteen Frank was the youngest of the family

---

Martin H. Fuller.

MARTIN H FULLER, deceased, was a native of Vermont born near Poultney, Rutland County on the 12th of December, 1829 His father was Hooker Fuller, and the family numbered seven children, four sons and three daughters The parents both died when Martin H was only about seven years of age, and he then went to live with an uncle, by whom he was reared to manhood His educational privileges were those afforded by the common schools He had no special advantages in his youth, but he endeavored to make the most of his opportunities, and his life was a successful, as well as an honorable and upright, one

At the age of twenty-two, Mr Fuller began to earn his own livelihood by working as a farm hand by the month Attracted by the West and the better advantages which he believed it afforded, he emigrated to Michigan about 1851, locating in Marquette, where he continued his residence for fifteen years. On the expiration of that period, in 1866, he came to Minnesota, locating in Saratoga Township, Winona County Here he purchased the farm which [illegible] comprised eighty acres on section 30, and when it came into his possession was but partially improved In connection with his agricultural pursuits, he also carried on a distillery in Troy for about eight years. His farm was placed under a high state of cultivation, many improvements being made thereon, and it became one of the valuable and desirable places of the neighborhood

Mr. Fuller was twice married In 1854 he was united in marriage with Miss Bogart, and to them was born one son, John H who is now living in St Paul, where he was employed as assistant yardmaster on the "Soo Line" and the Chicago, Milwaukee & St Paul Railroad Mrs. Fuller died in 1856 and on the 5th of June, 1867, Mr Fuller married Miss May E. Dustman Three children graced this union, but Marian and Myrtle, twins, both died in infancy. Ralph H. resides at home and carries on the farm He is a wide-awake and enterprising young man, highly respected in the community, and after his father's death he succeeded to the office of School Treasurer.

Mr Fuller had served as School Treasurer for [illegible] He had also served as Assessor and Township Supervisor, and in these various offices had discharged his duties with a promptness and fidelity that had won him high commendation and led to his frequent re-election. He was always true to a trust, whether public or private, and thereby won the confidence of all with whom he was brought in contact. With the Masonic lodge he held membership. He owned one hundred and twenty acres of land, and thus left his family in comfortable circumstances. He took an active interest in public enterprises, and was recognized as a valued citizen. His death occurred July 7, 1894, and he was laid to rest in Saratoga Cemetery, amid the deep regret of many friends. His widow and son still occupy the old homestead and are prominent people of the community.

Wilson C. Brown.

WILSON C. BROWN, Chief Clerk of the Winona & St. Peter Land Company, and one of the highly respected citizens of this county, comes from the far-off state of Maine. He was born May 14, 1847, in East Wilton, Franklin County, and there remained until the age of ten years, when he removed to Kennebec County, Me., with his parents. His father, Charles T. Brown, was general agent for the North Wayne Edge Tool Company of Maine, and resided in the Pine Tree State until the year 1860, when he emigrated westward, becoming a resident of St. Peter, Minn. He represented his district, the Nineteenth, in the State Legislature continuously from 1866 to 1869, serving one term in the House and three terms in the State Senate, and from 1872 to 1874 he was United States Surveyor-General of the state. He was a prominent man in public affairs, his worth and ability well fitting him to be a leader of the people. He was also President of the Board of Trustees of the asylum at St. Peter from the time of its organization until his death, the building having been erected under his supervision. He died in St. Peter, November 30, 1879, and thereby Minnesota lost one of its most valued citizens.

Wilson C. Brown acquired his education in the common schools, and with his parents came to Minnesota in 1860, when thirteen years of age. At the age of seventeen he entered the United States land office at St. Peter in the capacity of clerk, and thus served for five years under Abner Tibbits, and later with ex-Governor Swift. In that office he remained until 1869, when he came to Winona, and entered the service of the Winona & St. Peter Railroad Company as chief clerk of its land department. Later, in 1876, he held the same office with the Winona & St. Peter Land Company, a position which he has filled continuously since in a most creditable and acceptable manner.

The Winona & St. Peter Land Company acquired by purchase from the Winona & St. Peter Railroad Company about five hundred thousand acres of land, included in the latter's Congressional grants, located from Winona westward in the various counties along its line of railroad. This domain, comprising a fine body of agricultural lands, has been disposed of in small tracts to actual settlers at low prices and on easy terms thus enabling many people to obtain a desirable home in southern Minnesota who could not otherwise have done so. Mr Brown has established branch offices at various places for the accommodation of settlers, and has thus disposed of a large amount of property. He attends carefully to all the details of the business, is alive to the company's interests, and his faithful service has won him universal confidence. In addition to his other interests, Mr Brown is a Director in the Citizens' State Bank of Redwood County.

On the 21st of September, 1869, in St Peter, Mr Brown was married to Miss M Alice Dunning, of that place. Their union has been blessed with two children, a son and daughter, Carleton W and Maude D.

Nic Lambert.

NIC LAMBERT, who is living on section 18, Wilson Township, where he operates a valuable farm, is one of the wide-awake and enterprising young men of the community He was born on a farm in Oneida County N Y December 26, 1861, and is a son of Michael and Elizabeth (Killian) Lambert, both of whom were natives of Germany. During his boyhood the father came with his parents to the New World the family locating in the Empire State During the first few years after his arrival he worked at railroading, and then sought a home in the West, coming to Winona County in 1865 Two years later he purchased a farm of one hundred and twenty acres on section 18, Wilson Township and afterward added to it until he now owns one hundred and sixty acres This he placed under a high state of cultivation, transforming the once wild prairie into rich and fertile fields He placed thereon many excellent improvements, including all the accessories and conveniences which are found upon a model farm There may be found a comfortable residence, good barn and outbuildings and well kept fences Mr Lambert has retired from active business life and is now living in Winona, at the age of sixty-six [illegible] prosperous [illegible] rest from all care, for a competence acquired through his own exertions supplies him with all the necessities and many of the luxuries of life.

To Mr and Mrs Lambert were born seven children, all of whom are yet living in this county namely Barbara, now the wife of John Redick, a resident of Winona, Mike, who is living in Winona Township, Nic, of this sketch; Philip and Adam, at home, Mrs Mary Redick; and Annie, who is still under the parental roof

Mr. Lambert, of this sketch, was a child of only four years when he was brought by his parents to this county In the usual manner of farmer lads the days of his boyhood and youth were passed He attended the district schools in the winter season, but during the greater part of the year his time and attention were given to farm work He continued under the parental roof until he had attained his majority, when he started out to earn his own livelihood, working as a farm hand and at carpentering

As a companion and helpmate on life's journey Mr. Lambert chose Miss Tracy Einhorn, their wedding being celebrated on the 13th of April, 1884 Her father, Michael Einhorn, was born in Germany, [illegible] in farming. He [illegible] ulturists of Winona County To Mr and Mrs Lambert have been born eight children, five sons and two daughters, who in order of birth are as follows Michael, Nic, Elizabeth, Philip, Johnnie and Angeline, and an infant son.

In his political views Mr Lambert is a Democrat He is now serving as School Clerk and the cause of education finds in him a warm friend He has, however, never sought public office, its honors and emoluments having no attraction for him. He is connected with the German Catholic Church Mr. Lambert has spent almost his entire life in this county, and has therefore become widely known He has many warm friends, among whom are those who have known him from boyhood and have been witnesses of his well spent life and straightforward career As a citizen he manifests a commendable interest in everything pertaining to the welfare of the community and bears his part in the work of public advancement.

Oliver W. Tibbetts.

OLIVER W TIBBETTS is one of the enterprising wide-awake and valued citizens of Dakota, Winona County He is engaged in contracting, also operates a stone-quarry for the Government, and carries the mail from Ridgeway to Dakota. Mr Tibbetts is a western man by birth for he claims Linn County, Iowa, as the place of his nativity He was born December 28, 1853, and is a son of Jeremiah W and Catherine (Maynard) Tibbetts, the father a native of Indiana the mother born near Ottawa province of Ontario, Canada The father was a farmer by occupation, and in 1819 emigrated to Minnesota, locating in Dresbach, where he engaged in business as an Indian trader for a time. He then removed to Iowa, but after a year spent in the Hawkeye State, took up his residence in the village of Dakota this county For several years he spent much time going back and forth between the two places, but at this writing, in the fall of 1894, he is located in the city of Winona

Oliver W. Tibbetts was reared under the parental roof, remaining at home until the day before he attained his majority. At that time, December 27, 1874, he was united in marriage with Miss Alice Wilson, daughter of J G and Sarah (Brown) Wilson, both of whom were natives of New York, but now reside upon a farm in this county Four children were born to Mr. and Mrs Tibbetts, three of whom are yet living Ethel May, born October 9, 1875, and Edith C, born December 12, 1877 are still at home, George W., born October 18, 1879, is the only son and the pride of the family Alice M, born March 21 1885, died on the 2d of November of the same year

Mr. Tibbetts had no capital at the time of his marriage, but possessed a young man's bright hope of the future, and a determination to succeed, and with a resolute purpose began farming on rented land. He worked hard, and practiced economy, and at the end of a year was enabled to purchase forty acres of land, to which he removed With characteristic industry he began its development, and five years later purchased another tract of forty acres He then sold out, paid off all indebtedness and began work at day labor. He he now owns some property in the village, besides his stone-quarry, all of which has been acquired through perseverance, industry and good management. He also owns an imported Clydesdale, which has taken more prizes than any other horse ever took in the show ring, being one of the finest heavy draft horses in the United States.

Mr. Tibbetts manifests a commendable interest in everything pertaining to the welfare of the community, and the cause of education finds in him a warm friend. He had no special school privileges himself, but resolved that his children should not lack in that direction, and is giving them good advantages. He is now serving as Constable of Dakota, a position he has filled for about six years with credit to himself and satisfaction to his constituents. He votes with the Republican party, and in his religious views is an Episcopalian.

Samuel W. Spalding.

SAMUEL W. SPALDING. The pioneer residents of Winona County have witnessed many changes within the past thirty years—wild tracts of land transformed into fields of waving grain, elegant structures where once stood the log cabin of the frontiersman, and schools and churches where once the savages roamed unmolested. Among those who have aided in effecting this happy result, and who have lived to see the fruit of their labors, is the subject of this present sketch, who is still living on his fine farm in Pleasant Hill Township.

Mr. Spalding was born in Canada, March 16, 1829, and is the son of Joseph Spalding, who was of Welsh descent. He had six brothers and three sisters, four of whom were born in the Dominion, where our subject remained for the first five years of his life, the others were born in New York State. At that age he accompanied his parents on their removal into the State. They made location in Essex County, N. Y., [illegible] manhood and was given a good education in the schools near their home. One year after attaining his majority he began to earn his own money by working out for others on farms. He continued in this manner for three years, and then, being fond of the sea, was engaged as fisherman on a schooner for two summers, the vessel being employed off the coast of Newfoundland. After his experience as a sailor, young Spalding came West, by way of the Erie Canal and Lakes, and first located in Will County, Ill. He only remained there for six months, however, when he removed to what is now Houston County, Minn. While here he took up a quarter-section of Government land, on which he erected a rude log cabin. After clearing this tract he sold it and entered another claim for a like amount. On it Mr. Spalding and his sister resided for two years, when the former came to Winona County, and located on the estate which he still owns and occupies, in March, 1856. [illegible], which his thorough knowledge of agriculture has enabled him to cultivate and improve in a most profitable manner. The greater portion of the claim was covered with a heavy growth of timber, and in order to get this property in readiness for cultivation, he expended much time and toil.

When ready to establish a home of his own, Mr. Spalding was married, in 1857, to Miss Sarah Jane Hatch. To them was born one son, Franklin, who is now a farmer living in this township. Politically our subject has always been a stalwart Democrat. He has been Supervisor of his township, and aided in the building of the first schoolhouse in his home district. He has ever been true to the various duties and responsibilities imposed upon him, and few men in any community deserve or receive higher esteem.

Joseph J. Hillmer.

JOSEPH J. HILLMER, Professor of Ancient and Modern Languages in the high school of Winona, was born in Rottenmann, Styria, Austria, on the 9th of March, 1841. His father, Joseph Hillmer, was an extensive brewer and a prominent citizen of Rottenmann. One of his daughters still owns the old homestead, a summer resort in the Alps. One son, A. Hillmer, was a captain in the Austrian army, and for distinguished services received the golden cross and gold medal. His death resulted from exposure during the service. He had just been promoted to be captain of the Hoch und Deutchmeister Regiment of Vienna, the leading regiment of the army.

J. J. Hillmer spent his boyhood days in his father's home, and attended the public schools until eleven years of age, when he entered the gymnasium at Gratz, where he pursued his studies eight years taking the regular preparatory course for the university. At the age of twenty he entered the Imperial University at Gratz, where he remained for three and a-half years. From his boyhood days he had expected to enter the Romish priesthood, which course had been decided upon by his mother. He pursued the regular theological studies, devoting himself to oriental languages—the Arabic, Hebrew, Syriac, Chaldaic and Armenian. He had previously studied the Greek, French, Italian and German languages, and had now become proficient in ten different tongues. The professors in the university were among the most prominent teachers in the world.

Professor Hillmer's studies had awakened in him a love of liberty, and, deciding to come to the United States, he left the university just before completing the regular course, in order to avoid ordination and thus be under the control of the bishop. He crossed the Atlantic in 1867 and went to St. Paul accompanied by a classmate. He reached his destination December 24, this being the loneliest Christmas eve he had ever experienced. Professor Hillmer was induced to go to St. Paul through correspondence with a friend at Belle Plaine, and in that city was ordained for the priesthood in April, 1868, by Bishop Grace. He then went to Minneapolis to take charge of St. Boniface's German Church in St. Anthony. He removed the house of worship from the outskirts of the town to the main street in St. Anthony, near where Germania Hall now stands. The school was already established, and in 1869 he succeeded in introducing the now famous Faribault plan, credited to Bishop Ireland. This consisted in getting the school board to pay the teachers and combing with the public schools, retaining the Catholic teacher and religious instruction, which was to be given after regular school hours. After a year this was discontinued, but it was the beginning of the famous Faribault plan of education.

Mr. Hillmer also had charge of two missions, one in Crystal Lake Township and the other in Medina Township, near Minnetonka. In the year 1870 he erected St. Joseph's Church in North Minneapolis, which was named in his honor and he was aided largely by Jacob Barge, John Orth and other prominent German citizens. For some time he had charge of that church, there being then only three priests in Minneapolis, the others being Father McGolrich, now Bishop of Duluth, and Rev. Father Tissot, lately deceased. Father Hillmer had charge of the church until November, 1870. About this time a change in his views occurred. He became acquainted with Rev. D. B. Knickerbocker (the rector of Gethsemane Episcopal Church of Minneapolis, but now Bishop of Indiana), whose liberal and broad views had a great influence on the church and also upon Mr. Hillmer. His natural love of liberty led him to accept these ideas. About this time the infallibility of the Pope was declared, a view which he could not accept, nor would he submit to the arbitrary rulings of the ecclesiastical authorities, whose demands were at times extreme and unjust. He decided to leave the priesthood, and carried out the resolution in November, 1870. He sent his resignation to Bishop Grace, who would not accept it, but Mr. Hillmer was thoroughly disgusted with the lives of priests, saw much insincerity in their doctrines and could not consistently remain in the Catholic Church. He has, however, still retained his intimacy with his old parishioners, whom he always visits while in Minneapolis.

It was the intention of Mr. Hillmer to join the Episcopal clergy. He went to Faribault, where Bishop Whipple resides, and in accordance with the canons of the church he spent six months in study for the ministry, and was then received as a minister of the Protestant Episcopal Church, on the 21st of June, 1871. He was placed in charge of Trinity Church at Stockton, Winona County, where he city he was married, September 1, 1871, to Miss Emma J. Booth, then a student in St. Mary's Hall, of Faribault, Minn., which city was her home. Her father was a prominent merchant of Hamilton, Fillmore County, where he located at an early day. David L. Booth will be well remembered by the old citizens of Winona, as he had intimate relations with many of the pioneer settlers. To Mr. and Mrs. Hillmer have been born the following children: Jennie Monica, a teacher in the city schools; Joseph Booth, cashier in the United States Express Company's office; Nona Theresa and Elsie Corinne.

During the year passed in Stockton, Professor Hillmer was also rector of a church in Minnesota City. In October, 1872, he went to St. Charles, Minn., and first conducted services in the parlor of his home; he afterwards held meetings in a hall until Trinity Church was erected. He also conducted services occasionally in Chatfield and Eyota. In connection with his ministerial work he taught private classes in German in Rochester, and thus began his career as a teacher. He came to Winona in August, 1876, having been elected teacher of German in the public schools. At the same time he held regular services on Lord's Day in Rushford and Minneiska, and at times during the absence of the rector filled the pulpit of St. Paul's Church in Winona. In 1890 he became rector of Grace Church at Wabasha, and spends Saturday and Sunday of each week at that place, where his work has been extremely successful. He is now teacher of languages in the high school of Winona, having classes in Latin and Greek, four classes in German and one in French. He thoroughly enjoys his school work, and makes it a delight to the students. The relations between them are ever of the most pleasant, and the pupils all have the highest regard for Professor Hillmer. The degree of Doctor of Philosophy was conferred upon him by Galesville University, of Galesville, Wis. For some time he was also associated with Dr. Teschan in the publication of the Winona *Adler*, a weekly German paper.

Professor Hillmer is very prominent in Masonic circles. He was made a Mason in Rising Sun Lodge No. 19, A. F. & A. M., of St. Charles, and

rees in Chatfield,

and the Royal Arch degree in Winona. He then joined the Winona lodge and chapter and was Worthy Master at this place in 1886 and 1887. For many years he was Chaplain, and at this writing he is serving as Secretary. He is also Secretary of Winona Chapter No. 5, R. A. M., Prelate of Cœur de Leon Commandery, and has been a delegate to the Grand Lodge. While serving as Master he introduced the dramatization of the Masonic work, introducing the stage, and in this his labors have been most effective. He acted as King Solomon and still holds the position. Only one other lodge in the state has adopted this most excellent feature in conferring degrees.

In 1885 Professor Hulmer visited the old Austrian home, where he spent the vacation months, meeting many of his old friends and classmates and some of his former professors. He also spent many pleasant hours with his brother, the Captain, who died the following year. A love of liberty has been one of Professor Hulmer's chief characteristics, and in accordance with this he is a man of broad mind, whose views on no subject are narrow or contracted. To others he accords the same right of far-reaching thought, and in consequence is charitable and liberal in his judgments.

Marshall Ney Pierce.

MARSHALL NEY PIERCE, who resides at No. 170 Broadway Street, Winona, claims Illinois as the state of his nativity, his birth having occurred in Galena, on the 17th of November, 1819. He was a son of Marshall B. Pierce, then Sheriff of Jo Daviess County, Ill., and one of the prominent citizens of that locality. The subject of this sketch was reared in Savannah, Ill., and continued in his native state until June, 1870, when he came to Winona and secured a position as bookkeeper with Langley & Hatcher, a prominent commission firm. With this company he was connected until April, 1872, when he engaged with Joseph Reynolds, who was known throughout the Northwest as "Diamond Jo." He became a great favorite of Mr. Reynolds, was given at once responsible positions, and had the confidence of his employer in an unlimited degree. He was first made bookkeeper for E. B. Strong & Co., Mr. Reynolds being the principal stockholder in that company, and in August, 1878, when Mr. Strong removed to Chicago, Mr. Pierce became general manager for the Reynolds grain business at this place, and had charge of the grain which was shipped by the "Diamond Jo" steamers, used in the business on the Upper Mississippi. This business was afterward transferred to Dubuque.

Mr. Reynolds was a man whose interests were varied, and at the time of the transfer of the grain business to Dubuque, Mr. Pierce was placed in charge of other interests, being given the position of Auditor and local Treasurer of the Hot Springs Railroad. He entered upon his duties in December, 1881, and served in that capacity until the death of his employer. He was also a Director of the road, of which Mr. Reynolds was President, Secretary and Treasurer. After the death of the latter Mr. Pierce, in March, 1891, was elected Secretary and Treasurer of the company. He was also serving as Auditor and local Treasurer, and as such had charge of all the receipts and disbursements. The position therefore was a very responsible one, and he continued to act in that capacity until June, 1893, when on account of failing health, he was forced to resign, and was succeeded by Capt. Fred A. Bill, who is well known to the people of Winona.

On the 22d of November, 1882, Mr. Pierce was united in marriage with Miss Frances Medora Lewis, daughter of John P. Lewis, formerly a merchant of Winona, who died in Indianapolis, Ind., in 1891. Mrs. Pierce was reared in this city, and by her marriage has one daughter, Frances Gertrude, who is eleven years of age. Mr. Pierce possesses most excellent business and executive ability, is enterprising and progressive and sagacious and far-sighted. He gives close attention to all details, is true to every trust, and thereby merits the confidence of all.

Ole Nelson.

OLE NELSON, a native of Norway, is the owner of a good farm in Wiscoy Township. He is a veteran of the late Civil War and a valiant soldier of several of its important campaigns. He is now identified with the Grand Army of the Republic, and on all occasions may be found discharging his duties as a patriotic citizen of his adopted land. He is progressive and public spirited, striving to uphold measures calculated to bring prosperity to this community. Though he has never been an office-seeker, he once served as Constable in the burgh of Wilson, being the first to hold that office. In politics his ballot is deposited in favor of Republican nominees.

Our subject was born May 7, 1835, and is one of five sons and five daughters whose parents were Andrew and Josephine Nelson, the others being as follows: Caroline, Nels, Anna, Dolan, Katherine, Abraham, Ericker, and two who died in infancy. Our subject's early years were passed on his father's farm. He [illegible] common schools, and in 1849, with his parents, set sail for America. After seven weeks on the Atlantic, they landed in New York City, from where they proceeded to Buffalo by canal, and thence to Milwaukee by way of the Lakes. At that time the city was a mere fishing village. Our subject continued to reside in the place where the family first located until 1846, when he went to the vicinity of Baraboo, Wis., where his father had taken up some Government land. The latter's death occurred in April, 1846, and in the following fall his faithful wife followed him to the silent land.

When Ole Nelson was left an orphan he was only thirteen years of age, and he was then thrown upon his own resources to rise or fall, as the case might be. For five years he worked for his board and clothes in the employ of a farmer, and on the expiration of this period continued with the same man for a year on small wages. For about three months he was in the employ of the North-Western Railway Company [illegible] helped to survey. In the spring of 1853 he went to Appleton, Wis., and attended Lawrence University for the following year.

In 1854 Mr. Nelson went to Wilson Township, where he purchased one hundred and sixty acres of Government land, paying at the rate of $1.25 per acre. He erected a log cabin, to which he brought all his belongings by ox-teams. After living on the farm for four years he sold the place and purchased one in Houston County, this state, and engaged in its cultivation until 1862, when he enlisted in defense of the Union. He was mustered into the ranks as a private soldier of Company D, Seventh Minnesota Infantry, at Ft. Snelling, on August 14. He was then sent on a campaign through the Dakotas, where the Indians were taking advantage of the grave situation in this country's affairs to pillage and devastate the farms of the settlers in the Northwest. Mr. Nelson's first engagement was with a band of Indians numbering about four or five hundred, and he took part in an important battle with them, besides numerous skirmishes. In the spring of 1863 he was sent across the Missouri River on the trail of the marauding red-skin, and was thus employed until the next fall, when he was discharged on account of disability at Ft. Snelling. He was mustered out of service December 29, 1863. Soon afterwards he took up his abode in Winona County, where he rented land for a few years, and then settled on the farm which he now owns. This is located on sections 25, 26 and 35, Wiscoy Township. Mr. Nelson owns altogether some two hundred and forty acres, a portion of which he rents to responsible tenants. He is a practical and thrifty agriculturist and a good business manager.

June 17, 1860, occurred the marriage of our subject and Miss Caroline A., daughter of D. B. Clarke, of Pleasant Hill Township. Fourteen children were born of their union, namely: Andrew, who died March 11, 1884; Effie, whose death occurred October 3, 1891; Aline, who died September 12, 1880, and Willie, Charlie, Fred, John, Frank, Albert, Caroline L. and Amy J. The mother of these children was called to the silent land June 27, 1881. The family are much respected in this locality, where they are very well known and are esteemed among its best citizens. Mr. Nelson is truly a self-made man, as he began life entirely without capital, and, undaunted by the difficulties in his way, pressed steadily onward to the goal he had in view, that of becoming well-off in this world's goods and of occupying an honored place among his fellow-men.

Berend Ballmann.

BEREND BALLMANN, a worthy German-American citizen of Hart Township, is an early settler of this locality, and is entitled to a place in its annals, for he has always to the best of his ability supported all public measures and improvements in the community where he makes his home. He owns a well improved homestead, situated on section 1, and this place, now equipped with substantial farm buildings, fences, etc., bears little resemblance to the one of former years, on which stood only a log cabin. For a quarter of a century our subject has been Township Clerk, and for a like period of time has been Justice of the Peace. In educational matters his influence has always been felt in favor of good schools and teachers and better facilities for the young. In 1888 he was elected on the Democratic ticket to the position of Register of Deeds of this county, and acceptably discharged the duties pertaining to the office for a period of two terms, or four years.

Our subject is one of three sons and eight

daughters. He was born August 20, 1838, in Germany, and passed his boyhood on a farm. He received a good education in his mother tongue, and started out in life for himself on reaching his majority. He took passage on a sailing-vessel bound for the United States and arrived in New York City at the end of seven weeks. For the following year he remained in the metropolis, and finally, in 1860, came to Minnesota. He soon took up his abode in Hart Township, purchasing a part of the farm where he now lives, a tract of one hundred and sixty acres. As the years have passed he has been greatly prospered in his financial undertakings, and is now the proprietor of four hundred and forty acres of land, situated in one body and most of it under cultivation.

In 1864 Mr. Billmann married Miss Louisa Yaco and the following children came to bless their union: Bernard, John, William, Winnie, Helen, Otto, George, Martha, Mamie, Betty and Alice.

In addition to managing his large estate with marked ability, Mr. Billmann has been interested in various other enterprises, and was one of the organizers of the Farmers' Insurance Company and the Rolling Stone Fire Insurance Company, being Treasurer of the former.

Jacob Johns.

JACOB JOHNS. The progress made by Winona County in commerce and agriculture is largely due to the energy, perseverance and industry of its foreign-born citizens, many of whom have here gained prosperity, if not affluence. One of this class is Mr. Johns, a wealthy and progressive agriculturist, who owns a fine estate in Hart Township. He is a native of Germany, but since his fifteenth year has dwelt within the limits of this county, with the development and history of which he has been prominently identified up to the present time.

The parents of our subject were Jacob and Maggie (Jahn) Johns, the former of whom was a native of Germany, and is now living in Winona County, having attained the age of ninety-four years. Our subject was born August 5, 1842, and at the age of three years was brought by his parents to America, the journey across the ocean consuming two months. After landing in Baltimore, Md., they proceeded to Missouri and made their home in that state for the ensuing seven years, after which they went to Hazel Green, Wis. In 1856 they c[illegible] Hart Township, where our subject grew to manhood and began the battle of life for himself. At the age of eighteen he began to work for farmers by the month, and was thus employed until the outbreak of the late war.

August 15, 1862, Mr. Johns enlisted as a private soldier in Company E, Sixth Minnesota Infantry, and was mustered into the service at Ft. Snelling. His first engagement was at Birch Coolie, September 2, 1862, in one of the Indian reservations, and the second battle was Wood Lake, September 23, 1862. He was mainly employed in looking after the redmen of the Northwest until the spring of 1864, when he was sent southward. He participated in the battle of Helena, Ark., and the sieges of Spanish Fort and Ft. Blakely, and also took part in many other engagements of less renown. He was never wounded nor taken prisoner, and served from first to last as a private soldier. His final discharge was dated August 19, 1865.

On his return home Mr. Johns rented land for a year, and at the expiration of that time, by strict economy and industry, he was enabled to lay aside [illegible]ty acres of land

This property was located on section 28, Hart Township and proved the nucleus of his present possessions. As he could afford he extended his domains, until now he is the proprietor of four hundred and forty acres. He has been equally successful as a general farmer and as a stock-raiser, and most enterprises undertaken by him have been carried through to a successful consummation.

May 18, 1868, Jacob Johns married Miss Theresa Kryzer, and they became the parents of twelve children named as follows: Mary, Sophia, Lizzie, Emma, Annie, Jacob, Henry, Rose, Willie, Hannah, Eddie and George. In religion Mr. Johns and family are identified with the Catholic Church. He uses his franchise in favor of the Democratic party, and has held the position of Township Supervisor and Constable, in both of which he made a good record for himself and gave full satisfaction to his constituents. Socially he is a member of the Grand Army of the Republic.

William Garlock.

WILLIAM GARLOCK, deceased, was one of the most valued citizens of the county, and on his death was widely missed, but his life was a long and useful one, and the reward prepared for the righteous is surely his. His influence will long be felt and the best interests of the community bear the impress of his character. He was a man of sterling worth, ever true to his business, his friends and himself. He was filled with no vain ambition to stand on more exalted pinnacles, but to those who counted him as an associate in his less prosperous days he remained the same unobtrusive, warm-hearted man. He loved truth and honesty and was opposed to anything under-handed. His affairs would always bear the light of strong investigation and his career was ever honorable and straightforward. A close student of economic questions, he had the keen insight into the future course of commerce that can only be obtained from a careful study of business history. He was not quick to jump at conclusions but gave due credit to the opinion of others, and when his mind was made up and a course adopted it was seldom his plans were changed or that a necessity for change existed.

William Garlock possessed many of the characteristics found in the sturdy ancestry from which he came. He had the indomitable pluck and perseverance of the Puritan forefathers, without their intolerance, and the keen-sightedness and adaptability of the later New Englanders. He was born on the 15th of January, 1818, in Montgomery, N. Y., and six weeks later was taken to Onondaga County, where the family settled. There he grew to manhood, becoming inured to the hard labor necessary to farming operations in a new country. But little is known of his parentage, or of the ancestry of the family, but there is no doubt as to the spirit of application and perseverance, and the lessons of integrity and honesty that were instilled into him in all his boyhood years. In October, 1841, when in his twenty-fourth year, he was united in marriage with Miss Julia Horton, a lady of merit, who proved through life to be a valuable helpmate and companion to her husband on every occasion. They had one daughter, Mrs. J. N. Selover, of Winona, and a son, William H., now cashier of the Second National Bank of Winona.

Mr. and Mrs. Garlock had a desire to cast in their lot with the people who were emigrating westward, and as Minnesota was then drawing hundreds from the East we find them early in June, 1856, located in Winona. Mr. Garlock at once became associated with the now venerable L. C. Porter in purchasing an interest in a sawmill from Wyckhoff & Highland, and they did a fairly successful business until 1860. This was before the lumber interests had assumed extensive proportions and the financial panic of 1857 coming on, the business was of comparatively slow growth.

We learn that in 1858 Mr. Garlock purchased the first load of wheat ever offered upon the market, paying for it in lumber. This he had ground into flour in Huff's old mill, and in turn traded the flour for pork, from which he managed to realize some cash. This was his first start as a grain dealer, but he soon turned his attention more fully to that business, becoming an extensive and successful operator in grain, purchasing at various points on the river, as well as on the lines of railway in the interior. His business in this line was continuously successful and in his career he always refrained from having anything to do with board of trade speculations. In no sense a gambler, his operations were of a strictly legitimate nature, he only selling that which he had the ability to supply. His clear-sightedness was soon recognized by other business men, who sought association with him in strictly financial matters, where just the qualities he possessed were in demand. In 1858 the Bank of Southern Minnesota was established, the principal stockholders being Mr. Garlock, L. C. Porter and Thomas Bennett. In 1861 this was re-organized, becoming the First National Bank, and L. C. Porter was made President, William Garlock Vice-President, and Thomas Bennett Cashier. Mr. Garlock's relations with the institution lasted for ten years, when he disposed of his stock, and with Messrs. Burbank, Prentiss and others organized the Second National Bank, of which he remained Director until his demise. While never in personal charge of the bank, as a Director his counsel was freely sought and given, and it is in a large measure due to his conservative course, in harmony with his associates, that this bank now occupies an enviable position among the financial institutions of the state.

For some years before his death Mr. Garlock attended more particularly to his private interests, and was carrying out a long-cherished desire to erect such a home for his declining years as he and his wife had decided upon, and when the dread summons came the new residence was well advanced in its course of construction. Politically Mr. Garlock affiliated with the Democratic party, being a liberal man, however, he was not strictly bound by traditional ideas, but recognized the good found in other men and measures. He had no political aspirations, and the only public office he ever held was in the City Council, at the time the efficient water system was established and his ideas were largely embodied in the accepted plan. He had the fullest confidence of his supporters, and all knew that his business sagacity and strict integrity precluded any but honest work being done for the public so long as he remained in the council.

Mr. Garlock never attached himself to any social or religious order, although he was in sympathy with the foundation principles of both and was a liberal contributor to every enterprise that had for its object the elevation of mankind. His was a life that was free from taint and taught the lessons of Christian charity not in harangue or public prayer, but in the silent daily walk of an honest thoughtful, generous man. He had no vices himself, but had a great sympathy for those less strong, and was in touch with every move that tended to strengthen the weak and fallen. Free from eccentricity, he was not an enthusiast, but with a clear brain and healthy body he was at all times a level-headed, conservative business man.

Zaphna Henry Lake.

ZAPHNA HENRY LAKE was born on the 5th of June, 1827, in Conneaut, Ashtabula County, Ohio. His father, Zaphna H. Lake, Sr., was a native of the Buckeye State, and the grandfather was one of the early settlers of Ohio. The former was a prominent anti-slavery man, and his home was one of the stations on the famous "underground railroad." He married Harriet Wright, who also belonged to one of the old families of Ashtabula County.

Our subject was reared on a farm, and during the greater part of his youth was in delicate health. He began his education in the district schools, and afterward attended Ashtabula College for a time. Mainly on account of his health he made a trip to California in 1849, in company with a physician. In Sacramento he secured a hotel which had been formerly conducted by an aunt, who transferred it to him on the condition that he run it as a temperance house. Thus he carried on hotel-keeping for four or five years, and was joined in California by his father, who had been a merchant in Conneaut, Ohio, and was the owner of two or three lake vessels. He afterward went to Chicago, and became interested in real estate and also in property in Aurora. While on a business trip to the latter place, he was stricken with apoplexy, and died at the age of sixty-three years.

About that time Zaphna H. Lake went to Chicago to settle up his father's estate. He had formerly made a location in La Crosse, Wis., and in company with A. W. Webster opened a grocery store. Subsequently he came to Winona and established what was known as the Winona Deposit Bank, on the site of the present Savings Bank. Mr. Webster, his partner, who was originally from Kingsville, Ohio, continued with him in business until they closed out the bank, when he removed to Chicago, where he now lives. Mr. Lake withdrew from the banking business about 1865. His venture in that direction had proved a successful one. The bank had been carried through a financial crisis without injury, and yielded to the stockholders a good return. Mr. Lake found it necessary to withdraw on account of failing health, and in 1865 he turned his attention to the loan and insurance business, associating himself with R. B. Bisford. He was a man of great energy, and applied himself so closely to his business that it proved detrimental to his health. In 1871 he was forced to seek a change, and went to California, where in a great measure he regained his health, and on his return resumed business. In 1876 he was again forced to leave home, but in March of the next year was brought back, and for two months lingered along until, on the 27th of May, death ended his sufferings.

Mr. Lake took an active interest in public affairs, and did all in his power to promote the general welfare. In early life he was a stanch Republican, but afterward became one of the followers of Horace Greeley, and later formed no political ties. He was a man of firm convictions, and adhered closely to whatever he believed to be right. He had strong sympathy for those in need, and took a very active part in aiding the soldiers and others in distress during the late war. He made friends wherever he went, winning the confidence of all by his honorable, upright life, and his loss was deeply mourned.

Mr. Lake was married, on the 29th of October, 1862, to Miss Fannie E. Ehle, daughter of Joseph H. and Fannie S. (Hyde) Ehle. Her father was an active commission man on the river, and did a good business. For some years he served as Assessor. He was a native of New York, came to Winona in 1857, and after several years' illness, died, January 30, 1870, at the age of sixty-four. His wife survived him until June 30, 1894, passing away in her eighty-fifth year. She had made her home with Mrs. Lake for some years previous to her death. She was a woman of strong and lovely character, possessed more than average intelligence, was an extensive reader and had a wonderful memory, stored with historic facts, being well versed in both modern and ancient history. She took an active part in church and social work and was one of the leading members of the Congregational Church. Mrs. Lake was born in Calhoun County, Mich., and removed thence to Southport, now Kenosha, Wis., where she lived until coming to Winona. She, too, is prominent in church work, and delights in doing good. Those in distress find in her a friend, and sympathy and substantial aid are always given to the needy.

David A. Murray.

DAVID A. MURRAY takes a leading part in advancing the agricultural interests of Winona County, where he has one hundred and seventeen acres on section 29, Pleasant Hill Township. He was born near Amsterdam, Montgomery County, N. Y., June 30, 1837. He was there trained to farm pursuits, and when a lad of seventeen began the struggle of life on his own account. About that time he made his way west to Wisconsin, and for two years was identified with the farm life of La Crosse County.

Young Murray then removed to Minnesota, and taking up school land in Pleasant Hill Township, this county, was occupied in its cultivation until joining the ranks of the Union army. This was in 1864, when he [illegible] Company C, First Minnesota [illegible] into the service with his regiment at Ft. Snelling. From there they were ordered to Chattanooga and placed on garrison duty, serving in that capacity until the establishment of peace, when our subject received his honorable discharge and with his comrades returned home.

In the year 1870 Mr. Murray became the owner of a quarter-section of land, on which he lived for one year, and then disposed of the tract to good advantage. Four years later we find him residing on his present fine estate, where he is winning from the soil an abundant share of the various grains and in this way secures for himself and family all of the comforts and many of the luxuries of life.

The lady to whom Mr. Murray was married March 1[illegible] 1869, was M[illegible] Warwick, the widow [illegible] W[illegible] name previous to her union with that gentleman was Jane Lemon, and her birth occurred February 27, 1811 in Ireland. By her marriage with Mr Warwick there was born a daughter, Sarah E., who is now the wife of Edward Hesselgrave. To our subject and his wife there has come a family of four children: Etta, Jeanette, the wife of Edward Besaw, residing in this county; Lester A. and Royal R.

Mr Murray possesses intelligent views on all subjects of general interest, particularly on political questions, and is an ardent supporter of the Democratic party. He has been before the public in the capacity of Assessor and Chairman of the Board of Supervisors. He holds membership with John Ball Post No. 15, G. A. R., in the workings of which he is greatly interested and takes a leading part. Mr Murray is a self-made man, and his sketch will do honor to our volume and prove interesting to his many friends, who hold him in the highest possible esteem.

Oscar J. Gates.

OSCAR J. GATES, who for many years has been prominently connected with the business interests of Winona as a contractor and builder, dates his residence here from the year 1865, and is therefore one of the early settlers. He claims New York as the state of his nativity, his birth having occurred in Essex County, on the 10th of December, 1841. His parents were Willis and Almira (Hulet) Gates. The father was a native of Connecticut, and there spent the days of his boyhood and youth. When a young man he removed to New York, where he engaged in farming and also carried on a sawmill, which undertakings constituted his life work. His remaining days were spent in New York, where his death occurred at the advanced age of eighty-one. His ancestors for several generations were natives of this country, and little is known concerning the early history of the family. His wife was born in Washington County, N. Y., where her death occurred at the age of seventy-six years.

Under the parental roof Oscar Gates was reared to manhood, and the common schools afforded him his educational privileges. He remained at home until the 11th of August, 1862, when, having attained his majority, he responded to the country's call for troops and enrolled his name among the boys in blue of Company F, One Hundred and Eighteenth New York Infantry. He went through the services as a private, and when the war was over was honorably discharged at Richmond, Va., on the 11th of June, 1865. He participated in many important engagements, including the battles of Fair Oaks, Wilderness, Cold Harbor and Richmond, and was ever a loyal soldier, who stood at his post and faithfully defended the Old Flag and the cause it represented until the Stars and Stripes were planted in the capital of the Southern Confederacy.

When his country no longer needed his services, Mr Gates returned to his home in New York, but remained there only a short time, and in September made a location in Winona. The West was rapidly settling up, and he believed that to a man in his business a good opening would be found. He embarked in contracting and building, which he has since followed with excellent success. He has erected many of the most important buildings in the city, including business blocks, public buildings and private residences. He is an expert workman, and thus capable of superintending his men. He always faithfully fulfills his part of a contract and has the confidence and respect of all with whom he has had business dealings. Success has crowned his efforts, and he now has a pleasant home and a competence which supplies him with all the comforts of life.

On the 7th of October, 1880, Mr. Gates was united in marriage with Miss Maggie McQuay, of Minneapolis, and their union has been blessed with one son, Leonard J., now a youth of ten summers. They are well known people of this community and in social circles hold an enviable position. Mr. Gates votes with the Republican party, and in his social relations is connected with the Masonic fraternity, the Knights of Pythias lodge and John Bell Post No. 45, G. A. R.

Franklin Staples, M. D.

FRANKLIN STAPLES, M. D., a physician and surgeon of Winona, was born in Raymond, now Casco, Cumberland County, Me., on the 9th of November, 1833, and is one of a family of two sons and three daughters born to Peter and Sarah (Maxwell) Staples, natives of Maine. Only two of the children are now living, the Doctor and his sister, Emma, who resides with him. His only brother, Edwin, was a Union soldier in the War of the Rebellion, and was killed in battle in Virginia in 1864. His sister Harriet died after removing to the home of her brother in Minnesota, and one sister died in early childhood. The father was a farmer and lumberman of the Pine Tree State, and there died at the age of seventy-four years. The mother of the Doctor passed away when he was a boy of eleven years. The paternal grandfather, Peter Staples, Sr., was a farmer in Maine, and was of English descent. His death occurred at the advanced age of ninety-six. He was one of the first settlers of the town of Raymond, having removed there from Cape Elizabeth, Me., at an early age. At the age of twenty-one he married Sarah Dingley, who was then sixteen years of age, and was also born in Cape Elizabeth. They lived together for more than seventy years, and reared a large family. The mother died at the age of ninety-nine. The maternal grandfather of the Doctor, William Maxwell, was born in Maine, and was also of English lineage. He made farming his life work, and died at the age of about seventy. The ancestors of the Staples and Dingley families of New England on coming to this country first settled in Kittery, York County, and in Cape Elizabeth, Cumberland County, Me.

Franklin Staples during his early life lived in Buxton, York County, Me., the family moving there when Franklin was four years old. He received an academical education in the common school in Buxton, at Parsonsfield Seminary, and at Limerick and Auburn (Me.) Academies. He taught school [illegible] the Pine Tree State, and for a term of four years in the city of Portland He began the study of medicine in the office of Dr Charles S D Fessenden, of Portland, Me, in 1855, attended lectures in the medical department of Bowdoin College in 1856, and was one of the first students in Portland School for Medical Instruction under the instruction of the late Prof William C Robinson and Prof Israel T Dana, now of the Maine Medical School In 1861 he entered the College of Physicians and Surgeons (the medical department of Columbia College), New York, and graduated therefrom in March 1862 He first became assistant to the late Prof David Conant, of the Maine Medical School, as Demonstrator of Anatomy for that year In the summer of 1862 he established himself as a general practitioner at Winona, Minn

The Doctor was married on the 4th of June, 1863, to Helen M Harford, daughter of the late Ezra Harford, of Portland, Me. Of their four children, two are living. The eldest, Gertrude, is the wife of Seward D Allen, an attorney residing in Duluth, Minn The children of Seward D and Gertrude (Staples) Allen are Franklin Staples and Seward Ralph Helen Ford Staples is with her parents Annie and Mae both died at the age of four and a-half years.

The Doctor and his wife are members of the Congregational Church, and have done active work therein and in educational work in the city and state Dr. Staples was one of the founders of the Winona Preparatory Medical School In 1871 he was elected President of the Minnesota State Medical Society, and in 1874 was appointed a member of the Minnesota State Board of Health which position he continues to hold having been President of that association since the year 1889 He is a member of the American Public Health Association and of the American Medical Association, was one of the Judicial Council of the association in 1875 and 1877, and Vice-President in 1877 During the years 1883 and 1887 he held the chair of the Practice of Medicine in the medical department of the University of Minnesota, when the faculty of the university constituted the Medical Examining Board of the State He was the first President of the Southern Minnesota Medical Association which society was organized in 1892 His writings on medical and surgical subjects have from time to time been published in scientific and professional journals, but of late years his attention and interest have been largely given to sanitary science and to practical work in this direction Among the first of his writings in this line was his report on "The Influence of Climate on Pulmonary Diseases in Minnesota," published in the Transactions of the American Medical Association in 1876 Among his other publications are A Report on Diphtheria" in 1878, a part of the State Board of Health work, "The Treatment of Fracture of the Femur," State Medical Society work, 1878, and an article relating to progress in modern surgery, entitled "Some Notes and Suggestions on Aseptic and Antiseptic Surgery of the Present Time," 1893 His writings other than professional have been published from time to time in various journals

Dr Staples has been known especially by his study and practical work as a surgeon, and has been able to witness and have a part in the great progress which in the last quarter of a century our country and the world has witnessed in this department of scientific work. His abilities, both natural and acquired, have won for him prominence in his profession, and it may be said of him that he has enjoyed the confidence and respect of his profession and of the community where has been his field of labor Coming to the then new state of Minnesota in 1862, he has been able to witness the growth and development of this now great commonwealth and to have some part in the work of its progress

C. A. Bierce.

C. A. BIERCE, who is engaged in the real-estate and insurance business, was born in Claverack, Columbia County, N. Y., March 7, 1830, and is the eldest in a family of six children, five sons and a daughter, who were born of the union of Cornelius B. and Catherine (Sigendorph) Bierce. The father was a native of Connecticut, born about 1808. During his boyhood days he came with the family to New York, where he lived for forty-two years, following the occupation of farming during the greater part of that time. In 1850 he bade adieu to home and friends in the East, and with his wife and children emigrated to Michigan, settling in Jackson County, where he lived until 1881. In that year he came to Winona, and for four years made his home with his son C. A. He was a quiet, unassuming man, of retiring disposition, but the excellence of his character and his sterling worth were recognized by those who knew him best, and he thus won many warm friends. He was much interested in educational and religious matters, aided in the founding of Leoni College at Leoni, Mich., and was prominent in church circles. His wife was a daughter of Nicholas Sagendorph, who was born in Germany, and on crossing the Atlantic to America settled in New York, where he spent his remaining days, dying at an extreme old age.

The paternal grandfather of the subject of this sketch was Austin Bierce. He, too, was a native of the Nut[illegible] pursuits as [illegible] Connecticut until middle life, when he emigrated with his family to New York, where he spent his declining years. He and his wife died within two days, and were buried in the same grave, as were his parents before him, a remarkable circumstance.

C. A. Bierce was reared to manhood under the parental roof and on attaining his majority was married, in Michigan, to Miss Frances C. Adams, a native of Genesee County, N. Y., and a daughter of Lockwood and Fannie J. Adams. Her parents were both natives of Connecticut, and their family numbered five daughters. The father, who was a millwright and carpenter, possessed much mechanical genius and carried on business along those lines during his entire life. He passed away when in the prime of life, but his wife long survived him, and died in 1891, at the ripe old age of eighty-four years.

Mr. and Mrs. Bierce were married in 1851, and began their domestic life in Michigan, where they made their home until 1857. They then located west of the Mississippi, settling in Osage, Iowa. Mr. Bierce had previously been engaged in merchandising in Michigan, but, like hundreds of others, suffered severe losses in the financial panic of 1857, and after going to the Hawkeye State turned his attention to teaching school. For five years he was Principal of the schools of Osage and then taught for three years in Bradford, Iowa. On the expiration of that period he once more [illegible] ...ning a store in [illegible] ...ntinued for three years He was then numbered among the merchants of Northwood, Iowa, for one year after which he became a resident of Mankato, Iowa, whence he came to Winona in 1872 Soon after he embarked in the real-estate and insurance business, which he has since followed with good success For several years he has been one of the Directors of the Gates City Carriage Works, and has assisted in the establishment and promotion of many of the leading enterprises of the county

Throughout his entire life Mr Bierce has been a Prohibitionist in principle, and on the organization of the third party in Minnesota became its first Secretary He has been the candidate for Probate Judge Secretary of State, and for other offices, but on account of the numerical strength of the old parties could not win election While in Michigan he was a member of the Methodist Church, but is now connected with the Congregational Church, and in its work is deeply interested His life has been well and worthily passed, his career has been an honorable and upright one, and in this volume he deserves mention.

Thomas Brady.

THOMAS BRADY, who owns a valuable and highly improved farm of one hundred and sixty acres on section 20 Saratoga Township, is a native of the Emerald Isle He was born in County Cavan Ireland, in 1828, and is one of a family of four children, three sons and a daughter, whose parents were Mathew and Susan (Farley) Brady The days of his childhood and youth were passed upon his father's farm, where he was early inured to hard labor, beginning work in the fields at a tender age This, however, gave him experience and developed his self-reliance and the training then received has proven of incalculable benefit to him in his later years His educational privileges were necessarily limited, and he seldom attended school, except at the night sessions

On the home farm Mr Brady continued his labors until 1851, when at the age of twenty-six years, he resolved to try his fortunes in America He had heard much of the advantages and privileges here afforded, and resolved to test the truth of these reports hoping thereby to benefit his financial condition Taking passage on a sailing-vessel bound for the New World, after a voyage of nine weeks and three days he landed in New York City, from where he made his way to Cambria County, Pa For two years he worked on a railroad in that state, and in the spring of 1856 came to Minnesota, settling in Fillmore County, that locality being then on the frontier. Mr. Brady entered land from the Government, and thereon made his home until 1857, when he came to Winona County and established a grocery in Troy For five years he carried on business along that line, and then traded his store for eighty acres of land.

Mr Brady removed to his farm in the year 1865, and until a short time ago continuously carried on agricultural pursuits He has prospered in his undertakings, and his labors have brought him a comfortable competence As his financial resources were increased, he extended the boundaries of this farm until it now comprises one hundred and sixty acres of rich and arable land. This he rents, the income from the same being sufficient to enable him to lay aside business cares and live a retired life.

Mr. Brady holds membership with the Catholic Church. He is a pleasant, genial and popular gentleman, who has made many friends throughout this community, and by his quiet and unassuming, yet honorable, life he has won the confidence of all. He is a self-educated and self-made man whose success is deserved, and in the history of his adopted county he well deserves representation.

Nelson Breed.

NELSON BREED, a horticulturist of Winona County, living in the village of Homer, has made his home in this locality during the greater part of the time since 1865, and is therefore numbered among its early settlers, almost thirty years having passed since his arrival. He was born on a farm in Broome County, N. Y., June 11, 1850, and is a son of Lemuel and Hannah (Decker) Breed, the former a native of Virginia, and the latter of the Empire State. In his younger years the father learned the trade of shoe-making, and also the mason's trade, and for some time carried on the two occupations. He also engaged to a limited extent in farming. He was in humble circumstances, and with the hope of benefiting his financial condition he emigrated westward in 1855, locating in Homer in the month of June. Here he remained until 1865, when he went to Iowa, where he has since resided with the exception of one year spent in Nebraska. He is now engaged in the hotel business. He started out in life empty handed, having nothing on which to depend for a livelihood [illegible] have brought to him success, and he is now in comfortable circumstances.

To Lemuel and Hannah Breed were born three children, and when they were quite young their mother died, being called to the home beyond in January, 1861. Nelson was the eldest. Mrs. Itasca Rolland, now of Iowa, was the second, and Mrs. Eva Denton, the wife of an engineer, was the youngest and died in Dakota when about twenty-five years of age. After the death of his first wife the father was again married.

Nelson Breed remained at home until the death of his mother, which occurred when he was only thirteen years of age. In the following February he offered his services to the Government, enlisting in Company I, Second Minnesota Cavalry. From Homer he went to Rochester, and thence was sent to Ft. Snelling, Minn., where he was engaged in Indian warfare until the 17th of November, 1865, when he was honorably discharged. He served as a private under Capt. Isaac Bank, and was ever a faithful soldier.

[illegible] Mr. Breed returned to

Homer and later went to Iowa, but after a short time left that state for Chippewa Falls, Wis. He has always considered this place his home, however, and it has been his permanent abode for some time. He now owns nine acres of land, which he has placed under a high state of cultivation. The improvements upon it were all made by him and the buildings were among the best in the village. He is engaged in small farming and fruit culture, and the products which he places on the market find a ready sale, for they are always of good variety. He also owns some sixty acres of other lands. In this way Mr. Breed has achieved a comfortable competence and is now supplied with all the necessaries and many of the luxuries of life.

Mr. Breed was married, on the 26th of May, 1874, to Miss Mary L. Hanes. She was a native of Canada, and came to Homer on a visit. Here she met Mr. Breed, and, the friendship ripening into love, they were married on the above date. Four children have been born of their union: Itasca M., born March 12, 1875, Claude G., February 21, 1877, Rolland E., November 22, 1881, and Mary E., November 29, 1884. All are still with their parents.

Mr. Breed has long served as School Treasurer, his efficiency leading to his repeated re-election. He belongs to the Grand Army of the Republic, and is a Democrat in politics. His duties of citizenship are faithfully performed, and his many acquaintances and friends know him to be a high minded and honorable gentleman, in whom they can place all confidence.

Prof. Hermann Rohweder.

PROF. HERMANN ROHWEDER, of Winona, was born in Holstein, Germany, May 3, 1842, and is a son of Jurgen and Margaret (Schlueter) Rohweder. At the age of fifteen he came to the United States, locating in Winona in 1857, with his father, who died in Wabasha County, September 11, 1871, at the age of seventy-five. He had spent the last years of his life on a farm with his daughter. On coming to Minnesota, he had made a home in the eastern part of Winona, where he lived a retired life. His family at that time consisted of William, Mary and Hermann. The first-named was formerly a contractor and builder, and served as Alderman of Winona, where he was recognized as a prominent citizen. He now lives at Goodwin, S. Dak. Mary is the wife of Jurgen Jacobs and at this writing, in the fall of 1894, resides in California.

Professor Rohweder began the study of music at the age of seven years, receiving instruction on the violin from very able teachers. He studied wind instruments also, fitting himself for orchestral work. His teacher was the leader of an orchestra, and at the age of eleven years Hermann joined an orchestra, playing a violin and flute. He continued his connection with the same until fifteen years of age. The work demanded constant practice, and all he received for orchestral playing went to his instructor, Hermann being allowed to keep only what he received from outside engagements He would often play at weddings and public gatherings, and as a boy he earned considerable money. In 1857 the steamboat "Banjo," a minstrel boat built for the purpose of giving entertainments lost its leader, who was taken sick, and on reaching Winona inquiry was made for a leader Mr Rohweder was called upon, and accepted the position of leader of the band at $10 per month. He then went to St. Paul and during the summer gave entertainments on board the boat, which was built like a theater, and was capable of seating one thousand people. This orchestra visited nearly all of the leading cities on the upper Mississippi, and went up the Illinois River to La Salle While thus engaged, however Professor Rohweder was taken sick and returned home, where he suffered an illness of twelve weeks The next summer he engaged with the George Washington De Havens Great Union Circus as leader of the band, and traveled with that organization for three seasons in Minnesota, Wisconsin, Illinois, Michigan Indiana and Iowa He made Winona his home, and during the winter months was leader of an orchestra, which was engaged for balls, parties, etc

Professor Rohweder was married, November 22, 1863, to Miss Margaret Dickmann of Greenwood Prairie, Wabasha County She was born in Holstein, Germany, August 9 1843, and came to the United States with her parents in 1852 Mr Rohweder, already settled in Winona gave his chief attention to music, but also had to work along other lines in order to make a living Later, however, his profession furnished him a livelihood, and in 1869 he organized the Germania Band and Orchestra, which attained a wide reputation and was appreciated by the public He also gave instruction on the violin and other string and wind instruments When he came to Winona, he found only one musical enthusiast here, George Frederick Storey, a colored boy, little older than himself, who possessed a love and genius for music, but knew little of its principles After receiving instruction, he played the harp, and Professor Rohweder playing on the violin, they furnished good music Mr Storey has since been connected with the Professor and has been a member of his family for about thirty-seven years He is a well read man, who speaks German as well as English fluently, and is especially well versed in music

Professor Rohweder also organized and taught dancing classes The Germania Band, which he organized in 1869, still exists, and he has arranged much music for bands and orchestras To the Professor and his wife were born two children: Dora, who died at the age of two and a-half years; and Sophia an expert musician, who is now the wife of P W Froemke, agent of the Green Bay, Winona & St Paul Railroad Company Mr. Rohweder is one of the oldest members of Prairie Lodge No 7 I O O F, of this place, and also belongs to the Encampment and to the United Workmen

In connection with his other work, the Professor is interested in real estate In 1887 he platted Rohweder & Brochlow's Addition to Winona, comprising several acres in the southwestern part of the city Much of this he has improved, and has sold many houses and lots He now has several tracts of land, and both residence and business property His home at No 163 Liberty Street is a fine two-story residence He has two hundred and ten feet frontage of improved business property on Third Street, has erected a number of business houses, and has a fine block of two stores He has also handled farm property and his speculations in real estate have proved advantageous, bringing him a handsome income.

Hon. Thomas Simpson.

HON. THOMAS SIMPSON, prominent in public and political affairs, and now a leading member of the Bar of Winona County, was born in the north of England, of Scottish ancestry, May 31, 1836. He is a son of Anthony and Elizabeth (Bonson) Simpson. The paternal grandfather, Nathan Simpson, was born in the same country and throughout his business career was interested in mining. He was a hardy and vigorous man, possessing a self-reliant character, which enabled him to go through life dependent entirely upon his own efforts. At the age of sixty his death occurred. The maternal grandfather, Robert Bonson, was a physician, and spent some years in America, although he died in England. He crossed the Atlantic in 1825, and established the first lead furnace at Galena, Ill., and also in Dubuque, Iowa. He was a member of the Methodist Church, and reached the allotted age of threescore years and ten.

Anthony Simpson was Superintendent of an English mine in Swaledale, Yorkshire. About 1837 he emigrated to the New World, locating in Dubuque, Iowa, where he engaged in mining and smelting for many years. He also carried on farming, and there made his home until his death, which occurred in 1866, at the age of fifty-seven years. His wife survived him until 1871, passing away at the age of sixty-one. In England they belonged to the Wesleyan Church, and after coming to America joined the Methodist Episcopal Church, in which Mr. Simpson long served as an officer. He was prominent in public affairs, and was a highly respected man. In the family were ten children, six sons and four daughters, of whom three sons and four daughters are now living, namely: Nathan, of Dubuque; Thomas; James, of Dubuque; Mary, widow of Rev. J. L. Kelley, of Dubuque; Ellen, wife of Dr. I. V. Coldren, of Topeka, Kan.; Margaret, widow of James Cortes, of Dubuque County, Iowa; and Caroline, widow of Rev. J. P. Mather, and a resident of Dubuque.

Thomas Simpson was only a few months old when his parents came to America. He was reared and educated in Dubuque, and during his younger years engaged in mining, smelting and farming. At the age of sixteen he finished a course of study as a civil engineer under the instruction of the prominent clergyman, Rev. L. S. Norris, who had formerly been State Surveyor of Maine. In the winter of 1853 Mr. Norris was given the contract by the United States Surveyor-General at Dubuque, Iowa, for running the guide meridians and standard parallels, the base lines of the Government surveys of Minnesota Territory. He took Mr. Simpson with him as one of his assistants, but the work was soon turned over to our subject, who completed it in 1855, and a record of the same is in the United States Surveyor-General's office at St. Paul. In the latter part of 1855 he was sent by the Government to Green Bay, Wis., to determine the boundaries of the Menominee Indian Reservation and protect the Indians in their lumber and timber interests, and while there he also did some surveying of public lands for the Government.

On the 1st of January, 1856, Mr. Simpson came to Winona to make his home, and has lived here continuously since. He began business as a loan agent, and also sold land-warrants and dealt in land, continuing operations along these lines for several years. Throughout his life he has been a student and in his earlier years he studied law. Soon after his arrival in Winona he met Rev. George C. Tanner, an Episcopalian minister, who aided him greatly in his studies. In 1858 he was admitted to the Bar, and has practiced continuously since. In his early days he formed a friendship, which has continued through life, with Rev. Edward Eggleston, author of "The Hoosier Schoolmaster" and other popular works. From early life Mr. Simpson has been a communicant of the Methodist Episcopal Church and from 1856 until 1892 was Superintendent of the Sunday-school of the Central Methodist Church of Winona, besides filling other important offices in the church.

One of the most important events in the life of Mr. Simpson occurred October 30, 1860, when was celebrated his marriage with Miss Isabella Margaret Holstein, daughter of George and Elizabeth (Black) Holstein, natives of Pennsylvania. Three children were born to them: George F., James K. and Earl. The mother died December 21, 1888, and in an article widely published in the public journals of the county, entitled "A Living Epistle," a most worthy tribute was paid to her memory. She was born in Lewisburg, Pa., March 25, 1837, and was a daughter of Christian parents, in whose home she received careful training. She was educated in a private academy in her native town, in Lewisburg University and in the Wesleyan Female College of Wilmington, Del. For several years she was a teacher in the public schools. In Wilmington she joined the Methodist Church, and during her long residence in Winona she was indeed "a living epistle" of the Christian faith. During the war, as Secretary of the Soldiers' Aid S . . . . . . wounded, and her memory is enshrined in many a soldier's heart. When the State Soldiers' Orphans' Home was located in Winona, she was appointed a director, and proved a mother to the little ones whom war had left desolate. She was an inspiration to the hundreds of state normal pupils with whom she was brought in contact, and for twenty-four years she taught a large Sunday-school class, mostly normal students, through whose lives her influence is felt throughout the country. In the various missionary societies, in temperance and charitable work she was a leader, working in organized bodies, and by herself performing many acts of which none knew save the recipient of her kindness. The helpless, the desolate and the poor found in her not merely an alms-giver, but a friend. In all her public work her home was not neglected, and it was there, perhaps, that her best qualities of love, tenderness and helpfulness were displayed. She was a woman of vigorous intellect, of sound judgment and wonderful skill and tact, as well as a woman who possessed the tenderer qualities of nature. Fitted by nature and education to shine in the highest social circles, she sought out the lowly and lost, carrying to the dark abodes of sin and want and woe the light of God which shone in and about her. She was plain and unassuming in manner, taking no credit to herself, content to let her light so shine that others, seeing her good works, would glorify their Father in heaven. For four years prior to her death she was a sufferer from physical ailments, but did not seek the sympathy of others, striving constantly, instead, to bring brightness and happiness with her wherever she went. Her Christlike character has made the world better for her having lived.

Mr. Simpson was one of the charter members of Prairie Lodge No. 7, I. O. O. F., and is now an honorary member. In politics he is a Republican. Soon after attaining his majority he was elected and served for two years as Justice of the Peace and was then made Secretary of the consolidated school districts of Winona. He has been Alderman of the city of Winona three terms, and was the first President of the Board of Education of this city. In 1864 he was appointed a member of the Normal . . . M . . . its President for many years and continued one of its members until 1881. In 1866 he was elected to the State Senate for a term of two years, and was an honored member of the General Assembly. He has owned large landed interests in Minnesota and also has a fine home in Winona. He came to Minnesota when there were probably not six thousand people in the territory. He has been prominently connected with the manufacturing and financial interests of Winona, and was one of the organizers of the Second National Bank of Winona, serving as its President for many years. He is now Secretary and General Counsel for the Winona & South-Western Railroad Company, and was one of the promoters of that enterprise. His name is inseparably connected with the history of this community, and among the most prominent citizens of southwestern Minnesota Thomas Simpson is always mentioned.

Asa Forsyth.

ASA FORSYTH, deceased, was born in Chautauqua County, N. Y., on the 22d of February, 1812, and was a son of Charles and Abigail (Killand) Forsyth, both of whom were of Scotch descent, and were reared in Connecticut. The grandfather was one of the heroes of the Revolution, and the great-grandfather was an old sea captain. Charles Forsyth served in the War of 1812 for a short time, and was stationed at Black Rock. In the family were ten children who grew to mature years, four sons and six daughters, but only two of the number are now living. The Forsyths removed to Chautauqua County, N. Y., at an early day, and in 1808 Charles Forsyth took up three hundred acres of land on the Lake Shore & Buffalo Road, six miles east of the Pennsylvania state line, four miles west of Westfield, N. Y., and about a mile distant from Lake Erie. He had one of the most beautiful farms in western New York, and his home commanded a fine view of the lake and surrounding country. The household was noted for its hospitality, and the friends of the family were many. The descendants of Charles Forsyth are still in possession of the homestead, but none of the name are living. He was one of the most substantial citizens of Chautauqua County, and his last days were spent on the old farm, his death there occurring in 1861.

Asa Forsyth remained under the parental roof until eighteen years of age, attending the common schools and aiding in the labors of the fields. He possessed much mechanical genius, being an expert with all kind of tools, and his services were therefore valuable. On leaving home he assisted a gentleman to take a raft of logs to Pittsburg, and when sold the money was intrusted to him by the owner to carry safely home. This he did, putting the money in an old hand-bag, which he thought would arouse no suspicion as being the repository of anything of value. Until twenty-five years of age he was employed in various ways, scorning no work that would give him an honest living. He then purchased an interest in a carriage and wagon factory in Meadville, Pa., and the firm soon won an enviable reputation and gained an extensive business.

On the 8th of December, 1840, Mr. Forsyth was united in marriage with Miss Sarah Liephart, of

Meadville, and to them was born one son, Charles H, but on the 15th of May, 1876, he, then only child, was called to the home beyond, his death occurring in St. Paul, Minn He followed the river, having served as pilot, captain, and in other capacities, and was on board his father's vessel, "The Julia,' when he took his last trip to St Paul.

Mr Forsyth continued in the carriage business in Meadville until 1845, and then sold out on account of poor health Hoping that outdoor life would prove beneficial, he then spent three years in charge of the old homestead, and in 1849 returned to Meadville with the intention of joining a company en route for California, where he wished to establish a sawmill, but owing to a lack of funds on the part of some members of the company he abandoned the idea. In connection with W Bartlett he then started a wholesale grocery in Meadville, which he carried on for ten years On the expiration of that period the firm purchased an interest in a canal-boat, for all freight was then carried on the Erie & Pittsburg Canal, and they believed the venture would be successful, and so it proved Another ten years passed and Mr. Forsyth, on account of ill health, was again forced to seek a change of climate. He came to Winona in April, 1858, after having visited other portions of the western country, including St Anthony and St Paul Here he opened a loan office and dealt in real estate until 1860, when he embarked in the grain business, forming a partnership with H D Moss He afterward had other partners, and carried on operations along that line for some time At first he would furnish the capital, his partner furnishing the experience, but he found he often lost in this way, and it was not until he gave his personal attention to the business that he met with success Soon after his arrival in Winona he invested in a large tract of land in Olmsted County, the title of which was defective, and for a time he thought it would be a total loss to him and the land would revert to the Government About 1868, through the efforts of the late Hon H M Rice, of St Paul, while in the United State Senate, his title was made good, and what at one time appeared a total loss proved a valuable and profitable investment

On the 1st of June, 1866, Mr Forsyth lost his wife, and on the 12th of December, 1870, he was again married, his second union, celebrated in Winona, being with Miss Julia A Liephart, a younger sister of his former wife

From 1870 until 1876 Mr Forsyth owned a small steamboat, "The Julia," named for his wife, which he used mainly for rafting purposes, his son being pilot and captain on the same He made judicious investments in real estate, and obtained several residences and other city property His home, located at No 158 West Broadway, was erected about twenty years since His death occurred September 27, 1891 He had no church relations, but donated the lot on which was built the First Episcopal Church of Winona, and was ever a warm friend to the ministry and to all work which was calculated to elevate humanity In business he was conservative. In politics he was a stanch Democrat, and when General Taylor made a tour through Pennsylvania he took as much delight in the General's reception as though he had been a candidate of the Democracy To his home and family he was very devoted, and as a friend he was ever loyal and true. Mrs Forsyth has been an active worker in the church and gives freely to the poor and needy Her husband had full confidence in her ability to manage the property interests, and they were a happy and devoted couple.

William Hiltz.

WILLIAM HILTZ, a well known resident of Winona, was for many years a leading farmer of the county but is now living retired in the enjoyment of a rest which he has truly earned and richly deserves. He was born in Herkimer County, N. Y., January 12, 1831, and is a son of Solomon S. and Catherine (Folts) Hiltz. The family is of German origin, and was founded in America in the early part of the eighteenth century by the great-grandfather of our subject, who left the Fatherland and emigrated to the New World, taking up his residence in Herkimer County, where occurred the birth of the grandfather, father and that of William Hiltz. The grandfather served in the War of 1812.

The father was reared on the old homestead, and after he had attained his majority was united in marriage with Miss Folts, who was born in Herkimer County, N. Y., in 1801. Her parents were also natives of that locality and her grandparents were natives of Germany. On leaving the Empire State Solomon S. Hiltz removed to Kane County, Ill., where he made his home until 1861, when he came to Winona. He settled on a farm in Saratoga Township, and to agricultural pursuits devoted his energies for many years. His death there occurred at the advanced age of eighty-one. His wife still survives him, and at the age of ninety is living on the old home farm. Both were highly respected people, and became well known citizens of this community.

At the age of nine years William Hiltz left home and began working on the Black River Canal. He was also engaged on the construction of the New York & New Haven Railroad for a time. In 1819 he accompanied his father to the West and settled in St. Charles, Ill., where he worked on the construction of the Illinois Central Railroad. Seven years were passed in that state, after which he came to Minnesota, and in April, 1856, took up a claim in Winona County, entering from the Government one hundred and sixty acres of land in Fremont Township. This he at once began to improve for it was then a wild and uncultivated tract, on which not a furrow had been turned. With characteristic energy he began to clear and plow it, and in course of time the once wild prairie was transformed into rich and fertile fields, which yielded a golden tribute to the thrift and enterprise of the owner. Good buildings were erected, and as the years passed his place became one of the model farms of the neighborhood.

As a companion and helpmate on life's journey, Mr. Hiltz chose Miss Helen A. Duncan, and their wedding was celebrated on the 26th of July, 1852. The lady was born in Elgin, Ill., May 27, 1836, and is a daughter of Craig and Jennette (Havens) Duncan. Her father was born in Madison County, N. Y., May 1, 1811, and his parents were natives of Vermont. His father was of Scotch extraction and made farming his life work. Mr. Duncan was both a farmer and carpenter. He emigrated westward in 1835, settling in Illinois, where he made his home until 1856, when he came to Winona County, and took up a homestead in Fremont Township. There he remained for several years, after which he removed to Fillmore County, Minn. His death occurred at the age of sixty-five years. His wife was born in Le Roy, N. Y., and was called to her final rest at the age of fifty-five. Her parents were also natives of this country, and were of Scotch-Irish lineage.

To Mr. and Mrs. Hiltz were born two children. Mary F., the elder, became the wife of George J. Orline, and died at the age of thirty-nine years, leaving two sons, Gray H. and William H., who are now living with their grandparents. Charles L. was the first white male child born in Fremont Township, the date of that event being August 13, 1856. He is yet living, and until March, 1893, operated the homestead, but now lives with his parents.

Mr. Hiltz votes with the Republican party, and keeps well informed on the questions and issues of the day, but has never sought or desired the honors or emoluments of public office. During the greater part of his life he was a farmer, and in his agricultural pursuits met with success. As his financial resources increased, he added to his land until he now owns a valuable tract of four hundred and forty acres. He resided upon the farm until 1890, when he came to Winona, where he has since lived retired. He has taken no prominent part in public affairs, yet his life has been a busy and useful one, and his career has ever been straightforward and honorable. Few men have started out to make their own way in the world at an earlier age. His early life was not an easy one, yet by being thus early thrown upon his own resources he developed a self-reliance and force of character which have proven of incalculable benefit to him. He is indeed a self-made man, and his example may well serve to encourage others.

John Harders.

JOHN HARDERS, a contractor in brick and stone work, doing business at No. 173 East Broadway, came to Winona in 1866, and has resided here continuously since. He at once began business in the line of his trade, which he carried on successfully until ten years ago, when he began contracting. He is now the senior member of the well known firm of Harders & Gatz, his partner being August Gatz. They do a general line of brick and stone contracting, and have built up an immense business employing during the season of 1894 seventy-five men. Their business averages about $16,000 annually. On all sides may be seen evidenc[illegible] their handiw[illegible] and [illegible]ntly they have erected the Polish Catholic Church, the Knights of Pythias Building, the schoolhouse in Spring Valley, a dispensary for Dr. Watkins, the Madison School and the Sugarloaf School.

Mr. Harders is a native of Germany, his birth having occurred in Hamburg, on the 30th of January, 1841. The days of his boyhood and youth were passed in the Fatherland, but when twenty-four years of age he determined to seek a home beyond the Atlantic, hoping thereby to benefit his financial condition. It was in 1865 that he sailed for the New World. After spending one year at Paterson, N. J., he came to Winona, Minn., hav-in[illegible] a [illegible]-in-law [illegible] who resided near this place For two years he was in the employ of Charles Butler engaged in making scaffolding, and in 1868 he began to learn the stone and brick mason's trade, being in the employ of others until about 1881, when he embarked in business for himself

Mr Harders was married on the 8th of December 1865, the lady of his choice being Miss Lena Ladewig. By their union have been born seven children four sons and three daughters, namely Willie, who is now in Oregon, Henry, a bricklayer, who is working with his father, and Rudolph, Harry, Lizzie, Ella and Meda, all of whom are at home with their parents

The success with which Mr Harders has met in his undertakings is indicated by the volume of business which he now does He learned his trade in a careful and systematic way, and is thoroughly familiar with the work in all its details, so that he is now capable of managing others and having them work to the best advantage He is enterprising and progressive, and although he came to this country in limited circumstances, he is now the possessor of a comfortable competence

---

Hon. Orville Morell Lord.

HON. ORVILLE MORELL LORD While Winona County has much in the way of natural resources and commercial transactions to commend it to the public, the chief interest centers in the lives of those citizens who have achieved success for themselves and at the same time benefited the community in which they reside Prominent among these men is the subject of this sketch, who was long identified with public affairs in this section of the state For a number of years past he has been to some extent retired from public life and now devotes his entire attention to the growing of small fruits, in which enterprise he has met with noteworthy success He makes a specialty of raising the "rolling-stone" plum, which is one of the finest in the state.

Mr. Lord was born in the town of China, in what is now Wyoming County, N. Y., April 20, 1826 He is the son of Stephen S and Caroline (Badger) Lord, the former born in Saratoga County in 1778, and the latter in Cayuga County, N. Y, in 1803 The ancestors of the family had removed to New York from Tolland and Hartford Counties, Conn In 1831 Stephen S Lord removed with his family to Dunkirk, N Y, and in 1837 came to Michigan, settling in Metamora, Lapeer County The father was a blacksmith by trade, and also gave some attention to the cultivation of a small farm

The subject of this sketch was in the winter seasons a pupil in the district schools until he was seventeen, after which he attended a private school at Pontiac, Mich for three months Afterward he taught school during the winter months until he was twenty-two In 1848 he married Miss Martha L Deming, of Oxford, Oakland County, Mich, and they have had five sons and two daughters, of whom three sons and one daughter are now living. In the spring of 1852 Mr. Lord came to Minnesota, arriving here on the 2d of May. His wife and two children arrived in July of the same year. He brought with him all his household goods, a span of horses and farming tools, intending to make agriculture his exclusive business. It is worthy of note that his horses were the first brought into the county. Instead of settling upon a claim, as he had at first intended, he located in the village of Minnesota City, where he bought several lots and built a house.

Having acquired some knowledge of blacksmithing when he was young, Mr. Lord bought the tools of a blacksmith and carried on the business for a year or two, his shop being the only one in the county at that time. In 1852 he shod the first span of horses ever brought into the county by a settler, and the first ever shod here. In July, 1853, he was appointed Coroner for Fillmore County by Governor Gorman. At the election held in the fall of 1853 he was elected Representative to the Territorial Legislature from this district. The session was held from January 4 to March 4, 1854. Among the acts of which he secured the passage were the original charter for the Transit Railroad, the division of Fillmore County, the creation of Winona County, and the establishment of the county seat at what is now the city of Winona. The present boundaries were defined by Mr. Lord and submitted to some of the leading citizens of Winona for their approval. He also secured the passage of a memorial for a post route from Minnesota City to Traverse des Sioux, and carried the mail semi-monthly in 1855. This was the first mail route established in the territory south of the St. Peter River, and was afterward extended from Minnesota City to Winona, terminating at the St. Peter River instead of Traverse des Sioux.

In 1854 Mr. Lord built the first sawmill in the county, this being in Minnesota City. In 1857 he was appointed by the Governor as commissioner for selecting land for the Transit Railroad Company. October 12, 1857, the appointment of Notary Public was conferred upon him by the Governor, both appointments having been unsolicited by him. In 1859 he was a candidate for the Legislature, but was defeated by Judge Orlando Stevens. He removed to Michigan, and resided near Kalamazoo from 1861 until 1864, when he returned to Minnesota and again took up his abode at Minnesota City. In 1871 he was again a candidate for the Legislature, but was defeated by seven votes. Two years afterward he was elected to that body, and served in the next session.

In September, 1875, Mr. Lord was appointed County Superintendent of Schools to fill the vacancy caused by the resignation of Rev. David Burt, who had been appointed State Superintendent of Public Instruction. He was re-elected to the office of County Superintendent several times. In the interests of popular education he has always been an active worker, and in addition to his other official positions has served almost continuously as one of the School Committee in Minnesota City since the first school was started there in 1852. Fraternally he has been a member of the Masonic order since 1862. Though not identified with any denomination he contributes liberally to the churches, and believes in putting the Golden Rule into practice in daily life. Doubtless there is no citizen in the county who has more friends and fewer enemies than he. As a man of upright character, irreproachable life and strict integrity, he enjoys the esteem of all who know him.

Amasa Gleason.

AMASA GLEASON. This gentleman, who is a native of Saratoga County, N. Y., has been a resident of Winona County since 1853, and has done good work by aiding in the rapid development of Pleasant Hill Township. He has been successful in his efforts to acquire a good home, and has accomplished his purpose by strict attention to business and thorough responsibility in all he undertakes. He owns and occupies one hundred and twenty acres of land on sections 3 and 10 which is well stocked and thoroughly tilled. The entire work of improvement has been done by its present owner. The house, barn and other buildings are substantial, conveniently located, and adequate for their respective purposes.

Mr. Gleason was born September 15, 1825, and was the son of Joseph and Jemima Gleason. His education was confined to the district school, which he attended during the dull seasons of farm work. His father died when he was a child of three years, and he was therefore carefully trained by his widowed mother. Amasa remained at home until nineteen years of age, when he began earning money by working out on farms by the month. He was thus occupied for two or three years, when he determined to try his fortune in the western country, and in 1848 went to Michigan by way of the canal and Lakes. He located in Lenawee County, residing there for two years, and then went to Wisconsin and purchased land in Fond du Lac County. The tract was in its original state of wildness, and after working hard to improve it for three years, our subject sold out and removed to La Crescent, this county, where he took up another claim of Government land. He cleared a small portion of this and lived there until 1856, when he sold out and became identified with the agriculturists of Pleasant Hill Township. His claim here consists of one hundred and twenty acres of Government land, for which he paid $1.25 per acre. It is located on sections 3 and 10, Pleasant Hill Township, and is regarded as one of the finest and most thoroughly improved farms in this locality.

On first making his home in this county Mr. Gleason erected for his family a log cabin, which was 14x14 feet in dimensions. As years passed by and he grew more prosperous this rude structure was replaced by a more commodious and modern dwelling, and the family was made more comfortable. Mr. Gleason has received substantial aid in what he has accomplished from his devoted wife, who was formerly Miss Harriet Spalding. They were married March 30, 1856, and immediately moved onto a wild tract of land, which they improved in a profitable manner. Their children are five in number: Joseph W., who was born January 10, 1857, and is a prosperous farmer of this county; Mary, born August 27, 1859; Roland, who was born January 19, 1862, and is living in Martin County, where he is following farming pursuits; George, who was born June 19, 1864, and is also a farmer, living at home; and Ednah J., who was born June 16, 1867, and married George Wilson; she resides about half a mile from the old homestead.

Mrs. Gleason was born in Lower Canada, February 26, 1827 She crossed over to the States in 1854, locating at La Crescent, Minn, where her marriage with our subject took place They were subjected to great inconveniences in the early settlement of the county, but bravely overcame all obstacles which beset their path, and rose to a position of affluence Mr Gleason helped to organize the first school in the township, and has ever since been greatly interested in the cause of education He has been Supervisor and prominent in all matters pertaining to the welfare of his community For many years he has been identified with the Methodist Episcopal Church, and has greatly aided the spread of the Gospel in his township

William C. Swett.

WILLIAM C. SWETT, deceased, was one of the honored veterans of the late war A native of Ohio, he was born September 8, 1825, and died September 19, 1875, at the age of fifty years, respected by all who knew him The days of his boyhood and youth were spent in his father's home, where he remained until twenty-five years of age. He then started out in life for himself and gave his attention to farming, which he followed during his active business career.

On the 28th of September, 1849, Mr Swett was united in marriage with Miss Sarah S. Whitlock, daughter of Levi C and Emeline C (Sissan) Whitlock, both of whom were natives of Connecticut Her father was a native of that state and a farmer by occupation Emigrating westward, he located in Winona County, Minn in the year 1859, and died May 20, 1891, at the age of ninety years. He carried on agricultural pursuits during the greater part of his life, but during his last years lived retired in the town of Pickwick He had a family of eleven children, eight of whom are now living. His wife died about 1890.

Mr and Mrs Swett were in very limited circumstances at the time of their marriage, but decided to try [illegible] in the W[illegible] and coming to Winona County, Minn, entered eighty acres of land from the Government, to which he afterward added by purchase another tract of eighty acres. This he at once cleared, plowed and planted, and in course of time good harvests were garnered, and the wild land was transformed into rich and fertile fields Mr Swett continued his farming until after the breaking out of the late war, when he responded to the country's call for troops, and went to the South The rigors and hardships of army life, however, undermined his health, and after a year and a-half of service he was discharged in one of the hospitals of New Orleans. He then returned home wrecked in health and almost blind, but in these trying days his wife indeed proved a helpmate to him and by her capable management of the farm all indebtedness was paid off and financial affairs were placed in a good condition

After the death of her husband, Mrs Swett continued on the farm for ten years, rearing her family and managing the business interests About 1885 she removed to Dakota, where she has a good home, but did not dispose of the land until the fall of 1893 About the time of her husband's [illegible] but the petition was not granted until about four years later. She now receives $12 per month, to which she is justly entitled.

Four children were born to Mr. and Mrs. Swett, but only two are now living. Elbert W., born July 22, 1850, died on the 13th of July, 1867, being drowned in the Pickwick mill-pond when a youth of seventeen years. Levi B., born May 17, 1855, resides on the old homestead, where he carries on farming. Eliza W., born February 10, 1859, died on the 22d of July of the same year. Sarah J., born July 18, 1862, is now engaged in dress-making in La Crosse, Wis. In his political views Mr. Swett was a Republican, joining the ranks of the party on its organization, for he was a stalwart opponent of slavery, and the Union found in him one of its able defenders, and he continued among the loyal boys in blue until physical disability rendered his service no longer possible. He belonged to the Christian Church, as does his wife, and throughout the community was held in high regard. Mrs. Swett has many friends in Dakota, and, like her husband, deserves mention in the history of their adopted county.

Alexander Cramer Mason.

ALEXANDER CRAMER MASON, who is now living a retired life in Winona, was born in Chambersburg, Franklin County, Pa., on the 12th of April, 1818. His father, George Mason, who was a native of Virginia, kept a hotel on the old Pennsylvania Turnpike, and teamed across the mountains to Pittsburg. He married Catherine Reinhart, who died in 1827.

Alexander Mason spent his boyhood days upon the farm and in a country mill. At the age of twenty years he began learning the stonemason's and bricklayer's trade, serving a three-years apprenticeship, and when that time had expired he started out as a journeyman. Throughout his business career he followed those lines of trade. Later he went to Harrisburg, Pa., where he had previously worked for some time on the first railroad bridge at that point. Leaving that place in 1841, he started for the South, locating in Vicksburg, where he followed his trade until the spring of 1844. In that year he returned to Cincinnati, Ohio, and made his home in the Buckeye State until 1865, during which time he worked on the new court house in Cincinnati for a part of three years. He also worked in Toledo, but at length he determined to go further west, and Minnesota was chosen as the scene of his future labors.

On his arrival in this state Mr. Mason settled in Plainview, Wabasha County, where he remained for three years, when, in 1868, he came to Winona. Since that time he has made his home in this city and has been recognized as one of its leading citizens. For a part of one season he was employed on the construction of the normal school building. The following year he secured a small farm five miles from Winona, and there he lived for seven years, while through the summer months he worked as a contractor and builder in Winona. For eighteen years his present residence has been his home. He continued contracting for some years and won success in his undertakings, so that he is now enabled to live retired, resting in the enjoyment of the fruits of his former toil.

On the 7th of April, 1847, in Cincinnati, was celebrated the marriage of Mr. Mason and Miss Hester Maria Biles, who was born in Washington, Washington County, Pa., on the 16th of June, 1820. Mrs. Mason's parents were William P. and Mary (McCauley) Biles, both of whom were natives of the Keystone State. Mr. Biles was by trade a carpenter. They had a family of eight children, three sons and five daughters, only three of whom are now living. The eldest, Eliza, widow of William Donaldson, resides at Plainview, Wabasha County, Minn., and has attained the age of eighty-eight years. Mrs. Mason was the seventh child in order of birth. Margaret, the youngest, is the wife of Adam Keck, of St. Louis. Mr. Biles died in Ohio in 1851, at the age of nearly seventy-three, and his wife survived him several years, dying at the home of her daughter, Mrs. Mason, in Winona, in 1877, aged ninety-three years.

Mr. and Mrs. Mason became the parents of seven children, who grew to mature years. George Edwin is a leading contractor of Cincinnati, Ohio. William Alexander was reared in Winona, but for fifteen years lived in Cincinnati, where he was in partnership with his brother George. He married in that city, and there died at the age of forty-four years, just at twelve o'clock on the night of December 31, 1893, as the bells were announcing the death of the old and the birth of the new year. Mary Kate is now the wife of Henry Willis, a dealer in coal and lime of Winona. Franklin Biles, who is well known in Winona, where he served as bookkeeper and also carried on a store for a time, is now in St. Louis. Edwin Keck, who was in partnership with his brother Franklin in Winona until their store burned out, is also now located in St. Louis. Hester Ellen died July 31, 1884, at the age of twenty-six years. She was educated in the normal school, and at the age of twenty began teaching, being thus employed in the country schools of Winona and Renville Counties until failing health caused her to abandon that work. She died of quick consumption after six months' illness. She was a bright student and a faithful and successful educator. In her social relations she was considerate of her friends, always kindly disposed, and those who knew her held her in the highest regard. She held membership with the Methodist Episcopal Church, as does her sister, Emma Jeannette, who is the youngest of the family and is still at home.

In early life Mr. Mason was a supporter of the Democracy and voted with it until 1860, when he cast his ballot for John Bell. Since the organization of the Prohibition party he has been one of its most stalwart advocates. For forty-nine years he has not tasted a drop of liquor. On the 22d of August, 1845, he joined the Sons of Temperance, and to that old pledge taken so long ago he has ever been true. Mr. Mason is always found loyal to the cause he espouses and to a friend. He is a man of sterling worth and strict integrity, and his honorable, upright life has gained for him the confidence and esteem of all with whom he has been brought in contact.

Adam Bohn.

ADAM BOHN, the genial proprietor of the Riverside Fruit Farm, located on section 31 Homer Township, is doing a good business as a horticulturist and is well known throughout Winona County. He claims Germany as the land of his birth, which occurred in the town of Immenhausen, Hessen, on the 15th of January, 1849. His parents were Henry and Katie (Schwartz) Bohn. They, too, were natives of Germany and in that country the father carried on a hotel and owned a farm, which he operated until his emigration to America. In the year 1869 he bade adieu to home and friends, sailed for the New World and took up his residence in the city of Winona, where he secured a position with Conrad Bohn, a manufacturer of sash and doors and a general lumber dealer. The father was here employed until his death which occurred on the 11th of November, 1880. His wife survived him only a few months and passed away on the 17th of March, 1881.

This worthy couple became the parents of six children, all of whom are yet living in Winona County. Jacob Bohn is now employed as baggagemaster on the Chicago & North-Western Railway, a position which he has filled for the long period of twenty-six years. John now resides in Winona, and is engaged in the dairy business. Adam is the next younger. Mrs. Elizabeth Garrison also makes her home in the county seat. Dederick is now a retired merchant living in Winona, and Henry is engaged in the dairy business in this county.

Adam Bohn spent the first seventeen years of his life in his native land and then accompanied his parents on their emigration to America, remaining with them until he had attained his majority. In the public schools his education was acquired and in his youth he became familiar with farm work in all its departments. On starting out in life for himself he began work at the carpenter's trade, which he followed for twenty-four years, doing a good business along that line. He was an expert and faithful workman who thoroughly understood his business and always lived up to his contracts. He has been employed on many of the buildings of the county, and many good residences stand as monuments to his thrift and enterprise.

About 1890 Mr. Bohn purchased a tract of land on section 31, Homer Township for which he paid $1,800. Upon this he erected a good house and began the development of what is now known as Riverside Fruit Farm. All of the improvements there seen were placed upon the farm by Mr. Bohn and have made this one of the desirable and valuable properties of the township. He gives his entire attention to the cultivation of large and small fruits of good varieties, and these find a ready sale in the market, thus bringing him a fair income.

Mr. Bohn was married on the 26th of September, 1868, the lady of his choice being Miss Sophie, daughter of Thomas Heberer, who was a native of Illinois, and who came to Minnesota in 1853. He located upon a farm in Winona County, where for five years he made his home, and then removed to the city of Winona, where he resided until his death. He was one of the early settlers and was a man highly esteemed for his sterling worth. He passed away on the 8th of July, 1888, and in less than a year his wife was called to her final rest, departing this life in May, 1889. They were the parents of three children, all yet living: Mrs. Bohn, who was born in Illinois July 18, 1851; Louisa, now a resident of La Crosse, Minn.; and Mary, born January 16, 1848.

To Mr. and Mrs. Bohn have been born nine children, and the family circle yet remains unbroken. They are: Otto, the eldest, who was born November 11, 1870, and is now living in Winona; Mrs. Cora Langian, who was born October 21, 1874, and makes her home in Winona; Frank, born August 13, 1881; Clara, September 19, 1882; Rosie, on the 12th of August, 1884; Irena, December 17, 1886; Mabel, April 14, 1889; Walter, May 5, 1891; and Charlie, March 26, 1892. With the exception of the two eldest, all are yet with their parents.

The Bohn family is one of prominence in the community, and its members rank high in the social circles in which they move. Both Mr. and Mrs. Bohn are members of the Presbyterian Church, and in his political views he is a Democrat, but is not strongly partisan. He would not hold himself bound by party ties should he for any reason wish to support any other than a Democratic candidate. He is a good financier, a careful business manager, and his success has come to him as a result of well directed efforts.

Conrad Fakler.

CONRAD FAKLER, a retired farmer residing at his pleasant home on West Wabasha Street, Winona, well deserves the rest which he is now enjoying, for his life has ever been a busy and useful one. A native of Germany, he was born in Wurtemberg, on the 27th of November, 1827, and in the Fatherland spent the days of his boyhood and youth. His father was a mill-owner, and during his childhood Conrad learned the miller's trade. When he had attained his majority he sailed for the New World, hoping to benefit his financial condition. He sailed from Germany in March, 1848, about ten days before the beginning of the revolution of that year.

After reaching the United States Mr. Fakler made his way to St. Louis, Mo., where he secured work in a mill [illegible] therein. On the death of the head miller he was given his position, and thus served for about six years, receiving good wages. In 1860 he came to Winona. It was his intention to go to New Ulm, Minn., but on stopping at this place he decided to locate here, and soon secured the land which he now owns, paying for the same $3 per acre. The tract comprises one hundred and twenty acres and is situated in Wilson Township, eight miles southwest of Winona. At the time of Mr. Fakler's purchase it was all raw land, not a furrow having been turned or an improvement made. With characteristic energy he began its development, and soon transformed it into a fine farm, whose rich and fertile fields yielded to him a good income. Thoroughly understanding his business, he won success [illegible] most desirable places in the neighborhood. To farm work he devoted his energies until 1885, when he laid aside business cares.

While in St. Louis Mr. Fakler was united in marriage with Miss Catherine Fell, and to them have been born six children: Conrad, who is now living in Hillsdale Township; Joseph; George, who is living on his father's farm; August, who resides in Winona Township; Adam, and Bertha, wife of Arnold Wunderbee, a resident of Minneapolis. The family now reside on West Wabasha Street, where they have a pleasant home.

Mr. Fakler is independent in politics, and has never sought office. He is a self-made man, who since an early age has made his own way in the world, and therefore deserves great credit for his success. He has met with reverses, but overcame these by determined effort and persistent energy, and steadily pushed his way forward until he reached the goal for which he had striven. He is now possessed of a comfortable competence, which enables him to spend his declining days in retirement. He is a pleasant and accommodating gentleman, and a large circle of friends have for him the highest regard.

James Cleveland Blake.

JAMES CLEVELAND BLAKE, deceased, was a native of Connecticut, his birth having occurred in Winsted, Litchfield County, on the 12th of July, 1849. His parents were Charles H. and Jennie (Cleveland) Blake. His early boyhood days were passed under the parental roof, and at the age of fifteen he began clerking, which occupation he followed until twenty-two years of age. In that year he emigrated westward, seeking a home in Winona, hoping that a change of climate would prove beneficial to his health, which had failed.

In order to earn a livelihood, Mr. Blake sought and obtained a position as salesman in the grocery store of E. F. Curtis, and in 1872 became a partner in the concern, the connection continuing for four years. He then purchased an interest, in connection with Mr. Curtis and Thomas Simpson, in the Winona Carriage Company, now the Gate City Carriage Company. This connection continued until 1878, when, on the death of Mr. Curtis, the business was discontinued. He was instrumental in inducing the Rushford Wagon Company to locate at this place, and became a stockholder in the Winona Rushford Wagon Company, of which he was made Secretary and Treasurer. From this time until his death he was connected with that enterprise, and much of its success was due to his untiring efforts and good business ability.

Mr. Blake was married October 4, 1870, the wedding taking place in Winsted, Conn., Miss Anna Beecher, a native of that place, becoming his wife. To them were born the following children: Charles Beecher, James Bronson and Ward Mitchell, all at home; Susan, who was a student in the normal school, and died November 7, 1889, in her eighteenth year; Mary Cleveland, who died in infancy, August 8, 1876, and Harry, who also died in infancy.

Mr. Blake's residence was erected in the year 1884, and he left his family in comfortable circumstances. He was a member of the Board of Trade, and was an enterprising and progressive business man, to whom the life and prosperity of the city are largely due. He was a member of the Congregational Church, and took an active interest in its work and upbuilding Everything pertaining to the welfare of the community received his support, and he was recognized as one of the most valued citizens of Winona County He spent the winters of 1888-89 and 1889-90 in California In the fall of the last-named year he had to withdraw from business, and on the 15th of April, 1891, he departed this life his death resulting from lung trouble He was a man of genial and pleasant manner popular alike with his associates and employes and all who knew him mourned his loss

---

John Gordon.

JOHN GORDON has been identified with the development of Pleasant Hill Township ever since returning from the war with the exception of five years, when he was a resident of Witoka He now owns two hundred and ten acres of land, which is situated on section 31, and here he is engaged in general agricultural pursuits, in which he has met with success

A native of Ireland our subject was born July 4, 1828, and is one of six children, four sons and two daughters, all of whom are living The boyhood of our subject was passed on a farm, and his educational advantages were rather limited When he was fifteen years of age he began learning the tailor's trade, at which he worked for about two years.

In 1849 John Gordon took passage in a sailing-vessel, and at the end of a voyage which consumed thirty-three days landed in New York City Near the metropolis he found work as a common laborer until 1854, when he came westward as far as Janesville, Wis In that state he continued to live until the spring of the following year, when he came to this county and located in Pleasant Hill Township. Soon afterward he purchased one hundred and sixty acres of land at second-hand, which was heavily timbered, there being no improvements ed a log cabin, which is still standing and under the roof of which he continued to dwell until the breaking out of the late war

August 2, 1862 Mr Gordon enlisted as a private in Company K, Ninth Missouri Infantry, and was mustered in at Ft. Snelling There he remained until the spring of 1863, when with his regiment he was ordered out to quell the Indian troubles in the Northwest, and was in several more or less serious encounters with the rest of the men Later he was sent to Nidford, his duty being to help protect the settlers on the frontier In the fall of 1863 he was sent South, and his first regular battle was that of Raleigh Cross Roads He was unfortunate enough to be captured in this engagement, which took place June 10, 1864 He was taken to Mobile, and was detailed to take care of the wounded in the hospital Subsequently he went to Selma, thence to Montgomery, and finally to Macon, Ga He was there until Sherman had started on his raid from Atlanta, and was then sent with other prisoners to Andersonville He had made some money while working in the hospital, and, as his captors had not searched him he was much better off than most of the other prisoners, as he had the wherewithal to purchase rations from the guards Nevertheless he was con- ... lle Prison from

August, 1864, until May, 1865. Previously, at the battle of Brice's Cross Roads he had been wounded by a minie-ball, which struck his collar bone. When he went into the service he weighed one hundred and eighty-eight pounds, but on his discharge tipped the scales at only one hundred and twenty pounds. From Andersonville he was taken to Jacksonville, and from there to Annapolis, Md., where he was confined in the hospital from May 9 until July. He received his honorable discharge on the 2d of July, 1865, and at once returned home.

A short time after the last-named event our subject purchased ten acres of land in Houston County, just across the line from this county. His homestead now comprises two hundred and ten acres, which is a desirable and valuable piece of property, having been well improved and yielding abundant crops in return for the proprietor's care and industry. Politically he is a Democrat, and socially he is a member of the Grand Army of the Republic.

September 11, 1858, Mr. Gordon was married, and his union has been blessed with the following children: Catherine, who died February 20, 1885; Annie, who was called to her final rest July 1, 1882; Lizzie, wife of Frank Monohan, of Witoka; James, Mary J., William and Joseph. The family are members of the Catholic Church, and have hosts of sincere friends and well-wishers in the community where they dwell.

Henry Stinson.

HENRY STINSON has been for about thirty years identified with the upbuilding and growth of Winona County, as he located within its borders only a few months after the close of the war. With the exception of about three years since his coming here he has owned and operated the farm where he now has his home. This is situated on section 20, Pleasant Hill Township.

Henry Stinson is one of ten children, six sons and four daughters, born to Gilford and Lucy (Townes) Stinson. Their other children are named as follows: Adeline, Ann Jeanette, Colby, Ruell, Sumner, Elbridge, Solan and L. S. I. The brothers Colby, Elbridge, Ruell and our subject were all in the Union service during the War of the Rebellion, and Colby was killed on the battlefield of Pittsburg Landing. Elbridge died at Little Rock, Ark., in the hospital, from disease contracted during the service.

The birth of Henry Stinson took place in Lincoln County, Me., January 30, 1831. He was born and reared on a farm, and continued to live with his parents until he was twenty-six years of age. In company with the other members of the family he went to Wisconsin in 1849 and resided for a number of years in Racine County. Afterwards he was for a time a resident of Adams County. From there he enlisted as a private in Company C, Fifty-first Wisconsin Infantry, this event occurring March 17, 1864. His first service was in St. Louis, whither he had been sent by way of Milwaukee, and after spending some six weeks in the Missouri metropolis he was sent to Kingsville, in the same state. From there he proceeded to Madison, Wis., where at the end of the war he was discharged with the rank of Corporal.

For a few months after his return from army service Mr. Stinson lived at his old home in Wisconsin, but soon came to Minnesota and for three years rented land in Homer Township, this county. Afterward he settled on a farm in Pleasant Hill Township. The place where he now dwells is situated on section 20, Pleasant Hill Township, and has been placed under good cultivation and improvement since it came into his possession. The owner is a practical and thorough agriculturist, using the most advanced ideas as well as the old and tried in the management of the farm.

In 1854 Henry Stinson married Miss Candace Irene Gerry. They have become the parents of seven children, who are named respectively, Ida, Cyrus, Annie, Rena, Ada, Lydia and Jennie. They are all being given excellent school advantages and are being fitted to take their places in society and in the battlefield of life with credit to themselves and to their parents.

Politically Mr. Stinson is affiliated with the Republican party and is a member of the Grand Army of the Republic. He faithfully uses his influence and means to promote good citizenship and the prosperity of the locality in which his home is made. He bears a high reputation among his townsmen as a man of honor and high integrity in all his dealings.

Leonard L. Mann.

LEONARD L. MANN, who carries on farming on section 31, Wiscoy Township, and also engages in the work of the ministry, is one of the worthy and honored citizens that New York has furnished to Winona County. He was born in Schoharie County of the Empire State on the 22d of July, 1821, and is a son of Levi and Lucy R. (Greenwood) Mann. The father was a native of Worcester, Mass., and the family is of English lineage.

Leonard Mann is one of four children. He was reared on a farm, and the work connected with the life of an agriculturist was made familiar to him in early life. He attended the district schools and acquired a go [illegible] to become a tiller of the soil, and wishing to enter the ministry, when twenty-one years of age he went to Hamilton, N. Y., in order to prepare himself for that work. There he continued his studies for four years and for one year was a student in Worcester, Mass. He was licensed as a minister of the Baptist Church before going to Hamilton, and on leaving school he took charge of a church in Ulster County, N. Y. He continued in the active work of the ministry from that time until 1860, when he came to Winona County and located on the farm on section 31, Wiscoy Township, where he yet makes his home. He has eighty acres of land which he has placed under a high state of [illegible] ments thereon.

the neat appearance of the place indicating his thrift and enterprise. To some extent he has also continued his ministerial work, serving as a local preacher.

On the 26th of May, 1847, Mr. Mann was united in marriage with Miss C. Freeman, and to them were born three children. The mother of this family was called to her final rest in December, 1859, and in 1860 Mr. Mann was again married, his second union being with Miss A. Sinclair. Their union was blessed with three children, as follows: William, Minnie and Lenora K.

Mr. Mann votes with the Republican party, but has taken no active part in political affairs. He devotes all his time to his farm work and to the ministry, laboring earnestly in the Master's vineyard. His life has been a power for good, and his influence has been felt by many with whom he has come in contact.

INDEX.

BIOGRAPHICAL.

A

B

C

M

N

P

Q

R

S

T

V

W

Y

PORTRAITS.

CPSIA information can be obtained at www.ICGtesting.com
Printed in the USA
LVOW130608300312
275411LV00002B/525/P